THE GLOBAL CLINICAL MOVEMENT

THE GLOBAL CLINICAL MOVEMENT

EDUCATING LAWYERS FOR

SOCIAL JUSTICE

EDITED BY FRANK S. BLOCH

OXFORD
UNIVERSITY PRESS

OXFORD
UNIVERSITY PRESS

Oxford University Press, Inc., publishes works that further Oxford University's objective of excellence in research, scholarship, and education.

Oxford   New York
Auckland   Cape Town   Dar es Salaam   Hong Kong   Karachi   Kuala Lumpur   Madrid   Melbourne   Mexico City   Nairobi   New Delhi   Shanghai   Taipei   Toronto

With offices in
Argentina   Austria   Brazil   Chile   Czech Republic   France   Greece   Guatemala   HungaryItaly   Japan   Poland   Portugal   Singapore   South Korea   Switzerland   Thailand   Turkey   Ukraine   Vietnam

Copyright © 2011 by Oxford University Press, Inc.

Published by Oxford University Press, Inc.
198 Madison Avenue, New York, New York 10016

Oxford is a registered trademark of Oxford University Press
Oxford University Press is a registered trademark of Oxford University Press, Inc.

Library of Congress Cataloging-in-Publication Data

The global clinical movement : educating lawyers for social justice / edited by Frank S. Bloch.
   p. cm.
  Includes bibliographical references and index.
  ISBN 978-0-19-538114-6 ((hardback) : alk. paper)
  1. Law—Study and teaching (Clinical education) I. Bloch, Frank S.
  K103.S63G56 2010
  340.071'1—dc22   2010013069

1 2 3 4 5 6 7 8 9

Printed in the United States of America on acid-free paper

Note to Readers
This publication is designed to provide accurate and authoritative information in regard to the subject matter covered. It is based upon sources believed to be accurate and reliable and is intended to be current as of the time it was written. It is sold with the understanding that the publisher is not engaged in rendering legal, accounting, or other professional services. If legal advice or other expert assistance is required, the services of a competent professional person should be sought. Also, to confirm that the information has not been affected or changed by recent developments, traditional legal research techniques should be used, including checking primary sources where appropriate.

(Based on the Declaration of Principles jointly adopted by a Committee of the American Bar Association and a Committee of Publishers and Associations.)

You may order this or any other Oxford University Press publication by visiting the Oxford University Press website at www.oup.com

CONTENTS

PREFACE

Twenty-five years ago—and ten years into my law teaching career—I found myself in the office of Dr. N.R. Madhava Menon, then the head of the Campus Law Centre of Delhi University. I had heard from colleagues in the United States that he and a few others in India, most notably Professor Upendra Baxi, were seeking to introduce clinical methods into India's tradition-bound system of legal education by establishing university-based legal aid clinics. I was about to apply for a Fulbright grant to teach abroad during an upcoming sabbatical year, and I was looking for a host institution where I could concentrate on legal aid and clinical legal education. As we mapped out plans for what turned out to be a wonderfully rewarding year for me with Dr. Menon and his colleagues, I had a sense that my life as a clinical legal educator was about to change dramatically. But I could not have imagined the richness of the experience that global clinical legal education would bring to me, both personally and professionally. This book presents much of what I have come to learn about global clinical education—in the words of many of the people who have taught me so much over the past twenty-five years.

Another catalyst for this book is the Global Alliance for Justice Education (GAJE). This book is not about GAJE, but the organization has had a pervasive influence on its content and production. Not coincidentally, the idea of GAJE—a global alliance of law teachers and others committed to achieving justice through education—was first floated at an internationally staffed "refresher course" for Indian clinical teachers organized by Dr. Menon. The first concrete steps toward establishing the organization were taken during a clinical conference organized by the Section on Clinical Legal Education of the Association of American Law Schools at which Dr. Menon gave the keynote address titled, "In Defense of Socially Relevant Legal Education." Many of the topics discussed in this book reference GAJE activities; most of the contributors to this book are among GAJE's 700-plus members, and most of them have participated in one or more of the five worldwide conferences that the organization has held over the past ten years.

One of clinical legal education's more popular themes is collaboration; collaboration between teacher and student, collaboration among clinicians, and collaboration across disciplines. It was my honor to orchestrate this particular collaboration among a group of extraordinary clinical law teachers, and I cannot thank them enough for their hard work on this project—in the face of the heavy competing demands placed on them by an active clinical practice. It was a pleasure to collaborate with colleagues who truly value the act of collaboration. I must also thank Vanderbilt University Law School for summer grant support that allowed me to develop and carry out the project, and to my alma mater, Columbia University Law School, for hosting me as a Scholar in Residence for a semester of full-time editing. Finally, I want to offer special thanks to three Vanderbilt law students who provided me with invaluable research assistance: Colby Block (class of 2010), Erica Deray (class of 2011), and Donovan Borvan (who will graduate from the University of Chicago Law School in 2011).

The authors of several chapters wish to acknowledge persons who provided them with extraordinary assistance. The authors of Chapter 4 (Mariana Berbec-Rostas, Arkady Gutnikov, and Barbara Namyslowska-Gabrysiak) wish to thank Zaza Namoradze, director of the Budapest Office of the Open Society Justice Initiative and a pioneer in promoting and supporting the establishment of legal clinics in Central and Eastern Europe and countries of the former Soviet Union, for insights that he provided concerning the clinical movement in the region. The authors of Chapter 6 (Cai Yanmin and J.L. Pottenger, Jr.) would like to thank the many experts who reviewed earlier drafts of their chapter, particularly Jerome Cohen, James Feinerman, Jennifer Lyman, Pam Phan, Wang Chenguang, and Andrea Worden. The author of Chapter 8 (Diego Blázquez-Martín) wishes to thank his colleagues, Professor Maria Marques, Professor Antonio Madrid, and Vice Dean José García Añón, for providing additional information about clinical work at various universities in Spain. The author of Chapter 13 (Daniela Ikawa) wishes to thank Edwin Rekosh and Lusine Hovhannisian, colleagues at the Public Interest Law Institute, for their valuable comments on the chapter, and Adam Bodnar, Basia Namyslowska-Gabrysiak, Claudia Vazzoler, Filip Czernicki, Henrique Trevisani, Irene Maestro Guimarães, Renata Titina, Samuel Friedman, and Wanda Nowicka for agreeing to be interviewed and for the vital insights that they provided. The authors of Chapter 16 (Ajay Pandey and Sheena Shukkur) would like to thank Dr. Suri Sehgal, founder of the S.M. Sehgal Foundation and its Institute of Rural Research and Development (IRRAD) for the encouragement and support to the experiment of the unique legal literacy project described in the chapter, the villagers of Mewat and Ms. Aditi Jha and Mr. Navneet Narwal, colleagues at IRRAD who worked on the project, and also Professor C. Raj Kumar, vice chancellor of O.P. Jindal Global University and the dean of Jindal Global Law School, for his comments on the chapter. The authors of Chapter 19 (Margaret Martin Barry, Filip Czernicki, Izabela Kraśnicka, and Mao Ling) would like to thank the following clinicians for providing information concerning their respective countries: Dimitry Shabelnikov (Russia), Andrei Brighidin (Moldova), Maximilian Tomoszek (Czech Republic), Nigel Duncan (United Kingdom), Markiyan Duleba (Ukraine), Ernest Ojukwu (Nigeria), Jeff Giddings (Australia), Bruce Lasky (Southeast Asia), and Stephan van der Merwe (Republic of South Africa). Finally, the authors of Chapter 25 (Edward Santow and George Mukundi Wachira) would like to thank Professors Frank S. Bloch, Clark D. Cunningham, and Elizabeth Cooper for providing supplemental information about GAJE and GAJE activities.

—FSB
Nashville, Tennessee

LIST OF CONTRIBUTORS

Margaret Martin Barry is Associate Professor of Law at the Catholic University of America's Columbus School of Law in Washington, D.C., where she teaches in the Families and the Law Clinic. She has also taught at the University of Montenegro and the NALSAR Law University in Hyderabad, India. She is a member of the board of editors of the *Clinical Law Review*, and has served as chair of the Association of American Law Schools (AALS) Section on Clinical Legal Education, as President of the Clinical Legal Education Association (CLEA), and as the co-president of the Society of American Law Teachers (SALT).

Mariana Berbec–Rostas is Program Officer for the Human Rights and Governance Grants Program at the Open Society Institute–Budapest, where she focuses on human rights in health care and legal capacity building. She has assisted with the development of pioneer human rights, public interest, and legal empowerment university-based clinics in Eastern Europe, Southern and Western Africa, Southeast Asia, and the Middle East. She is a member of the Global Alliance for Justice Education (GAJE) steering committee and was actively involved in the organization of the 2008 international conference in Manila.

Diego Blázquez-Martín is Profesor Titular at Universidad Carlos III de Madrid in Spain. He has served as coordinator of the Human Rights Clinic at the Instituto de Derechos Humanos "Bartolomé de las Casas" since 2004. Professor Blázquez-Martin is a member of the Global Alliance for Justice Education (GAJE) steering committee. He is currently on leave serving as legal adviser at the Ministry of Equality of the Government of Spain.

Frank S. Bloch is Professor of Law at Vanderbilt University Law School in the United States, where he also served as Director of Clinical Education and as Director of the Social Justice Program. He has taught at the University of Chicago Law School and at Delhi University in India. Before joining the legal academy, he was a legal aid lawyer with California Rural Legal Assistance. Professor Bloch was a member of the interim steering committee that founded the Global Alliance for Justice Education (GAJE) and was co-chair of its inaugural conference; he has been a member of the steering committee since the organization was founded, serving as convenor and as treasurer.

Roger Burridge is Professor of Law and former dean at Warwick Law School, University of Warwick, in the United Kingdom, where he has taught in the law school's clinical program. He has also served as director of the UK Centre for Legal Education and was a barrister practicing in London with the Newham

Rights Centre. He has served as a consultant to the British Council, the European Union, and the US Agency for International Development on clinical development and training for trainers workshops around the world, including India, Ethiopia, Nigeria, Tanzania, Uganda, Malawi, Poland, Montenegro, and the United Kingdom.

Cai Yanmin is Professor of Law at Sun Yat-Sen University in the People's Republic of China, where she launched the clinical program in 2001 and continues to teach in a clinic focusing mainly on the rights of migrant workers. Professor Cai is also vice director of the Committee of Chinese Clinical Legal Educators (CCCLE). She has been active in promoting the expansion of clinical legal education in China, including training new clinicians from other universities around the country. Currently, she is working on a research project to revise the Civil Procedure Law of the PRC sponsored by the China National Fund for Social Science.

Erika Castro-Buitrago is Professor of Law and Director of the Environmental Law Clinic at the University of Medellín–Colombia. She has been a leader in establishing legal clinics in the public interest in the city of Medellín, specializing in the litigation of human rights and environmental cases. She is also an adviser to the public administration for the formulation of local environmental laws.

Anna Cody is Senior Lecturer and Director, Kingsford Legal Centre, at the Faculty of Law of the University of New South Wales in Australia, where she also serves as director of clinical legal education programs. She has worked on international development in East Timor and Indonesia and with the Center for Economic and Social Rights in New York, and has trained community lawyers in China and Australia. She worked previously with indigenous women in Alice Springs, establishing a domestic violence service and with indigenous organizations in Oaxaca Mexico around the right to water.

Liz Ryan Cole is Professor of Law and Director of Semester in Practice at Vermont Law School in the United States. She is a former president of the Clinical Legal Education Association and has served on the Board of Vermont Legal Aid. Before joining the legal academy, she worked as a legal aid lawyer in California. She also worked with the Legal Services Training and Advocacy Project and for the US Legal Services Corporation.

Filip Czernicki is President of the Polish Legal Clinics Foundation and was the co-founder of the Warsaw University Legal Clinic. He is a member of the Global Alliance for Justice Education (GAJE) steering committee and serves currently as its convenor. He has been active in promoting and establishing legal clinics in Poland and Eastern Europe, as well as lawyer pro bono activity. He has co-founded several nongovernmental initiatives and organizations, including the Polish NGO's Coalition for the International Criminal Court.

Nigel Duncan is Principal Lecturer at the City Law School, City University, London, where he introduced the first live-client clinical course in a professional program in the United Kingdom. He is also editor of *The Law Teacher* and a member of the Advisory Board of the UK Centre for Legal Education. He was a founding member of the Clinical Legal Education Organisation (CLEO), former chair of the Association of Law Teachers, and served on the interim steering committee that founded the Global Alliance for Justice Education (GAJE). He is co-founder of the interactive Web site: International Forum on Teaching Legal Ethics and Professionalism.

Nicolás Espejo-Yaksic is Professor of Law and Government at the Universidad Adolfo Ibañez in Chile, Professor of Law at the Universidad Central de Chile, and Founder and President of the Public Interest Foundation. He also serves as a Senior Human Rights Consultant for UNICEF–Chile. He is the former director of the Human Rights Center, Diego Portales University, the former representative in Chile of the Center for Justice and International Law (CEJIL), and has been a tutor in law at Exeter College, University of Oxford, and Warwick Law School in the UK.

Adrian Evans is Associate Dean (Staff), Monash University Faculty of Law in Australia, with teaching and managerial responsibilities in law school staffing, legal ethics, justice education, and clinical case supervision. At Monash, he also served as convenor of Legal Practice Programs and as coordinator of Springvale Monash Legal Service. He is a former member of the Global Alliance for Justice Education (GAJE) steering committee and co-chair of the Professional Ethics Committee of the International Bar Association.

Shelley A. M. Gavigan is Professor at Osgoode Hall Law School, York University in Canada, where she has served as Associate Dean, Director of Clinical Education, and as Academic Director of Osgoode's Intensive Program in Poverty Law at Parkdale Community Legal Services. Before joining the legal academy, she articled in a rural-based community legal clinic and continued to practice as a legal clinic lawyer and briefly as a human rights lawyer.

Jeff Giddings is Director of Professionalism and Professor of Law at Griffith University in Australia, where he is also the Convenor of the Graduate Program in Dispute Resolution. He was the founding director of the Griffith Law School Clinical Program, and was also lecturer and clinical supervisor at La Trobe Law School. He has delivered supervision training programs for various Australian clinical programs and was the convenor of Australian clinical legal education conferences held in 2003 and 2007.

Neil Gold is Professor of Law and Vice President, International at the University of Windsor in Canada, where he also served as Provost and Dean of Law. He is the former Director of Legal Assistance of Windsor and the Law Centre in Victoria.

He was a member of the interim steering committee that founded the Global Alliance for Justice Education (GAJE) and has consulted on legal education, clinical legal education, professional development, and dispute resolution in Africa, Asia, Australasia, South America, the United Kingdom, and the United States.

Richard Grimes is Director of Clinical Programmes at the University of York in the UK and a consultant with Talkinglaw, an independent service aiming to improve legal education and to support the development of community-based legal services. He also served as Director of Pro Bono Services and Clinical Education at The College of Law of England and Wales and as a member of the interim steering committee that founded the Global Alliance for Justice Education (GAJE). He has taught and trained around the world on access to justice issues, including legal aid, legal literacy programs, and pro bono services. Most recently he assisted in developing law-related capacity building programs in Afghanistan, Iran, and Nigeria.

Arkady Gutnikov is Vice President of St. Petersburg Institute of Law (named after Prince P. G. Oldenburgsky) in Russia, where he serves as Director of the Center of Clinical Legal Education and Coordinator of the Living Law/Street Law Center for law-related and civic education. He is also Vice President of the Russian Association for Civic Education and a member of the International Steering Committee of the European Human Rights Advocacy Center (EHRAC)/ Memorial Joint Project. He is the former program manager of the Clinical Legal Education Foundation (Russia) and has served as a trainer on clinical legal education, human rights education, and other civic and law-related education programs.

Daniela Ikawa is Legal Officer at the Public Interest Law Institute (PILI) in New York. She established a pilot NGO-based human rights clinic in Brazil and has taught International Human Rights Law at various Brazilian universities, graduate schools, and civil society organizations. She has also taught a course on teaching law, human rights, and ethics at the Central European University Summer School. She was managing editor of *Sur–International Human Rights Journal* and has practiced as a lawyer before the Interamerican Commission on Human Rights.

Peter A. Joy is Professor of Law and Vice Dean at the Washington University in St. Louis School of Law in the United States, where he also served as Director of the Criminal Justice Clinic. He was also Professor of Law and Director of the Milton A. Kramer Law School Clinic at Case Western Reserve University School of Law and a consultant to the American Bar Association Asia Law Initiative in Indonesia. He is a member of the board of editors for the *Clinical Law Review* and has served as president of Clinical Legal Education Association (CLEA) and as chair of the Association of American Law Schools Section on Clinical Legal Education.

Susan L. Kay is Associate Dean for Clinical Affairs and Clinical Professor of Law at Vanderbilt University Law School in the United States, where she teaches in the Criminal Law Clinic. She also teaches courses on professional responsibility, evidence, and criminal law. She has served as president of the Clinical Legal Education Association (CLEA) and as a visiting attorney at the NAACP Legal Defense and Education Fund.

Catherine F. Klein is Professor of Law at Catholic University of America's Columbus School of Law in Washington, D.C., where she also serves as director of Columbus Community Legal Services, the university's live-client clinical program. She is also co-director of Catholic University's Families and the Law, a clinical program designed to address the issue of domestic violence through individual representation, community outreach and education, and legislative advocacy. She is a member of the Global Alliance for Justice Education (GAJE) steering committee and has worked extensively in Central and Eastern Europe to support the development of law school clinics and other innovative teaching methodologies in the region.

Izabela Kraśnicka is Associate Professor in the Department of Public International Law of the Faculty of Law at the University in Bialystok in Poland, where she teaches Public International Law, Law of the European Union, and Introduction to the American Legal System. She is a member of the Board of the Polish Legal Clinics Foundation.

Bruce Avery Lasky is a Founder and Director of the Bridges Across Borders–Southeast Asia Community Legal Education Initiative (BABSEA CLE), which focuses on the development of university-based clinical legal education that carries out community legal, human rights, and access to justice education programs, with the aim of empowering vulnerable and under-served individuals and communities worldwide. He is also an adjunct professor or visiting professor at a number of universities in the Southeast Asia region, including Chiang Mai University in Thailand, where he assists in the further development of their clinical programs. He is a member of the Global Alliance for Justice Education (GAJE) steering committee and a founding director of Sustainable Cambodia.

Jennifer Lyman is Adjunct Professor of Law at Catholic University of America's Columbus School of Law in the United States and an organization development consultant. She was a clinical professor at George Washington University Law School and American University's Washington College of Law. Before joining the legal academy, she worked as a public defender in Washington, D.C. She has consulted and collaborated with criminal defense attorneys and law professors around the world, including Russia, Poland, Chile, and China.

Margaret (Peggy) Maisel is Associate Professor and Founding Director of the Clinical Program at Florida International University College of Law in the United

States, where she teaches an interdisciplinary community development clinic. She also taught at the University of Natal (now the University of KwaZulu-Natal) in South Africa, where she helped restructure the law clinic and co-authored two text books for first year courses, and at the University of Maryland School of Law, Antioch School of Law, and Harvard Law School. She has served as a member of the Global Alliance for Justice Education (GAJE) steering committee, on the Board of Governors of the Society of American Law Teachers (SALT), and as a consultant on clinical legal education in Africa, Haiti, and the United States.

Mao Ling is Associate Professor at the Law School of Zhongnan University of Economics and Law in the People's Republic of China, where she was vice director of the clinic center and taught the clinic course. She also teaches courses on civil procedure law, the law of evidence, and litigation and arbitration. She is a member of the Global Alliance for Justice Education (GAJE) steering committee and an individual member of the Committee of Chinese Clinical Legal Educators (CCCLE).

N. R. Madhava Menon is the founder of the National Law School of India University in Bangalore, the National University of Juridical Sciences in Kolkata, and the National Judicial Academy in Bhopal. Before that, he was head of Delhi University's Campus Law Centre, where he first introduced clinical methods to India through the Delhi Legal Services Clinic. He was a member the interim steering committee that founded the Global Alliance for Justice Education (GAJE) and served as co-chair of its inaugural conference. Currently, he is a member of the Government of India's Commission on Centre-State Relations and its Task Force on Restructuring Legal Education. He continues to train clinical law teachers as Chairman of the Menon Institute of Legal Advocacy Training.

Shigeo Miyagawa is Professor of Law at Waseda Law School in Japan, where he serves as director of the Institute of Clinical Legal Education. He teaches the immigration and refugee law clinic, as well as courses on comparative law between Japan and the United States. He is president of the Japan Clinical Legal Education Association and a trustee of the Japan Society of Comparative Law and the Japanese American Society for Legal Studies.

David McQuoid-Mason is Acting Director and Professor at the Centre for Socio-Legal Studies of the University of KwaZulu-Natal in South Africa, where he also served as dean of the Law School. He is the former director of the South African Street Law program and a past president of the Commonwealth Legal Education Association. He was a member of the interim steering committee that founded the Global Alliance for Justice Education (GAJE) and has been a member of the steering committee since the organization was founded. He has consulted on clinical education and conducted Street Law-type training workshops in Africa, Central and Eastern Europe, the Middle East, South America, and throughout Asia.

Les McCrimmon is Professor of Law at the Faculty of Law, Business and Arts at Charles Darwin University in Australia. He is a former full-time commissioner at the Australian Law Reform Commission and the former Director of Clinical Programs at the University of Sydney. He was a member of the interim steering committee that founded the Global Alliance for Justice Education (GAJE) and has served as a senior teacher and member of the management committee of the Australian Advocacy Institute and as a consultant to the Government of Botswana on the establishment of a law reform commission.

V. Nagaraj is Professor of Law and Registrar at the National Law School of India University in Bangalore, India, where he teaches the Alternative Dispute Resolution Clinic. He is also the supervisor of the National Law School's Legal Aid Clinic. He also taught at Havanur College of Law in Bangalore and was a visiting professor at Vanderbilt University Law School in the United States. He consults on alternative dispute resolution (ADR) and clinical legal education throughout India and has conducted a number of training sessions for Indian clinical law teachers.

Barbara Namyslowska-Gabrysiak is Assistant Professor in the Faculty of Law and Administration at Warsaw University in Poland, where she is affiliated with the Institute of Criminal Law of the Department of Comparative Criminal Law. She teaches courses in criminal law and is coordinator of clinic sections on criminal law and discrimination based on sex. She is a member of Warsaw University's Human Trafficking Studies Centre and has been active in various projects concerning women's rights.

Mary Anne Noone is Associate Professor and Coordinator of the Clinical Legal Education and Public Interest Postgraduate Program at La Trobe University in Australia. She pioneered a clinical course focused on legal ethics and professional responsibility and also developed a public interest law externship program. She is a member of the Editorial Board of the *International Journal of Legal Education* and a board member of Victoria Legal Aid and the West Heidelberg Community Legal Service. Currently she is working on models for providing legal aid services within health and community organizations.

Ed O'Brien is the founder and former executive director of Street Law, Inc., in Washington, D.C., where he currently holds the title of Executive Director Emeritus. He also taught the Street Law Clinic at Georgetown University Law Center. He has consulted widely on the structure and management of Street Law programs and has trained clinical teachers from Street Law clinics across the United States and throughout the world.

Ernest Ojukwu is Deputy Director General and Head of Nigerian Law School, Augustine Nnamani Campus and president of the Nigerian Network of University Legal Aid Institutions (NULAI). He conducts workshops on clinical legal education for law teachers throughout Nigeria and assists in the establishment of university-based law clinics. He is also director of the Nigerian Bar Association's Institute of Continuing Legal Education and chairman of the NBA's Academic Forum, and was secretary of Nigeria's National Committee on the Reform of Legal Education (2006–2007).

Ajay Pandey is Associate Professor and Assistant Director of Clinical Programs at Jindal Global Law School in India. He has worked with nongovernmental organizations (NGOs) on issues of human rights, consumer rights, the right to information, good rural governance, and legal aid to the poor. He was director of the Policy, Governance and Advocacy Centre of the Institute of Rural Research and Development (IRRAD), where he continues to be associated as an advisor, and a program officer in the Legal Aid Department of the Indian Social Institute, where he was editor of *Legal News and Views*.

Philip Plowden is Dean of Northumbria Law School in the United Kingdom, where he also served as Associate Dean and Director of the Northumbria Student Law Office. He is also a National Teaching Fellow of the Higher Education Academy of England and Wales. He is a former convenor of the Clinical Legal Education Organisation and the former editor of the *International Journal of Clinical Legal Education*.

J. L. Pottenger, Jr. is Nathan Baker Clinical Professor of Law at Yale Law School in the United States, where his clinical teaching includes housing, prisoners' rights, community and economic development, and legislative advocacy. He also served as director of Clinical Studies at Yale's Jerome N. Frank Legal Services Organization. He has taught at Harvard Law School and Oxford University and has consulted on clinical education for clinical programs in the United States, the United Kingdom, and China. He is a member of the board of the New Haven Legal Assistance Association, the Yale-China Association, and Dwight Hall, the Center for Public Service and Social Justice at Yale, and a former member of the board of the Clinical Legal Education Association (CLEA).

M. R. K. Prasad is Assistant Professor of Law at V. M. Salgaocar College of Law in India and Coordinator of The College of Law's Legal Aid Society. He is also secretary of the Forum of South Asian Clinical Law Teachers and has organized or participated in numerous clinical teacher training programs throughout India. He also served as a member of the National Coordination Committee that conducted the Louis M. Brown International Client Counseling Competition.

Mariela Puga is Chair Professor of Public Law at Catholic Cordoba University, Professor of Law and Social Change at the University of Palermo, and Associate Professor of Law at Cordoba National University School of Social Work, all in Argentina. She is also director of the Cordoba Public Interest Law Clinic. She is a member of the Public Interest Law Institute's Advisory Committee on

Legal Education Reform and has consulted on clinic development throughout Latin America. She was director of the Tucuman Public Interest Law Clinic and Coordinator of the Palermo Public Interest Law Clinic, and was chair of the 2006 Global Alliance for Justice Education (GAJE) worldwide conference.

Edward Santow is Senior Lecturer at the Faculty of Law of the University of New South Wales in Australia. Before joining the legal academy, he was a practicing lawyer and a legal officer at the Australian Law Reform Commission. He is also director of the Charter of Human Rights Project at the Gilbert + Tobin Centre of Public Law and legal adviser to the Legislation Review Committee of the New South Wales Parliament, which is responsible for assessing whether Bills of Parliament infringe unduly on human rights. He is a member of the Global Alliance for Justice Education (GAJE) steering committee and serves on the board of a number of NGOs, including the Refugee Advice and Casework Service and the Australian Human Rights Group.

Barbara Schatz is Clinical Professor of Law and a former director of the clinical program at Columbia University Law School, where she teaches the Community Enterprise Clinic. She is president of the Public Interest Law Institute (PILI), which promotes the use of public interest law internationally, and a member of the board of Human Rights First. Prior to joining Columbia, she served as executive director of the Council of New York Law Associates (now Lawyers Alliance for New York), where she administered a city-wide legal services program for community organizations. She has trained and consulted with law professors interested in establishing clinical programs in China, Central and Eastern Europe, and countries of the former Soviet Union.

Sheena Shukkur is Assistant Professor at the National Judicial Academy in India. Previously, she was Lecturer in Law at the School of Legal Studies of Kannur University in India, where she also served as head of the department. She has been active in involving students in legal literacy projects in association with the Kerala State Legal Services Authority, focusing on the rights of women and other vulnerable groups in Kerala State.

Takao Suami is Professor of Law at Waseda University Law School in Japan, where he teaches in the Civil Justice Clinic. He is the former director of the Waseda University Legal Clinic and the former secretary general of the Japan Clinical Legal Education Association. He is currently a member of the JCLEA Board.

Karen Tokarz is Charles Nagel Professor of Public Interest Law and Public Service, Professor of African and African American Studies, and Director of Dispute Resolution Program at Washington University School of Law in the United States. She is the former director of Clinical Education at Washington University and the current director of its Civil Rights and Community Justice Clinic. She was a visiting scholar at the Harvard University Program on

Negotiation and a Fulbright Senior Specialist at the University of KwaZulu-Natal in South Africa. She has served as president of the Clinical Legal Education Association (CLEA) and as chair of the Association of American Law Schools Section on Clinical legal Education.

Marta Villarreal is Coordinator of the Clinical Legal Education Program and the Public Interest Law Clinic at the Department of Law of the Instituto Tecnológico Autónomo de México (ITAM) in Mexico.

George Mukundi Wachira is Africa Regional Coordinator for the Transitional Justice Program at the Centre for the Study of Violence and Reconciliation in South Africa. He was a founding member of the Students Association for Legal Aid and Research (SALAR), a student-led legal aid clinic at the University of Nairobi. He was a member of the Global Alliance for Justice Education (GAJE) steering committee and served as the organization's first general secretary.

Charles D. Weisselberg is Shannon Cecil Turner Professor of Law at the University of California, Berkeley School of Law in the United States, where he was the founding director of the Center for Clinical Education and taught in a federal practice and a death penalty clinic. He also taught at the University of Southern California Law School and the University of Chicago Law School. He was a public defender before joining the legal academy. He is a former chair of the Association of American Law Schools Section on Clinical Education and has lectured and consulted on clinical legal education and criminal justice in Japan, China, and Australia.

Richard J. Wilson is Professor of Law and founding Director of the International Human Rights Law Clinic at American University's Washington College of Law in Washington, D.C. He has also taught at the City University of New York Law School. Before he joined the legal academy, he was an appellate public defender and also coordinated defender efforts at the National Legal Aid and Defender Association. He has consulted on clinical legal education and access to justice throughout the world, primarily in Latin America and Central and Eastern Europe, but also in Africa, China, South Asia, the Middle East, and Western Europe.

Judith A. Zimmer is Deputy Director of Street Law, Inc. in Washington, DC, where she has worked since 1985. She has supervised many of Street Law's programs and has co-authored several of its curricular materials, and has worked as a teacher trainer and curriculum developer in Northern Ireland, Azerbaijan, and Nepal. Prior to joining Street Law, Inc, she ran the Street Law Clinic at Cleveland-Marshall College of Law and helped run the law program for Cleveland's Law and Public Service Magnet High School. She is currently working with UNICEF to integrate democracy education into the formal and non-formal education system.

INTRODUCTION

FRANK S. BLOCH

At a workshop preceding the inaugural conference of the Global Alliance for Justice Education (GAJE) held in India in 1999, participants were asked to imagine a law school whose primary mission is to reduce injustice. The exercise started with the premise that law schools tend to see "the law" as the core subject of their educational mission and therefore tend to offer instruction that qualifies law students in an academic discipline rather than to practice in a profession. The exercise was intended, therefore, to highlight the need to focus law study not only on the concept of justice—as distinct from the law—but also on preparing future lawyers to root out injustice. A workshop setting was chosen to encourage the participants to approach the question of how to place justice—and how to achieve justice—at the center of legal education concretely and pragmatically. What would such a law school look like? What would make such a transformation possible? Are there any models now in existence? What barriers would block such a transformation? A wide range of proposals emerged during the workshop, with some concentrating on various ways a law school could be organized with justice as its central theme, while others focused on how law schools could target specific instances of injustice.

Two features of that workshop capture the essence of this book. First, the goal of the exercise was to begin a process of transforming legal education into justice education—and the obvious choice of means to achieve that transformation, as reflected in the proposals developed during the exercise, was clinical legal education and its core methodology of actively involving law students in their future professional role. Second, the workshop—and the full conference that followed—brought together an internationally diverse group of clinical teachers eager to share ideas and experiences in an effort to promote legal education reform around the world. This book is about a global clinical movement that first came to its own at that inaugural GAJE conference and its ongoing efforts to transform legal education into justice education by training lawyers for social justice.

GLOBAL CLINICAL LEGAL EDUCATION

There is a strong appeal these days to approaching just about any topic from a global perspective. But is there really something particularly meaningful about global clinical legal education—something more than simply that clinical legal education, like everything else, is "going global"? The answer is not all that obvious, at least at first blush. There is an easier, more obvious case for global legal education in general. In today's world, no law school can afford to ignore global perspectives in its curriculum. And unlike traditional international law studies, which could be seen as relevant only to a handful of policy-makers, academics, and highly specialized practitioners, today's "global law" has a pervasive influence on people's lives and touches on almost every lawyer's law practice. That is why New York University touts its "Global Law Program," and why the Jindal Global Law School recently opened its doors outside New Delhi.

But clinical legal education is different. Clinical legal education is hands-on, professional skills training coupled with instruction in—and initiation into—lawyers' public and professional responsibilities. Clinicians teach law students about what lawyers do, what they should do, and how they should do it. And they teach about lawyering with experiential learning methods that place students in the role of a lawyer, preferably in a real-world setting in which they not only face, but also address, social injustice. Clinics are also where students learn about the local community and its legal needs—and how law and lawyers can address those needs. As a practical matter, therefore, clinical teaching has an inherently local dimension. And the same is true when one looks at clinical law teachers, at least as compared to their traditional academic counterparts. Most clinicians, and all who teach in real-client settings, are licensed lawyers. More often than not, they have had years of experience in the field that produced ties to the local community and the local bar. When they write, their best scholarship is informed by what they encounter in the field—often in their local clinical practice as clinical teachers—and many step out of academia for a tour in local law practice, public interest work, or government.

So what is the point of examining clinical legal education globally? First, and most obviously, is its global reach. Clinical programs exist today, in one form or another, at law schools throughout the world. Second is its commitment to providing "socially relevant legal education," a mission that resonates across any local-global divide. Finally, there is the collective energy of clinical law teachers throughout the world seeking out and joining with colleagues to share experience and advance common goals: the global clinical movement. These three aspects of what is happening in clinical legal education today—its global reach, its social justice mission, and its emergence as a worldwide movement—make the case for taking global clinical education seriously. Each is explored further below and in the chapters that follow, as they are also the themes of the three parts of this book.

THE GLOBAL REACH OF CLINICAL LEGAL EDUCATION

The chapters in Part I document the global reach of clinical legal education. Included in these chapters are descriptions of clinical programs in selected countries in the Americas, Europe, Africa, Asia, and Australasia. Moreover, a comprehensive worldwide review of clinical legal education would reveal a global reach that extends to many more countries than those discussed in this book. There are, for example, a number of established clinical programs in various countries in the Middle East and there seems to be a growing interest in clinical education at law schools in Western Europe. Today, one could compile a list of clinical programs operating at law schools in every region of the world.

The fact that an impressive worldwide list of clinical programs can be compiled does not mean, however, that all clinical programs on the list meet some narrowly defined set of criteria that qualifies them to be listed. The list of clinical programs around the world consists of a variety of different types of clinics and clinical courses that can look quite different from one country or region to another—community legal centers in Australia, legal literacy projects in India, legal aid clinics in the United States, and *clinicas jurídicas* in Chile. Some differences are due to structural factors, such as whether law is taught as an undergraduate or a graduate course or whether additional postgraduate training is required before entering law practice. Others are due to economic and political conditions that influence the role that lawyers may or may not play in addressing social needs. What brings all these programs within the global reach of clinical legal education—despite inevitable differences in structure and content—is that they offer experientially based training in professional skills and values that emphasize critically important areas of professional and public interest that have been left out of the traditional law school curriculum.

The global reach of clinical legal education has importance beyond impressive numbers of law school clinics. With its focus on new areas of study, its links to social action, and its use of dramatically different teaching methods, clinical education has not been an easy sell. Clinical education's increasingly global presence gives the field a certain credibility that helps reformers establish new clinical programs. And as its global reach extends further—and the number of law school clinics grows—a momentum has begun to develop that has helped sustain existing clinical programs and ease the path toward institutionalizing clinical education. In other words, the global reach of clinical legal education has aided and facilitated its growth and acceptance. For example, the existence of clinical programs around the world has helped the Committee of Chinese Clinical Legal Educators push for expansion of clinical programs in China. Prominent examples of support for new clinical initiatives that reached across borders include South Africa's Association of University Legal Aid Institution's work in Nigeria that resulted in the establishment of the Nigerian Network of University Legal Aid Institutions and the efforts by the Polish Legal Clinics Foundation, the Russian Clinical Legal Education Foundation, and others to bolster clinical programs throughout their region.

THE SOCIAL JUSTICE MISSION

The chapters in Part II describe various aspects of clinical legal education's social justice mission and demonstrate how the global reach of clinical education has resulted in its social justice mission having an important global dimension as well. Although there has always been a strong link between clinical programs and legal aid or other forms of social justice work, those links were at first decidedly local. Many clinical legal education programs began as what amounted to law school-based legal aid offices. There are also many instances where law school projects focused entirely on a local social justice mission played a key role in developing new clinical programs. Promising to provide legal aid or other types of legal services to the community has been a very effective way to bring in funding for new clinical programs, particularly in developing countries. As a result, clinicians continue to work with their students mostly on cases and projects aimed at addressing social injustice in their local communities. And they have been concerned, for the most part, about legal education and legal system reform in their home countries.

This has begun to change, however, with the rise of a global clinical community. Clinicians and their students can now explore different ways that their clinical practices can serve not only their local clients but also those of their clinical colleagues around the world. A global approach to clinical education encourages faculty and students to become involved in projects dedicated to achieving social justice across borders and in other regions of the world. And as part of a global network, clinics can engage in a global social justice practice through a variety of specialized clinical projects.

Street Law is an example of a form of clinical education with a strong social justice component that has developed its mission and expanded its influence through the global clinical movement. The primary motivation of the first Street Law programs was local social justice; law students at Georgetown University went to local high schools in Washington, D.C., to instruct students about their legal rights. That experience was then shared with clinicians in other countries, which led to Street Law becoming part of the clinical curriculum at law schools around the world—in a variety of different forms tailored to meet the educational goals and social justice needs of the particular country. For example, Street Law came to South Africa when the country was beginning to free itself from the apartheid era, and Street Law clinics became a powerful tool for social change by demonstrating to law students their capacity—as public-minded lawyers—to promote greater awareness of civic rights. Insights gained while operating what was basically a locally framed project in South Africa modeled on a project begun in the United States have served to inform and enrich Street Law clinics throughout the world.

While practically any type of specialized clinical program can have a global dimension, two areas of specialized clinical practice involve obviously globally significant work: human rights and immigration. In some human rights clinics, clinical teachers and their students literally cross borders to investigate and prosecute a wide range of human rights claims. In other instances, a particular case handled in a human rights clinic may benefit a local client but might also have implications for others around the world. Either way, clinical legal education's educational mission—and most particularly its social justice mission—includes engaging students in these types of matters as members of a socially responsible profession. Human rights clinics can have, therefore, an important influence on how future lawyers see the role of the law and the legal profession in a global society. Immigration clinics benefit from global clinical education in a different way. Typically, students in an immigration clinic carry out a local service; the client just happens to come from a foreign country. The global aspect comes with the need to cross borders and cultures while representing a local client. Thus, students handling an immigration case—whether the client is seeking refugee status or simply wants to continue a course of study—will often need to consult the law or investigate facts in another country. These types of clinics have flourished with the aid of personal and professional connections among clinicians across borders and regions that would not exist without a global clinical community.

THE GLOBAL CLINICAL MOVEMENT

Finally, we come to the global clinical movement. Does it really exist? As noted above, there is no doubt that clinical legal education has gone global. There are clinical programs at law schools all over the world, and clinical law teachers have been meeting together regularly at international conferences for many years. But a movement connotes something more than a widespread network of like-minded persons. Moreover, there are a number of substantial obstacles ahead. As noted above, much of what clinical education is all about—training future lawyers in professional skills and values—has an inherently local focus. Add to that the conservatism of the two institutions that clinical education seeks to reform—the legal profession and legal academia—and one might be inclined to bet against the chances of mounting a global clinical movement. The evidence on the ground shows otherwise.

The chapters in Part III demonstrate that a global clinical movement is already underway, one that draws on a commitment—shared by clinicians around the world—to reorienting legal education toward educating lawyers for social justice. While it is necessarily a multifaceted movement, it is gaining strength worldwide through the emergence of a common set of goals tied to preparing students for competent and ethical law practice. It gains strength also by maintaining a flexible approach to how clinical methods can be used to carry out those goals. There is, after all, more to global clinical legal education than the global clinical movement. The process of forming a global clinical movement has itself brought about important advances in clinical education as clinicians have worked together at conferences, in workshops, and on specific clinical projects. With that in mind, the global movement should focus on what it is uniquely positioned to achieve, without undercutting valuable informal networking among clinicians or seeking to replace existing national and regional clinical organizations.

What we have today is a fledgling global clinical movement with tremendous opportunities for future growth. Communication across borders has never been easier. GAJE is the natural organization to coordinate the next steps in the evolution of the global clinical movement, but it need not—and should not—go it alone. National clinical organizations have begun to look beyond their own borders to support new clinical programs in their regions, most notably in Africa and Central and Eastern Europe. But the opportunity is not just to grow in numbers. If the global clinical movement is to take on the project that was simulated in the GAJE workshop exercise—transforming legal education into justice education—it must find ways to identify, encourage, and support innovative developments in clinical legal education around the world that can help achieve the movement's educational and social justice goals. This book seeks to set the stage for the global clinical movement to move that project forward.

PART I

THE GLOBAL REACH OF CLINICAL
LEGAL EDUCATION

The chapters in this part, except for the last one, present the stories behind clinical legal education in different countries and regions of the world. The last chapter examines the global reach of clinical education in the context of debate over charges of "legal imperialism" ascribed to the law and development movement. Each of the first eight chapters tells its story from its own perspective and while each offers a full account of key developments, none is intended to be a comprehensive report on all that has happened in the field. Nor are all eight chapters together intended to provide a complete accounting of all clinical programs worldwide. They do not include, for example, programs that have existed for some time in several countries in the Middle East, nor do they cover all of the new programs in continental Western European countries that until recently have not been part of the clinical movement. These chapters do, however, provide an overview of most of the major clinical programs existing today—together with discussion and analysis of the various challenges that clinical programs face around the world.

Chapter 1 covers four countries that were among those that opened the era of modern clinical legal education. It describes the emergence of clinical programs in the United States, Britain, Canada, and Australia in the 1960s and 1970s and examines some of the key elements of those programs that have influenced the spread of clinical education around the world. Chapter 2 looks at the development of law clinics in selected countries in Southern, East, and West Africa, with somewhat more extensive discussion of pioneering work in South Africa. It also describes different approaches that clinical programs in the region have taken to the sometime competing goals of providing legal services and access to justice and teaching law students practical skills. Chapter 3 covers a group of Southeast Asian countries that have adopted clinical education relatively recently—Thailand, Malaysia, Indonesia, the Philippines, Vietnam, Laos, and Cambodia—along with India, which has been a leader in clinical legal education in South Asia since the 1970s. The chapter examines shared lessons and experiences in an effort to chart a way forward for clinical legal education in South and Southeast Asia.

Chapter 4 covers Central and Eastern Europe and includes a brief history of the development of clinical legal education in selected countries including Poland, Hungary, Bulgaria, Bosnia and Herzegovina, Serbia, Croatia, Russia, and Ukraine. The chapter examines the role that clinical programs can play educating a new generation of lawyers from the perspective of countries in transition from totalitarian or authoritarian regimes to democracy. It also includes some observations about the opportunities and challenges for legal clinics within the wider European context. Chapter 5 looks at four countries in Latin America—Argentina, Chile, Colombia, and Mexico—and how clinical legal education has evolved in the region since the 1960s, when some early clinics received funds from the United States with the specific goal of training a cadre of modern lawyers to use law to address problems of social injustice and political corruption.

Chapter 6 examines the relatively recent but rapid rise of clinical legal education in China and how these new clinical programs operate within the current Chinese legal system. The chapter also looks at challenges clinics face and opportunities for further development in the larger context of social, economic, and political change taking place as a result of modernization. Chapter 7 analyzes the special case of clinical legal education in Japan, where clinical programs have been introduced as part of recent major reforms to the Japanese system for educating lawyers. While noting that the reforms recognize the need to train future lawyers in skills and professional values, the chapter identifies a number of institutional challenges that Japanese clinics continue to face. Chapter 8 looks at recent developments in Spain, one of the few countries in Western Europe other than the United Kingdom to implement clinical programs in the law school curriculum. In addition to describing various law school clinics in Spain, it explains how clinical legal education can serve to meet the goals of the Bologna Process throughout Europe.

This part concludes with Chapter 9, which explores the question whether the major influence that clinical legal education in the United States has had in other parts of the world can be considered imperialistic. The chapter finds no basis for such a charge, based on its analysis of the critique of the law and development movement from the 1970s onward—as well as its assessment of the social action role that clinical programs play in countries outside the United States and their focus on promoting the ethical responsibilities of the legal profession.

1. THE FIRST WAVE OF MODERN CLINICAL LEGAL EDUCATION
The United States, Britain, Canada, and Australia

JEFF GIDDINGS, ROGER BURRIDGE, SHELLEY A. M.
GAVIGAN, AND CATHERINE F. KLEIN

INTRODUCTION

This chapter considers the experiences of a group of early adopters of clinical education in the United States, Britain, Canada, and Australia. While important early developments occurred in other countries and in other parts of the world, clinicians in these countries laid the groundwork for the modern clinical movement and set the stage for its spread around the world.

There are many accounts of the history of particular clinical programs, generally written by an insider, someone involved in the clinic being described. The same attention has not been given to comparative accounts and to drawing together common threads. Why do clinics develop in particular ways in different countries? The emergence of clinics often appears tied to the development of legal education more broadly, but there are a number of other significant factors—social conditions, happenstance, regulation, as well as influential individuals and groups. In this chapter, we identify similarities in the emergence of clinics as well as variations around service expectations and the prominence of clinics within the academy. The similarities may tell us something about the essence of clinic-based learning.

THE EMERGENCE OF CLINICAL LEGAL EDUCATION

Clinics developed in each of these countries amid much broader social changes.[1] In the United States, the modern clinical movement "was born in the social ferment of the 1960's." (Schrag & Meltsner, 1998 at 3) In 1960s Australia, many law teachers at the newly established "red-brick" universities (as opposed to the well-established sandstone ones) were young "baby boomers" interested in developing new teaching approaches to enhance the case method of law teaching. The clinical movement burgeoned in Britain in the fertile environment of post-1968 Europe.

---

1. The influence of the legal aid movement on clinical education in these countries and others is discussed in detail in Chapter 10.

Against the background of youthful disillusion and labor dissatisfaction that changed the shape of European governments, the student unions and law schools of England established voluntary legal advice centers as part of a purposeful, measured movement that promised radical reform of legal education. In Canada, the movement for clinic-based legal education was inextricably bound up with the movement for community-based access to justice and other broader movements for social change and social justice in the 1970s. (Gavigan, 1999; Gavigan, 1997; Ewart, 1997) A cohort of law students and progressive faculty across the country challenged their law schools to provide a curriculum that addressed the lives and areas of law that affected the poor and dispossessed, while also challenging the legal profession to accept new ways and sites of providing legal services.

Many of these early clinical programs developed from volunteer arrangements. In the United States, for example, committed students at Yale began providing legal aid services—without receiving academic credit—in the late 1920s. "The academic faculty allowed the students to work in the legal aid offices but refused to award academic credit, considering the work to be outside the academic domain." (Holland, 1999 at 510) By 1930, Bradway noted five law schools with student volunteer clinics and another seven involved in "experimental efforts to use students in legal aid work." (Bradway, 1930 at 174) The strong community service focus of these fledgling clinics continued to be prominent in the more formal, for-academic credit clinical programs that emerged later, particularly in the late 1960s and 1970s.

Storefront legal clinics also began to appear in Canada in the early 1970s. "For the first time, law schools began to be pressed by students who wanted something different." (Gavigan, 1997 at 444) In 1970, Harry Arthurs had noted the "dramatic appeal" of clinical programs and the "outlet and reinforcement for the creativity and idealism of law students" they provided. (Id. at 448) Student commitment to legal aid service delivery was important in the establishment of Australia's first clinical programs as well. At Monash, volunteer students were pivotal in the establishment of Springvale Legal Service in 1973. From 1977, legal studies students at La Trobe University extended this commitment beyond law students, working as paralegals in a legal service center for fellow students. At the University of New South Wales (UNSW), law students were closely connected to the Redfern Legal Centre in the late 1970s. Although Redfern did not become the site for the UNSW clinic, a clear culture of voluntary involvement among students had been established.

Early Clinics in the United States

As law schools began to flourish in the early twentieth century, administrators attempted to distinguish their offerings from the apprenticeship path by focusing on analysis of legal doctrine stemming from appellate decisions. Although several institutions had nascent clinical programs, such as the University of

Pennsylvania's Legal Aid Dispensary established in 1893, this form of legal education was not given much weight as many future lawyers continued to opt for apprenticeships. A contrasting view was provided by a 1921 study by the Carnegie Foundation for the Advancement of Teaching, which noted that legal education was lacking in "clinical facilities or shopwork" as compared to engineering and medical education. (Rees, 1921 at 281) Around the same time, Reginald Heber Smith published *Justice and the Poor*, calling for the expansion and development of legal aid in order to make justice more accessible and fair. Suggestions that law schools should reach out to the burgeoning legal aid organizations to provide students with real world experience were met, however, with concerns about "practicability" from many school administrators. (*Id.* at 286) Throughout the 1930s and 1940s, a vocal minority of legal scholars criticized legal education for its inability to train lawyers to serve competently upon graduation and lauded the use of clinical programs to not only supplement students' education experiences, but to also bring legal services to those who needed them the most. (Frank, 1933; Bradway, 1930)

During the 1950s, the desire to focus on teaching students the "art of lawyering" resulted in the inclusion of research and writing courses, trial skills courses, and clinical programs in the curriculum. By the end of the 1950s, more than one-quarter of accredited law schools provided some sort of clinical education. The standards for these programs varied widely, as did the models used; a small number of schools even mandated participation in a clinical program, but at many schools students did not receive academic credit. (Barry et al., 2000) The level of supervision of the students varied greatly as well, with some clinical programs giving experienced students the responsibility for supervising less-experienced students. (Stevens, 1983) The major social issues of the 1960s and 1970s—poverty and civil rights, the women's movement, the Vietnam War—had a profound influence on the direction of clinical programs, leading to greater student demand and more specific focus on providing legal services in areas such as poverty law, civil rights, women's rights, consumer rights, and environmental protection.

Probably the most important factor at this time, from the late 1960s through the 1970s, was the decision by the Ford Foundation to fund the Council on Legal Education and Professional Responsibility (CLEPR). CLEPR and its president, William Pincus, built the foundation of clinical legal education in the United States as it is known today. Although many CLEPR grants— awarded to nearly half of the then-existing law schools within the first few years of its existence—were only temporary sources of funding, the resulting clinical programs were able to take root. Of the schools that received funding, few, if any, ceased operating the clinical programs after the funding ran out. Many other schools that witnessed the success of CLEPR-funded clinical programs were inspired to start programs of their own. (Schrag & Meltsner, 1998)

Early Clinics in Britain

The conditions in the 1970s were conducive to change. The impetus of social reform promoted by Sir William Beveridge and implemented by the post-war Labor government had introduced significant developments in health and education. Basic legal services were also available for a few, which had proved sufficient to reveal the inequalities of access to the vast majority. Unmet legal need had become a rallying call for those seeking further welfare reform. Both main political parties were alert to possible solutions, and in 1971 the government conducted a comprehensive review of legal education.[2]

A 1973 survey of legal advice in universities and polytechnics revealed wide provision of services to students by staff and/or students, with many extending services to the local community. (Britton, 1973) However, none of these advice centers were incorporated in the curriculum of a law school. The first clinic to be incorporated into the undergraduate curriculum in England was established at the University of Kent in 1973, followed by Warwick University in 1975. (Rees, 1975; Sherr, 1995) Other early clinical ventures were pursued at the polytechnics of the South Bank and Trent and the University of Brunel.

The Kent program for undergraduate law students was centered upon a law office that provided the full gamut of legal services to the local community. The clinic was led by a solicitor and volunteer practitioners who served as frontline advisers and supervised the students. Student experiences ranged from legal adviser and representative, to observer and participant in the administration of the clinic. A clinical law course was introduced into the curriculum at Warwick in 1975. It emanated from student, staff, and local practitioner collaboration in establishing local legal advice centers, initially for university students and subsequently for people with legal problems from surrounding communities. It began as a one-year elective course during which students attended local advice sessions with law school staff and soon became a fully operational live-client clinical course. The main objective of the Warwick Legal Practice Program, however, was "to provide a special form of legal education to law students" rather than a primary commitment to provide legal assistance. (Sherr, 1995 at 109) Other clinical programs at Warwick have included smaller courses focusing upon placements, practice-oriented research projects, and Street Law programs.

Clinical programs have flourished in the United Kingdom periodically at a significant number of law schools. Often because the live-client clinic has not been the sole or even main focus for clinical activities, they have evolved over time into different expressions of practical engagement. These developments have been the product of new blood, adjusted pedagogical objectives, resource pressures, educational policy, and political expediency. Kent's program is no exception.

---

2. *Report of the Committee on Legal Education*, under the Chairmanship of Sir Roger Ormrod (Cmnd. 595).

In 1976 the clinic became embroiled in a political struggle with the factions in the university and the local legal community. (Smith, 1979) The incident was indicative of the sensibilities of university authorities and professional interests. It proved only to be a temporary setback for Kent, although it gave rise to wider anxieties for those contemplating setting up a clinic. The experience encouraged Warwick, for example, to outsource its advice clinics and distance the service element from the campus and university.

Clinics were neither as abundant nor as specialized as they have become in the United States. The UK engagement with clinical approaches has been distinctive because of the educational, professional, and social context that has shaped the process of lawyer education and training. Thus, while examples of simulations and role-play are widely used in UK law schools, a 1995 survey showed that only eight of the seventy-nine universities polled offered live-client clinics. Two law schools in the survey offered a full representation service, and six institutions offer advice only or partial (tribunal/arbitration) representation. (Grimes, 1995) On the other hand, Street Law as a form of clinical legal education has become quite prominent.[3]

Early Clinics in Canada

One might say that there were two expressions to the "first wave" of law school clinics in Canada in the early 1970s. Many law schools supported the creation of law student clinics housed in the law schools, often funded by provincial legal aid plans. Examples include University of Manitoba Legal Aid, Student Legal Services at the University of Alberta, Downtown Legal Services at the University of Toronto, Community Legal Advice Services Program at Osgoode Hall, and Community Legal Aid at University of Windsor. The law students in these clinics often were volunteers who received little or no academic credit for their clinic work. Their legal work, including representation of low-income clients, was supervised by one or two staff lawyers with little faculty involvement. In the province of Ontario, the model of these clinics was a student-run "student legal aid society," which provided an opportunity for students to represent clients in various matters.

Another model of the first wave found expression in clinics that were established and located in communities. In 1971, the federal government provided funding for four community legal clinics, three of which were deeply affiliated with law schools: Community Legal Services, Inc. of Point St. Charles in Montréal, Dalhousie Student Legal Aid, Osgoode Hall Law School (for Parkdale Community Legal Services (PCLS)), and Saskatoon Legal Assistance Society (associated with the College of Law, University of Saskatchewan). Each of these

---

3. Street Law clinics in the United Kingdom and elsewhere in the world are described in Chapter 15.

clinics had a broader vision of access to justice than conventional delivery of legal services and legal representation by law students for low-income people. They were committed to social change, the elimination of poverty, and community organizing and law reform. (Zemans, 1978; Garth, 1980) In 1974, the faculty of law at the University of Windsor added Legal Assistance Windsor (LAW), with its express commitment to an interdisciplinary approach of law and social work/social policy, to this pioneering cohort of clinics. (Voyvodic & Medcalf, 2004)

The legal educational implications of the first wave's social justice objectives cannot be overstated. For Parkdale's first director, Fred Zemans, Osgoode's development of this poverty law program had two central elements: "exploring the possibilities of clinical legal education and developing an alternative model of legal aid services." (Zemans, 1997 at 503) There was, however, a "dynamic tension" from the beginning between the law school and the clinic—not least because in the early period, clinical education was called "clinical training," and this appellation ensured that concern, if not outright resistance, would be expressed by some faculty members. For Osgoode's Harry Arthurs, a formidable skeptic, the "role of intellectualism [would] be further diminished." (Gavigan, 1997 at 449) Its academic rigor thus suspect, clinical education was also seen as a "competitor for the soul of legal education ... [and] a device for anchoring the law school more solidly with the legal profession." (Voyvodic & Metcalf, 2004 at 106 n. 13) New clinical programs have continued to be created at Osgoode Hall; these programs are smaller, involving fewer academic credits and fewer students, but they still provide students with the opportunity to work with clients while integrating theory and practice.

Emergence of Early Clinics in Australia

As noted earlier, Australia's earliest clinical programs—at Monash University, La Trobe University, and the University of New South Wales (UNSW)—involved newly established law schools with young academics and socially active students. Monash Law School developed Australia's first clinical program, with students being the driving force behind its establishment in 1975. The La Trobe University clinical program can be traced to the 1974 establishment of the La Trobe Legal Service by staff from the Legal Studies Department. La Trobe did not offer a law degree at that time, but had developed related socio-legal studies; there was strong student demand both for the provision of legal services to the student population and for involvement in the delivery of those services. (Evans, 1978) The UNSW law school explored the possibility of developing a clinical program with the Redfern Legal Center, but this met with resistance from some involved in the center due to independence concerns. The law school established its in-house clinical legal education program in 1981 with the opening of Kingsford Legal Centre, a move prompted in part by the recently established UNSW seeking to challenge the preeminence of Sydney University.

Interest in clinical legal education was reactivated following a range of reforms to the university sector in 1987 that expanded the number of law schools dramatically, with a number of the newly established "third-wave" law schools considering the establishment of clinical programs. (McInnis & Marginson, 1994) The mid-1990s saw the establishment of prominent clinical programs at Newcastle University, Murdoch University, and Griffith University. The live-client model has been most prominent, with some law schools also characterizing simulation-based and placement activities as clinical. Clinic appears to have been viewed by some new law schools as a means of differentiating themselves from other new law programs in an increasingly competitive environment. The clinic-oriented law degree at the University of Newcastle is the largest and most ambitious of these new programs. The Newcastle program enables students to combine the academic and vocational stages of their law studies, satisfying the practical legal training requirements by way of involvement in a range of clinical activities. (Boersig, 1996) Most Australian clinical programs have benefited greatly from continuity of key staff. Monash and La Trobe have both had senior academics remain involved in their respective clinical programs for more than twenty years, while UNSW has benefited from a series of long-term contributions. Griffith and Murdoch have also had key staff remain involved since the inception of their programs in the mid-1990s.

COMMON AND CONTRASTING EXPERIENCES

This section examines common threads from the different countries as well as those aspects where the experiences differ. External factors impacted on these early clinics as they developed their particular approaches to law teaching and service delivery. Resourcing issues have been prominent in the development and continuing operation of these clinical pioneers.

Impact of Education Policy

Most law schools in the United States now extol the virtues of their clinical offerings to a wide range of constituencies. However, had CLEPR—and later the US Department of Education—not provided substantial external funding to law schools to develop clinical programs, clinical legal education would likely have remained a marginal development. Since that time, clinical programs have had to compete with other parts of the law school for their share of the budget. Although many law schools have now embraced the value of having strong clinical programs and some have obtained sizable endowments to guarantee ongoing funds, clinics remain vulnerable—especially at law schools where clinical faculty have only a limited role in law school governance.

The environment has been conducive to the introduction of clinical methods in the United Kingdom since the 1980s, when undergraduate education became a focus for government regulation and quality assurance. Higher education reforms have promoted experiential and practice-oriented learning, promoting problem-solving approaches and diversity of learning methods. However, not all of the government's policy initiatives have been beneficial for clinical programs. The professions became more distanced from the academies as national and European education policy, rather than professional competence, became the primary lever of higher education reform. Moreover, the rapid expansion of higher education exacerbated the resource tensions. Professional supervision of student casework by clinical teachers for large numbers of students has always fared badly in comparison with the traditional "pile-them-high-and-teach-them-cheap" lecturing model. The government's funding model continues to treat law among the cheapest disciplines to teach. Successful clinical programs have consequently either been elective or purely voluntary. On the other hand, the government has supported a recent trend for large-scale student engagement in the community. The attorney general, in conjunction with city firms and the bar, are vigorously promoting pro bono student activities—emphasizing, as have law school clinics, professional altruism alongside educational improvement and career development.

The impact of changes in education policy on clinical education has been most dramatic in Australia, where moves toward a mass participation model of higher education contributed to the emergence of new law schools. The sweeping reforms to higher education instituted by the federal Labor government in the late 1980s freed up the processes required of universities to establish new schools. With the number of law schools doubling between 1989 and 2003—from twelve to twenty-four—the newer law schools were a significant force in building the momentum of the Australian clinical movement. (Johnstone & Vignaendra, 2003)

Opposition from Outside
Canadian clinics faced early opposition from the practicing profession. The clinic at the Windsor law school, for example, "faced concerted opposition from Windsor's private bar, which strenuously opposed the entry of law students into the city's courtrooms on the grounds that they lacked professional qualifications and would therefore put clients at risk. Some members of the judiciary also expressed this opposition, refusing to permit law students to appear." (Voyvodic & Medcalf, 2004 at 112) The clinical program established by the Osgoode Hall Law School in the early 1970s faced initial opposition from the Law Society of Upper Canada, particularly in relation to the clinic's role in the delivery of legal aid services. The law school agreed that the clinic would only assist people who could not obtain legal services elsewhere, and that it would neither act for paying clients nor compete with private practitioners who handled primarily criminal and family law cases under the judicare scheme. (Zemens, 1997) The fledgling Parkdale Clinic subsequently enjoyed great support from significant others in the legal profession, not least the then Attorney General (and later Chief Justice of Ontario)

Roy McMurtry, Samuel Grange (later a judge of the Ontario Court of Appeal), and numerous lawyers who gave generously of their time and expertise to support students and the board of directors. (Ellis, 1997)

The UNSW law school encountered significant resistance from the Law Society of New South Wales to the establishment of its clinical program, Kingsford Legal Centre. This resistance was due in part to the law school's links to Redfern Legal Centre, a very prominent and radical community legal center. Staff and volunteers at Redfern were behind the establishment of the Australian Legal Workers Group, which was setting itself up as the alternative law society for radical young lawyers. The director of the UNSW clinic thus had to negotiate with the President and Secretary of the Law Society not only about the opening of Kingsford, but also about what type of practicing certificate the law society would give him. After several months of difficult negotiations, the Law Society backed off and issued him the required practicing certificate.

In England, the Kent clinic faced early difficulties on a range of fronts. While receiving considerable support from radical practitioners and some elements within the professional establishment, self-interested local solicitors were concerned that "some of their potential clients were obtaining free legal services at the clinic." (Smith, 1979 at 10) In addition, the university senate became unhappy with the political and public nature of the cases taken on by the clinic. These included a series of cases where the clinic acted for students against the university, represented city refuse collectors in an action against the city council, and led an inquiry into the management of a psychiatric hospital, one of whose board members was the wife of the university vice chancellor. (McFarlane, 1988 at 149; Smith, 1979 at 9) The clinic also represented a journalist accused of spying on the Central Intelligence Agency of the US government.

The highly politicized nature of the legal work done by some clinical programs in the United States—together with the limited availability of alternative legal aid services—have resulted in certain clinics facing very strong opposition from powerful political interests, including state governments. Indeed, some attempts have been made to have universities close down clinical programs. In a comprehensive outline of attempts at such political interference, Kuehn and Joy explain that the "interests of politicians and of university alumni and donors add an additional level of outside interest and potential interference in law school clinic activities." (Kuehn & Joy, 2003 at 1974)

Interest in Professionalism and Ethics

Much has been written about the suitability of clinic-based learning while at law school for fostering the ethical awareness and professional responsibility standards of practicing lawyers.[4] Concerns regarding ethics were clearly prominent in both the establishment and development of clinical programs in the United

---

4. Ethics and professionalism is the topic of Chapter 12.

States and Canada, and have become increasingly significant for Australian and UK programs.

The Canadian experience with clinical legal education, notably in those clinics engaged in community-based poverty law legal services, afforded myriad opportunities for student engagement with—and critical interrogation of—legal ethics and professional responsibility. As one of the early clinicians in Canada observed, in reflecting upon his own experience in the 1970s, "the concept of a community-based legal clinic delivering legal services is an inherently radical idea" rendered even more complex when law students possessed of "disconcertingly high ideals but often little experience" are on the front lines. (Ellis, 1997 at 571)

From the outset, the Parkdale Clinic challenged the profession's strictures against advertising; even more challenging were some of the early client services decisions that the clinic made, including a policy not to represent landlords, even indigent landlords, in landlord and tenant disputes. (Zemens, 1997; Elis, 1997) One of the most controversial policy decisions taken by the Parkdale Clinic involved a decision not to represent male clients in matters where spousal assault is an issue, unless unable to find other legal representation for the man. These policies illustrate the sorts of challenges that these clinical programs presented—not only to the traditional approach to the delivery of legal services, but also for students who were required to grapple with the transformative potential and political (and educational and professional) implications of alternative approaches to the practice of law. (White, 1997; Mosher, 1997) Significantly, students in these programs have made significant contributions to the professional literature that reflect their experience with their clients and the community, their critical engagement with clinic polices and professionalism, and poverty law and law reform more generally. (*e.g.*, Robertson, 1997; Romano, 1997; Rachin, 1997)

As noted earlier, improving law school training in professional responsibility was one of the key goals of CLEPR as it was funding the US clinical movement in the 1970s. In addition, at around the same time, the legal profession was deeply affected by the aftermath of the Watergate scandal of the early 1970s. The large-scale involvement of lawyers in the Watergate cover-up (Richard Nixon himself was a lawyer), prompted a public demand for federal regulation of the profession. The then Chief Justice of the United States, Warren Berger, spoke out on the subject. As a result, the American Bar Association (ABA) instituted several major reforms regarding professional responsibility and ethics, including the mandate that all students at ABA-accredited schools take a course in professional responsibility and ethics. Many students and administrators recognized that clinical programs served as training grounds for this new focus in legal education by presenting students with ethical dilemmas in practice and testing their ability to solve those problems.

Clinics, particularly live-client clinics, have long been recognized in the United Kingdom for the opportunities they present for ethical inquiry and development inherent in the student-client experience. The capacity for clinics to address ethical concerns has also been recognized in government proposals for legal education reform.[5] Clinical teachers have consistently espoused the professional importance of clinical methods as a vehicle for ethical awareness and appreciation. Experiential methods are at their most valuable when they can embrace ethical issues as part of a holistic approach to legal understanding. (Webb, 1996) In this regard, it is salutary to reflect on the pedagogic implications of Kent Law School's experience of the "politics of representation" described above.

The ethics focus of Australian clinical legal education has been articulated more clearly in recent years. Styles and Zariski have referred to the increasing importance of legal education goals related to the development of professional ethics and student-centered learning, along with the development of student understanding of the relationship between theory and practice and the development of technical skills. They consider clinics well placed to counter some of the negative influences of traditional legal education on students' commitment to the public interest. (Styles & Zariski, 2001) Dickson and Noone rightly note that the clinical setting "constantly gives rise to spontaneous and various ethical questions which challenge and test students." (Dickson & Noone, 1996 at 847) Given that written ethical conduct rules cannot cover every possible circumstance, clinics provide students with opportunities to develop the ability to identify and address ethical issues in relation to a wide variety of matters, including conflict of interest, confidentiality, and legal professional privilege. The 2007 Best Practices Report published in the United States has similarly called for law schools to expand their use of experiential education as "a powerful tool for forming professional habits and understandings." (Stuckey and Others, 2007 at 123)

POINTS OF CONTRAST

Clinics develop in ways that reflect the particular circumstances and concerns of different nations. The clinical movement in the United States is considerably more prominent than in the other countries addressed in this chapter. It has achieved a greater sense of critical mass, in large part through the presence of professional accreditation requirements that promote clinic-based learning for law students. Nonetheless, as recently as 2007 the Carnegie Report referred to clinical training in the United States as "the underdeveloped area of legal pedagogy." (Sullivan et al., 2007 at 24)

The Academic–Professional Divide in Legal Education
In the United States, a written examination—administered by each individual state—is now the standard method for qualifying for admission to the bar.

---

5. Lord Chancellor's Advisory Committee on Legal Education and Conduct, First Report on Legal Education and Training, ACLEC 1996, HMSO, London.

Obviously, the need for law schools to prepare graduates for entry into the profession is particularly acute in a system that does not rely on or require apprenticeships. This absence of a requirement for law graduates to complete a vocation-focused professional program prior to admission to practice has thus shaped the expectation in the United States that law schools play a substantial role in preparing students for the practice of law. It is also likely to have fostered the greater prominence of clinics in the United States as compared to Australia and the United Kingdom, where legal education continues to be divided into academic and professional stages, albeit with some law schools delivering both stages.

More clinics might have developed and flourished in the United Kingdom were it not for the success of the vocational postgraduate programs organized by the Law Society and the General Council of the Bar. The UK professions, unlike their US counterparts, have long required the successful completion of a year-long program of practical education and training for those seeking admission to practice. Such practically oriented training relieves the "academic stage" providers from the obligation to incorporate professional concerns in their degrees or conversion programs. As a result, many vocational programs have become active in promoting clinics. The Inns of Court School of Law, for example, offers live-client opportunities in conjunction with the charity, the Free Representation Unit. The College of Law, which delivers professional programs at seven centers in England, runs five legal advice clinics. The Bar Council—and recently the Bar Standards Board—encourages providers of its Bar Vocational Course to include clinics as an option. The University of Northumbria offers a program unique in the United Kingdom, combining the academic and vocational stages in a single curriculum.

While relying on a system of professional education similar to that of the United Kingdom, Australian vocational programs, with the exception of Newcastle Law School, have not been as prominent as advocates for clinic-based learning. Newcastle was the first Australian law school to offer a program combining completion of a law degree with this professional requirement. Newcastle law students could choose to complete either a standard law degree or to enter the "Professional Program," which enabled students to obtain a restricted right of legal practice immediately upon graduation. Other Australian law schools which operate professional programs have continued to rely heavily on simulations, supplemented by work placement arrangements which do not involve close direct supervision by program staff. Monash clinicians were heavily involved in the development of the law school's vocational program in 1999, incorporating a substantial clinical component. However, that program was discontinued in 2007 due to university requirements that such postgraduate programs generate substantial revenue streams.

Accreditation Requirements

The American Bar Association (ABA) has strongly supported clinical programs in the United States through its authority to accredit law schools authorized to graduate students qualified to sit for the bar examination in every state. The requirements for law schools to gain ABA accreditation include making clinical experiences available to students. The ABA has also given preference to in-house models of clinical education over externship arrangements; ABA scrutiny of externships is more detailed, and limits are placed on the amount of credit that can be given to clinical work that does not involve direct supervision by law school faculty or staff employed by the law school. (Joy, 2004) The ABA also promoted the student practice rules critical to running live-client clinics and, as discussed below, supported efforts to increase the status of clinical faculty.

This strong institutional support of clinics by the practicing profession contrasts with the relative lack of prescription in both the United Kingdom and Australia, where the professions have not been as actively supportive. The focus of Australian legal professional regulators has been on ensuring coverage by each law school of particular areas of substantive law rather than on the approaches used to foster student learning. Regulators have also relied on the practical orientation of the vocational phase of Australian legal education to prepare law graduates for practice. The implications of the split pathways to professional qualification in the United Kingdom—between a knowledge-focused academic stage and a practically oriented professional one—have marginalized the holistic potential of clinical methods. The academic undergraduate stage of legal study concentrates on the acquisition of the knowledge and analytical skills appropriate for a liberal higher education program and is reflected in the career destination of graduates, less than 50 percent of whom enter the legal profession.

Funding

A key difficulty for law teaching and a factor limiting the further development of clinical legal education in Australia is the Relative Funding Model used by the federal government since 1991 for the allocation of operating grants to universities. Law was placed in the bottom discipline cluster, along with economics, accounting, and various humanities. The least expensive ways of teaching have become the default position for Australian law schools. In the absence of a strong tradition of clinic-based experiential learning in law and with law funded at a minimal level, it is less likely that law schools will prioritize clinical programs given that they are a relatively expensive form of legal education. The establishment of the Southern Communities Advocacy Law Education Service (SCALES) by Murdoch University in 1997 was therefore a significant development, as SCALES was the first clinical program to receive direct federal government funding—and continues to receive funding—as one of four programs supported by a small clinical legal education funding program included in the 1998 federal budget. For the past decade, the federal Attorney-General's Department has directly supported the clinical programs at Griffith, Monash, Murdoch, and UNSW.

The UK experience is similar to that in Australia, with the funding of undergraduate law programs in the lowest band for government support of university teaching. Moreover, the government awards additional funding to those universities and law schools which are most research-active; although opportunities for law schools to achieve significant research funding are relatively scarce, the quest for research outputs and scholarly reputation further eclipses clinical ventures.

Clinical legal education is funded in the United States for the most part through each university's regular budget process. This places clinical programs in a relatively strong position, as they are an important component of both public and private law schools. The problem, as noted earlier, is that clinics must compete with other law school programs and can be vulnerable—given their relatively higher cost—in times of economic stress. Clinics might be thought to have an advantage at public universities since they provide a direct public service, but most publicly funded law schools receive only a small percentage of their support from state funds.

Clinics in Canada have had to face funding uncertainties—the Dalhousie clinic was almost forced to close when the law school experienced a funding crisis in the early 1990s—related not just to supporting clinical legal education, but also support for legal aid more generally. The Saskatoon Legal Assistance Clinic (and the College of Law) had made an enormous, shaping contribution to the form of the first comprehensive legal aid plan in Saskatchewan in 1974. But then, following a change in government and subsequent restructuring of legal aid (notably the elimination of any form of community governance or boards), the legal aid plan withdrew from its partnership in the clinical program in 1983—and the College of Law was unable to continue it on its own after the 1986–87 academic year.

Treatment of Clinical Academics

Wherever clinics have been established, concerns have been raised in relation to the marginalization of clinical academics. This may be more of an issue in the United States because of the broader acceptance of clinical teaching. The more you have, the more you have to lose.

Clinical teachers in the United States, as a group, have always been treated to some degree as second class by the legal academy. In the 1970s, CLEPR provided a series of grants to augment the salaries of clinical faculty relative to those of classroom teachers, in an effort to aid in the recruitment and retention of skilled clinical faculty. By doing so, CLEPR hoped to bring legitimacy not only to the role of the clinical faculty within law schools, but also to clinical legal education as a whole. (Joy & Kuehn, 2008) While some progress was made, Schrag and Meltsner noted—referring to a 1978 CLEPR report that only 14 percent of full-time clinicians held tenure-track positions—that the lack of status and equal treatment of clinic staff was "the most difficult issue facing clinical legal education." (Schrag & Meltsner, 1998 at 8) In 1980, the ABA and the Association of American Law Schools issued a joint report on clinical education that echoed many of CLEPR's concerns and suggestions regarding the role of clinical faculty, but at the same time left any action at the discretion of each law school's administration. The reality is that "[t]he clinical educator is in a double, if not a triple, bind. If clinicians devote too much time to skills training, then they neglect legal scholarship. If they spend too much time on scholarship, their supervisory duties may suffer, and, after all, it is close supervision that makes skills education successful." (Tomain & Solimine, 1990 at 312–13)

If clinics are to become more prominent in the United Kingdom and Australia, issues related to the status of clinicians will no doubt require close attention. It is likely to be challenging for significant progress to be made in addressing the relative lack of status without support from the practicing profession. This may prove to be difficult as there is a lack of interest among the professions for clinical programs in the academic stage, and the problem is compounded by a widespread disdain felt by many law teachers for legal practice, believing it to be a distraction from the intellectual mission of undergraduate scholarship. Tony Bradney has summed up the distaste for practitioners prevalent in many UK law schools: "[T]hrough the century, university law schools have progressively sought to distance themselves from the legal professions, arguing that their academic role was incompatible with close contact." (Bradney, 1992 at 5)

THE LASTING LEGACY OF THESE EARLY CLINICS

The early clinical experiences described in this chapter have had a major impact on the development of clinical legal education—and legal education generally—in each of the four countries, and on the shape that clinics have taken in other countries around the world. As seen in the other chapters in Part I on the global reach of clinical education, traces of these first-wave clinics are seen to some degree wherever clinical programs exist today. The question remains, however, whether these early clinics will leave a lasting legacy, not only in their own counties but also elsewhere in the world.

The comparatively slow development of the UK clinical movement has defied its early promise despite the environment being, in many ways, more conducive to the introduction of clinical methods. First, education policy has sought to ensure that public education is more responsive to the needs of the professions, employers, and business. Second, the protectionist apprehension expressed by some local practitioners soon turned into support as the clinics generated new clients; in some areas niche law firms diversified to meet the newly identified needs. Third, successive reports on legal education from government enquiries, official committees, and professional reviews have almost universally recommended the adoption of clinical approaches. Finally, research has confirmed the pedagogical effectiveness of clinical courses. In a competitive market, law schools might have been expected to seek advantage by adopting a clinical approach, but only Northumbria University has done so at an institutional level.

Clinical legal education has faced challenges in the United Kingdom from the combined forces of academic indifference, vocational provision, and inadequate funding. Moreover, the lack of government and professional leadership or coordination of the academic stage of legal education has undermined efforts to establish live-client clinics as a staple offering in undergraduate programs. Instead, law schools have developed a variety of clinical approaches in their teaching, borrowing models from elsewhere and developing their own distinctive programs. Warwick University provides a prominent example, where clinical initiatives now include a Death Penalty Internship program, a Discrimination Awareness Campaign, a Community Justice Project, and a long-established simulation clinic.

In the Australian context, the key to shaping clinical programs had been the backgrounds of the people working in the clinics. These programs tend to have been—and continue to be—staffed by people with a strong commitment to access to justice issues. This has brought with it an abiding emphasis on community service and using the law and legal system to achieve community development objectives. (Giddings, 2003) Another important factor is that Australian clinical programs have served multiple masters. Many students are drawn to clinics by a range of factors, including the opportunity to be part of much-needed community services, to find a practical context for their other law studies, and to develop legal practice skills. Law schools and universities have viewed clinics as valuable student learning environments as well as sites for significant community service contributions. Law schools have also used clinics to distinguish themselves from neighboring law schools in terms of the learning opportunities provided to students. New funding opportunities may become available as governments are increasingly interested in the contributions clinics can make to the delivery of legal services.

Clinical law teachers in the United States have spent the last forty years training themselves to be teachers and lawyers who are attentive to the transmission of knowledge, skills, and professional values to students who (hopefully) will be critical thinkers who do not accept the existing order as being the only way possible—and who will be advocates for the improvement of the legal system and profession. Clinical education has added a uniquely important dimension to the law school's mission of preparing students for the practice of law through its own methodology: clinics place students in positions where they have to take responsibility for another human being, where their words and actions matter, and where their hard work or failures have consequences for people other than themselves.

The history of Canadian clinics and clinical education is an uneven one, and not always a happy one. And yet, even periods of dearth have not been complete. As noted above, one of the first Canadian clinics and clinical programs was forced to close its doors, and for almost twenty years Saskatchewan saw no clinical education. However, in 2005, a new generation of Saskatchewan law students—in collaboration with the inner city community in Saskatoon—began to work on a new community legal initiative: Community Legal Assistance Services for Saskatoon Inner City (CLASSIC). With the prospect of a renewed clinical legal education program at this law school, it is fitting to end this discussion of the Canadian clinic experience with this new promise expressed through CLASSIC's mission statement, resonant as it is of the spirit and vision of the first wave:

> The purpose of CLASSIC is to provide legal assistance to low-income, histori-cally disadvantaged Saskatchewan residents (with particular attention to the needs of Aboriginal peoples) through a legal clinic that meets the needs of the community. This provides students with clinical experience, new insights into the social reality of law, and also fosters ethic of social justice and cultural understanding.

The Canadian legacy is one of struggle, growth, loss, and renewal. Clinical edu-cation in Canada, notably in the poverty law movement, has helped to redefine the scope of poverty law and the communities to be served. Never static, always in transition and transformation.

CONCLUSION

These first-wave histories highlight the distinctiveness of clinical legal education as a point of both strength and vulnerability. The need to respond to casework demands and the intensive nature of clinical supervision mark clinicians as dif-ferent to their legal academic colleagues, as do the closer links clinicians maintain with the practicing profession. These histories also demonstrate a complex foun-dation of the global clinical movement. Having emerged during progressive times in the late 1960s and early 1970s, clinics and their staff have influenced the practi-cal and ethical frameworks of their students for some four decades. While this longevity is a significant achievement, challenges remain to the sustainability of clinical movements in these four first-wave countries and the rest of the world.

LIST OF REFERENCES

BRIAN ABEL-SMITH, MICHAEL ZANDER, & ROSILAND ROSS, LEGAL PROBLEMS AND THE CITIZEN (Heinemann 1973).

Jennie Abell, *Ideology and the Emergence of Legal Aid in Saskatchewan*, 16 DALHOUSIE L.J. 125 (1993).

Margaret Martin Barry, Jon C. Dubin, & Peter A. Joy, *Clinical Legal Education for This Millennium: The Third Wave*, 7 CLINICAL L. REV. 1 (2000).

John Boersig, "Clinical Legal Education: The Newcastle Model," paper presented at the Australasian Professional Legal Education Council

International Conference, *Skills Development for Tomorrow's Lawyers: Needs and Strategies*, Conference Papers, Vol. 1, at 463 (1996).

Anthony Bradney, *Ivory Towers and Satanic Mills: Choices for University Law Schools*, 17 STUD. IN HIGHER EDUC. 5 (1992).

John S. Bradway, *The Nature of a Legal Aid Clinic*, 3 S. CAL. L. REV. 173 (1930).

Philip Britton, *Students and Legal Advice: A Survey Report*, LEGAL ACTION BULLETIN (1973).

Jennifer Corcoran, *Legal Aid—A Developing Need*, 7 L. TCHR. 161 (1973).

Judith Dickson & Mary Anne Noone, The Challenge of Teaching Professional Ethics, Australasian Professional Legal Education Council International Conference, *Skills Development for Tomorrow's Lawyers: Needs and Strategies*, Conference Papers, Vol. 2, at 847 (1996).

S. Ronald Ellis, *The Ellis Archives—1972 to 1981: An Early View from the Parkdale Trenches*, 35 OSGOODE HALL L.J. 535 (1997).

Adrian Evans, *Para-legal Training at La Trobe University*, 3 LEGAL SERVICE BULL. 65 (1978).

Doug Ewart, *Parkdale Community Legal Services: Community Law Office, or Law Office in a Community?*, OBITER DICTA, Sept. 30, 1971 at 8, *reprinted in* 35 OSGOODE HALL L.J. 475 (1997).

Jerome Frank, *Why Not a Clinical Lawyer-School?*, 81 U. PA. L. REV. 907 (1933).

BRYANT G. GARTH, NEIGHBOURHOOD LAW FIRMS FOR THE POOR (Sijthoff & Noordhoff 1980).

Shelley A. M. Gavigan, *Poverty Law, Theory, and Practice: The Place of Gender and Class in Access to Justice*, *in* LOCATING LAW: RACE/CLASS/GENDER CONNECTIONS 208 (Elizabeth Comack ed., Fernwood Publishing 1999).

Shelley A. M. Gavigan, *Twenty-Five Years of Dynamic Tension: The Parkdale Community Legal Services Experience*, 35 OSGOODE HALL L.J. 443 (1997).

Richard Grimes, *Legal Skills and Clinical Education*, 2 WEB J. CURRENT LEGAL ISSUES (1995).

Jeff Giddings, *A Circle Game: Issues in Australian Clinical Legal Education*, 11 LEGAL EDUC. REV. 38 (1999).

Jeff Giddings, *Clinical Legal Education in Australia: A Historical Perspective*, 3 INT'L J. CLINICAL LEGAL EDUC. 7 (2003).

Laura G. Holland, *Invading the Ivory Tower: The History of Clinical Education at Yale Law School*, 49 J. LEGAL EDUC. 504 (1999).

RICHARD JOHNSTONE & SUMITRA VIGNAENDRA, LEARNING OUTCOMES AND CURRICULUM DEVELOPMENT IN LAW: A REPORT COMMISSIONED BY THE AUSTRALIAN UNIVERSITIES TEACHING COMMITTEE (2003).

Peter A. Joy, *Evolution of ABA Standards Relating to Externships: Steps in the Right Direction?*, 10 CLINICAL L. REV. 681 (2004).

Peter A. Joy & Robert R. Kuehn, *The Evolution of ABA Standards for Clinical Faculty*, 75 TENN. L. REV. 183 (2008).

Robert R. Kuehn & Peter A. Joy, *An Ethics Critique of Interference in Law School Clinics*, 71 FORDHAM L. REV. 1971 (2003).

Lord Chancellor's Advisory Committee on Legal Education and Conduct, First Report on Legal Education and Training (1996).

Michael Meltsner & Phillip G. Schrag, *Scenes from a Clinic*, 127 U.PA. L. REV. 1 (1978).

Janet E. Mosher, *Legal Education: Nemesis or Ally of Social Movements?*, 35 OSGOODE HALL L.J. 613 (1997).

Les McCrimmon, *Mandating a Culture of Service: Pro Bono in the Law School Curriculum*, 14 LEGAL EDUC. REV. 53 (2003–2004).

Julie McFarlane, An Evaluation of the Role and Practice of Clinical Legal Education, With Particular Reference to Undergraduate Legal Education in the United Kingdom (unpublished Ph.D dissertation 1988).

CRAIG MCINNIS & SIMON MARGINSON, AUSTRALIAN LAW SCHOOLS AFTER THE 1987 PEARCE REPORT 13 (Australian Government Publishing Service 1994).

ROGER ORMROD, COMMITTEE ON LEGAL EDUCATION, REPORT, 1971, Cmnd. 595.

Leah Rachin, *The Spousal Assault Policy: A Critical Analysis*, 35 OSGOODE HALL L.J. 785 (1997).

ALFRED Z. REED, TRAINING FOR THE PUBLIC PROFESSION OF THE LAW: HISTORICAL DEVELOPMENT AND PRINCIPAL CONTEMPORARY PROBLEMS OF LEGAL EDUCATION IN THE UNITED STATES WITH SOME ACCOUNT OF CONDITIONS IN ENGLAND AND CANADA (Carnegie Foundation for the Advancement of Teaching 1921).

William M. Rees, *Clinical Legal Education: An Analysis of the University of Kent Model*, 9 LAW TEACHER 125 (1975).

Cherie Robertson, *The Demystification of Legal Discourse: Reconceiving the Role of the Poverty Lawyer as Agent of the Poor*, 35 OSGOODE HALL L.J. 637 (1997).

Diana A. Romano, *The Legal Advocate and the Questionably Competent Client in the Context of a Poverty Law Clinic*, 35 OSGOODE HALL L.J. 737 (1997).

PHILIP G. SCHRAG & MICHAEL MELTSNER, REFLECTIONS ON CLINICAL LEGAL EDUCATION (Northeastern University Press 1998).

Avrom Sherr, *Clinical Education at Warwick and the Skills Movement: Was Clinic a Creature of Its Time?*, in FRONTIERS OF LEGAL SCHOLARSHIP 116 (Geoffrey A. Wilson ed., John Wiley & Sons, 1995).

Peter Smith, *Developments in Clinical Legal Education in England*, Council on Legal Education for Professional Responsibility, Vol. 11, No. 3 (1979).

ROBERT STEVENS, LAW SCHOOL: LEGAL EDUCATION IN AMERICA FROM THE 1850S TO THE 1980s (University of North Carolina Press 1983).

ROY STUCKEY AND OTHERS, BEST PRACTICES FOR LEGAL EDUCATION (Clinical Legal Education Association 2007).

Irene Styles & Archie Zariski, *Law Clinics and the Promotion of Public Interest Lawyering*, 19 LAW IN CONTEXT 65 (2001).

WILLIAM M. SULLIVAN ET AL., EDUCATING LAWYERS: PREPARATION FOR THE PROFESSION OF LAW (Jossey Bass 2007).

Joseph Tomain & Michael Solimine, *Skills Skepticism in the Postclinic World*, 40 J. LEGAL EDUC. 307 (1990).

William Twining, *The Benson Report and Legal Education: A Personal View, in* LAW IN THE BALANCE—LEGAL SERVICES IN THE EIGHTIES 186 (Philip A. Thomas ed., Robertson Publishing 1982).

Rose Voyvodic & Mary Medcalf, *Advancing Social Justice Through an Interdisciplinary Approach to Clinical Legal Education: The Case of Legal Assistance of Windsor*, 14 J.L. & SOC. POL'Y 101 (2004).

Rose Voyvodic, *"Considerable Promise and Troublesome Aspects": Theory and Methodology of Clinical Legal Education* 20 WINDSOR Y.B. ACCESS TO JUST. 111 (2001).

Julian S. Webb, *Inventing the Good: A Prospectus for Clinical Education and the Teaching of Legal Ethics in England & Wales*, 30 LAW TEACHER 288 (1996).

Lucie E. White, *The Transformative Potential of Clinical Legal Education*, 35 OSGOODE HALL L.J. 603 (1997).

Frederick H. Zemens, *The Dream Is Still Alive: Twenty-five Years of Parkdale Community Legal Services and the Osgoode Hall Law School Intensive Program in Poverty Law*, 35 OSGOODE HALL L.J. 499 (1997).

Frederick H. Zemans, *Legal Aid and Advice in Canada*, 16 OSGOODE HALL L.J. 663 (1978).

2. CLINICAL LEGAL EDUCATION IN AFRICA
Legal Education and Community Service

DAVID McQUOID-MASON, ERNEST OJUKWU, AND
GEORGE MUKUNDI WACHIRA

INTRODUCTION

In most African countries, university law clinics were established to serve live clients with two purposes in mind: to provide legal services and access to justice, and to teach law students practical skills. In several African countries, particularly in South Africa and in East and West Africa, postgraduate law schools provide vocational training to law graduates, and some of those have also introduced clinical legal education programs involving work in law clinics.

The genesis of modern law clinics in the United States during the 1960s and the South African clinical movement in the 1970s were both closely linked to access to justice. (Franklin, 1986; McQuoid-Mason, 1982; Haupt, 2006) "Live client" clinics tend to be the norm in Africa, rather than simulated clinics, because African universities are frequently surrounded by seas of poverty and often the services provided by national legal aid schemes are minimal. Many African law schools feel, therefore, that they cannot afford the luxury of running purely simulated clinical legal education programs as is sometimes done in the developed world. As the element of social justice education tends to distinguish clinical law courses from ordinary practical legal training courses, one of us has defined clinical legal education as "teaching legal skills in a reflective social justice context." (McQuoid-Mason, 2008 at 2) Clinical legal education thus seeks to relate the teaching of legal skills to the social justice issues that law students experience through dealing with indigent and marginalized clients.

Modern forms of law clinics were first established at universities in Africa during the 1970s, for example, in Ethiopia, Uganda, Tanzania, South Africa, and Zimbabwe, with others following in the 1980s and 1990s. In some instances the early attempts at establishing clinics were undermined by political events, in countries such as Ethiopia, Uganda, and Nigeria. Law clinics were established for the first time in a number of other African countries at the beginning of this century—and reestablished in Nigeria and Ethiopia.

The first law clinics in South Africa were established during the apartheid era for different reasons at different universities. At the historically "White" English-speaking liberal universities, law clinics were established primarily to help the victims of apartheid—and other poor persons whose human rights had been violated—to access legal advice and assistance, while at the same time allowing law students to gain practical experience. However, at the historically "White" Afrikaans-speaking universities, the emphasis was on exposing students to practical skills rather than assisting with human rights violations. A similar approach to that of the Afrikaans-speaking universities was adopted by most of the historically "Black" universities during the apartheid regime, when the majority of their teaching staff were vetted by the apartheid authorities. In other Southern African countries, such as Zimbabwe, Botswana, Swaziland, Lesotho, Namibia, Zambia, and Mozambique, law clinics were established in order to provide a service to the poor and to teach law students practical skills. The establishment of law clinics in Zimbabwe and Mozambique were influenced by developments in South Africa, while the law clinics in the other Southern African countries tended to develop independently.

In East Africa, the earliest law clinic was established in Tanzania to enable law student to assist people facing human rights violations. In Kenya, Uganda, Ethiopia, Rwanda, and Somaliland, the emphasis was on providing law students with opportunities to gain practical experience, as well as to assist the poor. In West Africa, law clinics were established in francophone Africa outside of university law faculties in order to provide legal services to the poor. The same impetus motivated the University of Sierra Leone law clinic. By contrast, in Nigeria the main thrust has been to reform legal education by introducing clinical legal education methods into the curriculum at both university and the postgraduate law school levels, while at the same time assisting the poor. These developments have been influenced in part by the South African experience. In Sierra Leone, the emphasis has been on human rights, similar to that in Tanzania.

This chapter provides a short history of the development of law clinics in Southern, East, and West Africa and also describes, for each region, why the clinics were needed, the basic clinical program requirements, and the type of training offered to clinical law students, including evaluation methods.

SOUTHERN AFRICA

Short History of Law Clinics in the Region

Live-client law clinics began operating in Southern African countries such as South Africa and Zimbabwe in the early 1970s, Botswana in the mid-1980s, and Swaziland in the 1990s. More recently law clinics have been established in Lesotho, Namibia, Zambia, and Mozambique, while Malawi has been in the process of setting up a clinic during the past two years. (McQuoid-Mason, 2007)

The first legal aid clinic in South Africa was established by law students at the University of Cape Town in 1972. The clinic was managed and staffed entirely by law students, with supervision being done by legal practitioners from outside the university. The clinics were held in poor neighborhoods during the evenings in churches or town halls. The program differed from subsequent law faculty programs in that nobody employed by the law school supervised the students and no office, equipment, or other facilities were provided by the university. The first law faculty staff-initiated law clinics were established at the universities of the Witwatersrand and Natal (Durban). The Ford Foundation funded a legal aid conference in South Africa in 1973, which was the catalyst for the law clinic movement in the region. At the time of the conference the only clinics in the country were at the universities of Cape Town and the Witwatersrand, but within two years five others had been established. (McQuoid-Mason, 1982)

By 1981, law clinics had been established at fourteen South African universities: Cape Town (1972), the Witwatersrand (1973), Natal (Durban) (1973), Port Elizabeth (1974), Natal (Pietermarizburg) (1974), Western Cape (1975), Stellenbosch (1975), Durban-Westville (1978), Zululand (1978), Rhodes (1979), the North (1980), Pretoria (1980), South Africa (1981), and Rand Afrikaans University (1981). Most of these early initiatives existed without funding from outside donors and relied entirely upon the law faculties providing limited support in the form of office accommodation, equipment, and materials. Staff members often supervised and administered the law clinics in a part-time capacity without receiving any reduction in their regular teaching loads. (McQuoid-Mason, 1982; De Klerk, 2005) At present, there are law clinics at seventeen South African universities. These include, in addition to those listed above (some of which were merged), the universities of the North West (formerly the Universities of Potchefstroom and Bophuthatswana), Venda, Limpopo (formerly the North), the Free State, Fort Hare, and Walter Sisulu University (formerly the University of the Transkei).

Nearly all law faculties and law schools at universities in South Africa operate live-client law clinics. South African university law clinics employ directors who are practicing attorneys or advocates, who may or may not be employed in the faculty as law teachers with tenure. In some universities, law clinic staff and the directors are employed on a contractual basis without tenure because the law clinics depend upon donor, rather than university, funding. In either case, if the director is a practicing attorney, the clinic will be accredited by the local law society and candidate attorneys may be employed—for admission purposes—as legal interns doing community service.

Some clinics evolved in relation to curricular needs. The University of Zimbabwe law clinic, for example, was used as the core component of the final year of the postgraduate LLB degree when first established in 1974. The University of Zimbabwe LLB degree was unique to the Southern African region at the time, because it was the first university to place clinical legal education at the heart of its law degree program. The final year is devoted to the procedural law courses, and all students are required to work in the law clinic, which is fully integrated into the program. The students are divided into law firms and supervised by a law teacher who is an admitted legal practitioner. The students provide legal advice and assistance to poor people under the supervision of a qualified practitioner employed by the university.

The Legal Practitioners Act of 1981 resulted in fusion of the attorneys and advocates professions in Zimbabwe, and after 1985 the University of Zimbabwe law degree was the only means of admission to the legal profession. This meant that the LLB degree became a practical degree. Articles of clerkship were abolished, and the law clinic was required to provide practical training for law graduates before they entered the legal profession. By 1983 Zimbabwean law students were providing legal advice and assisting with the drafting of pleadings for litigation up to the pretrial stage, all under the supervision of a qualified legal practitioner employed by the university. They were also able to attend pretrial conferences involving clients and lawyers under the supervision of the clinic director. (Smith, 1985) These practices have continued, but have been disrupted at times due to the unsettled political situation in the country.

The University of Botswana program is unique because the university has had to carry the brunt of providing legal aid for the country. Its law clinic was established as "a legal aid service" institution at the same time it introduced the LLB degree in 1984–85, which requires all final-year law students to do the clinical law course. The students spend a period of time working either in the campus law clinic or with some other organization that provided legal services, including nongovernmental organizations (NGOs). They then write up their experiences in a case book, which is submitted for examination.

In Swaziland, a cooperation agreement was entered into in 1990 between the Department of Law at Swaziland University and the Department of Legal Aid at the Council of Swaziland Churches. The Department of Legal Aid educates people regarding their legal rights, provides limited legal aid to indigent people, and does limited research into family law and inheritance issues. The agreement allowed law students to work in the department on these matters on a voluntary basis. (Iya, 2000) The law clinic in Lesotho was established at Roma University together with a clinical law course in 2000. Students are trained to conduct interviews and give advice, as well as to do legal research. (Letsika, 2002) They are also placed in internships where they are monitored. (Open Society Justice Initiative, 2004)

Other law clinics were established in the early 2000s in Namibia, Zambia, and Mozambique. The law clinic in Namibia operates off-campus in Katurura, a suburban township. It is a general practice clinic that provides legal advice, counseling, and representation before the courts of law. Skills taught include interviewing, drafting of documents, and advocacy. The clinic is staffed by two supervisors and enrolls about thirty students a year. The legal aid clinic at the University of Zambia works closely with the Law Association of Zambia. The clinic trains students in counseling and the giving of advice. The clinic also trains paralegals and conducts legal awareness programs. Some students are placed in government internships. (Open Society Justice Initiative, 2004) The legal aid clinic at the Centre for Practical Legal Studies at the Eduardo Mondlane University in Mozambique is located on the university campus and deals with labor law, civil law, and criminal law, with students providing legal advice, counseling, and representation before the courts. The University of Malawi Department of Practical Legal Studies plans to mainstream clinical law into the LLB program. (Open Society Justice Initiative, 2004) At present an informal Street Law–type clinic is run by law students.[1]

Why Were Law Clinics Needed?

As previously mentioned, most of the law clinics in Southern Africa developed because of the need to provide legal services to the poor and to give students an opportunity to obtain practical experience. The liberal universities in apartheid South Africa primarily tried to assist the victims of apartheid, while the universities that supported the apartheid regime tended to focus on practical skills. In the other Southern African countries, law clinics focused on the dual purpose of helping the poor and teaching law students practical skills. In most of those countries, apart from Namibia, there is no functional national legal aid program and reliance has to be placed on NGOs and the law clinics to provide legal advice and assistance to the poor.

Often law clinics in Southern Africa are described as "legal aid clinics" rather than "law clinics" because the service element of the programs is emphasized rather than the teaching and learning of skills. But this terminology also reflects the fact that the students benefit not only by learning practical skills but through the experience of providing legal services to poor and marginalized members of society.

Although during the early years of the African clinical movement members of the legal profession were often suspicious of law students doing the work of lawyers and taking away their clients, increasing numbers of practitioners joined with university to law schools to assist with the programs once they realized the value of law clinics as learning laboratories. Experience in the law clinic was also seen as being beneficial to newly graduated law students, who began to emerge from law schools with some practical legal skills rather than simply a theoretical knowledge of the law.

The benefits to the recipients of legal services from law clinics has also been recognized; provided that the law students are properly supervised, they receive competent legal services not otherwise available to them. This is particularly true in countries with very limited government-funded legal aid services or no legal aid services at all.

Program Requirements for Law Clinic Students

The program requirements for law clinic students vary from university to university and country to country. Some law schools have integrated student work in

---

1. Street Law clinics in Africa and other countries are discussed in Chapter 15.

their law clinics into the law curriculum; this is true of most of the South African universities, as well as the universities of Zimbabwe, Botswana, Lesotho, Namibia, and Mozambique. At the University of Swaziland, legal aid work is voluntary.

In South Africa, law clinic models include those located on campuses—used by most universities—as well as some that operate off-campus. In Zimbabwe, Botswana, Lesotho, and Mozambique the clinics are on campus, while in Namibia and Malawi they operate off-campus. The universities of Botswana, Zambia, and Swaziland use internship placements.

Clinic operations have been formalized in some countries. Most of the South African law clinics have in-house law clinic manuals, and the Association of University Legal Aid Institutions (AULAI) has sponsored a textbook entitled *Clinical Law in South Africa*. An *African Law Clinicians Manual* has been produced under the auspices of the Open Society Justice Initiative.

Type of Training and Evaluation

As in the case of the program requirements, the type of training law students receive in their clinical law programs and how they are evaluated varies from university to university and country to country. In most South African universities where clinical law courses are offered, they are regarded as full courses with the same amount of credit rating as other full LLB courses—even though the demands on the time of clinical law students are much higher than those for regular LLB courses. The same applies to most other universities in Southern Africa that offer clinical law courses for credit.

All the South African universities use legal practitioners employed by the law clinics to teach legal skills and to supervise the work of the students. Indeed, for a law clinic in South Africa to be accredited by the relevant provincial law society, the director of the clinic has to be a qualified attorney (solicitor) or advocate (barrister). In other Southern African countries, the clinics are also usually directed by members of staff who are qualified legal practitioners. Outside practitioners may, however, be used to supervise students in their work with the public when in-house practitioners are not available, or when students are farmed out to other organizations or work as interns.

In some instances in South Africa, law students are graded on their work in the clinic as well their work recorded in written reports or reflective journals. In other instances, the evaluation consists of an ongoing formative assessment, or even a formal practical examination. During formative assessments, students receive continuous feedback; in the case of written reports and journal, they only receive feedback as and when the work is handed in for assessment. In most of the other Southern African countries, the clinic students are graded on their work in the clinic and may be subjected to an examination. In Botswana, the students are graded on a case book they produce after they have served their internship either in the campus clinic or with an outside body such as an NGO or government legal office.

EAST AFRICA

Short History of Law Clinics in the Region

As is the case in Southern Africa, some of the law clinics in the East Africa emerged in the early 1970s. Tanzania had a law clinic at the University of Dar-Es-Salaam in the 1970s. The University of Addis Ababa, Ethiopia, also established a legal aid clinic in the 1970s, but it was closed down after the ouster of Emperor Haile Selassie in 1974. There were also early attempts in the 1970s to set up law clinics in Uganda at Makerere University, but—similar to what happened in Ethiopia—they did not survive some of the political turmoil that affected the country during the reign of Idi Amin. Law clinics emerged in Kenya, Rwanda, and Somaliland in the late 1990s and early 2000s.

During the last decade law clinics have proliferated in East Africa but they still remain largely driven by law students and alumni, with support of law practitioners and law lecturers. In Kenya, for example, live-client law clinics are found at two publicly funded universities—the University of Nairobi and Moi University, Eldoret. The legal aid clinic at the University of Nairobi is run by law students as a voluntary Students Association for Legal Aid and Research (SALAR). The clinic networks with NGOs that deal with children's rights, violence against women, refugee rights, and land matters. The legal aid clinic at Moi University is more advanced than Nairobi University's, and is formally incorporated into the law curriculum. The clinic divides its students into law firms where students are exposed to preparatory clinical components as part of their legal studies in the first three years of the LLB degree, with practice at the clinic reserved for final-year students in their fourth year. Students conduct live-client interviews in the clinic or are seconded to work with human rights NGOs.

In order to be admitted to practice law in Kenya, students must have completed a four-year law (LLB) degree. They should also attend compulsory two-year postgraduate training at the Kenya School of Law alongside a one-year practical training with law firms known as *pupilage*. The Kenya School of Law is in the process of starting a law clinic where its students will work with live clients on specific issues, involving mainly labor, land, and children's rights. There are also discussions underway about the prospects of establishing law clinics at the newly founded law faculties at Jomo Kenyatta University of Agriculture and Technology, Kenyatta University, and the Catholic University of Eastern Africa.

Ugandan universities do not have live law clinics since the collapse of the one previously established at Makerere University in the 1970s. However, clinical legal education is applied in one of the core courses taught as part of the undergraduate LLB curriculum at Makerere University. For example, the law degree course includes: interviewing, counseling, communication, simulations and externship, negotiation, trial practice and advocacy, ethics and legal responsibility, judicial conduct, civil and criminal clinics, arbitration and alternative dispute resolution, administrative procedures, and legal aid. The Law Development

Centre, which offers a postgraduate legal practice diploma for aspiring legal practitioners, is the only institution that has a law clinic. The Law Development Centre's clinic provides legal advice, counseling, legal representation, and legal awareness training, and also develops teaching materials.

A human rights law clinic has been in existence in Tanzania since the 1970s at the University of Dar-es-Salaam, which incorporates a four-year clinical program including internships. (Open Society Justice Initiative, 2004) As in Kenya, on completion of the LLB degree, students who wish to practice law in the High Court and subordinate courts must undertake a two-year internship or pupilage with law firms.

A legal aid clinic (*clinique juridique*) was established at the National University of Rwanda in the academic year 2000-2001. (Musiime, 2007) The clinic educates the public about their rights, and helps them to assert their rights and obtain easy access to justice. The clinic also provides legal advice and assistance with court cases and in dealing with administrative bodies. It also provides mediation services for family disputes. (Open Society Justice Initiative, 2004)

The legal aid clinic at the University of Addis Ababa in Ethiopia is a student-run voluntary program, like that at the University of Nairobi in Kenya. The clinic is run by the faculty of law in collaboration with its alumni association, the judiciary, and local NGOs involved in human rights outreach programs. A law clinic was established at Mekelle University in 2002 that provides general legal advice and advice on women's issues, and also runs a public awareness program. The clinic has influenced the new legal education reform underway in Ethiopia and led to the incorporation of clinic-specific courses, such as a child rights clinic, into the curriculum.

A legal aid clinic was established in Somaliland at the University of Hargeisa in 2004. The clinic, which is staffed by nine legal aid lawyers assisted by law students, also operates in the towns of Baromo and Gabilay. The clinic provides free legal services to poor and vulnerable groups, such as women, children, refugees, internally displaced persons (IDP), persons on remand in criminal cases, and minority groups. The clinic also gives practical legal training courses to third-year law students.

Why Were Law Clinics Needed?

As in Southern Africa, law clinics in Eastern Africa were established by law students and law lecturers principally to bridge the gap between imparting practical legal skills and theory. They were established also in response to the growing need for basic legal advice by indigent populations in the region. The law clinics provide free basic legal advice to poor communities and individuals and equip law students with practical legal skills in the process of providing legal service.

Program Requirements for Law Clinic Students

In East African countries, a law degree is typically a four-year undergraduate program. Since the majority of the law clinics are voluntary and not part of the formal curriculum, students do not earn academic credits for their work at the clinics. (Open Society Justice Initiative, 2004) However, with increased appreciation of the added benefit of equipping law students with practical legal skills, a number of law schools have mooted infusing their law clinics into the law curriculum. At the University of Nairobi, for example, there is a proposal under consideration for the incorporation of the voluntary students' legal aid clinic into the mainstream legal curriculum, which will also translate to students' eligibility to earn academic credits. (Asiema, 2003)

Type of Training and Evaluation

Students who participate at the law clinics receive basic training on legal drafting, research, negotiating, and oral advocacy from law teachers and practitioners who volunteer to work on a part-time basis at the clinic. The training is done on an ad hoc basis, depending on the availability of the practitioners and law teachers and on the identified needs of the students at any particular time. There is also a unique from of practical legal training akin to clinical legal education in Kenya, which entails a compulsory two-month attachment to magistrates' courts for students at the end of their second-year. The students are placed in courts vested with limited criminal and civil jurisdiction. They attend court sessions and interact with lawyers, court officials, and magistrates. They may also have an opportunity to assist in research and draft judgments, as they engage and brainstorm with magistrates on some of the court's cases. The students are supervised by their lecturers and the magistrates to whom they are assigned. At the end of the placement, they submit a report on their experiences and lessons learned.

As in most of Southern African countries, Eastern Africa law clinics are supervised by law faculty members who are qualified legal practitioners. Law practitioners—normally alumni—are also often invited to guide, train, and supervise students in their work with clients, or to provide internships. However, since most of the law clinics in East Africa are not part of the law curriculum of the universities, the work by students is not assessed for purposes of grading. Rather, it is done as a continuous evaluation of their performance and comprehension of the issues they deal with in their clinical work. That assessment is done by the law teachers and volunteer law practitioners who work with the students, in order to give the students feedback and guidance on their understanding and application of legal theory to legal problems.

WEST AFRICA

Short History of Law Clinics in the Region

The history of clinical legal education in West Africa is particularly varied, in part because of differences between anglophone and francophone countries in the region. For example, law clinics have been established in anglophone West Africa at university law faculties in Nigeria and Sierra Leone. In francophone Africa, law clinics involving university law students have operated in NGOs outside of the law faculties. Morocco, which is not technically regarded as West Africa but lies to the west of North Africa, is included in this section as well because it is the only Maghreb country in Africa with a law clinic.

In Nigeria, there were some early initiatives in the 1980s to introduce clinical legal education on a limited scope at Abia State University Uturu (formerly Imo State University Okigwe). The history of law clinics in Nigeria really began, how- ever, only at the beginning of this century as a result of funding and training initiatives following the First All Africa Colloquium on Clinical Legal Education at the University of Natal (now KwaZulu-Natal) sponsored by the Open Society Justice Initiative in June 2003 and the first Nigerian Clinical legal education col- loquium held in Abuja in February 2004. Another key development was the establishment of the Network of University Legal Aid Institutions (NULAI Nigeria) in October 2003, to provide a vehicle to advocate for the introduction and development of clinical legal education in Nigeria.[2] With the support of interna- tional donor agencies, including the Open Society Institute and the MacArthur Foundation, university-based law clinics were established at Abia State University (2005), Adekunle Ajasin University Ondo (2004), University of Maiduguri (2005), University of Uyo (2004), Ebonyi State University (2005, commenced service in 2007), Faculty of Law University of Ibadan (2007), Ambrose Alli University Ekpoma (2007), University of Abuja (2008), and Nigerian Law School Agbani Enugu (2008). There are also student-run law clinics at the University of Lagos, where students play only administrative roles, and at Ahmadu Bello University Zaria, which is run as an outreach/Street Law program. The clinical program at the Nigerian Law School also includes a placement component.

In Sierra Leone, the Fourah Bay Law Clinic at the University of Sierra Leone is a student-run operation with premises on the university campus. The clinic runs a number of projects, including legal aid and assistance in the Human Rights Centre, schools education through Human Rights Clubs, a newsletter entitled *Human Rights Watch*, human rights activities on the campus through panel discussions, mock trials, symposiums, and public lectures, and internship programs whereby students do a fourteen-day placement. (Open Society Justice Initiative, 2004)

In francophone Africa, law clinics operated by NGOs involve law stu- dents from universities in Benin, Burkino Faso, and Senegal. In Benin, the Association de Femmes Juistes de Benin uses law students from the University of Abomey-Calcayi and the National University of Benin. Arrangements for clinic students to work at NGOs are in place in Burkino Faso with the National

---

2. NULAI's contributions to clinical legal education in Nigeria, and elsewhere in Africa, are discussed in Chapter 19, which covers national and regional organizations.

University of Burkino Faso and in Senegal with the Université de Gaston Berge, St Louis. (*Id.*)

In Morocco, a Human Rights Clinic Program was established by the American Bar Association Rule of Law Initiative in 2005, in partnership with the Law Faculty of Mohammedia at the University of Hassan II. (American Bar Ass'n, 2007)

Why Were Law Clinics Needed?

Law clinics in Sierra Leone and francophone Africa were created to provide a much-needed social service to poor and marginalized people in those countries. In Nigeria and Morocco, similar reasons prevailed—but there was also an important emphasis placed on the clinical legal education's capacity to provide training in professional skills and values.

The reasons for—and reasoning behind—the establishment and development of clinics in Nigeria were thought through carefully when the Network of University Legal Aid Institutions (NULAI) was formed in 2003. The law teachers who founded NULAI as a platform for advancing clinical legal education recognized "that law degree programmes and teaching methods in Nigerian Universities are not adapted to participatory and interactive learning and teaching; and that the law curriculum is not skills focused and lacks opportunity for community service and the development of the mentality in using law for social change and development." (NULAI, 2007 at 11)

Program Requirement for Law Clinic Students

Clinical programs have not been fully integrated into the law degree programs in Sierra Leone and francophone Africa. As a result, student work in law clinics does not qualify for academic credit. On the other hand and as explained in more detail below, academic credit is awarded for clinical coursework at most Nigerian universities with law clinics—as is the case in the one Moroccan clinical program.

In Nigeria, legal education is divided into two parts: five years training at the universities (bachelor of laws) and one year vocational training at any of the campuses of the Nigerian Law School, leading to a call to the Nigerian bar. So far in most universities where clinical legal education and law clinics have been established, students receive academic credits for the academic component of the program and for clinic work. A standard clinical curriculum has been adopted by the clinics, which provides sixteen units of credit for courses in four semesters in the fourth and fifth years of the law degree program. In the fourth year, simulations and role plays are used, while in the fifth year law students engage in actual live-client clinic work. Clinic work is compulsory for all law students at Abia State University and Adekunle Ajasin University; at the Nigerian Law School, the placement clinic is compulsory.

In Morocco, students obtain academic credit for the clinical law program, which includes class sessions and field work in the clinic. The course work includes training in practice skills; at the clinic, which specializes in labor law problems, the students provide free legal advice to the public under the supervision of a lawyer.

Type of Training and Evaluation

In Nigeria and Morocco, clinic students receive training on research, writing and drafting, negotiation and mediation, interviewing, public interest lawyering, access to justice, ethics, and professional responsibility. The placement clinics at the Nigerian Law School involve attachment of law students for about two months to the courts and to various types of law practice settings, including legal aid offices, alternative dispute resolution venues, and legal advice centers. The students then return to the law school to submit a report before the assessment panels of teachers and legal practitioners described below.

The clinic in Morocco and the faculty-based law clinics in Nigeria are supervised by law teachers who are qualified to practice. Most of the programs are integrated into the curriculum of the faculties and students earn credits from assessment of their work. The placement clinics at the Nigerian Law School are supervised by the judges and lawyers to whom they are attached. Upon their return to the school, assessment panels made up of law teachers and private legal practitioners review the students' reports and portfolios. Those who fail to score up to 70 percent are required to repeat the attachment and be reassessed; only those who pass are called to the bar on passing the bar examination.

CONCLUSION

University legal aid clinics in Africa, and in developing countries elsewhere, can play a valuable role in supplementing the work of the national legal aid bodies. National legal aid schemes can enter into partnership agreements with university law clinics to compensate them for providing legal aid services for poor people that cannot be reached by the national body. Law clinics can also be contracted to provide backup legal services to clusters of paralegal advice offices, as occurs in South Africa. Such contractual agreements also help to make law clinics more financially viable.

More than twenty-five years ago, the role that law clinics can play in Africa was described as follows: "The well-supervised use of law students will significantly ease the limitations under which most of the legal aid programmes in Africa now have to work; it is only through student programmes that there is any possibility in the near future for legal services becoming widely available to the poor." (Reyntjens, 1979 at 37) The above statement applies equally today—not only to Africa, but to other continents as well.

LIST OF REFERENCES

American Bar Ass'n, Rule of Law Initiative, Morocco Human Rights Legal Clinic Formally Incorporated into University of Hassan II Law Faculty Curriculum (June 11, 2007).

Joy K. Asiema, The Clinical Programme of the Faculty of Law of the University of Nairobi: A Hybrid Model (paper presented at the First All Africa Colloquium on Clinical Legal Education, Durban 2003).

Brook K. Baker, *Teaching Legal Skills in South Africa: A Transition from Cross-Cultural Collaboration to International HIV/AIDS Solidarity,* 9 J. LEGAL WRITING INST. 145 (2003).

Willem De Klerk, *University Law Clinics in South Africa,* 122 S. AFRICAN L.J. 929 (2005).

Neil Franklin, *The Clinical Movement in American Legal Education,* 1 NATAL U. LAW AND SOC'Y REV. 66 (1986).

Frans S. Haupt, *Some Aspects Regarding the Origin, Development and Present Position of the University of Pretoria Law Clinic,* 39 DE JURE 232 (2006).

Philip F. Iya, *Fighting Africa's Poverty and Ignorance through Clinical Legal Education: Shared Experiences with New Initiatives for the 21st Century,* 1 INT'L J. CLINICAL LEGAL EDUC. 13 (2000).

Grady Jessup, *Symbiotic Relations: Clinical Methodology—Fostering New Paradigms in African Legal Education,* 8 CLIN. L. REV. 377 (2002).

Qhalehang A. Letsika, The Future of Clinical Legal Education in Lesotho: A Study of the National University of Lesotho's Legal Education and Its Relevance to the Needs of the Administration of Justice in Lesotho (unpublished LLM thesis, University of Natal 2002).

Qhalehang A. Letsika, *Clinical Legal Education in Lesotho: Some Reflections on Experiences in Teaching Lawyering Skills,* 38 LAW TEACHER. 213 (2004).

Peggy Maisel, *Expanding and Sustaining Clinical Legal Education in Developing Countries: What We Can Learn from South Africa,* 30 FORDHAM INT'L L.J. 374, 376 (2007).

DAVID J. MCQUOID-MASON, AN OUTLINE OF LEGAL AID IN SOUTH AFRICA (Butterworths 1982).

David McQuoid-Mason, *The Delivery of Civil Legal Aid,* 24 FORDHAM INT'L L.J. 131 (2000).

David J. McQuoid-Mason, *History of Live Client Clinics in Africa, in* David J. McQuoid-Mason & Robin W. Palmer, DRAFT AFRICAN LAW CLINICIANS MANUAL (Open Society Justice Initiative 2007).

David McQuoid-Mason, *Law Clinics at African Universities: An Overview of the Service Delivery Component with Passing References to Experiences in South and South-East Asia,* 2 J. JURID. SCI. 9 (2008).

Eunice Musiime, Rwanda's Legal System and Legal Materials (April 2007), *available at* http://www.nyulawglobal.org/globalex/Rwanda.htm.

Nulai Nigeria, 2004–2006 Activities Report (Nigerian Network of University Legal Aid Institutions 2007).

Open Society Justice Initiative, Report on First All Africa Colloquium on Clinical Legal Education June 2003 (2004).

Filip Reyntjens, *Africa—South of the Sahara*, *in* Perspectives on Legal Aid: An International Survey (Frederick H. Zemans ed., Greenwood Press 1979).

Frank Smith, *The Legal Aid Clinic, University of Zimbabwe, Harare*, *in* Legal Aid and Law Clinics in South Africa (David J. McQuoid-Mason ed., University of Natal 1985).

3. THE CLINICAL MOVEMENT IN SOUTHEAST ASIA AND INDIA

A Comparative Perspective and Lessons to be Learned

BRUCE A. LASKY AND M. R. K. PRASAD

INTRODUCTION

Clinical legal education has become, in one form or another, an important element of legal education in many countries in South, Southeast, and East Asia. Two of these countries—China and Japan—are discussed in separate chapters in this book. This chapter focuses on a number of Southeast Asian nations, including Thailand, Malaysia, Indonesia, the Philippines, Vietnam, Laos, and Cambodia, as well as on India, whose recent efforts to develop and expand serious clinical programs can serve as a positive example for the future expansion of clinical education throughout the region. Drawing on the experience of these countries, the chapter explores the means and methods utilized—and challenges faced—in establishing these programs. Before examining the development of clinical legal education, however, a brief general overview of legal education in the region will help place the challenges faced by the clinical movement in context.

Prior to the establishment of formal and independent programs, legal training in most of Southeast Asia was tied directly to each nation's European colonizing power. In Singapore and Malaysia, for example, nearly every lawyer was trained in England; in Indonesia, the Dutch colonial government established a law program to train administrative clerks. Indonesia's colonially established clerk training program would eventually become, in 1950 and after independence, Indonesia's first official law faculty at the University of Indonesia. Formal legal education came even later in other countries: in 1957 in Singapore, in 1972 in Malaysia, and in 1976 in Vietnam. (Tan et al., 2006) The lack of officially regulated or standardized academic legal institutions was not limited to Southeast Asia, but applied to India as well. Standardized law programs were a rarity in preindependence India, and the majority of persons seeking higher forms of legal education often went to Britain for their training.

Legal education began to reform in India after independence, but—similar to Southeast Asian countries—continued to focus on the academic study of law rather than on training in lawyering skills or values. (Krishnan, 2004) While today India has incorporated mandatory clinical legal education, this is a relatively recent development, the challenges and successes of which will be discussed shortly. Most law schools in Southeast Asia, on the other hand, continue to use an archaic lecture-oriented pedagogical method adopted at the time of their establishment.

In Southeast Asian law schools, many students are required to learn via rote memorization, and courses on skills and practice are frequently nonexistent. Because many academics believe that teaching lawyering skills can encourage a type of trade school mentality within law programs, teaching lawyering skills is considered best left to the legal profession following a student's graduation. Coupled with the lack of classroom-based skills and practical instruction is the fact that most law faculties do not promote social justice lawyering. Students are not exposed to human rights cases, and there is little emphasis on the ethical obligation to provide legal aid to the poor. As a result, most graduating Southeast Asian law students neither enter the public service field nor engage in any policy geared at alleviating the plight of and empowering marginalized communities—despite an endemic problem of people's disempowerment and a great need for legal services and advocacy on behalf of the poor.

THE CLINICAL MOVEMENT IN SOUTHEAST ASIA

The basic model of clinical legal education, simply defined as students and university faculties somehow involved in the provision of basic legal consultation services, has existed in some Southeast Asian countries for more than two decades. More than twenty-five years ago, Thammasat University in Bangkok established a clinic that focused on providing a broad variety of legal services to the public. Other Thai universities, such as Chiang Mai University (CMU), followed Thammasat University's lead and model and created programs centered on providing free legal advice and consultation to members of the community. Established in 1994 and staffed by students and professors on a volunteer basis, the CMU program not only provides free legal counseling to the community, but also serves the additional function of instilling the idea of duty and public service into the minds of the participating law students. Similar types of noncredited, voluntary legal aid or legal service clinics have been established at a variety of universities in Indonesia, including the University of Indonesia in Jakarta, where students and professors work with actual clients. A number of other programs allow for students to work alongside lawyers at legal aid societies as a type of internship experience. In Malaysia, limited clinical programs began more than twenty years ago at Universiti Teknologi MARA, where final-year students learned lawyering skills through a simulated program requiring them to work in a mock legal firm or clinic.

Despite the existence of all these programs, there was no consistent clinical legal education model which provided both a social justice mission and simultaneously integrated the program into an accredited legal education course; the Philippines, however, was an exception. Strongly influenced by developments in the United States, the clinical movement in the Philippines was much more expansive than those of its neighboring countries, taking root first at the

University of the Philippines and then spreading outwards to universities such as the Ateneo de Manila. The structured programs in the Philippines, unlike those at law faculties elsewhere in the region, were not only incorporated into the university curriculum, but also charged with the mission of providing much-needed legal services to socially vulnerable, marginalized, and economically deprived members of the community. These clinical programs and the schools which incorporated them are currently involved in an almost-religious mission to spread clinical legal education throughout the country, with some schools making clinics a mandatory course and others setting them up as an elective subject.

More recently, the model adopted in the Philippines—once an anomaly in Southeast Asia—has been recognized increasingly as an effective means of creating a more social justice-minded legal profession and a more progressive legal education pedagogy. For example, Pannasastra University of Cambodia (PUC) established a fully accredited, social justice-oriented, clinical program in 2003 with support from the Open Society Justice Initiative (OSJI), which had a long history of assisting in the development of clinical legal education in Eastern Europe and Africa, and, some time later, the not-for-profit organization Bridges Across Borders Southeast Asia Community Legal Education Initiative (BABSEA CLE).[1]

PUC's clinical program began as a two-section clinic, with one section involved in Community Legal Education activities—often referred to as Street Law—and the other section working as a live-client legal services clinic where students worked with a local nongovernmental organization (NGO) to provide legal aid services to indigent criminally accused persons. The strategy was to establish this type of program and then use it as a demonstrative model to promote clinical legal education within Cambodia and in neighboring countries. By late 2005, a significant number of outreach activities had occurred in nearby countries, including Thailand, Indonesia, Laos, Malaysia, Vietnam, and Singapore. Potential additional partners and supporters had been identified, and other organizations began to show interest in the development of clinical legal education in select Southeast Asian countries. For example, the United Nations Development Program (UNDP), having noticed the benefits of clinical programs, began to work with the Vietnam Lawyers Association in its efforts to further clinical education. Another local Vietnamese NGO, the Institute on Policy, Law and Development-Vietnam (PLD-Vietnam), has also begun to organize training and otherwise facilitate the development of new clinical programs throughout Vietnam, in conjunction with BABSEA CLE and UNDP.

---

1. The contribution of OSJI and BABSEA CLE to the global clinical movement is discussed further in Chapter 19, which covers national and regional clinical organizations.

All of these activities resulted in the first Southeast Asia Clinical Legal Education Conference held in Phnom Penh, Cambodia, in November 2005. The conference, using the PUC Legal Clinic as a type of model, provided a forum to discuss opportunities and challenges for creating clinical programs at Southeast Asian universities, as well as the role of clinical legal education in promoting access to justice and a culture of pro bono service. Aimed at fostering an environment in which participants could exchange ideas for promoting clinical programs, the conference was attended by more than eighty representatives from universities, the legal community, and Southeast Asian civil society—as well as regional and international experts on clinical education and access to justice. Many who attended came from countries in Southeast Asia interested in establishing clinical programs, while others were already engaged in clinical legal education and were interested in expanding their programs to include both a social justice theme and an accredited course program.

A companion workshop to the Phnom Penh conference—the First Southeast Asia Clinical Legal Education Training of Trainers Workshop—was held at the Ateneo de Manila Law School in Manila in early 2007. Similar to the first conference, the Manila workshop acted as a means of training nascent clinicians, focusing on the development of clinical programs, clinical teaching methods, and administrative skills. The workshop also served as an opportunity to expose the participants to, and develop linkages with, more established clinical programs, further cultivating network contacts among clinicians in the region initiated at the Phnom Phenh conference.

Both the Phnom Penh and Manila events seem to have achieved much of their desired objectives, having played a part in the establishment of a number of additional accredited social justice-oriented clinical course programs. For example: the University Malaya launched the first accredited clinical program in Malaysia in 2008; in 2009, Chiang Mai University, after operating a completely volunteer-supported, in-house consultation clinic for fifteen years, approved and implemented a two-section, fully accredited clinical program consisting of both an in-house consultation clinic and a parallel Community Legal Education section; and in 2009, the National University of Laos Faculty of Law and Political Science began taking steps to approve its Community Legal Education program to be included as one of the selective options for mandatory student field studies requirement. The bona fide potential for a significant number of other such programs in Southeast Asia continues.

Current Strategic Means and Methods for Establishing Clinical Programs in Southeast Asia

Building on the successful methods of the Phnom Penh conference and Manila workshop, BABSEA CLE and OSJI decided that the next logical and strategic steps would be to work simultaneously with a variety of potential university partners. Initially these partners included Chiang Mai University (Thailand),

Pannasastra University of Cambodia, Universiti Teknologi MARA (Malaysia), University Malaya (Malaysia), Vietnam National University (Hanoi), the National University of Laos Faculty of Law and Political Science, International Islamic University (Indonesia), and Pasundan University (Indonesia). Other universities, including many in Vietnam, have since joined the core group.

Partnering with universities from so many different countries enabled OSJI and BABSEA CLE to develop pilot clinical legal education (CLE) programs throughout Southeast Asia. This strategy was critical to carrying out effective outreach efforts, since each country in the region has a different type of legal and educational system.

Conducting outreach activities with a variety of university partners—each with successful clinical programs—made it easier to demonstrate the applicability and usefulness of clinical legal education in a multitude of legal and educational systems—and would help overcome any possible challenges by opponents who might argue that clinical education was a Western pedagogical method not appropriate for their educational venues and legal systems.

Because all of the programs were somewhat similar in nature, many with a two-section clinic model, the partners could learn from each other as their programs developed. In working closely with each of their partners, BABSEA CLE and OSJI were able to apply and share working models and systems, lessons, curriculum, etc., from each of the programs, and also help the new programs avoid certain known obstacles that could arise during their development. Additionally, as most of the programs started at approximately the same level, training workshops and exposure visits at one partner university were applicable to staff and students at other partner universities as well.

The fact that much information and training could be adapted and modified from one partner university to another contributed greatly to reducing the amount of money and resources needed for technical assistance. Moreover, because representatives from each of the partner universities had already begun working and learning together in formulating their clinical programs, it seemed natural to work with them as much as possible as a collective unit.

Implementation of Clinical Programs

During the initial stages of implementation for each university-based clinical program, special attention was paid to curriculum development, new and progressive interactive work-centered teaching methodologies, case management, training workshops, administrative procedures, and manual production, as well as general office setup. In order to try and ensure acceptance of the programs by faculty department heads, deans, university senates, and, often, governmental ministries, significant time was allotted to the development of detailed and comprehensive clinical course syllabi.

The general consensus among most, if not all, of the CLE programs was to take small steps and not move too fast. Thus, many new programs, including

Vietnam National University/LERES Center, Universiti Teknologi MARA, University Malaya, and National University of Laos Faculty of Law and Political Science, began as volunteer student associations. Other, more established programs began to outline ways to achieve full accreditation for their social justice-oriented clinics. Chiang Mai University, for example, developed an accredited course proposal that was approved in 2009. Still others, like the National University of Laos Faculty of Law and Political Science, opt for a middle ground between a volunteer-based program and a fully accredited program that includes working to make the clinical program an option for a required student internship, attachment, and/or community service program.

Significant Focuses of the University Clinical Programs

Each of the clinical programs developed in Southeast Asia since the 2005 Phnom Penh conference and 2007 Manila workshop is unique. Like clinical programs worldwide, each has its own strengths, weaknesses, opportunities, and challenges. At the same time, they are also quite similar in nature. Many of the programs include, or intend to include in the future, a clinic comprised of two independent sections, one of which focuses on providing in-house legal consultations—mostly to socially vulnerable and marginalized communities—while the other teaches about legal and community empowerment.

Unlike many clinical programs operating in other regions of the world which tend to specialize in specific legal areas, Southeast Asian clinics have tended to adopt a more general client services approach. As a result, clinical programs in the region have focused on such diverse areas as criminal law and procedure, juvenile justice, family law, consumer protection law, employment and labor law, minority rights, gender law, Shari'ah law, HIV/AIDS-related legal issues, land law, housing rights, civil law and procedure, discrimination issues, administrative law, human rights, and environmental law.

Many clinics in the region also incorporate legal and community empowerment teaching by promoting and assisting in the implementation of university-based community legal educations programs (CLEPs). Often referred to as "Street Law" or "Practical Law" programs, CLEPs have been implemented over the years at many universities around the world. Law students learn about various areas of the law, including human rights and civics, and also how to teach in a student-centered, participatory environment and manner. The students then take both their substantive legal knowledge and their newly acquired pedagogical skills and transfer them to marginalized communities.[2] The communities in which students have carried out CLEP programs are varied and wide-ranging. They have included prisons, juvenile detention centers, community centers,

---

2. The goals and methods of Street Law and its place in the global clinical movement are discussed in detail in Chapter 15.

domestic violence shelters, life skills teaching organizations, youth organizations, religious organizations, ethnic minority communities, single mother shelters, drug rehabilitation centers, and lower socio-economic high schools. The programs target communities in both rural and urban areas where there is little to no understanding of the law or of people's legal rights. Additionally, CLEP students have frequently involved themselves in nonlaw-related projects in order to gain a better understanding of the hardship of others. Which specific communities CLEP programs target depends to a great extent on demand from—and cooperation with—the communities themselves. For example, the clinical program at International Islamic University Indonesia, working through an NGO specializing in community empowerment and access to justice, focused its CLE program in 2007 on areas most devastated by the catastrophic 2006 earthquake.

Successes and Challenges

Clinical legal education has grown significantly in the region since Phnom Penh and Manila, both in quantity and quality of a majority of clinical programs. While, as expected, implementation was not as rapid and/or smooth at some universities as compared to others, overall the universities' clinical programs seem to be moving forward steadily and are picking up steam. Additionally, important and continued linkages have occurred, with clinicians and clinical students participating regularly in thematic trainings and exchanges. For example, during academic year 2007–08, the Chiang Mai University Community Teaching section reported providing legal knowledge and community empowerment training to over 2500 community members.

Another demonstrable success—this one from the Pannasastra University of Cambodia Legal Clinic (PUCLC)—is that 70 percent of legal studies students who completed PUCLC programs either go on to work in fields related to legal education, advocacy, and legal representation of the indigent or proceed further in their legal education. Additionally, PUCLC is being run entirely by former program graduates, which supports program sustainability and illustrates the positive impact the program has had on its graduates.

With each success comes a challenge and while each clinical program in the region has its own particular challenges, there seem to be consistent and general themes applicable to most, if not all, of them. First and foremost, because clinical legal education is a new and unfamiliar concept to many university faculty and staff, clinical programs face great hurdles in securing adequate faculty support for approving the program as a credited course. As many programs are not credited, universities allot only a limited amount time for their students to engage in program functions and activities. In addition, the lack of full accreditation poses the problem of requiring an increased workload from the students while not giving them course credit in return.

There has also been the challenge of a desire on the part of some faculty members to move too quickly—to expand their CLE program too quickly once it's been proven effective—while others have shown an initial reluctance to utilize interactive clinical teaching methods. Another significant problem is that many faculty members lack formal and practical lawyering skills training.

Clinical programs also face logistical challenges. First of all, there are statutory prohibitions on law professors engaging in actual practice of the law. With the exception of Cambodia and the Philippines, most public university law professors throughout Southeast Asia are prohibited from practicing law. As a result, in-house clinics focus primarily on providing consultation and referral services, rather than direct client representation. Additionally, there have been difficulties in receiving cooperation and permission from government authorities for the operation and engagement in certain activities. And finally, there are basic hurdles such as securing adequate facilities and funding for clinical programs and activities, and the lack of reliable manuals and materials written in local languages.

Moving Clinical Legal Education Forward in Southeast Asia

Despite the many challenges it faces, clinical legal education continues to move forward in Southeast Asia. The current developmental approach is a slow and sustained engagement between national and regional partners to develop networks of programs that can learn from both each other's successes and set-backs. All of the Southeast Asian clinical programs require further support—not simply financial, but, more significantly, technical and institutional—if they are to mature into fully accredited programs that are valued by university faculty, students, and community members alike.

As clinical education progresses in Southeast Asia, the clinical movement will undoubtedly look to other countries' experiences for lessons and examples. Nations such as Mongolia, those in Eastern Europe, and former civil codes countries can all provide the Southeast Asian clinical movement with examples of how best to proceed with developing such an important part of formal legal education. India, too, having a much longer history of CLE than most other countries in South and Southeast Asia, can act as a positive example for future regional CLE expansion.

THE CLINICAL MOVEMENT IN INDIA

With roots in both the legal aid and legal education reform movements, clinical legal education in India aspires to be a complete curriculum that addresses both professional skills and professional social justice values. The history of clinical legal education in India not only confirms that view, but also sets the stage for its realization in the years to come.

Early initiatives in India to develop clinical programs were prompted by two influential reports that attempted to integrate legal education with efforts to encourage the legal profession to contribute to positive social change. In 1973, the Expert Committee on Legal Aid of the Ministry of Law and Justice recommended introducing clinical legal education in law schools with the idea that student exposure to actual legal problems of the poor would simultaneously benefit students, the legal aid scheme, and the legal system as a whole. In 1977, the Committee on National Juridicare: Equal Justice–Social Justice urged law schools to participate in legal aid by establishing legal clinics, believing that law school clinics would offer the opportunity not only to provide skills training, but would also sensitize students to the broader social obligations of the legal profession. (Gov't of India, 1973; Gov't of India, 1977)

In a related development, the Committee for Implementing Legal Aid Schemes (CILAS) concluded in 1981 that court or litigation-oriented legal aid programs could not alone provide social justice in India. CILAS therefore recommended that legal aid clinics be established in law schools and universities as a way to mobilize and motivate law students to provide legal aid to the poor. (Gov't of India, 1981) The legal aid movement in India thus benefited and gained legitimacy from institutional support in its early developmental stage, typically in the form of legal aid clinics. And clinical legal education gained a foothold when some universities and law colleges established their own legal aid clinics, either as voluntary, extracurricular programs or, in a few instances, as a part of their curriculum.

Unfortunately, the momentum gathered by the legal aid movement for the development of clinical legal education in India was confined, for the most part, to student extracurricular activity. Efforts by faculty were also for the most part voluntary, and no substantive attempts were made to institutionalize and integrate clinics into the curriculum. Only a few universities, such as Delhi University, established permanent legal aid clinics. There were, however, some exceptions.

Banaras Hindu University introduced a limited-enrollment optional course in the early 1970s that included court visits, participation in a legal aid clinic at the law school, and an internship in lawyers' chambers. Aligarh Muslim University introduced a course on advocacy in the 1980s, which exposed students to topics such as factual investigation, legal research and writing, and litigation strategies. This same university also organized a few legal aid camps in the mid-1980s. These early clinical programs in India were established by the efforts of some inspired faculty and students, echoing the current development of clinical legal education in Southeast Asia. This can be taken as a lesson to be learned by Southeast Asian institutions as they work not only to develop their own programs, but as they work with other partner universities in their home countries and regionally.

In response to the general failure of voluntary methods adopted by individual law schools, the Bar Council of India (BCI) intervened in 1997 by issuing a circular directing all universities and law colleges to revise their three- and five-year law curricula to incorporate clinical-type programs and courses. (Bar Council of India, 1997; Bloch & Prasad, 2005) Current clinical courses required in all Indian law faculties include: moot court; student chambering; attendance, observation, and reflection of both civil and criminal trials; drafting pleadings and conveyances; professional ethics; and training in legal aid. After introducing the required courses, the BCI allowed for considerable flexibility in teaching and evaluation methods. Each university or law school is permitted to adopt teaching and evaluation programs suitable to prevailing regional conditions. Law schools may also identify local resources in adopting a particular kind of clinical program to teach these courses.

Successes and Challenges

The introduction of clinical courses in India has had significant successes. Similar to some of the developing in-house consultation clinics at universities in Southeast Asia, several law schools in India have established legal aid legal consultation clinics. Most of these consultation clinics offer only legal advice and limited paralegal services due to the fact that—as in most Southeast Asian countries—students and full-time professors are banned from practicing law. Yet even with this restriction, these legal aid consultation clinics provide valuable free services to the community and also give the students the opportunity to refine important skills such as interviewing, counseling, and drafting. Providing paralegal services to low-income and disadvantaged members of the community—such as drafting affidavits, assisting with voter registration and the registration of marriages, births, and deaths, and filling out various forms for social welfare benefits—increases a sense of social responsibility among the students. Learning from this example, similar paralegal support services are being incorporated into university clinical programs throughout Southeast Asia.

Despite the ban on students and faculty representing clients, law school clinical programs are able to engage in public interest litigation (PIL), a uniquely open process that allows nonlawyers to raise issues of public interest before the Supreme Court of India and the various state High Courts. (Mugunthan, 2008; Basavaraju, 2003; Singh, 2000) Clinical students and their faculty supervisors have brought PIL cases on a wide variety of issues, taking responsibility for the full range of tasks involved including appearing before the court, thereby offering students the opportunity to developed important advocacy and litigation skills. (Bloch & Prasad, 2005; Paranjape, 1991; Menon, 1982)

Law school clinical programs in India also play a major role in informing the public about their legal rights and duties. Much like many of the programs in Southeast Asia, many programs in India encourage and train their students to carry out street plays, skits, and public performances for legal literacy, addressing such important issues as untouchability, gender discrimination, domestic violence, children's rights, and the environment. As part of these activities, students often also advertise the free legal aid available at their law schools.

These types of community education and legal literacy projects not only help the public, but also allow students to develop important organization, research, oratory, and translation skills.[3]

Despite the successes of some Indian clinical programs and the Bar Council's mandatory directive to include clinical courses in the law school curriculum, clinical legal education still remains in a developing stage in India and faces numerous challenges. In looking at the structure and implementation of the mandatory courses, a number of difficulties can be discerned. Often only a few students are able to participate in national, regional, and international moot court competitions, with most students participating only in often poorly supervised moot courts conducted by their respective law schools. Most law schools have also failed to supervise students' placement in lawyers' chambers. The same thing has happened with the requirement that students attend and observe a civil or criminal trial. Courses on drafting, pleading, and conveyancing, as well as professional ethics, are taught mostly by practicing lawyers and are confined usually to the classroom with evaluation largely through examination. These courses, which are very similar to the simulated honors program taught at Universiti Teknologi MARA in Malaysia, neither allow for any actual client interaction nor do they include any true social justice component.

Even the required course in legal aid is confined at some law schools to teaching the Legal Service Authorities Act and some text-based public litigation skills. Other schools, however, meet this requirement with legal aid clinics and legal literacy programs—as described above—and some also provide academic incentives for students to attend and participate in the more informal and flexible arbitration-like people's courts (*lok adalats*).[4]

One of the greatest challenges overall, and one of the strongest lessons that can be learned, is the fact that while every law school in India is compelled to offer clinical legal education, the programs and courses are implemented with little to no direction or preparation. While proper oversight could exist via the Bar Councils, unfortunately this has not materialized. Because of the highly political nature of the BCI and the Indian State Bar Councils, neither the BCI nor the State Bar Councils are seriously involved in strengthening legal education. Law schools receive recognition from the BCI by merely satisfying specific guidelines regarding infrastructural requirements. As the BCI is the primary body which controls legal education in India, critics feel that the BCI needs to play a more active role in shaping the implementation of clinical legal education.

On the other hand, some other institutions have stepped up to support clinical education, most notably by sponsoring training workshops for clinical teachers. During the early 1990s the National Law School of India University organized a

---

3. Legal literacy clinics in India are discussed in detail in Chapter 16.

4. *Lok adalat* programs are discussed in Chapter 17, which covers alternative dispute resolution clinics.

series of refresher courses on clinical legal education in association with the University Grants Commission. These courses resulted in the publication of a handbook on clinical legal education in 1998. (Menon, 1998) In 2005, delegates at a conference on clinical legal education sponsored by the V. M. Salgaocar College of Law resolved to establish the Forum of South Asian Clinical Law Teachers; the Forum, in association with Menon Institute of Legal Advocacy and Training, has since conducted five regional workshops to train law faculty involved in clinical legal education in Bangalore, Bhopal, Pune, Delhi, and Kolkata. In addition to these training programs, several other initiatives have been taken for assessing and strengthening clinical curricula.

Not surprisingly, one of the major challenges facing clinical legal education is a lack of financial resources. In this regard, there is a large gap between a relatively small number of well-financed institutions, including the elite public universities, the new system of national law schools begun in Bangalore in the 1990s, and some private law colleges, and the vast majority of law schools that are either operated or aided by the government. These latter schools tend to struggle financially, as there is no private funding for any of their programs; as a result, they find it difficult to promote legal aid, legal literacy, or any other type of clinical program.

Finally, stringent rules for qualifying to become a teacher of law and the existing incentive structure for faculty discourage advocates from becoming law teachers and discourage law teachers from becoming involved in clinical teaching. Meager salary packages for adjunct teaching faculty also hinder part-time involvement in clinical programs by would-be enthusiastic advocates. Compounding the problem is the fact that due to a shortage in full-time faculty, clinical hours—though technically countable as teaching hours—often are not recognized as such and therefore become, to many faculty members, an extra and unpaid burden.

It is difficult to balance the successes of and challenges facing the clinical movement in India. Because India is a vast, multilingual and multiethnic nation, a single clinical teaching program is not possible to implement. Due to geographical differences and language barriers, each law school has had to adopt its own clinical program to suit local conditions. Significant differences between urban and rural lifestyles require law schools to adopt different approaches. Particularly when it comes to legal aid services, students must have sufficient knowledge about the culture, living conditions, ethnic problems, and, most importantly, the local language. It is clear, however, that there is a rich history in India of law school-based legal aid activity and other social justice-oriented law school programs that, together with more forceful support from the Bar Council of India and other professional bodies, has set the stage for further expansion and development of clinical legal education as an integral part of the Indian law school curriculum.

SHARED LESSONS AND EXPERIENCES: THE WAY FORWARD FOR CLINICAL LEGAL EDUCATION IN SOUTH AND SOUTHEAST ASIA

While much has been accomplished in recent years, clinical legal education in Southeast Asia is by no means a static movement. Growth continues, spurred by a belief in the efficacy of clinical legal education and aided by experience and learning.

India and the Philippines, with fully accredited and governmental-sanctioned—if not fully supported—clinical programs, offer positive examples and lessons to be learned in the effort to strengthen clinical programs in other regional nations. Full accreditation means not only giving time to professors and students to engage in the programs, but also—perhaps more significantly—signals the accrediting university's support for and belief in the importance and power of clinical legal education. In the future, clinical programs in Southeast Asia must work to gain full accreditation by their supporting universities, work already underway in many countries in the region. And while hurdles still exist even with support from governmental institutions, as indicated earlier in discussing the challenges facing India's clinical movement, the benefits of governmental support and approval cannot be discounted.

Southeast Asian clinical programs will also benefit from looking at developments in other nations and regions. In particular, clinicians in Southeast Asia should look to other parts of Asia, such as Mongolia and China, as well as Eastern European nations and other former civil code countries—especially those countries where clinical legal education has been integrated successfully into their legal systems and law curricula.

CONCLUSION

While still relatively young, the clinical legal education movement in South and Southeast Asia is both important and dynamic. Much has been accomplished in the past twenty-five years, even more so in the years following the 2005 Phnom Penh conference and the 2007 Manila workshop. Yet the movement to bring fully accredited clinical programs that include a social justice aspect is far from complete. As seen in this chapter, clinical programs in the region have achieved similar successes and often face similar challenges, and they offer both positive and negative lessons to be learned.

If clinical legal education is to succeed in Southeast and South Asia, the mindset of the legal community must change. Promoting legal aid and social justice can no longer be treated as an extracurricular activity, but instead must be undertaken as a regular activity of the law school, fully integrated and supported not only in the law schools, but also in the community.

Clinical education can reinforce a law school's presence in the community, while the faculty will benefit from learning from and assisting with real-life legal situations. Such an enriched experience will strengthen the faculty members' theoretical knowledge of the law and, in turn, allow them to teach law in a social context to their students. By integrating social justice and a culture of pro bono service into clinical legal education and, therefore, by extension into the university law curriculum, law students will emerge from these programs and universities not only with stronger lawyering skills, but also with a strong sense of social responsibility and public service.

Considering the pace at which clinical legal education has spread throughout South and Southeast Asia in recent years and the growing support it appears to have, there is reason to be optimistic that the goal of bringing integral, fully accredited and social justice-oriented clinical programs into university law curricula will be achieved. By developing a network of clinical programs and lateral ties, by working together nationally and regionally in a slow but sustained engagement with each other, the budding clinical programs discussed in this chapter, as well as those that have yet to be born, have already begun to realize that goal.

LIST OF REFERENCES

Bar Council of India, Circular No. 4/1997 (1997).

C. Basavaraju, *Public Interest Litigation as an Instrument for Securing Social Justice*, 30 INDIAN BAR REV. 223 (2003).

Frank S. Bloch & M. R. K. Prasad, *Institutionalizing a Social Justice Mission for Clinical Legal Education: Cross-National Currents From India and the United States*, 13 CLINICAL L. REV. 165 (2005).

Gov't. of India, Ministry of Law, Justice and Company Affairs, Report of Expert Committee on Legal Aid: Processual Justice to the People (1973).

Gov't. of India, Ministry of Law, Justice and Company Affairs, Report on National Juridicare and Equal Justice–Social Justice (1977).

Cheng Han Tan et al., *Legal Education in Asia*, 1 ASIAN J. COMP. L. 1 (2006).

Jayanth K. Krishnan, *Professor Kingsfield Goes to Delhi: American Academics, the Ford Foundation, and the Development of Legal Education in India*, 46 AM. J. OF LEG. HISTORY 447 (2004).

Bruce Lasky & Wendy Morrish, The Continued Expansion of Community/ Clinical Legal Education Initiatives Throughout Southeast Asia and the Role of Bridges Across Borders Southeast Asia (2009) (paper presented at the International Journal of Clinical Legal Education/Australian Clinical Conference, Fremantle, Australia).

Carlos P. Medina, Law Schools and Legal Aid: The Philippine Experience (Jan. 30-Feb. 3, 2007) (paper presented at the First Southeast Asian Clinical Legal Education (CLE) Teacher Training, Manila, Philippines).

CLINICAL LEGAL EDUCATION: CONCEPT AND CONCERNS, A HANDBOOK ON CLINICAL
  LEGAL EDUCATION (N. R. Madhava Menon ed., Eastern Book Company 1998).

N. R. Madhava Menon, *Public Interest Litigation: A Major Breakthrough in the
  Delivery of Social Justice*, 9 J. BAR COUNCIL INDIA 150 (1982).

Sangeetha Mugunthan, *Scope & Limitations of Public Interest Litigation in India*,
  20 CENT. INDIA L.Q. 261 (2008).

N. V. Paranjape, *Social Justice and Public Interest Litigation*, CENT. INDIA L.Q. 4
  202 (1991).

Parmanand Singh, *Protection of Human Rights through Public Interest Litigation
  in India*, 42 J. INDIAN L. INST. 263 (2000).

Gov't of India, Ministry of Law, Justice and Company Affairs, Department of
  Legal Affairs, Report of Committee for Implementing Legal Aid Schemes
  (1981).

Panarairat Srichaiyarat & Bruce Lasky, Community Legal Education (Street
  Law) Program at Chiang Mai University: Accomplishments and Visions for
  the Future (Dec. 7-13, 2008) (paper presented at the Global Alliance for
  Justice Education Conference, Manila, Philippines).

4. CLINICAL LEGAL EDUCATION IN CENTRAL AND EASTERN EUROPE
Selected Case Studies

MARIANA BERBEC-ROSTAS, ARKADY GUTNIKOV, AND
BARBARA NAMYSLOWSKA-GABRYSIAK

This chapter proposes to look at the history, rationale, current design, and future potential of clinical legal education programs in Central and Eastern Europe.[1] First, the chapter describes the early developments of clinical legal education in the region and its main supporters. It then provides details of several selected programs drawn from the authors' experience—in Poland, Hungary, Bulgaria, Bosnia and Herzegovina, Serbia, Croatia, Russia, and Ukraine—and analyzes these programs' role in preparing a new generation of social justice and human rights lawyers. The chapter concludes by proposing potential directions for future development of clinical legal education in the region, looking at opportunities and challenges within the wider European context as well.

POST-COMMUNIST TRANSITION, RULE OF LAW, AND LEGAL CLINICS

The transition from a totalitarian or authoritarian regime to a democracy with a well-functioning institutional framework and practices based on the rule of law is a road that takes many years, if not decades, and places a major responsibility on the legal profession in a given country to revive and uphold the rule of law, to commit to human rights and the public interest. (Kleinfeld, 2006) The legal profession is always a tangent part of governing institutions and regimes, by participating actively in or assisting with drafting laws and upholding legal norms. Thus, in countries which underwent the communist regime changes and reforms during much of the twentieth century—as well as those dealing with any other form of nondemocratic rule—the independence, role, and status of the legal profession was affected to a significant degree in its ability to analyze, stand for, and uphold the rule of law and human rights. (Meyer, 1995; Grazin, 2000) The legal

---

1. The phrase "Central and Eastern European Region" is used here to encompass the wider geo-political regional experience of transition and includes countries formerly communist or under the Soviet sphere of influence (except Central Asia and Eastern Germany): Albania, Armenia, Azerbaijan, Belarus, Bosnia and Herzegovina, Bulgaria, Croatia, Czech Republic, Estonia, Georgia, Hungary, Latvia, Lithuania, FYR Macedonia, Moldova, Montenegro, Poland, Romania, Russia, Serbia, Slovakia, Slovenia, and Ukraine.

profession had a marginalized role in social affairs and development during communism in Central and Eastern Europe, in which it was reduced to solving petty civil matters and dealing with criminality issues. This resulted in the legal profession's inability, lack of competence, and/or reluctance to engage in rule of law, human rights, and public interest lawyering on behalf of the most vulnerable groups. Although reformed in terms of their independence, voice, and social status, such views and attitudes toward social change and protection of vulnerable groups still dominate professional associations in some of those countries.

It is against this background that a major focus on reforming the legal profession—judges, prosecutors, the private bar—was put in place at the beginning of 1990s in Central and Eastern Europe, and in the mid-1990s in ex-Soviet Union countries. The agenda of law reforms was quite ambitious: reform most legal institutions through drafting of new legislation that would comply with the democratic and rule of law principles, provide technical assistance, and promote capacity building. In addition, emphasis was placed on the need to educate and empower the new generation of legal professionals that could undertake the legal reform work over the long term.

Although the demand for an educated legal profession was growing, this did not necessarily improve the quality of the legal education. Reasons for that include the lack of quality law textbooks and committed teaching and academic staff, poor academic and physical facilities at the law schools, and the tradition of teaching law and theories of law with a very limited focus on practical aspects of legal knowledge, skills, and values. There was, and still is, a more fundamental problem: the universities did not see themselves as places for preparing lawyers for practical work and life after graduation; they focused on identifying and defining concepts of law rather than on the capacity to analyze and solve legal problems.

Taking all of these limitations and concerns into account, various initiatives sponsored by bilateral and international donor organizations were launched, starting in 1993, to train judges, prosecutors, and practicing lawyers on issues related to human rights, democracy, and rule of law. One of these initiatives consisted of promoting human rights and practice-oriented legal education. Starting in 1996, it developed into decade-long support for the establishment and operation of university practical law courses—called law or legal clinics—where senior law students would be trained in legal skills and values, and be involved in providing free legal aid. This initiative received support from many donors present in the region, such as the American Bar Association's Central European and Eurasian Law Initiative (ABA CEELI) and the Ford Foundation (Moscow office), but the primary sponsor and promoter of legal clinics was the Open Society Institute (OSI) and Soros Foundations Network, represented at that time by the Constitutional and Legal Policy Institute (COLPI) and local Soros Foundations. Since the late 1980s, OSI and the local Soros Foundations have been implementing and supporting a range of initiatives to advance justice, education, minority rights, public health, and independent media. COLPI was the rule of law initiative of OSI-Budapest mandated to promote and support legal reform programs in the fields of judicial and constitutional reform, capacity building, legal profession reform, and access to justice, including reforming legal education in the region. It was succeeded in 2003 by the Justice Initiative, a global rule of law and human rights program of OSI-New York and OSI-Budapest that has extended its support of clinical legal education worldwide to include Africa, Southeast Asia, and the Middle East.

From 1997 to 2002, COLPI launched initiatives with technical assistance from Columbia University's Public Interest Law Initiative (currently the independent Public Interest Law Institute, or PILI) that established more than seventy-five university-based law clinics in more than twenty countries, including Armenia, Belarus, Bosnia and Herzegovina, Bulgaria, Croatia, Czech Republic, Estonia, Georgia, Hungary, Kazakhstan, Kyrgyzstan, Latvia, Lithuania, Macedonia, Moldova, Montenegro, Poland, Romania, Russia, Serbia Slovenia, Slovakia, and Ukraine. (Rekosh, 2008) The majority of these clinics were financially supported by the Soros Network, with small portions and support from ABA CEELI and the Ford Foundation. Most of these clinics are recognized by their host universities as part of the university structure and—in some places—as part of the curriculum, while continuing to provide free legal assistance to the most vulnerable groups in society.

In addition to providing direct financial support, COLPI and a few other donors have engaged in initiatives aimed at building a cadre of clinical teachers and coordinators that would undertake the long-term development and advocacy for clinical programs. Between 1998 and 2004, COLPI and PILI co-organized English and Russian language teacher training workshops and meetings on teaching methodology, interactive problem-based learning, and clinical management and fund-raising issues for more than 250 law teachers and coordinators in the region. Since 2005, the Justice Initiative, PILI, the Ford Foundation and ABA CEELI have also engaged in establishing, supporting, and building the capacity of national clinical legal education organizations in Poland, Russia, Ukraine, and Moldova.[2]

The direct impact of these initiatives on the model and outcomes of legal education is hard to document, but there are substantial indications of success. (Justice Initiative, 2009) First, there is the fact, discussed later in this chapter, that most universities in the region eventually incorporated these clinical programs as elective specialized courses for senior law students. Second, in Poland, Ukraine, Russia, Bulgaria, and Moldova, legal clinics became a mandatory or a recommended component of national legal education through formalized recognition by the government. And finally, clinical legal education's successes in the region have stimulated introduction of legal clinics at several universities in Spain, Italy, and Germany—Western European civil law countries—where such

---

2. A number of these organizations are discussed in Chapter 19.

a development would have been unheard of a decade ago.[3] (Bucker & Woodruff, 2008; Wilson, 2009) In addition, clinical legal education has been presented through academic exchange programs and a number of presentations by clinicians from the region at various European forums, including the annual meetings of the European Law Faculties Association.

Given the historical, geo-political developments in the region, the impact of clinical legal education in the countries of Central and Eastern Europe can be understood ultimately only by taking into consideration differences in approaches and results in each of these countries. In most of the countries selected for this chapter, clinical legal education started as a pilot initiative either driven by significant support from outside, combined with enthusiasm from inside the legal academy, or started as small initiatives at grassroot levels that later received support from donor organizations. The next section will look at the development of a clinical legal education movement in different countries in the region and analyze their success and impact on the legal education reform.

LEGAL CLINICS IN CENTRAL AND EASTERN EUROPE: SELECTED CASE STUDIES

A typical legal clinic in the region is a one- or two-semester, in-house elective course for third-, fourth-, or fifth-year law students. The clinic usually operates as a law office—on or off the university campus—and focuses on providing both legal skills and values training to law students and the opportunity to work with real clients. Most clinic clients come from vulnerable or indigent groups, such as pensioners and the elderly, refugees and asylum seekers, indigent criminal defendants, minorities, women and children, and the unemployed. Although legal services vary significantly, law clinics typically provide legal information and advice, court representation, and conflict resolution services in family, employment, administrative, social security, and sometimes criminal matters. Specialization of clinical programs depends to a great extend on the academic and practice interest and specialization of the supervising teacher or attorney. The representation of indigent criminal defendants by students is restricted by the formal requirement of membership in the bar, although some clinics, such as those in Hungary and Moldova, have provided legal services to pretrial detainees and prisoners.

The academic component of clinical courses consists usually of sessions on practical knowledge and skills where law students study—often with simulated exercises—interviewing and counseling techniques, professional ethics and responsibility, types of representation and advice, and trial advocacy skills. In addition, they are instructed in analytical, research, legal writing and reasoning,

---

3. Clinical programs in the United Kingdom, which have been well-established since the 1970s, are described in Chapter 1.

and problem-solving skills. The students then have the opportunity to practice their skills and develop lawyering values by working directly with vulnerable groups and providing free legal services. This is among the most important functions of these programs, since they provide necessary—sometimes totally lacking—civil legal aid to the most vulnerable and poor segments of the population, especially during the ongoing political and economic transition in the region that has resulted in increased poverty and decreased standard of life across wide segments of society.

Legal Clinics in Poland

Legal clinics have been operating in Poland since 1997, with the establishment of the clinical program at Jagiellonian University in Krakow. The legal clinic at the University of Warsaw was set up a year later, followed by the clinic at the University of Białystok. Since that time, clinical legal education programs have been created at all law faculties in Poland. There were numerous reasons for such a broad interest in clinical programs, but two of them are especially important. First was a great need to provide legal advice to those who cannot afford professional legal assistance. The second reason was the need to offer practical training for law students. These legal clinics gave law students the opportunity to confront real-world lawyering for the first time, and to gain experience—while in the midst of their law studies—from solving a real person's legal problem. With their dual emphasis on clinical training and providing free legal advice, legal clinics have quickly become an attractive and interesting new element of legal education in Poland.

The clinical movement in Poland is therefore already beyond the organizational phase, which consisted of adopting a clinical model of teaching and popularizing the idea of organizing legal clinics, and is now in the process of developing into an essential component of the curricula at law faculties. Indeed, clinical legal education is practically a mandatory element at every law school, with legal clinics operating at all law faculties throughout Poland. The next phase of the clinical movement—preparing and drawing up clinical curricula that use the educational opportunities of clinical programs to the fullest—is underway, with the enhancement of clinical training its top priority.

The most popular organizational model of legal clinics is the division into so-called sections that correspond to particular fields of law. Thus, most clinics are divided into sections on civil law, criminal law administrative law, labor law, and refugees. Some sections operate more than one clinic, and some clinics have subspecialties, such as rights of prisoners, gender-related discrimination, and cooperation with nongovernmental organizations (NGOs). This guarantees a clear structure and good organization for the work at the clinic, and also enables students to acquire experience by working in teams. Each section has its academic supervisor, who usually is a faculty member but sometimes may be a practitioner in the relevant field. Students have steady contact with their supervisor and consult with them regularly. Although supervisors are not always incorporated formally into the structure of the clinic, students can consult with them during their standard office hours.

Legal clinics offer various classes within each section designed to introduce the students to the basic legal knowledge and skills necessary in the work of a lawyer. Over the course of the academic year, the following classes are conducted in the majority of legal clinics: general clinical seminars, sectional seminars, individual consultations for students, students' duty hours (meetings with clients), psychological training, and specialized training. In addition, simulated court proceedings are slowly being included in the clinic-based program. Law clinics conduct various types of simulations, including hearings before a court of first instance, hearings before a court of appeal, selected fragments of court proceedings (such as hearings on incarceration or release), as well as simulations of proceedings before international bodies such as the European Court of Human Rights. This method gives students a fuller opportunity to develop their skills as professional lawyers. During simulations, students become intimately familiar with the provisions of law in a given practice area, and at the same time learn the principles underlying reliable and just proceedings. They acquire the skills they need to appear in court proceedings in defined roles and gain experience from the perspective of the role they play. Another important reason for organizing simulated hearings as part of clinical studies is the fact that in Poland it is still not possible for clients to be represented by students before legal institutions.

General clinical seminars cover problems related to the practice of all legal professions. Students meet with representatives of particular legal professions and thereby learn the ethical principles of every legal profession. Real-life aspects of practicing particular legal professions are discussed, including disciplinary responsibility. During these classes students get acquainted with the organization of work in the clinic; for example, the client case filing system and the general functioning of the clinic office. The general clinical seminar also addresses the clinics' cooperation with NGOs. Representatives of particular organizations, such as the Office of the United Nations High Commissioner for Refugees (UNHCR) and the Women's Rights Center, discuss the social and legal problems that their organizations face in their everyday activities. One of the aims of these sessions is to sensitize the young lawyers-to-be to existing social injustices.

Sectional seminars are held once a week in each clinical section to ensure that the students are properly and thoroughly prepared to conduct matters within the scope of their section of the law clinic. Section classes are designed so that, over the course of the whole year, students will be exposed to and come to understand all of the legal and social issues relevant to the work of their section. These classes also serve to impart the knowledge and practical skills students will need in the legal profession more generally, to teach them how to carry out proper legal analysis, and to sensitize them to various societal issues.

The main purpose of the individual consultations is to teach students how to solve the problems that the clients bring to the clinic. When coming to the consultation or seminar, students should be ready to present a diagnosis of the problem and a thought-through course of action. The teacher's role during these classes consists of steady monitoring of the students' work and following their line of reasoning. The problems presented during the consultation or seminars are commented on by all participating students, which allows for a larger group discussion and exchange of ideas about the peculiarities of the work done in the clinic.

Students' duty hours are usually one-hour appointments with clients each week at the legal clinic office. During these duty hours, a pair of students meets with the client in order to learn in detail both the problem and the factual circumstances of the case about which the client approached the clinic. Prior to these meetings—during section seminars—the students are prepared on how to conduct client interviews and to verify the factual circumstances related by the client. The students are also instructed to check whether the documents provided constitute complete documentation for the matter, or whether any documentation or information that could or should be known to the client is missing.

The purpose of psychological training is to teach students interpersonal communication skills and other psychological skills that may be useful in their future clinical work, especially during meetings with clients. The basic psychological skills include conducting an effective interview with the client and providing the client with clear and understandable legal advice, as well training in the protection of one's health and mental integrity. Psychological training should take place at the very beginning of the academic year, before students start their meetings with clients during their duty hours. Thus, at the Warsaw legal clinic it has become a crucial element at the start of the yearly clinical training cycle.

Legal clinics throughout Poland also organize various specialized courses connected with their fields of activity. For example, the Warsaw clinic offers classes during which students get acquainted with the mechanisms of stereotypes emergence and the problems of intercultural communication, which is particularly useful in the refugees section.

As pointed out at the beginning of this section, legal clinics are operating at all law faculties in Poland. The key to improving clinical teaching in the future is the development of comprehensive programs of clinical training carried out applying active clinical methods. Clinical teachers in Poland have a unique opportunity to teach students real-life knowledge and skills necessary in their future job as lawyers, as well as to shape the new system of higher education.

Legal Clinics in Hungary

The first clinical program in Hungary opened its doors at the Eötvös Loránd University (Eötvös Loránd Tudomany Egyetem, or ELTE) Faculty of Law in February 1997. The Refugee Legal Clinic, a partnership between the human rights watchdog organisation Hungarian Helsinki Committee (HHC) and ELTE, was set up as part of COLPI's regional initiative to create several clinics in Hungary. The program focused primarily on providing training to law students on refugee and asylum law and legal counseling techniques, as well as instruction in human rights and Street Law methodology. The legal clinic is an optional course for which students receive academic credit. The students carry out a variety of tasks under the supervision of the professors and legal practitioners, including conducting legal research, interviewing and providing legal counseling to asylum seekers, preparing draft submissions, and representing clients (especially underage asylum seekers) at interviews with authorities.

In 1999, the Legal Clinics and Street Law Foundation (the Clinics Foundation) was established as a separate legal entity affiliated with the ELTE law school. The foundation operates clinic sections on criminal law (prisoners' rights, juveniles' rights), labor law (employment rights), After-Care law (probation), children's rights (family law), NGO law (civil society support), nondiscrimination and Roma rights, Street Law, and refugee law. In 2008, a new pilot clinic section was launched on freedom of information within ELTE's Sociology of Law Department, in cooperation with the Justice Initiative and the Hungarian Civil Liberties Union (TASZ) and with participation of four other transparency NGOs in the country. During a two-semester course, law students receive training in issues related to the application of the Freedom of Information Act and its importance for the transparency of governance. After the two months of introductory seminars led by transparency activists and practitioners, the students work with lawyers at participating NGOs in preparing and submitting freedom of information requests on budgetary, environmental, and other public interest issues. In addition to providing legal skills and public interest training, the clinics at the ELTE law school also provide leadership in new teaching methodology and the insertion of new subject matter into the curriculum, such as nondiscrimination, freedom of information, and women's and children's rights.

In addition to those at the ELTE law school, there are legal clinics at universities in Miskolc, Debrecen, and Pecs. The students in these clinical programs undertake a two-semester course involving practical training and field experience in refugee and immigration law, employment law, family law, and nonprofit organizations law. The clinics are led by a full-time professor that specializes in one of these fields.

Legal Clinics in Bulgaria

Clinical legal education was introduced in Bulgaria in late 1998 with the initial financial and technical support from COLPI and the local Soros Foundation/ Open Society Institute-Sofia (OSI-Sofia). The first legal clinics were established in 1999–2000 at the universities in Plovdiv, Sofia, and Rousse. The clinic at the University of National and World Economy in Sofia was created in 2002. Three more universities opened legal clinics a few years later, University of Veliko Trnovo, Varna Free Univeristy, and Bourgas Law School. Over the following ten years the concept of clinical education entered the legal education vocabulary and many universities accepted it as a legitimate method for training law students. Moreover, in 2005, existing clinical programs signed the *Academic Standards for the Organization and Activities of Legal Clinics*, an unprecedented success in unifying the model for clinical education in Bulgaria. In the same year, the Council of Ministers formally incorporated clinical training into the system of Bulgarian legal education by amending the Legal Education Ordinance. Although the clinical programs are not mandatory, this precedent-setting achievement provides for future sustainability of law school clinical programs and therefore is important not only in Bulgaria but throughout the region.

Legal clinics in Bulgaria differ significantly in terms of their scope and structure, as well as with respect to the type of matters that they handle. The University of Sofia operates four clinic sections providing legal services and representation in administrative, criminal, employment, and refuges and asylum matters. Clinic work involves both simulated and real-life clients. In the criminal law section, for example, the students work with a part-time teacher practitioner on real cases focusing primarily on civil redress within the criminal process and socio-legal assistance to convicted persons serving their sentences. Students in the employment law section carry out simulated discussions and negotiations of labor contracts, but also handle employment disputes. The University of Plovdiv also operates four sections of legal clinic, including criminal law and nonprofit law. The criminal law section engages students in cases related to domestic violence, rights of defendants, and civil claims within the criminal process. Students provide legal services in pairs under the supervision of clinical law teacher. The nonprofit law clinic students assist civil society organizations in the registration and re-registration process and taxation issues, and also work on specific cases brought to the clinic by small nonprofits. The University of Rousse operates two semester-long clinics in which students work on family, succession, and administrative matters. The administrative law section focuses on training students in administrative procedure and appeals of government decisions. Students engage in free legal aid and simulated activities under the supervision of a part-time clinical teacher specialized in administrative law. The University of National and World Economy runs a two-semester Civil Law Clinic in which the first semester is dedicated to various clinical subjects, while during the second semester the students work with real clients.

Recently, a number of clinical programs in Bulgaria initiated cooperation agreements with civil society organizations, which could have an indirect effect of building and mobilizing a future generation of public interest and human rights lawyers in the country. It appears that clinic students have a sustainable interest in issues of public interest. For example, the majority of students who have participated in the Plovdiv University prosecution clinic course were employed later by the prosecution services. Another indicative example is the NGO law clinic in Plovdiv, where almost all of the students turned out to be volunteering in the activities of their client organizations.

Legal Clinics in Western Balkans

Most law schools in the Western Balkans do not yet have clinical programs. There are exceptions, however, some of which are described below. Clinical legal education may have a significant role in promoting reform of legal education in the future as countries in this region strive to integrate into the European Union and institute greater rule of law reforms.

Clinical legal education arrived in Bosnia and Herzegovina (BiH) relatively recently, with the first clinical program opening in 2003-04 at the law faculty of the University of Banja Luka. The clinic was established with assistance from the Open Society Fund BiH and later the local ABA CEELI office with funding from the United States Agency for International Development (USAID). The clinic, which operates under the umbrella of the University's Human Rights Center, focuses on civil matters. The students receive in-class training on skills and simulated court proceedings provided by practicing attorneys, law professors, and judges, after which they intern with courts and law firms where they work directly with clients to prepare simple motions and other legal documents for court hearings. Banja Luka launched the first real-client clinical program in the country in 2006. Students in the clinic provide free legal aid in employment, access to information, property ownership, and inheritance matters under the supervision of two law teachers and three practicing attorneys. The University of Bihac established a simulation clinic in early 2007, in which law students are introduced to basic lawyering skills and values through in-class teaching and internship schemes.

Clinical legal education was first introduced in Croatia in 2002 at the faculty of law at Osijek University, with the technical assistance from PILI. The students in the clinic, which focuses on civil and administrative law, receive supervised in-house training and provide legal counseling in matters related to torts, assistance to nonprofit organizations, and small for-profit enterprises. Several clinical programs operate in Serbia under the auspices of law faculties of the universities of Belgrade, Nis, and Novi Sad, most of which cover issues related to nonprofit law, appeals of administrative decisions, and small civil claims. There is one clinic in Montenegro at the University of Montenegro that operates four sections focusing on civil, administrative, commercial, and criminal matters. Senior students participate in simulated classes and are then placed in internship programs at courts and law offices.

Legal Clinics in Ukraine

Clinical legal education developed in Ukraine over the course of several years starting from 2000. The key player in promoting and supporting the legal clinics was the local Soros Foundation, the International Renaissance Foundation (IRF-Kiev), with technical assistance from COLPI and its 2003 successor the Justice Initiative. The main criteria for obtaining support looked to agreements and plans with the faculty administration to provide assistance and the proposals for curriculum design and student work. From 2001 to 2007, more than thirty-seven law clinics across the country received grants. In 2005, a national Association for Legal Clinics was created to respond to the growing needs for accreditation, support, and standardization of the work performed by these programs.[4] A new clinic on health and patients' rights was established in 2006 at the Kyiv Mohyla Academy with support from OSI's Public Health Program, with the aim of training lawyers specialized in issues related to human rights in health care. Today there are clinics in all regions of Ukraine.

All Ukrainian clinics train students in lawyering skills or human rights education methods and provide free legal assistance and human rights teaching to poor and vulnerable groups in their respective cities and regions. In addition, they work on promoting legal awareness of the general population by preparing and participating in TV and radio programs and by teaching law in public high schools. Most clinical programs in Ukraine are two-semester courses that engage law students in providing civil and administrative legal advice and representation, with a few also teaching Street Law and legal literacy courses.[5] Typically the first semester is devoted to a classroom component on lawyering skills, with the practice component taking place during the second semester. Students usually are divided into groups for their legal services work and are supervised by a teacher and practitioner. All clinical courses award academic credits and are graded as are other optional courses at the faculty.

All clinical legal education programs in Ukraine are integrated and incorporated formally under the university structure. A Minister of Education's Order dated from 2006 required all law faculties hosting legal clinics at the time to fully integrate them and to allocate necessary funding and human resources. The Order also institutionalized previously agreed academic standards for the operation of university-based legal clinics, including curriculum recommendations and minimum requirements for clinical operations. The Association of Legal Clinics and its affiliated Legal Clinics Foundation hold the authority of conducting evaluations and assessments of clinical programs in the country.

Legal Clinics in Russia

The story of clinical legal education in Russia is tied inextricably to the dramatic changes in the education system following the collapse of the Soviet Union in 1991. The quality of education became an issue immediately. Liberalization of the educational market, the emergence of academic freedom, and opportunities for academic exchange created an environment for innovation for progressive educators seeking to learn from world experience and to adopt the best models of legal education. Looking just at numbers, there were 52 law schools in all

---

4. The association and the recently established Foundation for Legal Clinics in Ukraine are discussed in Chapter 19, which covers national and regional clinical organizations.

5. Street Law and legal literacy are discussed in Chapters 15 and 16.

15 Republics of the former Soviet Union; today, there are over 1200 institutions providing legal education in the Russian Federation alone.

Against this background, a number of law professors, students, practitioners, and human rights activists sought to introduce a more practical and social-oriented system of legal education, which has played out over four distinct periods. The first period, from 1995 to 1998, was a time of enthusiasm and optimism. The role of donor and partner organizations was critical for implementing the clinical methodology at Russian universities. A partnership program sponsored by the United States Information Agency coupled five law schools in the United States with five law schools from the Russian northwest to provide the first clinical materials. ABA CEELI provided extremely useful technical assistance, with CEELI liaisons making the first steps in teaching Russian clinicians and developing a clinical curriculum. The Ford Foundation supported "training of trainers" and an "Academy of Human Rights" for clinical students. The Open Society Institute provided small institutional grants for legal clinics and supported Street Law programs. COLPI (now the Justice Initiative) organized international study tours, exchanges, and internships for clinicians. There was also some modest support from the Russian Law Reform Foundation and the Ministry of Education for some legal clinics. Through all these efforts, the first law clinic was founded at Petrozavodsk State University in 1995. Within a short period of time, clinics had been launched all around Russia—and all of the clinics established at that time still survive and are among the leaders in the Russian clinical movement.

The years from 1998 to 2002 represented a "boom" period for clinical legal education in Russia. There were large numbers of clinical trainings and workshops, including seminars for potential supervisors (practitioners and young faculty), summer and winter schools for clinical students, seminars for drafting curricula, and internships at existing legal clinics. Several clinics (at Tver State University, North-Caucasus Technical State University in Stavropol, and Krasnoyarsk State University) served as resource centers. The Clinical Legal Education Center, established in 1998 at the St. Petersburg Institute of Law named after Prince P.G. Oldenburgsky, hosted groups of clinicians from Belarus, Caucasus, and Central Asia for training and internships.[6] In 1999, the Ministry of Education identified St. Petersburg State University as a center for the development of clinical legal education and its law department started an officially accredited 72-hour program of in-service training for clinical supervisors. By 2002, there were more than 100 legal clinics in Russia.

The period of 2002–2006 can be described as a "hard time" for legal clinics, with stronger state regulation of education and low interest in the social mission of universities. It was also a time of suspicion of "foreign" educational models,

---

6. Russian clinical organizations are among those described in Chapter 19.

and grant support from international donors decreased substantially. Some clinics, operated as short-term projects, were closed. A survey of Russian clinics revealed many serious problems in both the quality of the services they provided and their educational value for students. The vast majority of Russian clinics remained merely "supplementary" to traditional law courses in which law students were taught how to serve the existing legal system—rather than how to think critically about ways to improve the system and how to employ legal mechanisms to achieve much-needed social change.

The most recent period, starting in 2006, seems to mark a new "boom" of clinical legal education in Russia. The development of legal clinics is now a part of state policy. The President of the Russian Federation has requested that legal education take on a more practical character. The Association of Lawyers of Russia is trying to make pro bono work mandatory for entry into the legal profession. The Ministry of Justice has recognized legal clinics as providers in the framework of the system of legal aid. New state educational standards are being drafted and legal clinics have a chance to become a part of the regular curriculum in all law schools. By 2009, there were more than 150 legal clinics preparing a new generation of Russian lawyers—with a broadly stated mission of providing legal aid and human rights protection, teaching professional skills, improving the quality of legal education, and offering public law education.

Almost all clinics in Russia work on various civil matters, including housing, labor, family law, and social security. Some clinics work on criminal cases, tax law, refugee rights, and international human rights law. There are also clinics that specialize in domestic violence, not-for-profit law, soldiers' rights, small business, and children's rights. Most clinics teach a practical course to prepare students before working with real clients that covers professional skills (interviewing, counseling, case analyses, ADR, legal writing, trial advocacy) and professional ethics. Clinic students provide various types of legal aid—advice, counseling, representation before courts—as well as social-legal research, drafting laws, and public education through Street Law programs.[7] Legal clinic is an optional course at most Russian universities; however, there are some exceptions such as St. Petersburg State University where the clinic is compulsory for all students.

THE FUTURE OF CLINICAL LEGAL EDUCATION IN CENTRAL AND EASTERN EUROPE—AND BEYOND

Clinical legal education was born out of the need to fill in the lack of practice-oriented and value-based training for future legal professionals. It is a currently

---

7. Street Law programs are described in Chapter 15.

widely known truth that without a "critical mass" of judges, prosecutors, attorneys, and legal counselors that share similar values of upholding the rule of law, maintaining and defending fundamental human rights, and promoting a legal culture focusing on social justice and justice education, very few rule of law reforms might succeed beyond the formalistic adoption of new law and legal policies and the establishment of new institutions. The way to achieve this "critical mass" for the long term is to reform legal education.

This reform began in Central and Eastern Europe approximately fifteen years ago, and has just recently started to take on a new pace. The main focus of the reform so far in most countries has been adherence to the so-called Bologna Process, a higher education restructuring initiative creating the European Higher Education Area (EHEA) in the forty-seven participating European countries. This process, although still underway, has the potential to influence the way legal education is designed and implemented since it focuses on transferability of knowledge and skills across the European area. Although many issues regarding the Bologna Process and legal education still remain to be resolved, clinical legal education offers several benefits for the long-term adherence to the Bologna Process. (Hovhannisian, 2006) One of its main benefits is the clinical methodology's focus on problem-based learning techniques. There are many opportunities for incorporating clinical legal education as part of the Bologna Process and to meet the practical challenges that the process poses for legal education outcomes.[8]

In addition and related to the Bologna Process, in non–European Union (EU) countries—except perhaps Russia—promises and political commitments related to EU integration create other opportunities for institutionalizing and establishing long-term sustainability of legal clinics. This could occur as a result of rule of law and human rights political commitments that these countries need to show in order to receive an EU integration "green card." With significant rule of law and legislative reforms behind them, these countries could move toward discussing the quality of those reforms and the ongoing lack of human resources to sustain them. Such a discourse could advocate for inclusion of legal education reform into the rule of law agenda of EU institutions, and thus strengthen the sustainability of already well-functioning clinical legal education programs in the region.

In parallel with the reform of legal education, recent discussions and developments in several EU and non-EU countries demonstrate an interest in assessing and reforming the legal profession itself, which in turn could serve as a well-grounded support for legal education reform. It is impossible to talk about the quality of the services provided by the legal profession—and its transparency and

---

8. The role of clinical legal education in implementing the Bologna Process is discussed in Chapter 8, which covers clinical legal education in Spain.

accountability—without discussing the standards of legal education and access to justice. Such discussions and debates have the utmost potential for institutionalizing clinical legal education as a model for quality legal education in the region and beyond. Some law school administrations now understand the role of legal clinics in professional training, taking into account the modernization of higher education, the Bologna Process, and reform of the legal profession. The role of legal clinics in assisting in shaping the future profession is without any doubt a topic that should be constantly present in political negotiations and discussions within the legal profession and with regard to the long-term success of rule of law reforms.

LIST OF REFERENCES

Andreas Bücker & William A. Woodruff, *The Bologna Process and German Legal Education: Developing Professional Competence through Clinical Experiences,* 9 GERMAN L. J. 575 (2008).

John M. Burman, *The Role of Clinical Legal Education in Developing the Rule of Law in Russia,* 2 WYO. L. REV. 89 (2002).

Lusine Hovhannisian. Clinical Legal Education and the Bologna Process (PILI Papers, Number December 2, 2006), *available at* http://www.pili.org.

Rachel Kleinfeld, *Competing Definitions of the Rule of Law, in* PROMOTING THE RULE OF LAW ABROAD (Thomas Carothers, ed., Carnegie Endowment for International Peace 2006).

Edwin Rekosh, *Constructing Public Interest Law: Transnational Collaboration and Exchange in Central and Eastern Europe,* 13 UCLA J. INT'L L. & FOREIGN AFF. 55 (2008).

Stephen Golub, *Forging the Future: Engaging Law Students and Young Lawyers in Public Service, Human Rights, and Poverty Alleviation,* OPEN SOCIETY JUSTICE INITIATIVE ISSUE PAPER (2004).

Martin Gramatikov, *Efficiency Evaluation of Projects on Establishing Legal Clinics at Bulgarian Law Schools,* OSI-SOFIA LAW PROGRAM EVALUATION REPORT (2003).

Lawrence M. Grosberg, *Clinical Education in Russia: "Da and Nyet,"* 7 CLIN. L. REV. 469 (2001).

James C. May, *Creating Russia's First Law School Legal Clinic,* 23 VT. BJ & L. DIG. 43 (1997).

5. CLINICAL LEGAL EDUCATION IN LATIN AMERICA
Toward Public Interest

ERIKA CASTRO-BUITRAGO, NICOLÁS ESPEJO-YAKSIC,

MARIELA PUGA, AND MARTA VILLARREAL

INTRODUCTION

Clinical legal education in Latin America has a long and complex history, dating back to the 1960s. That history begins with a project ignited by both American legal liberalism and economic liberalism, which has evolved into a mixture of approaches. Although not yet consolidated in the region, new approaches to clinical education based on the ideological and practical tenants of public interest law (PIL) may, nevertheless, help provide new forms of conceiving the rule of law, provide access to justice to insular minorities, and provide remedies for more effective and fairer social policies. This chapter describes key aspects of that history and their influence on the development of clinical legal education in Argentina, Chile, Colombia, and Mexico.

Clinical legal education was sponsored initially in Latin America by the so-called "first generation of Law and Development movement" (Rodríguez, 2001), shored up by a raising faith in the capacity of law and courts to effect social transformation. (Gardner, 1980)[1] A first wave of funds came from the United States, primarily to Brazil, Chile, and Colombia. Lead by the US Agency for International Development (USAID), the Ford Foundation, and a group of American universities, including Yale, Harvard, the University of Wisconsin, and Stanford, these and other funding organizations sponsored various legal programs and endeavors. Despite having had some impact on specific universities—notably at the University of Los Andes in Colombia, where the case-method remains in widespread use—these programs were generally considered a failed attempt to shape law schools as the source of a critical mass of modern lawyers. (Trubek & Galanter, 1974; Wilson, 2002) Most studies pointed out the inefficiency of legal transplantation for socio-cultural transformation (Watson, 1993) or the failure to recognize idiosyncratic features of Latin America legal culture, such as the weakness of the state law in post-colonial societies, the expanded legal pluralism, and specially, the administration's tendency to enact law for self-legitimating proposes. (Rodríguez, 2001; Gardner, 1980)

---

1. The law and development movement and its influence on legal education in Latin America is discussed in some detail in Chapter 9.

By the 1980s and early 1990s, most Latin American countries had gone through authoritarian governments and moved to a transitional period charac- terized by a strong hope of reconstruction and a critical review of the past. The so-far dominant formalist legal culture was particularly susceptible to criti- cism and with a young generation of law teachers educated in the left-wing lib- eral tradition and a growing influence of human rights lawyers and intellectuals devoted to the questions of law and justice, both American legal formalism and economic liberalism became major targets of the critical agenda of law and social change. American legal formalism was seen as incapable of providing a mean- ingful and accurate answer to the structural challenges of inequality, social exclu- sion, and political corruption in Latin America. At the same time, economic liberalism proved insufficient for redressing the intense and increased levels of inequality in the distribution of wealth and a progressive social feeling of decom- position of social cohesion in the region. (Courtis & Espejo, 2007)

Building on a revised strategic move to a "Second Generation of Law and Development" aimed at reappropriating the public role of both lawyers and law schools in the South (González, 1999; Courtis, 2007; Bohmer, 2007), a second- wave of clinical legal education arrived in the region in the 1990s. Comprised originally of law schools from Argentina, Chile, Colombia, and Peru, a regional network of PIL clinics expanded gradually to other countries, including Mexico and even the United States. (González, 2001) These clinics charged directly against the formalist approach to law, focusing on public law issues such as free speech, minority rights, due process, human rights, treaty enforcement, and other issues related to democratization and the rule of law. They worked initially on strategic litigation, attempting to connect law schools with both social issues and new theoretical challenges for legal theory.

Clinical programs developed under the rubric of PIL clinics were based more directly on the imperatives of social justice and the respect for human rights, as opposed to the opacity of the agenda of the first wave of law and development. PIL litigation clinics tried to avoid a naive belief on swift transformation of legal education and also assumed the limited—although not less important— possibilities of structural social change via legal activism. (Brewer & Cavallaro, 2008) Furthermore, PIL clinics developed a less formalistic distinction between civil society and academia, allowing for joint projects such as the joint venture between Universidad de Buenos Aires and the Centro de Estudios Legales y Sociales [Center for Social and Legal Studies] described below, and also among the several legal disciplines involved in human rights cases.

Despite these accomplishments, the second generation of law and develop- ment remained rather focused on the national level, paying little attention to regional processes and strategies of intervention. PIL clinics concentrated for the most part on developing a local agenda, which included some international liti- gation (mainly before the Inter-American Commission and Court of Human Rights) but not the construction of an authentic regional plan. While PIL clinics have been particularly fertile in proposing new forms of judicial intervention (McClymont & Golub, 2000; CELS, 2008), they have just recently started to think more consciously about the limits of these strategies and the necessity to reconsider their role in both legal education and professional practice. (Puga, 2008) The next sections of this chapter examine this development from the perspective of four countries in the region with substantial clinical experience: Argentina, Chile, Colombia, and Mexico.

CLINICAL LEGAL EDUCATION IN ARGENTINA

Although there were already some law school–sponsored legal aid programs, clinical legal education emerged in Argentina in the 1990s along with the second generation of law and development, under the auspices of the Latin American Network of Public Interest Actions. Three clinics were initially sponsored by this program and a country director appointed to coordinate the Argentina branch of the network and its expansion.

One of the first Argentinean clinics was Comahue Public University School of Law, located in Neuquén Province. The Comahue Clinic was an extracurricular course conducted by a professor of criminal law. The clinic provided students training on strategic litigation before the local penitentiary system. The project lasted almost four years and gave the local penitentiary system considerable visibility for a while by denouncing the violation of the rights of inmates. Once the Ford Foundation support ended, however, the university no longer supported the clinic. Public law schools, which tend to have more prestige than private law schools in Argentina, have been especially reluctant to implement curricular innovation, particularly regarding new pedagogic methods in teaching law. This partially explains why the Comahue Clinic—despite its relatively positive impact—was kept out of the official curriculum and eventually suppressed.

The other two clinics sponsored by the network tell a different story; both survived the closing down of the network and continue in operation. They also became the model for organizing and structuring new clinics around the country.

One of these other two clinics was the UBA-CELS Clinic established by a nongovernmental organization (NGO), the Centro de Estudios Legales y Sociales (CELS), in collaboration with the Buenos Aires National University School of Law (UBA). The clinic was designed to train law students in two different settings: in weekly clinical seminars held in a classroom and led by CELS-appointed lawyers and in meetings at the NGO office with other lawyers and clients. The particular strength of this project was that it provided students with a unique opportunity to observe, reflect, and work alongside some of the most prestigious human rights lawyers—and at one of the most well-established human rights organizations— in the country. They conducted research, discussed and participated in CELS's case work, and the organization, in turn, benefited from the support work of the students. Several key cases were litigated by this clinic, such as the *Viceconte* case that determined the obligation of the Argentinean State—under both the Constitution and international human rights law—to complete the production of a vaccination that was vital for a rural community.

The UBA-CELS model rapidly became popular among the student community. The selection process of UBA students became more rigorous, so that today just a few of hundreds of law students who apply can participate in this clinic. The lucky few usually have the chance to do a large amount of interviewing and counseling work on human rights issues, participate in the clinical seminars, and help lawyers with their research and client representation. The model, as an externship agreement,[2] has been imitated over the years through collaborations between other organizations and the UBA and other public and private universities across the country, each adapting the program in its own way to allow students to learn in the field and profit from their work. One such example is another clinic at UBA that operates in collaboration with the Asamblea Permanente Por Los Derechos Humanos (APDH) [Permanent Assembly for Human Rights].

The other successful model was developed at a private university, Palermo School of Law. Conducted by a law school professor as part of the curriculum, the clinic operated as a sort of laboratory focused on PIL cases—inspired by theoretical discussion and an intensively deliberative decision-making process. The clinic had a particular dynamic provided by students' discussion of both strategic litigation and the criteria for selecting cases on their PIL merits. A significant part of the learning process for students thus took place while proposing, hearing, choosing, or discarding potential PIL cases. After that, they conducted research, prepared court presentations, and collectively took strategic decision. However, under this model the students have limited contact with clients; most client contact is with the NGOs that propose the cases to the clinic. Similar to CELS-UBA clinic, the Palermo clinic won a number of important cases on a wide range of issues, including bilingual education for indigenous communities, social services rights for people with disabilities, and legal recognition of sexual identity for transsexuals.

The Palermo model has been replicated by a few public universities, most notably in the clinics of Tucuman National University and Santa Fé National University. The Palermo clinic has also utilized, as an alternative, the joint venture CELS-UBA model in collaboration with organizations such as the Asociación por los Derechos Civiles (ADC) [Civil Right Association] and the Asociación Civil por la Igualdad y la Justicia (ACIJ) [Civil Association for Equality and Justice], while preserving some of the characteristics of its laboratory model. This hybrid

---

2. Externships are covered in Chapter 22.

model came about due to both growing interest by NGOs in student work and some obstacles faced by the original Palermo model. The university perceived an incompatibility between its business image (especially for corporation and private interest) and the socio-economic cases addressed by the clinic, explaining that clinics were doing the job that NGOs should do. In fact, however, while NGOs do similar work, the original Palermo clinic's unique "academic lab setting" for strategy discussion and case selection resulted in the clinic handling different types of cases and with different approaches. Abandoning that model is a loss for both the public interest and the students' experience. Palermo's challenge is to adjust to the case selection and other policies of the NGO while retaining the important public interest and clinical values of its original model.

Despite the Palermo and CELS-UBA clinics' successful PIL records and their capacity for sustainability beyond Ford Foundation support, neither has made comparable progress in developing their clinical methodologies. They have spent little time reflecting on or documenting their pedagogical experiences or the impact their particular work can have on reforming the dominant teaching practices in Argentina. Nonetheless, there have been some attempts to extend their experience to other universities. In this context, it is worth noting that the three original network-sponsored clinics held two annual meetings, one of which was a regional meeting with delegates from Chile, Peru, Colombia, Ecuador, Mexico, and Argentina. Students presented and discussed cases they were working on, while professors gave more abstract speeches on PIL, litigation strategies, and pedagogical issues related to clinical legal education. The main focus was on sharing strategies on PIL actions and building a discourse on clinics as an alternative to formalist education. The other meeting was at a national level, allowing the three Argentinean clinics to discuss common matters. The last formal meeting of the network was in 2005. Since then, there were two attempts to bring it back to life. One was a meeting held in Mexico in 2007 with participants from a clinics throughout the Americas, including Argentina, Chile, Peru, Ecuador, Bolivia, Colombia, Brazil, Puerto Rico, Mexico, and the United States. In 2008, American University in the United States and Torcuato Di Tella University in Argentina organized a meeting in Buenos Aires with clinicians looking to involve Latin American clinics in a collaborative work on international human rights litigation before the Inter-American court. Neither of these has as yet resulted in reviving a regional network.[3]

One other early clinical project, conceived as part of a research program financed by the Ford Foundation but never funded, was the Tucuman National University clinic. It was the first time that a public university curriculum included a clinic, with a provisional clinical chair, professors assigned to do the job, credits

---

3. The role of national and regional organizations in the global clinical movement is the topic of Chapter 19.

allocated for students, a university office provided for clinic meetings, and even some records kept on the clinic's internal organization and dynamics. The clinic lasted almost four years and had a significant academic and local impact, especially after having won the first case on child malnutrition in the country. But the local governor disliked this type of interference of the public university with public affairs, and, as a result, when the law school dean changed, the clinic disappeared from the curriculum and professors were relieved of clinic responsibilities. Recently, some faculty members regrouped in an effort to keep the clinic functioning under weaker institutional conditions. In the meantime, the Santa Fé National University adopted the Tucuman model, establishing Santa Fé as the only clinic at a public university taught by law professors as part of the curriculum with an office at the law school. The Tucuman model is also put forward regularly as a model to achieve in other Argentinean national universities by student organizations, which play a significant role in Latin American universities—especially in Argentina, where they have elected delegates in the university council. The Santa Fé clinic has joined with other clinic projects at public universities to develop joint institutional strategies in the search for sustainability.

Fortunately, the higher education rules started to change at the beginning of this century and the Comisión Nacional de Evaluación y Acreditación Universitaria (CONEAU) [National Commission for University Evaluation and Accreditation], the agency in charge of regulation and accreditation of university programs around the country, has shown more concern about the need for practical training, pedagogical change, and public education social impact. As a result, some law schools have turned their attention to short clinical experiences and are progressively incorporating different sorts of NGO agreements, interactive settings, some timid expansion in law school legal aid offices (just for counseling), and a few courses on human rights and interdisciplinary issues. While these reforms need to be celebrated, it is important to note their still embryonic character. Moreover, much of this is motivated by concern over accreditation so that changes may prove to be more symbolic than real. Nonetheless, the new educational framework increases the chances of positive developments in clinical legal education.

In Cordoba National University, for example, internship programs at state offices have grown rapidly, as well as optional courses on human rights, public issues, and interdisciplinary approaches to the law. The private Catholic University of Cordoba has established a legal aid clinic and the San Andrés University in Buenos Aires (also private) is planning a comprehensive clinical program focused on practical skills based on the Anglo-Saxon model. Meanwhile, Palermo University keeps adding successful agreements with NGOs for joint clinical programs.

In short, two trends can be identified in Argentina. Private and public universities have shown a growing concern for practical training of students, although some of them are avoiding institutional involvement in public affairs by either teaching only skills with no social content or by delegating training in both skills and social justice to NGOs. Only the Santa Fé National University clinics persist as a fully integrated clinical model. As a consequence, most Argentinean universities are still in between the familiar two options: accept again transplants from the North American clinical model as a way to fill the gap on professional skills training, which is heavily resisted by public universities; or insist on connecting legal education to public affairs. The latter option could mean separating practical legal education from public affairs by situating professional training at NGOs, or, instead, moving toward the original Palermo, Tucuman, and Santa Fé models. Either way, the future sounds promising.

CLINICAL LEGAL EDUCATION IN CHILE

Following some limited previous experience, clinical legal education was established regularly in Chile in the late 1960s and early 1970s. These early clinics were set up at some traditional law schools under the auspices of the Ford Foundation and the US Agency for International Development (USAID). Their purpose seemed to be both the promotion of the ideological framework of the first generation of law and development in Chile and the case-study system of legal education conceived in the United States. (Figueroa, 1978, Sierra, 2003) As in other countries of the region, the impact of these clinics on legal education was rather marginal. Apart from the limits of the first generation of law and development movement discussed earlier, the Chilean legal clinics created under this umbrella faced two problems. On the one hand, legal clinics lacked the academic and professional *know-how* and resources to carry on a demanding radical transformation within law schools. On the other hand, legal clinics were shocked by the military *coup d'état*, a political process which implied a strong step back for legal education and in universities overall. (Wilson, 2002) As a consequence, legal education in Chile continued to be based on *clases magistrales* (lectures) and the memorization of positive law as defined in the codes, paradigmatically the civil code. (Barrientos, 2000)

After the return to democracy in the 1990s, a process of reforming law school curricula started to take place. These reforms included a more decisive focus on specialization in specific areas of the law, leading sometimes to the creation of a Masters in Law following the current European trend, training courses on oral litigation or other professional skills, the replacement of annual courses in favor of trimesters or semesters, and, in some cases, the implementation of the Socratic method. Although these changes might have been instrumental for the reemergence of a new culture based on clinical legal education, this has not necessarily been the case.

By 2009, almost all of the so-called "traditional" law schools provided some form of clinical education, including Universidad de Chile, Pontificia Universidad

Católica de Chile, Pontificia Universidad Católica de Valparaíso, and Universidad de Valparaíso. Some operate under the label of *clinicas jurídicas* or *consultorios legales* (legal clinics), which are officially part of the curriculum. Legal clinics normally operate within the law school premises and are generally designed to provide access to justice for the poor. Under the supervision of one or two professors (usually part-time faculty), students conduct interviews, counsel clients, and participate in the writing and submission of legal documents in rather simple judicial and administrative procedures, such as inheritances, evictions, and debt-related commercial proceedings.

Other universities facilitate the creation of *consultorios legales*, a form of legal aid for economically disadvantaged communities which take place outside the formal curriculum, which means they do not award credit. *Consultorios legales* emerged in the 1960s, seemingly influenced by both the first wave of law and development and a more critical social consciousness of the role that law schools may play within poor or structurally unfair societies. These *consultorios legales*, many of which operate under the auspices of a local church or communitarian organizations, tend to provide the same sort of legal services as the traditional legal clinics (*clínicas jurídicas*), under the supervision of a lawyer and with an active participation of law students.

At the same time, "private" or "new" law schools have stepped in to provide their students with some sort of professional practice, whether in the form of legal clinics, for example, at Universidad Andrés Bello, Universidad Central, and Universidad Diego Portales, internships, for example, at Universidad de los Andes and Universidad Diego Portales, or litigation training, for example, at Universidad Adolfo Ibáñez. However, few of these programs have been able to represent a shift away from the main features of the Chilean legal culture: mainly positivistic regarding the sources of law, formalist in construing such sources, and legalistic in its understanding of the role that the body of rules plays in the development of collective life. (Squella, 1994; Fuenzalida, 2007) In other words, legal clinics have remained marginal in the process of transforming Chilean legal culture. In this respect, they have tended to be both conceived and implemented as a way to exhibit—to the legal community and the public in general—some sort of educational method that may add symbolic value to the program offered by law schools. Legal clinics have not, however, become a fundamental part—not even a significant one—within the process of legal education reform. One must also recognize that whatever form clinical education takes in Chile, all law students must engage in six months of mandatory legal practice before being granted a professional title of lawyer by the Chilean Supreme Court.

This general scenario may be complemented by some positive examples taken from the so-called second wave of law and development and, in particular, public interest law (PIL) in Chile. Both Universidad Católica de Temuco and Universidad Diego Portales developed innovative clinical programs under the umbrella of the

Latin American Network of Public Interest Law Clinics, which operated from the mid-1990s until 2007. These programs allowed students to conduct research and otherwise take part in "hard" cases—both domestic and international—involving important social issues such as discrimination of women, indigenous peoples, and sexual minorities, access to health for HIV patients, torture and inhumane and degrading treatment for detainees, and criminal prosecution of political critique against public authorities, among others.

Although the PIL network no longer exists, the role it played was crucial for the national public impact of these cases as well as the promotion and creation of PIL in other countries of the region. The public image provided by PIL litigation has been instrumental, in some cases, for the consolidation of comparative advantages for law schools in a highly competitive environment—and in providing law students with analytical and professional tools traditionally absent in mainstream legal education. PIL cases handled at the Diego Portales and Católica de Temuco University clinics included the submission of habeas corpus; injunctions on environmental cases; civil and criminal complaints related to health, education, labor, and nondiscrimination; and litigation of various cases at the international level (particularly before the Inter-American Commission and Court of Human Rights). In all of these cases, students had an active and protagonist role that provided them with a unique educational advantage for pursuing careers as human rights lawyers, academics, or public officers.

Particularly in the case of the Diego Portales PIL clinic, one of the main strategies was to establish a clear connection between the use of judicial remedies for access to justice and the empowerment of civil society organizations—such as the Organization of People Living with HIV/AIDS (*Vivo Positivo* [Positive Living])—which tended to operate as the real "clients" of the clinics. (Contesse & Lovera, 2008) At the same time, the high profile of the cases submitted, most of which were followed by the media, provided both an encouraging environment for students and the opportunity for academic debate on the convenience or inconvenience of the use of the judicial activism as a tool for social change. (Atria, 2000)

In a similar way, the school of law of Universidad Central de Chile (UCC) runs a successful clinical program based on both the development of advocacy skills for law students and the promotion, education, and defense of human rights for vulnerable groups. The UCC clinical program operates around thematic clinics on civil, criminal, family, and labor law, as well as mediation. In addition, the UCC clinical program has recently created two legal clinics especially devoted to children rights and environmental justice. Parallel to these litigation activities, lecturers and students have taken part in educational programs for migrants, indigenous communities, and street-buyers, among other groups. So far, the UCC clinic has trained more than 1500 leaders of urban and rural communities in the use of legal and judicial remedies for the defense of their rights. One remarkable aspect of the UCC clinic is the financial and administrative institutional support it receives from the university, including plans to open new clinics on thematic issues and to continue promoting human rights within Chilean civil society. (Universidad Central de Chile, 2009)

At the market level, PIL litigation was a pioneer in the collective use of law for the respect of consumer rights—a professional form of intervention nowadays much developed by several organizations and law firms. A prominent example is CONADECUS, one of the leading NGOs in Chile promoting and defending consumer rights. At the civil society level, PIL litigation ignited new strategies of judicial intervention by lawyer associations particularly concerned with civil and political rights, such as Libertades Públicas [Public Liberties], Fundación Pro Acceso [Pro Access Foundation], and Fundación Pro Bono [Pro Bono Foundation]. Those strategies have been pursued also by other NGOs, including those mainly concerned with gender litigation and activism, such as Humanas: Centro Regional de Derechos Humanos y Justicia de Género [Regional Center on Human Rights and Gender Justice] and MOVILH: Movimiento Chileno de Minorías Sexuales [Chilean Movement of Sexual Minorities]; those focused on indigenous rights, such as the Observatorio Ciudadano [Citizens Observatory]; and others with a wider mandate, such as Corporación Interés Publico (IP) [Public Interest Foundation], which makes systematic use of both national and international strategic litigation for local organizations defending the rights of sexual minorities, housing rights for the disadvantaged, labor rights, and access to public information, among others. By using, promoting, and developing new forms of PIL litigation, these new clinical programs and NGOs seem to be connecting legal practice with social justice, contributing in this manner to the consolidation of the second wave of law and development.

CLINICAL LEGAL EDUCATION IN COLOMBIA

The so-called first generation of law and development had a rather marginal success in Colombia. As a matter of fact, only one out of the five law schools at which reforms were attempted—University of Los Andes, founded at 1968—has been able to sustain the Socratic method of law teaching until today. (Rodriguez, 2001) Some regulations were enacted that established the obligation of law schools to provide legal aid practices for students (*consultorios jurídicos*) in an attempt to reject the traditional way of teaching law by hierarchical lectures and memorization of the codes. Although the majority of these *consultorios* ended up replicating some of the same vices of legal formalism and were generally structured and perceived as mere positive externalities of law schools, they did open new perspectives on clinical education in Colombia.

It was not until the 1990s, however, that legal clinics started to take the form that they have today. The 1991 constitutional reform established a series of new mechanism for both the administrative and judicial protection of human rights.

Legal clinics during this period began as more-or-less informal groups of students and professors reflecting on new constitutional procedures for access to justice brought by the reforms. They foresaw the opportunities opened to professional practice and started to litigate some cases. Soon they became an alternative to the *consultorios*, and students were able to engage in a more demanding professional environment.

One of the first Clinics started under this umbrella was the Grupo de Acciones Públicas (GAP) [Public Action Group] at the Universidad Colegio Mayor de Nuestra Señora del Rosario in Bogotá, which was established in 1999. Students in this clinic make use of the new constitutional procedures in cases involving both individual and collective rights. The setting is quite horizontal, based on case-by-case discussions and a substantial work load for the students. Los Andes University also took an early part of this wave, although under the influence of the second generation of the law and development movement. The university already counts three clinical projects—Grupo de Interés Público (GDIP) [Public Interest Group], established in 2005, Programa de acción por la igualdad y la inclusión social (PAIIS) [Program of Action for Equality and Social Inclusion], established in 2007, and Justicia Global y Derechos Humanos [Global Justice and Human Rights], created in 2008—which are part of the *consultorio* program but are concerned particularly with social justice issues. The main emphasis of these clinics has been the exhaustion of procedures for the judicial declaration of unconstitutionality in human rights–related cases. A second, similar clinic dealing specifically with environmental issues was established at the University of Medellin in 2004.

These clinics have thus been instrumental in Colombia for the redefinition of both the role and structure of classical *consultorios*, helping to transform them into critical tools of the legal system. This tendency has been confirmed recently by the creation of new clinics at Pontificia Bolivariana University and the Luis Amigó University Foundation, both situated in the city of Medellin. Although they were conceived initially as *consultorios*, they have developed into more selective and strategic sort of clinics. Among other relevant aspects, these clinics have the chance to select students, provide them with training on client interviewing (a special setting for case-by-case learning), and a particular system of evaluation.

Despite of the positive evolution of clinical legal education in Colombia, *consultorios* clinics have remained as rather marginal courses in the curriculum with a relatively small impact on the general learning process. As a consequence, most clinics confront several obstacles, such as the lack of full-time professors and insufficient budgets for caseload management and other basic aspects of professional litigation. Two notable exceptions are Universidad de los Andes and Universidad del Rosario, both in Bogotá, where part-time professors have full-time support from coordinators and a small budget. Nonetheless, clinics have advanced an outstanding caseload related to a variety of socio-economic issues, including the rights of vulnerable groups, displaced people, handicapped people, women, children, homosexuals, and indigenous people. Environmental rights have been a key area of concern for clinics, allowing interdisciplinary work and rich collaborative projects among academics and practitioners from several fields. Recently, following some strategies previously developed by other clinics of the region, Colombian clinics have collaborated with social communicators and journalists in order to reinforce the presence of these cases before a public audience.

Unfortunately, some of these achievements may be overshadowed by changes in the selection process of students (in some cases, no more interviews), the size of courses (too many students), and a lack of coordination (fewer weekly hours for clinic work, which makes it difficult to implement the clinic methodology). Also frustrating is the lack of resources and willingness to involve more than one professor in the clinic. And since academic rules require that courses follow a general quantitative model of evaluation, it is difficult to evaluate competences and skills in clinical work adequately. In a hopeful sign, the Medellin clinic received permission from the university council to use a different form of evaluation based on specific know-how and forensic skills. Overall, however, only the well-established legal clinics in Bogotá seem to operate in a proper institutional setting.

To some extent, difficulties faced by clinics in Colombia are the natural outcome of the pervasive legal formalism and its pedagogical counterpart in most law school in the country, plus the rigidity of the curricula and the academic bureaucracy. These hitches impact the quantity and quality of the legal aid that clinics provide in the regions of the country that are in most need. Nevertheless, and despite the obstacles, Colombian clinics have been tools for pedagogical innovation, the development of more interdisciplinary research, important legislative work, and legal support for local organizations advocating for the defense of human rights.

CLINICAL LEGAL EDUCATION IN MEXICO

For more than two decades, reforms in substantive and procedural law (including constitutional reform) have progressively modeled a different legal system in Mexico that, nevertheless, have not had much of an impact on the quality of legal education—including providing lawyers with necessary professional skills. (López & Fix-Fierro, 2006) A couple of exceptions, however, can be traced back to 2003. That year, the Centro de investigación y Desarrollo Económico (CIDE) [Center of Research and Economic Development] organized a meeting on clinical legal education with representatives of several law schools. In the same year, the Instituto Tecnológico Autónomo de México (ITAM) included a PIL clinic in its curriculum as an elective course.

Unlike the experience in Argentina, Chile, and Colombia, the development of clinical legal education programs in Mexico was supported initially mainly by the Open Society Justice Initiative, which did not impose an agenda of development but instead supported agendas compatible with its own, including legal capacity development, equality and citizenship, and freedom of information and expression. Both CIDE and ITAM—one a public institution, the other private—were neither the major nor the largest law schools in Mexico. Nevertheless, their clinics were established within universities with well-deserved reputations based on their liberal education and having the necessary skills to perform in the recently renovated government system.

CIDE and ITAM helped initiate a trend toward a clinical legal education marked not only by its difference from the traditional way of teaching law, but also from universities' typical response to social needs. These clinics allowed for the inclusion of new models of legal education based on important changes in the curriculum, particularly evaluation methods. They were also able to advance an openness to different theoretical conceptions of the law and to respond to both the legal and social needs that pressed law schools in Mexico. These clinics also demanded an allocation of resources, something not many schools were willing to accept since teaching law had always been extremely low cost and highly productive.

The clinical methods used by the two schools were different. CIDE first started to collaborate with an NGO, developing a so-called extern NGO-based clinic. The students' work was supervised by a lawyer at the NGO who relied on CIDE to provide the legal structure. ITAM was developing a concept of clinical legal education as a specialized field of legal education, and therefore tried to implement and test a variety of clinical education typologies.

ITAM's clinical program had three major streams. First, it included a basic clinical course where students took a class with two components: theory and practice. The theory component focused on public interest law concepts while the practice component was oriented toward getting the students to produce a project of public interest impact. Then there was an advanced public interest law clinic course with a major objective of having the students acquire lawyering skills and allowing them to participate in real cases. The third stream was the public interest law clinic, which acted as a coordinating office for volunteer students as well as a *servicio social* (social service). It also operated a Street Law project.

The cases taken by the ITAM public interest law clinic allowed students to acquire not only litigation skills but also other abilities related to the legal profession. The clinic took a variety of cases from a wide range of themes, some coming from national NGOs, organized citizens, single individuals, students, and international organizations or human rights lawyers, involving constitutional or criminal litigation in national or international arenas, as well as environmental, gender, or migration issues—the only unifying criteria being public interest.

Passing through the clinic program allowed future lawyers to figure out that there is a lot more to being a lawyer than litigation.

These clinical projects at CIDE and ITAM reflected the expansive demand in Mexico for reform in the way law is taught, which should be able to reconcile tradition with innovation. (Magaloni, 2006) For example, the need to incorporate clinical legal education into the curriculum of Mexican law schools has recently grown in importance due to the passage of a constitutional reform of the criminal justice system. In 2008, the Mexican Congress ordered a shift from the traditional inquisitorial procedural system—which had a focus on documentary presentation of evidence—to one based on adversarial accusatory trials. The successful implementation of this new criminal justice model is particularly important given that Mexico is in the middle of a public security crisis. Implementing this new system will require the introduction of oral advocacy skills alien to Mexican criminal law practitioners and students.

Yearly from 2003 to 2007, the CIDE and ITAM were involved in the promotion of clinical legal education, approaching the task from various perspectives but mainly interested in the creation of a national network. This never materialized, in part because although various law schools showed interest in the clinic model, most recognized that it would require too many challenges—not only to change the curricula but also to transform the conception of law that framed the way to teach law. During this time, both universities were engaged not only in strengthening their own models of clinics but were also working, jointly with the Open Society Justice Initiative, on the development of clinical legal education in Mexico. CIDE was changing from a model of an NGO-based clinic to a more independent one with its own agenda, heading for diversification in its public interest litigation. ITAM was very much focused on the changing tasks and roles in the learning process, paying a lot of attention to the supervision of students during the practice experience. It also undertook the difficult challenge of training its professors in clinical methods.

Inspired by the conception of the clinic as a motor of change—of transformation of the legal system into a more democratic one—ITAM made use of a variety of clinical methodologies: it supported cases from NGOs; in close collaboration with students, it got involved in supporting public interest cases on the decriminalization of abortion and legal migration reforms; it participated in promoting innovations to the judicial system. The most common clinical methodology used in Mexico is associating with NGOs or with other institution, such as the UNHCR, in the representation of a case—especially for public interest or strategic litigation. That is the case at two other law schools offering a sort of clinical experience in their postgraduate programs for a master in human rights, Facultad Latinoamericana de Ciencias Sociales (FLACSO) and Universidad Iberoamericana. These types of clinics could be valuable experiences for students, although they have also provoked some strong criticism about the methodology.

Ultimately, the importance of the development of clinical legal education lies in the growing analytical review of the traditional methods of teaching; that is, in the efforts of law schools to pursue new approaches to law and the prevalent legal system. There are, however, many complications in Mexico in implementing the clinical method, one of the most difficult being the component of change that clinics promote. The legal system is very much rooted to its own perpetuating practices, assuring the power for those who already have it and excluding most others from justice. Many law schools, although interested in gaining spaces for their graduated students, are more concerned with preserving the status quo. In some cases, recognition by the university has provided the ideal platform from which to launch a clinical program, but recognition can also play against a clinical program when its presence becomes public and its actions start to be perceived publicly. Unfortunately, the activities and outcomes of clinical programs are not always well perceived by their universities or by the legal system in general. In the case of ITAM, the university decided to discontinue the project after the clinic got involved in some public interest cases. Whether this decision amounts to a political statement remains to be seen. The challenge of strengthening both access to justice and critical legal thinking in Mexico continues to be a project of the utmost importance.

CONCLUSION: STILL CHALLENGING TIMES

Legal clinics have come to Latin America to stay. Innovations they brought in litigation and social perception of the role of law and lawyers in society deserve a worthy spot in public affairs and legal education. The pedagogical impact for students has shown its importance since many of them have already become successful professionals actively defending the method and its outcomes.

What is still in doubt is the extent to which clinics are going to grow, and specifically how much they are going to challenge traditional legal education. Although public interest law initiatives have situated some clinics in the educational program, most remain isolated from the curriculum or are facing marginalization. Latin American law schools remain largely trapped by pedagogical practices that are structurally hostile to both case study and the development of research abilities by law students. (Gonzalez, 2004) Accordingly, challenging times are still on the horizon for most Latin American clinics. Most of them still lack long-term strategies for sustainability, have not achieved an idiosyncratic effective way for advancing into legal curricula, and have been progressively suffering budget reductions from inside and outside supporters. At the same time, legal clinics—particularly those advocated to the defence of human rights—face the challenge of developing litigation strategies that not only protect civil and political rights, but also socio-economic rights within ideological settings traditionally hostile to the judicial enforcement of socio-economic rights. (Lovera, 2007; Espejo, 2009)

Nonetheless, their stand against formalism and the inspiration that some clinics' PIL cases have had on law students and professionals have made clinics an increasingly better known model for channeling expectations of legal education reform, which so far has been deeply disappointing for law students and the communities that the law and the legal system should serve.

LIST OF REFERENCES

Fernando Atria, *Revisión Judicial: El Síndrome de la Victima Insatisfecha* [*Judicial Review: The Syndrome of the Dissatisfied Victim*], 79 ESTUDIOS PÚBLICOS 347 (2000).

Javier Barrientos, La enseñanza del Derecho en Chile: del Ius Commune a la Codificacion [The Teaching of Law in Chile: From the Common Law to the Codification], Paper presented at II Jornadas Ius Commune-Ius Proprium en las Indias (2000).

Martín F. Böhmer, *Igualadores y traductores: La ética del abogado en una democracia constitucional* [*Equalizers and Translators: The Ethics of the Lawyer in a Constitutional Democracy*], in ENSEÑANZA CLÍNICA DEL DERECHO. UNA ALTERNATIVA A LOS MÉTODOS TRADICIONALES DE FORMACIÓN DE ABOGADOS [CLINICAL TEACHING OF LAW: AN ALTERNATIVE TO THE TRADITIONAL METHODS FOR FORMATION OF ATTORNEYS] (Marta Villarreal & Cristián Courtis eds., ITAM 2007).

James L. Cavallaro & Stephanie Erin Brewer, *The Virtue of Following: The Role of Inter-American Litigation in Campaigns for Social Justice*, 8 SUR–INT'L J. FOR HUM. RTS. 85 (2008).

CELS, LA LUCHA POR EL DERECHO [The Fight for the Law] (Centro de Estudios Legales y Sociales 2008).

Jorge Contesse & Domingo Lovera Parmo, *Access to medical treatment for people living with HIV/AIDS: success without victory in Chile*, 8 SUR–INT'L J. FOR HUM. RTS. 151 (2008).

Christian Courtis, *La Educación jurídica cómo práctica transformadora* [*Legal Education as Practicing Transformer*], in ENSEÑANZA CLÍNICA DEL DERECHO: UNA ALTERNATIVA A LOS MÉTODOS TRADICIONALES DE FORMACIÓN DE ABOGADOS [CLINICAL TEACHING OF LAW: AN ALTERNATIVE TO THE TRADITIONAL METHODS FOR FORMATION OF ATTORNEYS] (Marta Villarreal & Cristián Courtis eds., ITAM 2007).

CHRISTIAN COURTIS & NICOLÁS ESPEJO, POR UN "CONTRATO DE COHESIÓN SOCIAL": APUNTES EXPLORATORIOS, DIVISIÓN DE DESARROLLO SOCIAL, [FOR A "CONTRACT OF SOCIAL COHESION": EXPLORATORY NOTES, DIVISION OF SOCIAL DEVELOPMENT] (Social Policies Series No. 129, CEPAL, United Nations 2007).

Nicolás Espejo-Yaksic, Manual Sobre Justiciabilidad de Derechos Sociales para Jueces de Iberoamérica [Manual on Judicial Enforceability of Socio Economic Rights for Judges of Iberoamerica], L. Casas, M. Feddersen & A. Quesille (collaborators) (Oxfam, UDP, RIJ 2009).

Gonzalo Figueroa, *Hacia una nueva concepción de los estudios de derecho* [*Toward a New Conception of Legal Studies*], in DERECHO Y SOCIEDAD [LAW AND SOCIETY] (Gonzalo Figueroa ed., CPU 1978).

Edmundo Fuenzalida, *La cultura jurídica chilena y sus transformaciones* [*The Chilean Legal Culture and Its Transformations*], 25 ANUARIO DE FILOSOFÍA JURÍDICA Y SOCIAL [ANNUAL OF LEGAL AND SOCIAL PHILOSOPHY] 165 (2007).

JAMES A. GARDNER, LEGAL IMPERIALISM: AMERICAN LAWYERS AND FOREIGN AID IN LATIN AMERICA (University of Wisconsin Press 1980).

Felipe M. González, *Evolución y perspectivas de la red universitaria sudamericana de Acciones de Interés Público* [*Evolution and Perspectives of the South American University Network of Actions of Public Interest*], 9 CUADERNO DE ANÁLISIS JURÍDICO 21 (Universidad Diego Portales 1999).

Felipe M. González, *La OEA y los derechos humanos después del advenimiento de los gobiernos civiles: expectativas (in)satisfechas* [*The OEA and Human Rights after the Advent of Civil Governments: [Un]satisfied Expectations*], 11 CUADERNO DE ANÁLISIS JURÍDICO (Universidad Diego Portales 2001).

FELIPE M. GONZÁLEZ, EL TRABAJO CLÍNICO EN MATERIA DE DERECHOS HUMANOS E INTERÉS PUBLICO EN AMERICA LATINA [The Clinical Work in the Matter of Human Rights and Public Interest in Latin America] (Universidad Deusto 2004).

Domingo Lovera Parmo, *Implosive Courts, Law and Social Transformation: the Chilean Case*, 3 CAMBRIDGE STUDENT L. REV. 30 (2007).

Ana Laura Magaloni, *Cuellos de botella y ventanas de oportunidad de la reforma a la educación jurídica de elite en México* [*Bottlenecks and Windows of Opportunity of the Reform of Legal Education of Elite in Mexico*], in DEL GOBIERNO DE LOS ABOGADOS AL IMPERIO DE LAS LEYES. ESTUDIOS SOCIO-JURÍDICOS SOBRE EDUCACIÓN Y PROFESIÓN JURÍDICAS EN EL MÉXICO CONTEMPORÁNEO [FROM THE GOVERNMENT OF ATTORNEYS TO THE EMPIRE OF THE LAWS: SOCIO-JUDICIAL STUDIES REGARDING EDUCATION THE JUDICIAL PROFESSIONS IN MEXICO] (Hector Fix-Fierro ed., Instituto de Investigaciones Jurídicas, UNAM 2006).

Mary McClymont & Stephen Golub, Many Roads to Justice: The Law Related Work of Ford Foundation Grantees around the World (Ford Foundation 2000).

Mariela G. Puga, *Los desafíos de las clínicas jurídicas en Argentina* [*The Challenges of Legal Clinics in Argentina*], 9 CUADERNO DE ANÁLISIS JURÍDICO (1999) [English version: *Challenges for Legal Clinics in Argentina*, 37 LAW TEACHER (2003)].

MARIELA G. PUGA, LA REALIZACIÓN DE LOS DERECHOS EN CASOS ESTRUCTURALES. LAS CAUSAS VERBITSKY Y MENDOZA [THE REALIZATION OF RIGHTS IN STRUCTURAL CASES: THE CAUSES VERBITSKY AND MENDOZA] (Facultad de Derecho, Universidad De Palermo 2008).

César A. Rodríguez Garavito, *Globalización, reforma judicial y Estado de Derecho en Colombia y América Latina: El regreso de los programas de derecho y desarrollo* [Globalization, Judicial Reform and State of Law in Colombia and Latin America: The Return of the Programs of Law and Development], *in* ¿JUSTICIA PARA TODOS? SISTEMA JUDICIAL, DERECHOS SOCIALES Y DEMOCRACIA EN COLOMBIA [JUSTICE FOR ALL? JUDICIAL SYSTEM, SOCIAL RIGHTS AND DEMOCRACY IN COLOMBIA] (Norma 2001).

LUCAS SIERRA, DERECHO, CAMBIO SOCIAL Y LOS JURISTAS EN CHILE: DE LA ESTRIDENCIA DE LOS 60 AL SILENCIO DE HOY [LAW, SOCIAL CHANGE AND LAWYERS IN CHILE: FROM THE STRIDENCY OF THE 60 TO THE SILENCE OF TODAY] (Editores del Puerto 2003).

LA EVOLUCIÓN DE LA CULTURA JURÍDICA CHILENA [THE EVOLUTION OF THE CHILEAN LEGAL CLINIC] (Agustín Squella ed., Corporación de Promoción Universitaria (Agustín Squella ed., Corporación de Promoción Universitaria (CPU) 1994).

David M. Trubek & Marc Galanter, *Scholars in Self-Estrangement: Some Reflections on the Crisis in Law and Development*, 1974 WIS. L. REV. 1062 (1974).

UNIVERSIDAD CENTRAL DE CHILE, CLÍNICA JURÍDICA Y PRACTICA FORENSE: AÑO 2009 Y PROYECCIONES [LEGAL CLINIC AND FORENSIC PRACTICE: YEAR 2009 AND PROJECTIONS] (2009).

ALAN WATSON, LEGAL TRANSPLANTS: AN APPROACH TO COMPARATIVE LAW (2nd ed., University of Georgia Press 1993).

Richard J. Wilson, *Three Law Schools Clinics in Chile, 1970–2000: Innovation, Resistance and Conformity in the Global South*, 8 CLINICAL L. REV. 515 (2002).

6. THE "CHINESE CHARACTERISTICS" OF CLINICAL LEGAL EDUCATION

CAI YANMIN AND J. L. POTTENGER, JR.

I hear, and I forget,
I see, and I remember
I do, and I understand.
Confucius

Although Confucius himself bears witness to the venerability and value of experiential learning, the clinical movement in China is barely a decade old. Substantial success has been achieved in that short span of time. As the country's project of legal reform has provided fertile soil for law school–based clinics to take root and grow, the number of law schools with clinics has increased rapidly. But clinical methodology remains perched precariously on the periphery of both the legal educational establishment and the legal aid system, even as both of these sets of legal institutions have expanded exponentially in size and scope. Chinese clinical legal education thus faces great challenges—and a hopeful, but uncertain future.

This chapter seeks to provide a contextual analysis of the role that clinical legal education is beginning to play in China. We open with brief descriptions of China's efforts to strengthen its legal system and establish a "rule of law" society. We then discuss the early efforts to establish legal clinics and several of today's leading clinical programs, illustrated with a few case histories. We conclude with some of the key challenges to Chinese clinical legal education, and how we view its prospects.

CHINESE LEGAL SYSTEM

As the People's Republic of China celebrates its sixtieth anniversary, one of its many accomplishments is progress in building a maturing, increasingly important set of legal institutions. The slogan "rule of law" has begun to have at least a ring of truth, as "rights consciousness" becomes widespread and as the government has greatly expanded the number and importance of laws, lawyers, and judges. There has been a veritable explosion of "law," with thousands of new statutes and regulations, covering entire fields of law and aspects of society, adopted at an accelerating pace throughout the past three decades. These, in turn, have encouraged the assertion of a wide variety of "private," often commercial, legal rights and duties, both in and out of court.

The expansion of the legal profession, though relatively small for such a large country, is remarkable. The whole of China had only about 2,800 lawyers (in 800 offices) in 1957; due to the vast social upheavals during the two ensuing decades, there were even fewer (2,300 in 250 offices) in 1980. Today there are roughly 160,000 licensed lawyers; however, that represents only about one per 8,000 in population, compared to one lawyer for every 300 people in the United States—and far less than the goal of 500,000 lawyers that Deng Xiaoping announced as part of his "opening up" policy. These developments have been accompanied by new laws, potentially opening the government itself up to law-based challenges against its own actions and authority. The courts hearing such cases have expanded in size and skill since 1980. There are now more than 200,000 judges in China, and they are considerably better trained than the ex-military men and police who China originally assigned to the ranks of its judiciary. But courts in China are not an independent branch of government, and legal reform remains an unfinished effort.

"Rule of law" is sometimes translated into Chinese as "rule by law," which hints at the government's increasing reliance on these same legal institutions as a means to preserve social order by exercising official authority—whether over individuals, organizations, or other levels of government. China is still essentially an administrative party-state, with power in the hands of the Chinese Communist Party rather than formal governmental entities. Courts remain subject to party influence or control, are rather far down the hierarchy of power in socialist democracy, and often lack both authority and autonomy.

In part as a consequence, courts also suffer a lack of respect from Chinese citizens, who far more often instead seek redress through China's extensive, less formal petitions (or "Letters and Visits") (*xinfang*) system. (Minzner, 2006) Courts actually play but a small part in China's complex dispute resolution system, falling far short of being able to provide the impartial adjudication of disputes—and effective enforcement of their own rulings—which are the hallmarks of a real rule of law society. (Cohen, 2008) This is true to varying degrees at the local, provincial, and national levels. Indeed, the quasi-federal, "local protectionism" character of the Chinese political and governmental structures further complicates rule of law reform efforts. The ancient maxim ("Heaven is high and the Emperor is very far away") still applies and can lead to provincial favoritism, corruption, and noncompliance, even in the courts. (Note, 2007)

Another piece of China's legal puzzle is, perhaps surprisingly, the media. The glare of publicity has become a powerful tool. Lawyers—and law school clinics—have found that the semi-independent media can be a big asset in their work, and use their connections (*guanxi*) to seek favorable media coverage as a key strategy in many of their cases. On the other hand, the government also uses the media as part of its social control efforts, and appeals to "order" and obedience to law are commonplace in the party-state's continuing efforts to shape and control public opinion. The Internet and blogosphere also are beginning to play a growing role; as with the media, their impact can strengthen or weaken the rule of law reforms. (Liebman, 2005 & 2007)

This tension between these two conflicting interpretations of what "ruling the country according to law" (*yifazhiguo*) means in practice illustrates the ambiguous, evolving missions assigned to the courts, legal profession, and legal academy in the People's Republic. As a civil law society, albeit one with an overlay of Soviet (and, even, a few common law) elements, China's courts are not the focus of law-making or law-reform. Legal professionals' roles have evolved during the three decades since Deng Xiaoping first launched the "reform and opening up" policy of economic liberalization. Initially described as "state legal workers" (Interim Regulations, 1982), lawyers later were given a broader responsibility of "providing legal services to the public" (Law on Lawyers, 1996). Now their role is described in even more "professional" terms: "providing legal services for a client" (Revision to Lawyers' Law, June 2008). But lawyers remain subject to tight political and bureaucratic oversight, notably through licensing. Concerns have arisen in recent years over the treatment of the country's "rights lawyers" (*weiquan*). Government tactics have at times been harsh; according to Jerome Cohen, they have included "coerced . . . dismiss[als] . . . criminal prosecution . . . [even] physical intimidation . . . torture . . . and beat[ings]." (Cohen Remarks, 2009 at 3–5)

The situation in the legal academy is somewhat different. Legal education was substantially dismantled during the Cultural Revolution; in 1977, there were only three law departments (with 223 students). Today there are more than 634 law-training, degree-granting schools, or departments, with about half a million students enrolled. (Wang Chenguang, 2006) The decision to reestablish higher educational "Institutes of Politics and Law" in the early years after the Revolution shows that the Chinese Communist Party has always grasped the blurred distinction between those two disciplines—and put "politics" in first place. These institutes have graduated many of the leading cadres who staff the government's and party's legal and bureaucratic institutions, and they still do. Although eventually rebranded as "universities," they remained subject to oversight by the Ministry of Justice until 2000, even while university-based schools responsible for teaching "law" were under the Ministry of Education. This small example suggests that these twin tensions about the nature of China's rule of law society are reflected even within legal academia.

Chinese Legal Education

Whether in the institutes or universities, legal education in China remains fundamentally traditional in structure and delivery. About two-thirds of China's 450,000-plus law students are undergraduates enrolled in a four-year program, seeking their first university degree. Yet very few of these students will actually enter private law practice. Instead, most will take some sort of government job or go to private business. Undergraduate law students usually carry as many as six to eight courses per semester, necessitating fifteen to twenty hours in class each week. Nearly all of their teachers use that class time to lecture on the black-letter legal "rules" which comprise the heart of their civil law courses. Law faculty teach as many as six courses a term, although a more common teaching load is four or five courses for the younger faculty and two to four for the more senior professors. Few faculty practice law, or are formally qualified to do so.

The curriculum is nationally standardized; even the course textbooks are prescribed by the Ministry of Education. Perhaps as many as twenty courses are required of all law students, including half a dozen or so general courses on Marxism, Deng Xiaoping philosophy, and Chinese society (which are mandatory for all undergraduates). For graduate law students seeking a masters or higher degree, additional specific courses are required to specialize in one's chosen field of legal study (such as civil law, economic law, criminal law, or international trade law). On the other hand, course reading assignments in China are relatively light, lessening the burden imposed by the additional class hours. Nonetheless, the overall degree requirements come out to nearly double the credit hours demanded for a typical three-year, postgraduate law degree in the United States. (Wang Chenguang, 2006; Phan, 2005)

It is therefore easy to see why clinical methodology, with its interactive, discussion-focused format and its essential emphasis on skills and values, presents a pedagogical challenge to Chinese students and teachers alike. The real-world, client-centered focus on "facts"—and practice—which lies at the heart of clinical legal education could not be more different from the rest of the curriculum, with its virtually exclusive emphasis on rules, "law," and theory. Nor could the less hierarchical, interactive style adopted by many clinical teachers be in sharper contrast to the passivity-inducing lectures still used by many of their "infallible" colleagues. We shall explore the challenges and opportunities inherent in this contrast later in the chapter.

Legal Aid

Alongside its push to increase the production of law and lawyers, the Chinese government has sought to improve poor peoples' access to the strengthening and expanding legal system by introducing a program of legal aid. First established in the Ministry of Justice in the mid-1990s, the Legal Aid Center now directs and supervises the work of over 3250 official, government-funded legal aid offices, employing roughly 6000 full-time lawyers (and a similar number of additional staff). These activities cost over five billion RMB ($750 million) in 2007. Literally thousands of civic groups and organizations, including universities, women's associations, local groups, nongovernmental organizations (NGOs) (and government-operated NGOs), support legal aid through their efforts. Well over 50,000 volunteers participate, the majority of whom are university students. Although there has been an enormous expansion of resources devoted to legal aid, financial eligibility requirements restrict assistance to the very poorest of the poor; even under China's own measures of poverty, most of those classified as "poor" are ineligible for legal aid. (Fu, 2009)

The work handled by government legal aid offices is substantial, and varied. About half of the roughly 650,000 cases in 2006 were classified as ADR (alternative dispute resolution); the other half was about two-thirds civil (including a large volume of labor-related disputes over injuries and wages, and many government benefits cases) and one-third criminal. Only a small fraction of criminal cases are considered sufficiently "serious" (in terms of the exposure to punishment) to qualify for mandatory free legal aid, so most criminal defendants are not represented by counsel. The scarce resource of legal services is reserved for those who can afford them, or for those defendants the government deems particularly worthy of assistance, namely those who are disabled or face capital charges. Significantly, very few (under 5000) cases involved administrative litigation claims, which would require challenging government decisions. (Xiao, 2009)

In addition to this formal structure, lawyers are required to contribute pro bono services as part of their licensing and ethical responsibilities. Most of this work is handled through urban legal aid offices, though cash payments in lieu of actual hours are commonplace. Rural areas are generally served instead by a large corps (about 100,000) of paraprofessionals ("Basic-level Legal Workers") that operate out of over 25,000 small legal services offices. They are trained and licensed, and therefore able to charge a small fee, but their status has become insecure in recent years. (Alford, 2010) Self-trained, unlicensed "barefoot lawyers" are increasingly active in rural "legal" disputes. Estimates suggest that although some three million people have received legal aid help, barely one-fifth of needs were met. (Liebman, 2004)

Prominent among the "civic" organizations helping to supply legal aid are university-based legal centers, clinics, and student-run legal aid offices. Indeed, two of the earliest legal aid organizations in China are the Wuhan University Center for the Protection of the Rights of Disadvantaged Citizens (1992) and the Beijing University Women's Legal Aid Center (1995). Neither began as a clinic in the sense of being a for-credit, academic course, although both now include that element. As discussed in more detail in the next section, over one hundred law school clinics are reported to be operating across China today.

CLINICAL LEGAL EDUCATION COMES TO CHINA

The Wuhan Center is acknowledged as the pioneer. Started in the early 1990s by Wan E'Xiang, then a young faculty member at the prestigious Wuhan University (and now a Vice President of the Supreme People's Court in Beijing), the center was from the start an effort to create a Chinese model for collaborative law reform efforts uniting students and faculty with their community. Professor Wan had studied at Yale and Michigan law schools under the auspices of the Ford Foundation's long-running, influential Committee for Legal Education Exchange with China; there he saw US-style law school clinics and local legal aid offices firsthand. He naturally turned to the Ford Foundation for support, which provided some of the first funding for the Center. Its initial model included students and faculty as volunteers, which is how the clinical program at Yale—and many other law schools around the world—got started.[1] Most of the real legal work was performed by a group of paid, staff lawyers employed by the Center. A similar model was adopted a couple of years later by the Women's Legal Aid Center, which also found financial backing from the Ford Foundation, but was more loosely affiliated with Beijing University. Both centers successfully handled a variety of cases (large and small), developing strong, positive reputations with the public, media, and legal communities. As the government encouraged legal reforms and greater access to justice, student-run legal aid offices became increasingly common at universities with substantial law departments. Their longstanding tradition of "bringing law to the people," by setting up tables in city neighborhoods to educate the masses about their legal rights, evolved into permanent offices with regular student staffing and assistance on actual cases. Occasionally, faculty would be consulted with specific questions.

Against this backdrop, the Ford Foundation decided in the late 1990s to explore whether there might be interest among Chinese law faculty and administrators in experimenting with a more formal model of clinical legal education. Working in collaboration with the director of clinical education at Yale Law School, J. L. Pottenger, Jr., through the School's China Law Center, Titi Liu (then a Ford Foundation consultant) helped students at Fudan and East China universities formalize and strengthen their student legal aid offices, linking them more closely with interested law faculty. Liu also arranged to visit six Chinese law departments [Fudan and East China (Shanghai); Wuhan University and South Central University of Politics and Law (Wuhan); and Beijing and Tsinghua universities (Beijing)] with Pottenger, to speak to interested faculty and administrators about clinical legal education and to see whether they might be interested in seeking grants from the Ford Foundation to pilot such an experiment in experiential learning. All six applied for and received grants, as did Renmin (formerly People's University).

The seven schools prepared to launch their new clinical programs in the Fall Term, 2000. A week-long training conference, organized at Wuhan University in August of that year brought together a team of clinical teachers from the United States and the initial cohort of Chinese clinical teachers—at least two from each

---

1. This phenomenon is discussed in Chapter 10, which covers the legal aid origins of clinical legal education.

of the seven participating schools. The Chinese group included Wang Chenguang, soon to be named Dean of Tsinghua, his Tsinghua colleague Chen Jianmin, and Zhen Zhen of Renmin; they later assumed leadership roles with the Committee of Chinese Clinical Legal Educators (CCCLE). Another CCCLE leader (Wang Shirong) led a delegation of faculty from Northwest University of Politics and Law (Xi'an); they joined the training conference even though they had not been part of the planning, and then set up their own clinical program, which soon garnered support from the Ford Foundation. That autumn, one Chinese teacher from each of the first seven schools came to New Haven for another week-long training session at Yale's Clinic, the Jerome N. Frank Legal Services Organization. Then, in December 2000, Renmin hosted a successful Forum on Clinical Legal Education and 21st Century Legal Educational Reform.

The first year's experiment went well and the Chinese clinicians held their own training conference the next summer. This was but the first of an ongoing series of exchanges, trainings, and site visits the Chinese (and the Ford Foundation) conducted amongst themselves, developing a truly Chinese model of clinical legal education. The following year, four Chinese schools [Northwest University of Politics and Law (Xi'an); Sun Yat-Sen (Guangzhou); Sichuan (Chengdu); and Yunnan (Kunming) universities] launched their own clinics. Clinicians from the United States continued to be involved; a second round of US-based training was held late in 2001 (in New Haven and at Columbia University, in New York City) and clinical teachers from China and the United States began a series of law school exchanges and partnerships. Over the next several years, the Yale-China Association placed law fellows at a number of Chinese law schools to help support the nascent clinics. Sun Yat-Sen hosted another international conference (at Zhuhai) in the summer of 2002, during which the CCCLE was launched with the approval of the China Law Society, an important honorary society that is quite influential in the legal profession. The CCCLE assumes a leading role for the remainder of this story and continues to be the major player in Chinese clinical circles today.[2]

Overview of Current Programs

By October 2009, membership in the CCCLE had expanded to include a total of 115 institutions, 76 of which have formally integrated clinical education into their law school curricula. Because several law schools have multiple clinics, the actual number of law clinics nationwide had grown to over one hundred. So clinical legal education in today's China exemplifies Chairman Mao's advice: "Let a hundred flowers bloom. . . ."[3]

---

2. The CCCLE is described in detail in Chapter 19, which covers national and regional clinical organizations.

3. From *On the Correct Handling of Contradictions Among the People, in* THE COLLECTED WORKS OF MAO ZEDONG.

The clinics cover an extraordinary array of subjects and strategies, reflecting both the particular interests and abilities of their founding faculty and students and their unique communities and contexts. They differ dramatically in design, with some focusing generally on functional processes, such as litigation, legislation, or ADR, while others have developed their own specialities, serving particular clients or concentrating on certain claims. These include women's rights, labor rights, civil rights, rights of the disadvantaged, rural or farmers' justice, environmental protection, and criminal (including juvenile) justice. Clinics have been established in cities, on college campuses, in villages, and even in minority people's special areas. Incomplete statistics from the CCCLE Secretariat document at least 564 full-time legal educators teaching in clinics throughout the country, and another 132 (or more, including practicing lawyers, judges, and procurators) "adjunct faculty" doing part-time clinical teaching. More than 17,000 students have participated in law clinics at their schools; another 2300 join their ranks each semester. Together with their supervising faculty, clinic students have handled more than 3600 legal aid cases, and offered free legal consultation and advice in well over 25,000 issues or disputes. More than 1800 legal documents have been drafted, and well over 30,000 hours of legal services have been provided. (Secretariat, CCCLE, 2009)

The CCCLE has facilitated this growth in a variety of ways. Chief among them are the numerous training workshops and school-to-school "visits" (or "program inspections") that CCCLE and its member schools conduct each year. Most are organized for clinical teachers, though other interested academics also participate, as do government officials from the Ministries of Education or Justice, its Legal Aid Center, and the Chinese Academy of Social Science. Perhaps equally significant are CCCLE's efforts to prepare (or translate) textbooks, monographs, and training exercises—including actual cases as they were handled by clinical students. The Ministry of Education has even included the CCCLE's compilation of texts and materials for clinical methodology within the tenth Five-Year Program of National Higher Education Texts.

One of the CCCLE's goals—to develop models of clinical legal education "with Chinese characteristics"—has been at the forefront of everyone's efforts. Northwest University of Politics and Law (in Xi'an), for example, has developed four different clinics—each designed to serve students and clients in a unique fashion. Its innovative legislation clinic works with local governmental agencies and civic groups to analyze local problems and then propose legislative solutions to help disadvantaged social groups, such as the elderly or migrant workers. Teams of students gather information from a variety of public and individual sources and bring this knowledge into the policy-making process. One of their projects resulted in provincial-level legislation against domestic violence; another enhanced wage protections for rural migrant workers. Others yielded local legislation designed to benefit the urban elderly. Hundreds of students participated in these efforts, as did a wide array of faculty, lawyers, and judges. (Note, 2007)

Cases at Northwest's Litigation Clinic include criminal defense—a rarity in Chinese clinics—as well as more traditional civil cases. The school also has a public interest law clinic (designed to "raise issues of fairness and justice by analyzing social phenomena") and a community law clinic (with an explicit Street Law, "know your rights" educational design). Northwest has also been a leader in pioneering interactive advocacy training programs for new lawyers or faculty specializing in criminal defense work, partnering in this effort with People's and Sichuan universities.

The clinics at Sun Yat-Sen University (in Guangzhou), by contrast, focus on the problems faced by a specific client group (workers), a particular methodology (civil litigation), and a specialized field (environmental law). To date, the clinic reports its students have handled around a hundred cases, offered legal advice to about six thousand individuals, and drafted over a thousand legal documents.

In one of their workers cases, for example, the clinic students represented a migrant worker who suffered a serious knee injury at his job in a Guangzhou restaurant. The employer had denied that the injury took place on the job, and the worker's claim for "identification of workplace injury" had been rejected at two levels of local administrative review. In an administrative litigation case filed in the Guangzhou People's Court, the clinic succeeded in overturning the adverse administrative decision, which pressured the employer into reaching an agreement with the injured worker for compensation.

Professor Cai Yanmin's account of one of Sun Yat-Sen's early efforts conjures up the spirit of clinical legal education in China:

> I still vividly remember a legal aid service coordinated by the clinic and a grassroots organization of migrant workers in Guangzhou shortly after the clinical program was launched. It was a hot sunny afternoon. Sitting in a storage shed, forty students from Sun Yat-Sen University were divided into groups and tried to solve the legal problems encountered by the workers. Some of the workers had been injured at work and could not get timely treatment and compensation, and some had been fighting against their factories for back pay. A note of desperation combined with great expectation was felt in their voices, although lots of them were only a few years older than the students. The students soberly listened, diagnosed and dispensed solutions, completely different from what they had been in the classroom. Several supervisors walked around the teams, giving guidance from time to time. This sobering experience increased my understanding of the more participatory, interactive clinical model. More importantly, it made me turn to a reflection on the nature of clinical education and the relationship between legal education and social responsibility as well.

At Tsinghua University, the nature and focus of the clinics has evolved with experience—and the interests of students and faculty. The school's well-regarded labor rights clinic is a good example. The core focus on unpaid wages and workplace injuries has remained intact, but as the faculty's and students' experience has grown they have undertaken increasingly complex and sophisticated cases, including several group litigations. In one group case, the clinic succeeded in winning back pay for a group of migrant construction workers who had come to Beijing from Henan Province through a labor contractor. Although they worked at the building site all summer, when their contract time was up the contractor withheld 25 percent of their promised wages and gave his personal IOU note instead. Efforts to collect on the note went nowhere, so the workers came to the Tsinghua clinic for help. The clinic managed to get all the wages paid within a few months, by identifying the parent company of the general contractor and urging its home office to rectify this clear violation of public labor law and policy. This pressure from the prestigious university had its intended effect, and all the workers were paid in full.

The school's other initial clinical offering was a mediation clinic, in which the students worked closely with a local dispute-resolution center for the protection of consumer rights. It also thrived for several years, but as the times changed and the school became increasingly comfortable with clinical work, it was replaced with an affirmative "administrative litigation" clinic that sought to raise novel social and civil rights issues, including a special focus on farmers' problems. Tsinghua's location in Beijing and its supportive dean (himself a world-renowned scholar *and* a clinical teacher) made this high-visibility effort possible. But the pendulum of legal reform has swung back quite a distance in recent years, and that clinic is inactive. An "assistance to the disadvantaged" clinic was established as its successor. Due to a lack of teaching resources, only the labor dispute clinic is currently operating.

Clinical work at the Wuhan Center has perhaps evolved the most. Originally staffed by paid lawyers and volunteer students and faculty, the center and university have together forged a real clinical partnership in which faculty supervision is carefully planned and executed, even while substantial student autonomy is nurtured. The Wuhan clinic fits neatly into the center's six specialized divisions, five of which serve particular disadvantaged social groups (women, minors, elderly, disabled, and workers). The sixth handles one of the hottest potatoes in China's still-nascent effort to become a rule of law society: complaints in administrative litigation suits against governmental entities or officials. The clinic also includes criminal defense, mediation, and community education components. As Pam Phan observed in her excellent analysis of clinical legal education in China, the Wuhan clinic "teaches students about justice by exposing them to injustice." (Phan, 2005 at 131–32, quoting the Wuhan clinic's mission statement)

Like many of the clinics in China, the faculty at the Wuhan clinic selects students through a highly competitive process in which essays and interviews play major roles. The explicit, open way in which the Wuhan clinic and its students pursue its social justice mission cuts across all six divisions and is well-captured by this paraphrase of another excerpt from its mission statement: Wuhan students are to use their considerable talents to serve the most disadvantaged, thereby developing "their sense of social responsibility" and perhaps even "holding accountable a traditionally unassailable government." (*Id.*) With this emphasis on teaching law students social responsibility, Wuhan stands out within the CCCLE, for there is a range of views among its member schools and clinical faculty on the centrality of a social justice mission in Chinese clinical legal education. They all agree, though, that by exposing students to different strata of society, as well as how law and legal institutions actually function, clinical methodology helps law students learn how truly to "seek truth from facts."

An administrative litigation case brought by Professor Li Ao's Wuhan clinic exemplifies these principles. The clinic represented a group of factory workers who had been employed in a newly privatized, formerly state-owned factory in a semi-rural county in Hubei Province. The workers were detained by public security bureau police after they had joined with over a hundred fellow workers to lock the gates in order to protest embezzlement of the factory's profits and assets by the new "owners." The clinic's lawsuit sought to have the detention—which lasted fifteen days—declared unlawful, and to obtain compensation. The case was tried in the county where the factory was located. Although witnesses were at first afraid to testify against the public security police, clinic students helped persuade them it was safe to speak in court. The local court ruled against the claims, which came as no surprise, and the clinic took an appeal to the intermediate court, where a trial de novo was held. The police defendants were shocked as the evidence of their misconduct was presented and the law supporting the workers' claims was explained, so they quickly asked for a compromise. The presiding judge stepped in to mediate this messy, potentially embarrassing case, and a settlement was arranged; the police paid double the compensation claimed, and the appeal was withdrawn. The workers lauded the students and celebrated their victory, which reverberated back to the county officials and local police. As one of the clinic students who helped present the case in court wrote, this outcome profoundly affected both the students' and the clients' "trust of law," instilling a belief that "law can truly protect them." It also made the clinic's students realize that they "could do such a lot for others" despite their relative youth, and that "lawyers could be respected heroically" if they "do good for people and for society."

CHALLENGES AND OPPORTUNITIES

Despite these impressive achievements after only a decade, clinical legal education in China faces stern challenges and substantial obstacles. While some of these are unique to the Chinese context, others are hauntingly reminiscent of problems which remain unsolved elsewhere, including the United States. The then-chair of the CCCLE, Zhen Zhen (from Renmin) detailed many of these issues in a speech nearly five years ago; some were practical (if nonetheless difficult), while others were more abstract and theoretical. Most remain unresolved, still only partially addressed, today. (Zhen Zhen, 2005)

Status of Students When Representing Clients

Much of the actual advice and legal work conducted by Chinese clinical students and faculty takes place outside of the judicial system—just as it does in clinics in many parts of the world. A problem arises because, under the current Chinese system, law student representation in court is possible only because the student acts as a "citizen representative" of the client, not as a recognized legal practitioner. Their status is thus akin to a friend or family member, and their access to legal documents (or to incarcerated clients) is quite limited. This problem is more significant in criminal cases. Thus, students in Sichuan University's criminal defense clinic are able to first meet with their clients only at the courthouse, on the very day of trial.

Chinese clinicians are still striving to persuade the Ministry of Justice to promulgate something akin to a "student-practice rule" so that at least a quasi-legal status—together with enhanced representational rights—could be achieved. This would be a major boost for the creation of criminal defense clinics, of which there are very few. In Beijing, one of the local judges has exercised his discretionary authority over his own court to permit students from the clinic at China University of Politics and Law to appear as student practitioners. Although this is a civil clinic, perhaps it could become a pilot for broader acceptance. While the lack of a student-practice rule is widely identified as a significant problem, it has not prevented students and their supervising faculty from together representing the clinics' clients effectively in a range of civil matters. In fact, one of Cai Yanmin's clinical students specifically commented to her that "the role and what clinical students achieved, even without 'practicing certificates,' were quite close to those [accomplished by] practicing lawyers." So perhaps this problem actually is more symbolic than substantive—except in criminal cases.

Expense and Financing of Legal Clinics

There is no doubt that the financing of legal clinics is a real and significant concern. The very substantial Ford Foundation financial support, now in place for nearly ten years and dispensed (mostly) through the CCCLE, has been only slightly supplemented by other funders. While the schools themselves have contributed to the expense of running clinics, no replacement for the Ford Foundation has been identified. Although modest funding has been obtained recently through the US Agency for International Development (USAID), that is hardly a long-term solution—and brings its own baggage. China's Ministries of Justice and Education have thus far declined to provide major funding. If they continue to hold back and no "white knight" appears on the horizon, a serious funding crisis will occur—and soon.

In the United States, the Ford Foundation's exit from the funding scene was somewhat ameliorated by the arrival of federal funding through the Justice and Education Departments. We can only hope that continued efforts will yield a similar outcome in China. Certainly such funding would be consistent with the central government's announced policies in favor of enhanced access to justice as a key element in its overall rule of law project. The USAID funding mentioned above was for a rule of law initiative aimed at promoting advocacy skills training and clinical legal education. In view of the rising concern about handling politically sensitive cases, even in university-based clinics, however, more direct governmental funding may not be an unmixed blessing. Private philanthropy is just beginning to develop in mainland China (and flourishes in Hong Kong), so that sector might present an attractive alternative. The high demand for—and high satisfaction of—Chinese law students with respect to clinical opportunities underscores the value it offers to the nation.

Integration of Clinical and Traditional Legal Education

There are several aspects to this problem. Currently, both teachers and students are overburdened (and under-rewarded) for their clinical work. This problem is most acute for the teachers, as the overall incentives and compensation structures directly undermine a faculty member's possible desire (even preference) to work as a clinical teacher-supervisor. The demands of real casework are simply too great to allow any but the most selfless educators to sacrifice their pay, publication, and promotional prospects. Equally critical is the issue of scholarship in clinical teaching. Most of the traditional teachers (as well as some deans and presidents) regard clinical teaching as merely the repetition of practitioners' clichés and war stories, without academic value. This problem is exacerbated for Chinese clinical faculty because their clinical work often does not focus on their substantive area of academic specialization, through which much of their professional/professorial standing is measured. Only by reinventing the standards and rewards of legal academia—whether completely or for specialized clinical faculty—can legal clinics achieve real sustainability. Even the growing pedagogical advantages inherent in experiential learning will prove insufficient to overcome existing incentive structures.

This difficult challenge remains a very real aspect of clinical legal education throughout the world. China has some potential advantages in solving this dilemma, as its initial cadre of clinical teachers was drawn from the ranks of "regular" academics. Moreover, Chinese law students are required to fulfill an apprenticeship requirement (*shixi*), and several schools have allowed work in their own clinic to qualify. The Ministry of Education has approved clinical courses as optional "electives" and the Ministry is considering whether to encourage practical education in law schools more actively, although this advance may be complicated by the common confusion of "clinical" work with "practical training" of any sort. Thus moot court, advocacy training, and even Socratic teaching styles have been labeled "clinical" at some schools. But governmental policies in favor of legal aid, access to justice, and assistance to the disadvantaged would support actual client work in clinics. Perhaps China will show the way to a solution which can then be emulated elsewhere.

Coordination and Integration with the Legal Profession and Legal System

These challenges, too, are not unique to China. But the lack of a tradition of independence or autonomy within the profession, as well as concerns about corruption, makes them considerably more complex. So does the lack of a strong, well-developed "public interest" segment of the bar. There is no doubt that clinics are not well-connected to either the pro bono work of law firms (often themselves new and weak) or their local legal professional associations. Nor do they usually work closely with local legal aid offices. University-based clinics are able—and willing—to select somewhat more sensitive cases, so they could offer opportunities for more innovative pro bono work, if closer integration could be achieved. Any solution is probably closely linked to the funding and academic integration challenges listed earlier, for if they can be resolved, these obstacles also should be overcome. The path to success here lies with the students and clients, for their satisfaction is essential if this experiment is to succeed, and their satisfaction also may provide the solution to these challenges.

Fortunately, an exciting new program may offer promise in this regard. In the summer of 2009, the Ford Foundation and the Public Interest Law Institute (PILI) launched a public interest fellowship program. Thirty recent clinic graduates have been awarded two-year fellowships to serve in public interest practice settings throughout China. Modeled to some extent after the Skadden and Equal Justice Works Fellowships in the United States, this program may help create a public interest career path previously untrodden in China. Equally important, the work of these clinic graduates may further advance the role and reputation of the law school clinics that fostered them, and so advance their integration efforts.

Localization, Standardization, Improvement, and Assessment

Clinical legal education in China needs to adapt to the requirements of its own educational authorities, developing practices and techniques which preserve its experiential essence but also exhibit Chinese characteristics. One particular challenge is the continuing tension—even within the CCCLE itself—between ensuring competent representation and quality education and the desire to encourage experimentation and multiple models for clinics, sometimes with varying levels of case volume or faculty oversight. Strengthening institutional procedures within clinics is thus vital. The emphasis on social justice education also varies greatly, with some clinics highlighting it, while others focus almost exclusively on skills training.

These challenges, too, are not unique to China. The solutions, however, will need to meet the contextual requirements of Chinese society, including its legal and academic cultures. Here the answers must emerge over time, as each school and each clinic experiments within its own environment and learns how to cope and prosper. Perhaps ironically, it is quite possible that the increasing internationalization of the clinical movement actually offers the way forward to overcoming these challenges. Certainly it helps shift perspectives, making clinical work less of an exclusively "American transplant."

CONCLUSION

As mentioned immediately above, the increasingly integrated, international character of the clinical movement may itself offer the way forward for meeting and overcoming some of the most serious challenges now facing Chinese clinical legal education. Certainly, Chinese clinical teachers, led and supported by the CCCLE, already have made substantial strides along this path. Active participation in the Global Alliance for Justice Education (GAJE), close collaboration with clinical teachers from other countries (such as India, Poland, South Africa, as well as their US partners), and an eagle eye for innovation are fast becoming hallmarks of Chinese clinical legal education. Indeed, Chinese clinical teachers have made presentations recently in Poland, Argentina, and Africa, sharing their experiences with scholars from over fifty countries or regions.

The special character of the Chinese experience of modernization, development, and astonishingly rapid social change and economic progress offers valuable lessons for the rest of the world. It has been a particular challenge for legal reform in China to define the goal of legal education, especially when Chinese legal education has to respond adequately to the social transformations taking place in the course of modernization. It is clinical education that pushed faculty to think and shape legal education with stronger social responsibility, not simply to produce effective practitioners, but to create a legal profession with moral obligations.

As pioneers advocating for clinical legal education in China in the past decade, clinical faculty believe that in the course of modernization China cannot afford to neglect society's ills and social groups that have been far removed from the country's rapid economic and social growth. Neither can China afford to neglect legal professionals' potential for facilitating access to justice as a tool for the average citizen. The real challenge for Chinese legal education reform has been to determine what type of legal professionals it wants to train, and to transform the traditional style of legal education into a new one that is responsive to social movements. Clinical legal education takes on the challenge to teach students about professional values, legal ethics, and a sense of social responsibility aside from lawyering skills. In the past decade, it has become an integral part of China's legal education system, helping to set a higher standard for the legal profession. More and more law schools have expressed their willingness to develop clinical programs. There is still much room for the development of clinical legal education in China. The best prospect for transforming the legal profession lies with a collective effort.

We conclude with the wisdom of China's clinical students, who themselves are playing such a significant role in the development, and reinvention of Chinese legal education.

> The clinical program exposed me to "the real world" and I met setbacks I had never imagined to encounter at so early a stage of my career. Fortunately, the educators pulled me back from disenchantment with society. Clinic education means much to me, like a platform for the practice of law, a battleground to examine my quest for law, and a starting point for academic research.
>
> –Pan, former legal clinic student

> Clinical Legal Education is a new way of looking at the law. Once you have represented a client, you understand their problems are not theoretical and your work has real world consequences. It makes you jazzed up and a little scared.
>
> –From a student in Hunan (2009)

> The best thing of clinical legal education is that it teaches students about justice by exposing them to injustice. While the clinical program deepened my understanding of the imperfect society at an early stage of my career, it also encouraged me to keep faith in law and the commitment to justice.
>
> –Wang, former legal clinic student

LIST OF REFERENCES

William P. Alford, *"Second Lawyers," First Principles: Lawyers, Rice-Roots Legal Workers, and the Battle over Legal Professionalism in China*, in PROSPECTS FOR PROFESSIONALISM IN CHINA: ESSAYS ON CIVIC VOCATIONS (William P. Alford et al. eds., Routledge 2009).

Wang Chenguang, *The Rapid but Unbalanced Growth of China's Legal Education Programs*, 7 HARVARD CHINA REV. 83 (2006).

Jerome A. Cohen, Remarks before U.S. Congressional-Executive Commission on China Roundtable: China's Human Rights Lawyers: Current Challenges and Prospects (July 10, 2009), *available at* http://www.cecc.gov/pages/roundtables/2009/20090710/JerryCohen_remarks_20090710.pdf.

Jerome A. Cohen, *The Struggle for Autonomy of Beijing's Public Interest Lawyers*, 1 CHINA RTS. F. 8 (2009).

Jerome A. Cohen, Is There Law in China? Is There Justice?, DeWitt Higgs Memorial Lecture (March 4, 2008), *available at* http://www.uctv.tv/search-details.aspx?showID=14256.

Michael W. Dowdle, *Completing Teubner: Foreign Irritants in China's Clinical Legal Education System and the "Convergence" of Imaginations*, in EXAMINING PRACTICE, INTERROGATING THEORY: COMPARATIVE LEGAL STUDIES IN ASIA (Penelope Nicholson & Sarah Biddulph, eds., Martinus Nijhoff Publishers 2008).

James V. Feinerman, Remarks before U.S. Congressional-Executive Commission on China Roundtable: China's Human Rights Lawyers: Current Challenges and Prospects (July 10, 2009), *available at* http://www.cecc.gov/pages/roundtables/2009/20090710/Feinerman_remarks_20090710.pdf?PHPSESSID=64beed9c827d5b18289eb00ff2935abf.

Ford Foundation, MANY ROADS TO JUSTICE: THE LAW-RELATED WORK OF FORD FOUNDATION GRANTEES AROUND THE WORLD (Mary McClymont & Stephen Golub eds. 2000), *available at* http://www.fordfound.org/pdfs/impact/many_roads.pdf.

Hualing Fu, *Access to Justice in China: Potentials, Limits, and Alternatives*, in LEGAL REFORMS IN CHINA AND VIETNAM (John Gillespie & Albert Chen eds., Routledge 2010), *available at* http://ssrn.com/abstract=1474073.

Thomas E. Kellogg, *The Death of Constitutional Litigation in China?*, 9 (7) CHINA BRIEF, April 2, 2009, *available at* http://www.jamestown.org/single/?no_cache=1&tx_ttnews%5Btt_news%5D=34791&tx.

Benjamin L. Liebman & Tim Wu, China's Network Justice (Columbia Law Sch. Pub. Law & Legal Theory Research Paper No. 07–143, 2007), *available at* http://ssrn.com/abstract=956310.

Benjamin L. Liebman, *Watchdog or Demagogue? The Media in the Chinese Legal System*, 105 COLUM. L. REV. 1 (2005).

Benjamin L. Liebman, Remarks before U.S. Congressional-Executive Commission on China, at Roundtable: Access to Justice in China (July 12, 2004), *available at* http://www.cecc.gov/pages/roundtables/071204/liebman.php.

Titi M. Liu, *Transmission of Public Interest Law: A Chinese Case Study*, 13 UCLA J. INT'L L. & FOREIGN AFF. 263 (2008).

Elliott S. Milstein, *Experiential Education & the Rule of Law: Teaching Values through Clinical Education in China*, 22 PAC. MCGEORGE GLOBAL BUS. & DEV. L.J. 55 (2009).

Carl F. Minzner, *Xinfang: An Alternative to Formal Chinese Legal Institutions*, 42 STAN. J. INT'L L. 103 (2006).

Note, *Adopting and Adapting: Clinical Legal Education and Access to Justice in China*, 120 HARV. L. REV. 2134 (2007).

Hari M. Osofsky, Social Change through Active, Reflective Learning? Clinincal Legal Education in China and the United States (July 25, 2002) (unpublished manuscript).

Pamela N. Phan, *Clinical Legal Education in China: In Pursuit of a Culture of Law and a Mission of Social Justice*, 8 YALE HUM. RTS. & DEV. L.J. 117 (2005).

J. L. Pottenger, Jr., *Clinical Realism: How Law Students Learn Judgment*, 42 YALE L. REP. 6 (1996).

Stephen Wizner, *The Law School Clinic: Legal Education in the Interests of Justice*, 70 FORDHAM L. REV. 1929 (2002).

Xiao Yanhui, Lecture at Yale Law School (February 26, 2009).

Zhen Zhen, The Present Situation and Prosperous Future of China Clinical Legal Education, Speech at UCLA Arrowhead Conference (Oct. 7, 2005), *available at* http://cdn.law.ucla.edu/SiteCollectionDocuments/ workshops%20and%20colloquia/clinical%20programs/zhen%20zhen.pdf.

7. JAPAN'S NEW CLINICAL PROGRAMS
A Study of Light and Shadow

SHIGEO MIYAGAWA, TAKAO SUAMI, PETER A. JOY, AND
CHARLES D. WEISSELBERG

INTRODUCTION

Japan instituted a new system of graduate professional law school education
when sixty-eight new law schools opened their doors on April 1, 2004. The new
law schools are an integral component of far-reaching reforms that seek to
improve the administration of justice in Japan by increasing the number of lawyers, especially in grossly underserved rural areas, and better preparing attorneys for the practice of law domestically and internationally. Japan modeled the
new graduate professional law schools after schools in the United States. A large
number of the schools adopted clinical legal education programs—also substantially influenced by law school clinics in the United States. However, the context
for clinical legal education in Japan is very different from that in the United
States. Japanese clinical education faces severe and sustained difficulties due to
issues such as dramatically lower bar passage rates and substantial resistance to
law students participating in the delivery of legal services to clients.

This chapter analyzes why clinical education was introduced into legal education in Japan and why it is confronting serious obstacles. It begins with a brief
explanation of the recent reforms in Japanese legal education. It then describes
the status and structure of clinical education in Japan and addresses various
challenges to the future of clinical legal education. Next, it describes the teaching
and service goals of Japanese clinical education and the current emphasis on
simulation programs. Finally, it discusses some hopeful signs that clinical education is gradually taking root in Japan, such as the founding of the Japan Clinical
Legal Education Association. Nevertheless, the chapter concludes that Japanese
law schools are under strong pressure to transform clinical education towards a
model that is far removed from the prevailing model—in the United States and
elsewhere—in which law students participate in the representation of real clients. At this point in time, the future of clinical education in Japan is uncertain.

CLINICAL LEGAL EDUCATION IN CONTEXT—THE RECENT REFORMS

To understand the present educational reforms, one must first understand traditional legal education in Japan. During the US occupation of Japan at the end of

World War II, a system of legal education was put in place consisting of three major elements: undergraduate study at universities; the national bar examination administered by the Ministry of Justice; and practical training provided by the Supreme Court's Legal Training and Research Institute (LTRI) for those who passed the bar exam. (Miyazawa et al., 2008; Tanaka & Smith, 1976) Thus, one typically became an attorney (*bengoshi*) after completing four years of undergraduate study, usually in a university's law department, passing the bar examination required for admission to the LTRI, and completing training at the LTRI.

This was an unsatisfactory preparation for the practice of law for several reasons. First, undergraduate law departments provided a general education for those who planned to enter business or government as well as the very few who would eventually practice law. Because so few undergraduate law students entered the practice of law, the law departments did not view their mission as educating would-be lawyers; thus, their courses were disconnected from professional legal education and the practice of law.

Second, an undergraduate law degree was not required to take the bar examination. Rather than serve as a qualifying examination to practice law after a rounded legal education, the bar examination was a fierce competition for a limited number of seats at the LTRI. The number of bar passers was—and still is—kept artificially low by the Ministry of Justice. Due to these limits—approximately 500 persons per year until 1990, gradually increased to approximately 1000 persons by 1999—bar passage rates were very low, on the order of 2-3 percent throughout the 1980s and 1990s. (Miyazawa et al., 2008) To prepare, applicants attended year-long "cram schools" programs devoted to memorization of material likely to appear on the bar examination. (Miyazawa, 2002)

Third, those who passed the examination received two years (reduced to eighteen months in 1999) of apprenticeship training at the LTRI, the single program required to practice law as an attorney, prosecutor, or judge. Though the LTRI offers legal practice training at real practice-settings, such as in courts, prosecutors' offices, and attorneys' offices, this apprenticeship training was—and still is—unlike clinical legal education, or even professional legal education, in countries like the United States. (Joy et al., 2006) The training is mostly passive observation of existing law practice. (Takano, 2007) The LTRI does not educate trainees to reflect critically upon their work or the present legal system; its top priority is for trainees to observe, understand, and follow present legal practice. (Miyazawa et al., 2008) These features of the LTRI's apprenticeships derive partly from the fact that its faculty consists of temporarily assigned practitioners.

Due to these traditionally high barriers to entry into the profession, the number of practicing attorneys is very small for a highly developed country. Japan has only about 28,000 attorneys for an estimated population of 127 million, many fewer per capita than the United States and European countries.[1] The scarcity of attorneys was particularly significant and obvious in rural areas, where in the 1990s criminal suspects often could not receive legal assistance at important pretrial stages of a case. (Yonemoto, 1995) Even in city areas like Tokyo and Osaka, there was another type of shortage. Japanese attorneys traditionally were generalists and litigators, without a background other than in law. Major companies with experience with legal systems in other developed countries were frustrated with the poor quality of nonlitigation services provided by Japanese attorneys. (Miyazawa et al., 2008)

To address these and other problems, the Japanese government established the Justice System Reform Council in July 1999. In 2001, the Council issued recommendations for comprehensive reform aimed at expanding the rule of law covering a wide range of topics, including civil and criminal procedure, alternative dispute resolution (ADR), legal education, practicing attorneys, prosecutors, and judges. (Miyazawa et al., 2008) Two of the major pillars of reform are "Expansion of the Human Base," with the goal of raising both the quantity and quality of legal professionals supporting the justice system, and "Establishment of the Popular Base," with the goal of involving the citizenry in the legal system such as citizen participation in the role of lay judges for criminal cases.

The Council expressed its view that the Japanese people were not satisfied with the quantity and quality of the current legal profession. As a result, its reform proposals addressed both the number of lawyers and the system of legal education. To increase the ranks of lawyers, the Council recommended raising the target number of bar passers annually to 3000 by the year 2010. It was expected that, as a result, the total number of attorneys in Japan would reach about 50,000 by 2018, more than double in size from the 1990s. (Justice System Reform Council, 2001) Noting that under the traditional system bar exam-takers focused on "acquiring techniques for passing the examination" rather than a sound education, the Council called for training the new lawyers in new ways. (Justice System Reform Council, 2001 at ch. III, pt. 2) The new system combined legal education at graduate professional law schools, providing education specifically for the legal profession, a new national bar examination, and a somewhat shortened period of training in the LTRI. The new law schools would be at the core of the process of educating lawyers, and eventually only graduates of those law schools would be entitled to take the bar examination.

Because Japan used law schools in the United States as a model for professional legal education, the new Japanese law schools are similar in many ways to

---

1. However, if Japan's so-called neighboring professions—including tax attorneys (*zeirishi*), patent attorneys (*benrishi*), judicial scriveners (*shiho shoshi*), and administrative scriveners (*gyosei shoshi*)—are counted as well, the number of legal professionals per capita would approach that of European countries.

those in the United States. As with most law schools in the United States, the purpose of the new professional law schools in Japan is to educate students aspiring to become lawyers. Japanese law schools also have a three-year program, though there is a two-year curriculum mainly for graduates of undergraduate law departments. Students in the new schools have diverse academic and professional backgrounds; many were employed professionally prior to law school.

The teaching methods are also similar to those in American law schools. Rather than the "traditional one-way lecture style," which is still common in Japanese undergraduate law departments, teaching is interactive, often using the case method. As a result, class size is usually small; the largest classes have fewer than fifty students. In contrast to undergraduate education in Japan, where the course work is not difficult, the graduate professional law schools are quite demanding and the students are much more serious. Moreover, as in the United States, the new law faculties consist of both academics and practitioners.

However, there are still structural differences between law schools in the United States and Japan. The Council's recommendations included many compromises to appease lawyers and academics, especially those teaching in undergraduate law departments, many of whom were opposed to the concept of professional law schools. Universities continue to maintain undergraduate law departments, and there is still apprenticeship training at the LTRI for those who pass the bar examination. As we will explain, the undergraduate law departments and the LTRI have proven to be obstacles to the full development of Japanese professional law schools and to the development of clinical legal education.

DEVELOPMENT AND STRUCTURE OF CLINICAL LEGAL EDUCATION IN JAPAN

Although a major emphasis of the legal education reforms in Japan was to provide law students with a well-rounded and rigorous exposure to lawyering skills, such as legal analysis and problem solving, the Justice System Reform Council's recommendations did not specifically address clinical legal education. Clinical legal education was relatively unknown to the Council members when they began discussing the reform of legal education in 1999 and although a large number of Japanese scholars and practitioners had studied in the United States, developments in clinical education had not yet attracted their attention. Nor were the new schools expressly given a social justice mission. While overall justice system reforms include an emphasis on making lawyers more available, especially in underserved geographical areas, neither the reformers nor the designers of the new law schools emphasized social justice as part of the curriculum. This may in part reflect a norm in Japan that education should be "neutral" and insulated from what may be perceived as any type of political movement. The Japanese Supreme Court, which administers the LTRI, has emphasized that Japanese legal training should be free from anything that might be viewed as promoting a political or social justice agenda.

Once the Council decided that the purpose of new professional law schools was to educate students aspiring to become lawyers, educational reformers took a closer look at the types of programs that would best prepare students for the practice of law. To become a good lawyer, students must have an opportunity to acquire not only legal theories and knowledge but also lawyering skills and professional values. Since the law reform plan called for shortening the duration of the apprenticeship at the LTRI from eighteen months to one year, more training in the practice of law would be needed within the new law schools. Reformers thus began to see clinical education as an excellent educational tool. Japanese scholars and practitioners soon became interested as well, once legal education reforms moved forward.

Reformers saw clinical legal education as a way to develop a new kind of legal scholarship, to "bridge theory and practice." (Joy et al., 2006 at 429–31) Though both legal academics and practicing lawyers usually studied law at the undergraduate level, their training and career paths diverged after graduation and mobility between these paths was quite limited. Accordingly, most professors on law faculties did not have practical experience in law. This separation between legal academics and practicing lawyers and judges has resulted in few opportunities for interaction between scholars and practitioners, and legal scholars frequently ignored research topics that are important for legal practice. Under the Council's reforms, the professional law schools are expected to facilitate the development of a model of scholarship that bridges theory and practice. Clinical legal education is an excellent vehicle for promoting these interactions.

For these and other reasons, clinical legal education became widely recognized by many academics and practitioners shortly after the Council submitted its recommendations in 2001. Nevertheless, because the Council's recommendations neither explicitly required the new professional law schools to include clinical courses nor described a particular approach to clinical education, each law school has been left to decide for itself whether to offer clinical courses and to define what those might be. Even so, guided by the leading principle of the educational reform—that schools should build a bridge between theoretical and practical education—at least some form of clinical legal education has become rooted in a majority of Japan's new professional law schools. Although the content depends upon the policy of each law school, a majority of the new law schools are at least providing a course titled "clinic," and some—approximately six in the Tokyo area alone—have established in-house clinical law offices.

According to a 2006 study by the Japan Federation of Bar Associations, fifty-two out of the seventy-four new Japanese law schools claim to offer clinical courses. (Nakanishi, 2006) This study adopted a broad definition of clinical courses, including externship programs and simulation (skills) courses, as well as real-client clinics. In 2008, the Waseda Institute of Clinical Legal Education surveyed all Japanese law schools about "real-client clinical courses," that is, those where students are actually involved in legal practice for real clients and have direct contact with them. (The survey excluded purely skills classes and courses in which students merely observed the practice of clinical professors.) All seventy-four law schools responded to the 2008 survey, with thirty-eight schools, or 51 percent, reporting that they offer real-client clinical courses. (Kabashima, 2009) Given the fact that only courses where students are allowed to have direct communication with clients fell under the definition of real-client clinical courses, this percentage is quite high. Moreover, some of the law schools started their clinical courses in 2007 and the number of law schools with clinical courses has gradually increased. This may signal a trend that more schools will begin to offer real-client clinical courses in the future.

While clinical legal education appears to be spreading, Japanese clinical education still remains in its infancy. In addition to the data about numbers of clinical courses, the 2008 survey identified a number of salient features about Japanese clinical legal education that are particularly relevant to its future growth.

Limited Academic Credit and Optional Courses

Although many Japanese law schools offer clinical courses, whether or not "real-client clinical courses," they remain on the periphery of the curriculum. Clinical courses are either optional or "mandatory optional" (meaning that students are obliged to take one course among a group of courses that may include a clinic). In addition, most are offered for two units of academic credit, a very low amount since students in three-year programs need ninety-three academic credits or more for graduation. Some clinical courses are offered for no academic credit at all, with the students working as volunteers.

The subjects of real-client clinics are also limited due to strict regulations, discussed in more detail below. Thus, criminal justice clinics are quite exceptional in Japan because of opposition by many practicing attorneys and prosecutors to any participation of law students in defense lawyers' work. In contrast, a variety of subject-matter-specific civil clinical courses are offered, including refugee and immigration law, women's legal issues, international human rights, disability law, family law, and labor law, with some being implemented as experiments.

No Standard Approach to Clinical Legal Education

There is no single model of clinical legal education in Japan, though one approach—having students participate in legal advice and counseling—is present in most schools. Yet there are variations even among schools that have developed counseling clinics, particularly with respect to the extent of student involvement. Although not considered a real-client clinical course in the 2008 survey, some law schools simply provide opportunities for students to sit with an attorney in the counseling room and listen to the conversation. There are a few law schools (Waseda is an example) that provide a more extensive range of legal services, with students working under the close supervision of experienced clinical professors. (Joy et al., 2006)

These differences in the types of clinical experiences available to students reflect a variety of understandings about the objectives of clinical legal education. Some law schools take the view that clinical education should be limited to providing students with the opportunity to gain a real-life understanding about current legal practice principally by observation and participation in the delivery of limited legal services, such as advice and counseling. Others see clinical education as a means for students to reflect upon and become critical of current practice in order to reform it. Although the number of the latter-type schools is relatively small, they view legal clinics as a laboratory to develop new modes of practice. At these law schools, students are involved in the delivery of a wider range of legal services, such as interviewing clients and drafting documents for courts, and are actively engaged in critically examining the legal system.

Clinical Offices and Externships

According to the 2008 Waseda survey, fourteen out of the seventy-four law schools have their own clinical law offices on or near their campuses. Japanese regulations currently prohibit universities from operating law offices, so these clinical offices are not officially part of the law schools. They are independent of the universities and usually have special service contracts with the law school for the purpose of educating students.

Most law schools entrust their clinical programs to outside law offices. An attorney at the external law office is appointed as an adjunct professor and placed in charge of clinical courses. This arrangement blurs the distinction between law school-run clinical courses and externship programs, but is much more like the latter. Sixteen law schools have set up legal counseling offices for real-client courses. A legal counseling office is not a law office like the clinical law offices or external law offices described above; rather, they are offices specially established for the convenience of administering clinical courses in which clinical professors and students provide counseling services for clients.

In addition, almost all Japanese law schools have some form of externship program.[2] Some law schools send students to legal departments of large corporations as well as to traditional law offices. Others send students to offices of international organizations such as those that are part of, or affiliated with, the United Nations. The diversity of the externship placements means that some law students assist in the representation of underserved clients while others do not.

---

2. Externships are discussed generally in Chapter 22.

Clinical Faculty

In most clinical courses, students are supervised by clinical faculty who have many years of experience as practicing attorneys and are appointed as professors or adjunct professors. When the new law schools opened, nonclinical faculty had little interest in clinical education, though a small number of schools sought to bridge theory and practice by offering clinical courses taught by teams of academics and practicing attorneys. Academic professors are, however, becoming more involved in clinical courses; today, more than half of the thirty-eight schools with real-client clinics report that academic professors participate in some of their clinical courses.

Reflecting the relatively weak position of clinical education within the new law schools, the status of clinical faculty is not stable. Most clinical teachers are appointed as part-time adjunct professors with contracts of limited duration. The salaries of adjunct professors are not sufficient to cover the hours spent educating students, and the low pay becomes a disincentive for adjunct professors to focus on teaching. Others are appointed as full-time professors and receive a similar amount of salary as academic professors; however, they usually have an employment contract with definite duration and are not eligible for tenure or other long-term employment with the law school.

Clinical faculty need to develop special expertise in clinical education, including its philosophy, objectives, and methodology. However, most law schools do not fully understand the importance of this and do not structure their employment arrangements to facilitate the professional development of clinical faculty. As a result, in many law schools the first wave of full-time clinical professors in Japan is reaching the end of their contracts. They will either have to seek employment with different law schools or return to legal practice or other employment. This failure of Japanese law schools to structure continuing relationships with experienced full-time clinical faculty will likely make it more difficult to establish high quality clinics.

CHALLENGES TO CLINICAL LEGAL EDUCATION

Several problems have emerged during the early years of clinical education in Japan that have impeded its steady development. Some affect the system of the new professional law schools as a whole, while others are specific to clinical education.

As noted earlier, the professional law schools in Japan were based largely on the model of graduate professional law schools in the United States. However, the American model presupposes certain conditions that are not present in Japan. As a result, Japanese law schools and clinical programs are facing serious difficulties. The most critical issue to the success of the new Japanese law schools is the bar passage rate, which has remained much lower that the targeted 70-80 percent upon which the new law school system is premised. Japan has not made steady progress towards the Council's target of 3000 new lawyers each year. In 2008, the number passing the bar was 2065 and the bar passage rate was 32.98 percent. In 2009, the number passing the bar was fewer, only 2043, and the bar passage rate fell to 27.6 percent. The bar examination thus remains a competition for a limited number of positions rather than a qualifying exam for the practice of law.

Contributing to the continued low bar passage rate is that more law schools opened than were originally expected, and more students enrolled in these schools. With a higher number of bar exam-takers, it has become impossible to meet the expected high passage rate. Even if the number of bar passers eventually increases to 3000, the bar passage rate will remain low. Unless the target number of new lawyers is increased or the number graduating from the new law schools dramatically decreases, the bar passage rate may decline even more.

The relatively low passage rate affects every aspect of the new law schools and jeopardizes the success of graduate professional legal education in Japan. The decline of bar passage rate has led to a sharp decrease in law school applications. The drop in applications is particularly apparent among people with prior job experience and with educational backgrounds other than in law. Given the goal of developing new lawyers with diverse professional and educational experiences capable of serving a broader range of legal needs, it is unfortunate to lose many of these students. In addition, students are well aware of the low passage rates and tend to focus less on courses that are not directly related to the new bar examination. Law schools are under pressure to change from a broad professional education and, instead, to "teach to the test"—a regression to the "cram school" type of training that was expressly rejected by the Justice System Reform Council.

Clinical education cannot escape from these influences. In particular, there has been less demand for clinical courses than might be expected because they are perceived by both students and many professors as primarily preparing them for practice—an important goal of the legal education reforms—rather than directly helping them pass the new national bar exam. (Joy et al., 2006)

The development of clinics in Japan has been hampered also by two specific challenges distinct to clinical legal education. One stems from the relationship between law schools and the LTRI. The other is the lack of a student practice rule.

The new system for training lawyers combines education at professional law schools, a new national bar examination, and apprenticeship training in the LTRI. Although the new law schools should be the core of new system, the relationship between clinical programs and apprenticeship training at the LTRI is not clear. Some contend that clinical courses are not necessary because the LTRI provides practical training. But, as we have noted, the LTRI's apprenticeships differ significantly from law school clinical experiences in at least two respects: the apprenticeship training is based upon "learning by seeing" rather than "learning by doing," and the LTRI does not encourage legal trainees to reflect critically upon current practice and the legal system. These differences have not been fully recognized or appreciated by educators in the new law schools.

Moreover, most Japanese lawyers were inculcated to the norms of their profession at the LTRI rather than at university or in another setting. For many of them, clinical education is undermining or prejudicing the position of the LTRI, which was the only practical legal training they received. So long as the LTRI exists and most lawyers continue to receive the bulk of their training in professional skills and values in that setting, there will be a tension between clinical education at law schools and training at the LTRI.

Since the Justice System Reform Council's 2001 recommendations did not explicitly mention clinical legal education, there was no effort to pass a student practice rule or otherwise clarify the status of students within court procedures in the legislation that was adopted to implement the recommendations. This ambiguity causes substantial practical problems on a daily basis. (Rubinson, 2008) Moreover, the new professional law schools have a short history and many remain skeptical of law students' involvement in actual legal practice. At the same time, the status of legal trainees at the LTRI is not entirely clear under Japanese law. Though there was discussion in the 1970s about whether LTRI trainees could, for example, interrogate criminal suspects at the prosecutor's office, the status of apprentices has not been legally resolved. Nevertheless, the apprenticeship program has taken deep root and nobody contests that the trainees may be involved in legal practice under supervision of practicing attorneys, prosecutors, and judges. Although few trainees actually practice under attorney supervision, the decision to permit trainees to do more than simply observe legal practice has been left to the lawyers with whom they are apprenticed.

The problems caused by a lack of recognized status for students are particularly apparent in criminal justice clinics and are the primary reasons why the number of criminal justice clinics is quite small in Japan. The National Prosecutor's Office seems to have a view that law students are not allowed access to the evidence disclosed to the defense attorney for preparation for court, and the National Police Agency has taken the position that law school students are prohibited from participating in confidential interviews between clinical professors and criminal suspects in custody. These governmental agencies make a clear distinction between judicial trainees and law school students, as do some local bar associations.

There are difficulties in civil law clinics as well. In clinics that handle cases beyond the counseling stage, law school students are not allowed to sit with their clinical professors in court; they are forced to watch from the gallery like ordinary citizens. Needless to say, they cannot question witnesses. Some courts even prohibit students from participating in nonpublic pretrial procedures where litigants and their lawyers identify issues and evidence to be presented at trial. Law school students are not treated as prospective lawyers by the Japanese bench and bar.

EDUCATION, SERVICE, AND AN EMPHASIS ON SIMULATION

The designers of clinical law programs in Japan are well aware of two important goals of the American model of real-client clinical legal education: educating students in professional skills and values and providing legal services to socially and economically disadvantaged people. Nonetheless, Japanese clinical programs place a stronger emphasis on the education aspect rather than providing service because of the historical context in which clinical legal education started in Japan. Japanese law schools also tend to rely more on simulation methods than real-client clinics because of the barriers currently preventing law students from fully participating in the delivery of legal services to clients.

With very few exceptions, university-based legal education in Japan did not incorporate experiential learning methodology until the new professional law schools opened in 2004. Undergraduate law departments at Japanese universities offered academic courses on legal doctrines, but not professional courses on law practice. Moreover, prior to 2004 nearly all full-time law faculty in Japan had no legal practice experience, saw little value in teaching lawyering skills or law in the context of providing legal services to clients, and were often ill-equipped to do so. Under directives of the Ministry of Education and Science, approximately 20 percent of faculty members at the new law schools are to be practitioners with five or more years of experience. Many of these new practitioner-professors have found real-client clinics to be very good settings in which to provide practice training.

Nevertheless, there has been an emphasis on simulation methods in clinical programs due in part to the lack of a student practice rule and the persistent view that interactions with real clients by prospective lawyers is better suited for the LTRI's apprenticeship program. Simulation methods have been incorporated in a variety of courses with titles such as Basics in Law Practice, Legal Ethics and Professional Responsibility, and Lawyering Skills. In these courses, role-playing is widely used to teach lawyering skills and professional values, such as forming the client-attorney relationship, legal counseling, and preparing and examining witnesses. Students sometimes deal with simulated clients who are trained by the law school to serve as mock clients in order to evaluate students' performances.

In addition to typical role-playing methods, some Japanese law schools have developed unique simulation programs. A well-known example is Nagoya University Law School's Professional Skills Instruction Materials (PSIM), a database of video-recorded role-playings that are accessible by professors of PSIM membership universities via the Internet. Another example is a virtual law firm program developed by Kwansei Gakuin Law School. In this program, students experience aspects of law practice by participating in competing virtual law firms as counsel. (Symposium, 2008)

Some schools have also developed simulation courses for subject areas where there is little opportunity to develop a real-client clinic. For example, there are large sums at stake in actual cases involving corporate and commercial transactions, and business clients may be reluctant to employ a clinic. Clinical courses with simulation methodology can provide effective educational opportunities for students in this field. Waseda Law School, in collaboration with the University of Washington, offered a course on international mergers and acquisitions (M&A) contract negotiations using teleconference facilities. Students in Japan and the United States participated in the simulated M&A contract negotiations. The simulation materials were prepared and adopted from real business transactions by clinical professors at both law schools. (Hamabe, 2007)

There have been some benefits for Japan in having introduced clinical legal education relatively late in comparison with other countries. Japan was able to study other countries and choose the most cutting-edge methods in this age of global law practice and e-expertise. Japan has been able to establish innovative simulation courses, such as building video databases and using simulated clients to evaluate students' performances, as well as a number of significant real-client clinics. One of the strengths of clinical legal education is the reinforcement of students' ability to learn from their experiences and to think critically about existing law practices. Both simulation courses and real-client clinics can teach students to be self-critical and reflective.

Though clinical programs in Japan tend to emphasize teaching rather than service, the new law schools' clinics are in fact serving substantial numbers of socially and economically disadvantaged clients. In even the less extensive clinical programs, such as those providing legal counseling, students help to map out solutions for their clients' legal problems. This is a needed legal service for many unable to afford lawyers. Some law schools have developed, or are developing, clinical courses in fields where there is great need, such as child law and disability rights clinics. In addition, law students participating in externship programs work in a wide array of legal settings, including nongovernmental organizations, where they help provide much-needed legal assistance.

Japanese clinical programs are also helping to make legal services available to people in remote areas, such as rural agricultural communities and small islands, where there are very few or, in some locations, no lawyers. To name just a few, Hiroshima, Kagoshima, Ritsumeikan, Shimane, and Waseda law schools send students to isolated communities that lack lawyers. Many other law schools are interested in developing such programs.

An increase in service-oriented clinical courses for geographically, economically, and socially disadvantaged clients appears inevitable because Japan's system of for-profit-based legal services does not usually serve these clients. Law schools are well suited for providing these types of legal services, along with providing excellent educational opportunities. The exposure of law students to assisting traditionally unserved and underserved clients helps to instill in them a sense of their professional responsibility as lawyers in society. Clinical education's service goal is likely to become more important in Japan over time, as the number of law schools that develop clinical programs increases to cover many previously underserved areas.

POSITIVE SIGNS

Although clinical programs face a number of obstacles, there are several positive indicators for the future of clinical legal education in Japan.

The first positive sign is the relationship between law school accreditation and clinical education. Every law school is subject to examination every five years by at least one of three accrediting institutions authorized by the Ministry of Education: the Japan Law Foundation, the National Institute for Academic Degrees and University Education, and the Japan University Accreditation Association. Each accrediting institution has established its own standards for evaluating law schools, and it is noteworthy that each set of accreditation standards refers to clinical courses. It is therefore likely that accreditation standards will encourage more Japanese law schools to promote clinical legal education.

The National Institute for Academic Degrees and University Education requires law schools to offer, by 2011, optional or "mandatory optional" courses with four credits among moot court, lawyering, clinic, and externship. (National Institute for Academic Degrees and University Education, 2007) The Japan Law Foundation also requires law schools to set up clinical courses that include clinics, externships, and simulation courses such as moot court and lawyering, and to implement them properly. (Japan Law Foundation, 2005; Japan Law Foundation, 2006) The Japan University Accreditation Association imposes requirements similar to those imposed by the Japan Law Foundation. (Japan University Accreditation Association, 2005) Under the accreditation standard of the Japan Law Foundation, in particular, students are required not only to observe the lawyering tasks, but to be actively engaged in legal practice under proper instruction by clinical professors. In other words, the emerging accreditation standard is influenced by a model of real-client clinical legal education.

Though there are of course many challenges to overcome, clinical methods—whether employed in real-client clinics, simulated courses, or externships—are becoming rooted at Japanese law schools. One element that was lacking for the promotion of clinical legal education was a national network of clinical law teachers. To fill the vacuum, the Japan Clinical Legal Education Association (JCLEA) was formed in April 2008 with 212 founding members.[3] JCLEA is the first academic society that specializes in legal education in Japan, though there are many academic societies in established areas of law.

---

3. For a discussion of other national and regional clinical organizations, see Chapter 19.

JCLEA was established for three purposes. The first purpose is to establish a network of clinical law teachers to share their experiences and improve clinical legal education. Before JCLEA, educational efforts by clinical faculty were isolated and there were few opportunities to share pedagogical methods. That has changed. JCLEA holds annual national conferences, and its membership grew to 245 in 2010, including nine supporting organizational members. Another purpose for JCLEA is to provide an academic forum where clinical law teachers can gain different viewpoints from teachers in professions such as medicine, which have long used clinical methods that bridge theory and practice. Finally, JCLEA seeks to provide Japanese clinical law teachers with opportunities to learn about clinical legal education overseas. While the role that clinical legal education plays in a given country depends on the history of the legal system and the culture surrounding the relationship between lawyers and the public, Japanese clinical law teachers benefit from sharing information and experiences in other countries.

So while there are challenges ahead, there are also hopeful signs.

CONCLUSION

Japan's system of professional legal education is clearly in transition. The new law school system is premised on the understanding that in order to become good lawyers, students must have opportunities to acquire not only legal theories and legal knowledge, but also lawyering skills and professional values. The new law schools are designed to provide these opportunities for students, and clinical legal education is an excellent vehicle to provide students with such skills and values and to bridge theory and practice.

The newly established law schools are also designed to be at the core of professional legal education; however, their locus has been threatened by the low passage rate of the bar exam. There has also been resistance to coordinating the new law schools with the undergraduate law departments and the LTRI. It is notable that the duration of the apprenticeship at the LTRI was shortened from eighteen months to one year in the wake of the justice system reforms. As a result, many academics and practitioners believe that it is inevitable for Japanese law schools to teach lawyering skills and values. Still, the discussion to date has tended to focus on *what* to teach about law practice rather than on *methods* of teaching law practice that are most effective in law school settings. Clinical legal education was introduced to Japan along with the new law school system, but its goals of teaching lawyering skills and professional values while bridging theory and practice have not been fully attained.

Clinical legal education in Japan has achieved much in the six short years since its inception. Today there are many innovative clinical programs throughout Japan, and some are making legal services available to clients who cannot otherwise obtain counsel, thus involving students in access-to-justice efforts. In addition, the founding of the Japan Clinical Legal Education Association has created a network for clinical law teachers. It is not clear, however, whether clinical legal education will become a mainstream pedagogy for training lawyers in Japan. It may take many more years for clinical legal education to take a firm root in the framework of professional legal education in Japan.

LIST OF REFERENCES

Yoichiro Hamabe, *"Kokusai Keiyaku Kosho" Kamoku to Simyureshon: Waseda Daigaku [A Course in "International Contract Negotiation" and the Simulation Method: Waseda Law School]*, in HOSOYOSEI TO RINSHOHOGAKUKYOIKU [DEVELOPMENT OF LAWYERS BY CLINICAL LEGAL EDUCATION] 198 (Shigeo Miyagawa ed. 2007).

Japan Law Foundation, Hokadaigakuin Hyokakijun (Kaiteiban) [Accreditation Standards for Law Schools (Revised edition)] 15 (2005).

Japan Law Foundation, Hokadaigakuin Hyokakijun–Kaisetsu [Accreditation Standards for Law Schools with Annotations] 64 (2006).

Japan University Accreditation Association, Hokadaigakuin Kijun [Standards for Law Schools] (2005).

Peter A. Joy, Shigeo Miyagawa, Takao Suami, & Charles D. Weisselberg, *Building Clinical Legal Education Programs in a Country Without a Tradition of Graduate Professional Legal Education: Japan Educational Reform As a Case Study*, 13 CLINICAL L. REV. 417 (2006).

The Justice System Reform Council, Recommendations of the Justice System Reform Council—For a Justice System to Support Japan in the 21st Century (2001), http://www.kantei.go.jp/foreign/policy/sihou/singikai/990612_e.html (last visited Dec. 20, 2008).

Rinshohogaku Zenkoku Kurinikku Chosa [National Survey of Legal Clinics in Japan], 6 RINSHOHOGAKU SEMINA [CLINICAL LAW SEMINAR] 1 (Hiroyuki Kabashima ed. 2009).

Setsuo Miyazawa, *Education and Training of Lawyers in Japan—A Critical Analysis*, 43 S. TEX. L. REV. 491 (2002).

Setsuo Miyazawa, Kay-Wah Chan, & Ilhyung Lee, *The Reform of Legal Education in East Asia*, 4 ANN. REV. LAW & SOC. SC. 333 (2008).

Kazuhiro Nakanishi, *Hokadaigakuin niokeru Rinshohogakukyoiku [Clinical Legal Education at Japanese Law Schools]*, 1 HOSOYOSEI TAISAKUSHITSU HO [LEGAL EDUCATION BUREAU REPORT] 5 (2006).

Robert Rubinson, *The Ethical and Legal Basis for Student Practice in Clinical Education in the United States and Japan: A Comparative Analysis*, 4 OMIYA L. REV. 98 (2008).

Shimpojiumu: Hosogino no Tanren to Shimyureshon [Symposium: Training Lawyering Skills Through Simulation Methods], 5 Rinshohogaku Semina [Clinical Law Seminar] 1 (2008).

Takashi Takano, *Making a Criminal Justice Clinic in Japan*, 25 Waseda Bull. Comparative Law 41 (2007).

The Japanese Legal System, Introductory Cases and Materials, 566–88 (Hideo Tanaka & Malcolm D. Smith eds., University of Tokyo Press 1976).

The National Institute for Academic Degrees and University Education, Hokadiagagkuin Hyokakijun Yoko [Evaluation Standards for Law Schools] (2007).

Kazuhiro Yonemoto, *The Shimane Bar Association: All Twenty-One Members Strong*, 25 Law in Japan 115 (Daniel H. Foote trans., 1995).

8. THE BOLOGNA PROCESS AND THE FUTURE OF CLINICAL EDUCATION IN EUROPE
A View from Spain

DIEGO BLÁZQUEZ-MARTÍN

INTRODUCTION

If we understand *legal tradition* in J.H. Merryman's sense, as "a set of deeply rooted, historically conditioned attitudes about the nature of law, about the role of law in the society and the polity, about the proper organization and operation of a legal system, and about the way law is or should be made, applied, studied, perfected and taught" (Merrymanm, 1969 at 2), there is a strong relationship between legal tradition and an intrinsic model of legal education. And this is obviously true if we think of legal education, again using Merryman's words, as the contents, process, and means established in a given society in order to provide "the basic attitudes about the law: what law is, what lawyers do, how the system operates or how it should operate . . . to transfer legal culture from generation to generation." (Merryman, 1975 at 859) The main way to make possible the survival of a given legal tradition is through education: by training future members of the legal profession in the paths and limits of this given legal tradition.

For a long time, the two predominant Western legal traditions (common law and civil law) differed also in their models of legal education. Both models are now in need of reform because both legal traditions have experienced significant changes in some of their respective distinguishing features, just as law and legal practice have changed substantially over the last fifty years in Europe and around the world. Of course, these changes are due to many varied factors, from some as general as globalization to some very particular, such as university budgeting and finance; and they can be analyzed from an international, regional, or national perspective.

This chapter addresses the role that the so-called Bologna Process for the construction of a European Higher Education Area has played in promoting changes in Spanish legal education. More specifically, it analyzes the role that clinical legal education can play in the transition from a classical model of legal education to the model, methodology, and aims of the Bologna Process. Coming from the common law tradition of legal education, clinical education has had an impact at some of the leading law schools in Spain since the beginning of the implementation of the Bologna Process, and is considered to be one of the most significant changes introduced to achieve Bologna's reforms.

But above and beyond the institutional implications for this European higher education project, the introduction of clinical legal education into Western civil law legal education systems is an important step in the recent evolution from the "*code era.*" In fact, some comparativists have termed the present process as the "decoding era," characterized by the following guidelines: the *siege* of the codes (mostly specific laws developed over broad areas first regulated by the original codes, but not included in the codes); *replacement* of the codes (through constitutional texts or constitutional interpretation, so that the codes are no longer the first general normative authority); and code *freeze* (dozens of sections are no longer applied, given more current regulations, but not abrogated or annulled). (Bellomo, 1989 at 32)

These guidelines can be explained by two main facts: the constitution-based legal systems after World War II and the implementation of the welfare state. Law is no longer primarily the establishment of limits, but rather an instrument to achieve social goals. It has transformed to a more flexible and soft instrument to allow administrative agencies to solve problems as fast and as easily as possible, reducing certainty and accuracy in the process. This instrumental conception of law needs a new law-drafting methodology based on principles, objectives, and general commands or briefs—rather than detailed prescriptions.

Not only has the content of the law changed, but also the way the legal system works. A preeminent executive branch has created a massive body of regulations. The notion of a constitution as fundamental law has spread to the continental—or civil code—tradition, limiting parliamentary jurisdiction. Because of (more or less) welfare state policies, goal-focused legality moved legal language and law-drafting methods to new kinds of juridical rules, such as "principles" (Dworkin, 1978; Alexy, 1989), "soft law" (Thurer, 2000), and "standardization rules" such as those set out by the International Organization for Standardization (ISO). This new concept of law, known in Italy as "*ductile law*" (referring to its malleable nature and its ability to adapt to very different goals, attitudes, or means) (Zagrebelsky, 1992), suggests the relevance and final importance of promoting a kind of jurist capable of facing legal reality with imagination, an open mind, and the will to achieve the goals established by legislation. Law is thus recognized, from a generic and global perspective, as no longer *ratio scripta*: clear, precise, concise, and unequivocal rules, with an abstract scope and general target population. (Ruiz Miguel, 1996)

The truth of the matter is that "law in action," using Oliver Wendell Holmes's classical distinction, is more important and relevant than ever before. That is why—strictly from a theoretical point of view—legal education reform is necessary. Using terms from Roman law concepts, it is more necessary than ever to join the *scientia* and the *prudentia*. We should no longer select one and separate the one from the other; it will be necessary to teach not only legal *scientia*, but also legal *prudentia*. (Guastini, 1996) As Wolfgang Friedmann asserted, it "never has been so important that lawyers, legislators, judges or professors of law would be something more than skilful crafters." (Friedmann, 1966 at 17)

Consistent with these important ideas, clinical legal education can be one of the most useful tools to achieve the stated aims of legal education reform in continental Europe: updating, modernizing, internationalizing, and promoting social awareness. (Hovhannisian, 2006) The remainder of this chapter focuses on the case for—and future of—clinical legal education in the Spanish implementation of the Bologna Process. The next section presents a brief overview of the origins and state of legal education in Spain. It is followed by two sections that explain how the Bologna Process can influence Spanish legal education and discuss existing clinical programs in Spain. The chapter concludes with new initiatives and some conclusions.

LEGAL EDUCATION IN SPAIN

It is noteworthy how slowly law schools in Spain have changed their curriculum (or not) since 1953, considering how much the social and political, economic, and cultural conditions have changed. But when we speak of models of legal education, normally we forget that in many cases the real facts are not considered; legal education is based on a fiction to establish the relationship between a specific legal system and legal education. In the case of Spain, this is particularly clear because the legal doctrine—the so-called Science of Law—was one of the foundations of legitimacy of the Franco regime that imposed a system of legal education whose aims were to sustain its legitimacy and practical scheme, and whose first task was to tear down the more open experience of the European and cosmopolitan Second Spanish Republic university.

In this regard, it has to be noted that during the 1920s or 1930s, the so-called Silver Age of Spanish culture—which extended to law and legal studies—placed Spain at the forefront of scientific and cultural movements. (López & Sánchez, 2004) What has recently been called "the big cut" (Claret, 2006) illustrates the bleak picture relative to the faculties of law; of the dozen professors holding procedural law chairs in 1936, only three survived war or exile. (González, 2000) Moreover, this required the removal of the previous education model and the introduction of a new one. In the case of legal education, this process was streamlined in 1953 with the approval of the national compulsory curriculum and the regulation of the contents and forms of teaching. This curriculum was very similar to one discussed and rejected already in the 1930s after being proposed by José Castán Tobeña—at the time Dean of the Faculty of Valencia—who ended up being president of the Supreme Court of Spain for over twenty years and the official lawyer and most reputed legal head of the Franco regime.

The national compulsory curriculum was intended to introduce a legal culture that was uncritical, traditionalist, nationalist, Catholic, socially conservative, and economically liberal. Its purpose was to perpetuate the regime and to present the civil law as the core of law, as closed, abstract, and timeless. This claim was buttressed with the almost-monopoly publication of a few textbooks on civil law that could be studied for all legal professions, and whose abstraction, generality, and timelessness was at such a level that—even after the period of dictatorship and the approval of the Constitution—the editors would consider it not necessary to modify the text and, in some cases, even to mention recent legal changes.

With respect to legal education in public law, as Alfredo Galllego Anabitarte says, until 1939 (the end of the Spanish Civil War and the beginning of the Franco regime), "administrative law prevail[ed] on constitutional law, as a reflection of the administrative state," but with the new regime, Spanish public law "was quite discredited in the Faculties of Law." (Anabitarte, 2004 at 207–208) Once democracy was restored, the curricula of the faculties of law changed very little; thus, the Bologna Process will represent a first step in the evolution of legal education reform because it will require a comprehensive reform of the law school curriculum.

BOLOGNA PROCESS AND LEGAL EDUCATION

The signature of the 1998 joint declaration on harmonization of the architecture of the European higher education system in Bologna—the site of the first school of law in Europe—started the so-called process to create the European Higher Education Area. (Terry, 2008) The Bologna Process is based on the following ideas, at least as it has been understood and implemented in Spain: "self-learning" as a "matter of reference," professional guidance, learning and students' perspective, and social adaptation and professional requirements. Another objective of this process of reform, mentioned expressly in the original declaration but sometimes hidden in later documents, is the international competitiveness of European universities—especially relative to those in North American.

As for the impact of the Bologna Process on European legal education, it is, of course, very complicated to implement reform in institutions born some three quarters of a millennium ago. And it was especially difficult in law schools, usually considered as one of the most relevant elements in the institutional architecture of the nation state. Nonetheless, the European Law Faculties Association (ELFA), after discussing the issue since early 1999, reached a final position that it set out in a board letter to the European Union (EU) Commission and the EU Education Counsel in 2002 based on a consensus on four objectives: to promote effective quality assurance systems, to promote a system based on two cycles, to promote the mobility of students and faculty, and to improve the recognition of a system of degrees. (European Law Faculties Association, 2002) From a pragmatic perspective, the discussions and agreements about the new era of legal education in the European Union were about for whom, for how much, and for how long. In the same way, a common structure based on a double-cycle "bachelors + masters" in law was assumed. However, what type of education was going to be developed was not discussed despite the fact that all four of the core original proposals of the European Higher Education Area policy were to change university education. The institutions were concentrated instead on a bureaucratic agenda with a very inward vision of mobility, losing the aim of international competitiveness.

At the same time, to concentrate on the bureaucratic agenda is to misunderstand the higher objectives of the Bologna Process: the modernization of European universities in every respect and the promotion of the social dimension of higher education, relative to both professional standards and social awareness. In the case of legal education, it should be understood also relative to the earlier discussion about the effectiveness of the legal education model based on the change of law and the way law works today.

Moreover, there is an agenda other than the bureaucratic one; there is a pedagogical agenda as well, based on how to teach and how to learn law that is also part of the Bologna Process. As Lusine Hovhannisian of the nongovernmental organization (NGO) Public Interest Law Institute has noted, implementing clinical legal education into the curriculum would be one of the most efficient methods to achieve Bologna Process aims in the field of legal education. This point has been made not only from the NGO perspective, but also from within the legal academy. Thus, Andreas Bücker proposed recently to use clinical education in Germany to achieve the goals of the Bologna Process. In his opinion, now is the time for clinical programs to take advantage of recent innovations that allow law students to practice law through free legal advising under the supervision of a qualified professional, even though the German professor recognizes that there are some gaps in German professional regulation needed to open spaces for student practice. (Bücker & Woodruff, 2008)

Both of these observations—the external and the academic one—explain perfectly the experience of a large group of Spanish faculty in different schools for whom the Bologna Process opened the chance to renew their classes by enhancing professional skills and providing their students a faculty with a more realistic learning/teaching methodology, although, as in Germany, it was necessary to find open spaces for student practice. In the next section, I will report briefly on the endeavor of this group of law professors and offer some observations on how that project has evolved.

CLINICAL LEGAL EDUCATION IN SPAIN AT THE DAWN OF THE BOLOGNA PROCESS

During the discussion of the national strategy to fulfill the European commitments of the Bologna Process that took place between 2002 to 2005, the National Agency for Quality Assessment and Accreditation (Agencia nacional de evaluación de la calidad y acreditación, or ANECA), as well as the regional agencies, promoted a large number of studies and surveys of the university community's opinion of the present and future of the different educational programs. At the same time—or even before—some universities had considered independently the need to evaluate their programs and the professional success of their graduates. These studies showed how legal education was considered by students far from their own professional experience and that satisfaction with law studies among former law students was lower than among students in other degree programs (5.7 versus 7, on a scale of 1 to 9). In general, a wide range of students from different universities demanded more practice and more specialized education. At the same time, professionals appreciated skills and knowledge exactly in the opposite sense as skills and knowledge were given by the different degrees in law at the national level. (Jardí & Romeva, 2004; SOPP-Uc3m, 2003/2004)

This body of social research inspired a group of diverse, and at first unconnected, people to start to work on furthering clinical legal education in Spain. Even before this effort began in 2005, Rovira i Virgili University's School of Law at Tarragona, a new and small institution with a very young faculty, started a Penitentiary Legal Clinic, "Derecho y Cárcel" (Law and Prison), in the academic year 2002–2003. Its most important feature in the Spanish context, especially since it was a pioneer program, was its *Anglo-Saxon* profile. It was set up with the aim of providing legal advice to individual convicts through drafting various legal documents respecting divers aspects of penitentiary life, such as transfers, leaves, etc. After three years, however, the clinic closed as the result of some curricular changes. (Banqué, 2005)

More recently, in academic year 2008–2009, Rovira i Virgili University School of Law started a new clinical program on business and contract law. But the more influential and relevant pioneer clinical initiative at Rovira i Virgili School of Law is the Environmental Legal Clinic (Clínica Jurídica Ambiental, or CJA) that started in 2005. The CJA is part of the Center of Enviromental Studies of Tarragona (Centre d'Estudis de Dret Ambiental de Tarragona, or CEDAT), a multidisciplinary research unit at the Universitat Rovira i Virgili. CJA is a compulsory subject of the M.D. course on Environmental Law, the official specialization postgraduate course on environmental law, and is run by a multidisciplinary team of eight members of the legal faculty. The clinic's clients are all institutions that agreed with the university to collaborate on this project. Significantly, all public administrations present in the province of Tarragona are part of this consortium, including the Public Prosecutor Office, as well as some public services providers or public agencies (for example, water services). The cases all involve some aspect of environmental law, which is especially important to the economic life of Tarragona province since it is an important tourist center and the site of a major petrochemical corporation and a power plant.

Students are divided into small groups of between two and five to work on a given case provided by one of the clients of the clinics. The groups work on a double tutorship supervision model with one supervisor provided by the school and one from the client. Both supervisors grade the group's activity. Given the multidisciplinary nature of the cases, the clinical program requires a strong coordination effort by the faculty and staff involved in the project.

Tarragona's clinical team also works on theoretical aspects of clinical legal education, promoting different publications, and contributing to events on legal education at both national and international levels. The CJA was presented for the first time at the National Congress for the Innovation in Legal Education, held at Málaga in 2007. As an indication of a developing clinical movement in Spain, Professor Maria Marques hosts a Web site on legal education and promoted the two first national meetings of clinical faculty at Rovira y Virgili School of Law. She is also one of the organizers of a future Spanish clinical education network.

At about the same time, the Instituto de Derechos Humanos "Bartolomé de las Casas" started a clinical program on human rights at Universidad Carlos III de Madrid (UC3M), a public university in Madrid's southern suburbs, traditionally the working class metropolitan area of Madrid. It is also a new (in European terms) and small (in Spanish terms) university, with a primary concern for practical learning (25 percent of classes are based on practical methodology) and the first in Spain implementing the new Bologna curriculum. Instituto de Derechos Humanos "Bartolomé de las Casas" is a research and postgraduate teaching institution linked to UC3M with an M.D. and a Ph.D. program in Human Rights.

The first clinical program at the Instituto de Derechos Humanos was a Street Law course on human rights set up in 2005 as an option for the subject on human rights in the Licenciatura de Derecho (the undergraduate program on law). The UC3M Street Law clinic, like others around the world, trains law students to be teachers themselves.[11] One of the first instructions the students are given is: let your imagination go and teach just as you would have liked to have been taught. Since the program was established, students in the human rights course and students in the Instituto's Human Rights Ph.D program have participated as well. As a result, the Clínica Juridica has teachers, Ph.D students, law students, and high school students all working together. The program is financed by the City of Getafe, where the main campus is located, with a plan to expand the program to all of its high schools. Approximately sixty law students participate each year along with five full-time faculty members and six postgraduate students supported with fellowships. Together they teach human rights to around four hundred teenagers each year.

In 2007, Universidad Carlos III de Madrid started a law clinic on AIDS legal issues, financed by the National Ministry of Public Health and co-organized with

---

1. Street Law clinics are discussed in detail in Chapter 15.

the main NGO in the field, Coordinadora Estatal de VIH/SIDA [National Federation for HIV/AIDS] (CESIDA). Approximately two hundred students enroll in the clinic, which is staffed by twelve faculty members and five teaching or researching assistants. Conceived as a project of collaboration between the civil society and the academic world, the clinic provides two different services: legal service, with the aim of assisting the NGO and individuals with legal consultations provided by professors; and the promotion of broader solutions to given problems identified in collaboration with CESIDA, with the aim of offering a clinical education experience in different subjects where the students and the professors work together on a topic proposed by the NGO to promote a better quality of life of people living with HIV in Spain. Among the subjects and the topics that the clinic has worked on are: social security law (drafting revisions to the law on disability benefits and litigating the issue of noncontributive benefits for HIV-positive persons in prison); labor law (litigation support on the issue of discrimination); procedural law (a guide of juridical resources for people living with HIV/AIDS); right-to-health protection (restorative cosmetic surgery related to side effects due to high-effective treatment); and constitutional law (constitutional implications of prostitution regulation in the context of a welfare state).

Given the success of the Street Law program, it was established as a compulsory clinical subject in the M.D. program on human rights. Around twenty students per academic year choose a clinic among four options. Three of the options are in international law on human rights. In one of those clinics, a group of students worked on factual investigation with the accusing lawyers in the "CIA flights" case. In another, they prepared two different amicus curiae for the Inter-American Commission on Human Rights (IAHCR). In the third of these clinics, which focuses on the scope of human rights protection in Europe, they prepared a report on the national judicial effects of the European Court on Human Rights—one of the most controversial technical issues in the Spanish system of protection of human rights and a traditional complaint of human rights NGOs. The fourth clinic works in the area of human rights education programs.

Rovira I Virgili University in Tarragona and Universidad Carlos III de Madrid represent a model of schools (small, new, young faculty) that were created by regional governments during the late 1980s and early 1990s, which are perhaps more naturally inclined toward clinical legal education. But some of the larger, older "traditional" universities have developed clinical programs as well. This is the case with the Universitat Central de Barcelona and the Universitat-Estudi General de Valencia.

Valencia University was one of the *Estudis Generals* (universities in ancient Catalonia) of the medieval kingdom of Aragón, achieving the same university status as Bologna or Rome in 1502. Since then and up to modern times, the school of law of Valencia University has been particularly relevant to Spanish faculty and legal scholarship—including with respect to the origin of the 1953 national curricula discussed earlier. When the Bologna Process came along, a group of around twenty Valencia faculty members began reflecting on the coming changes and the need for new learning and teaching methods, drawing on the experience at Rovira i Virgili University Tarragona and Universidad Carlos III de Madrid. As a result of their efforts, the dean created a new position of Vice Dean for the Coordination of the European Convergence and Innovation. With the support of the new vice dean, Professor García Añon, a *Clínica Jurídica* was started in academic year 2006–2007 with five clinical courses on immigration law, gender violence crimes, environmental law, prison law, and pornography. Each course was coordinated by one professor, but all of the faculty could work with any of the students according their interest and each professor's specialty.

Clinical courses at Valencia University are offered as a noncompulsory subject. The cases are submitted by different public and private local or regional institutions that collaborate with the clinical program. The courses are structured to include some common issues and activities of general interest for all the students. At the same time, each coordinator can program activities needed for each individual case or even each step in the process. On a practical level, each dossier is divided in nine stages: reception and selection of cases, student case selection, first client interview, fact research, legal research, consultancy, first draft and assessment, rewriting, and presentation. The course expects a final dedication of one hundred twenty hours for the student and sixty-three hours for the professor with three students. At the end of the semester, the students have to write proposals for a maximum of three different cases.

This first experience was very well received and its results were presented at the International Seminar on Clinical Legal Education organized by Roviri I Virgili University in Tarragona, where Vice Dean Professor García Añon noted two classic challenging questions for the future of Valencia University's clinical program: the calculation of faculty teaching hours and the balance between the social interest of the cases and their "pedagogical" interest. The experience and results of the Clinica Jurídica at Valencia University were presented again during the Second Congress on Teaching Innovation in Legal Studies at the University of Málaga, on the theme "towards the European Higher Education System." As this was the first time that clinical legal education was treated as an academic issue in a national meeting in Spain, one could say that the Spanish clinical movement was born officially during this congress.

Valencia University School of Law ran three clinical courses during academic year 2007–08, again as noncompulsory subjects: prison law, environmental law, and a new one on human rights. The environmental law clinic was a collaboration with an ecologic NGO to develop new tax incentives for regional and local authorities to protect natural spaces. It was designed to teach tax law students alternative social values apart from those normally attributed to tax advisers or tax consultancies. Unfortunately, the Clinica could not be run during academic year 2008–09 due to some administrative problems. Nonetheless, the professors who were involved with the earlier clinical courses developed their own courses utilizing the clinical methodology. And most importantly, the University of Valencia has now recognized the Clínica Jurídica as one of its research units, formalizing and institutionalizing the efforts of clinical professors not only as a teaching activity, but also as a research action.

The other clinical experience at one of the older, large Spanish universities is the *Dret at Dret* Project (right to access to law, in Catalonian) of the Universitat Central de Barcelona. This project originated in academic year 2005–06 with a group of faculty members of the school of law of the Central University of Barcelona who were concerned with and committed to social responsibility of the university, and who were convinced of the formative power of bringing reality to the academic context. Their first efforts, which sought to link the networks of voluntary work at a number of NGOs, the legal assistance services provided by these organizations, and the official services of free legal aid, had an important impact both on the academic life and on the social life of Barcelona. This led to explicit support for the initiative on the part of the university when the faculty group insisted on the need to stabilize and institutionalize their work and asked the school to formalize the project. On March 23, 2007, the School of Law Faculty Assembly passed a regulation whereby the school assumed the administrative load and regulated the academic status of the students and teachers that participate in the project.

Dret al dret uses the traditional practicum period, found at some law schools in Spain and elsewhere in Europe, to provide quality legal assistance to some social disadvantaged sectors and, at the same time, specific vocational training to the students while they satisfy a legal professional need on the part of social organizations. In order to achieve this two-part aim, the students—supervised by professors—offer their services to social organizations that work with disadvantaged groups. *Dret al dret* is also building a network with all these organizations, since some joint initiatives and other types of coordination can make the legal aid offered more effective. For this reason, *Dret al dret* also provides the opportunity for some students to work on other cases or interests that are not specifically tied to a given collaborating institution.

The project is run in collaboration with the Bar Association of Barcelona, and it is financed by the City and the Catalonian autonomous government. There are also around twenty collaborating social entities. Twenty-two full-time teachers of the faculty take part in *Dret al dret*, and with this option the students cover the credits imputed to Practicum I and II. Institutionally, *Dret al dret* relies on a general coordinator and a series of teachers responsible for different areas of intervention, including penitentiary law, human rights and international law, immigration law, children's law, law of women, and social rights. In all these areas, *Dret al dret* offers social entities participating in the project the following services: production of documents that facilitate access to the juridical resources; workshops to find law-based alternatives; training groups to train associations or answer specific questions; production of informative material about legal topics; recording and broadcasting of radio programs; and the publication of Web pages to communicate their work in different areas.

CONCLUSION

Legal education in Europe faces great challenges with respect to its aims, its ways, and its influence. Great legal thinkers placed continental European universities at the vanguard of legal discourse around the world because they were at the same time the founders of a comprehensive concept of the law. But legal cultures are not so Western-dependent anymore, and this concept of law has become overwhelmed by dramatic changes in society, economy, culture, and technology—and law's contents and practice. The Bologna Process provides the means by which Europe can reform legal education to compete in today's globalized world.

In the case of Spain, the Bologna Process offers the opportunity to make decisions that should have been made twenty-five or thirty years ago, to make legal education and law more effective and to create progressive tools for social and cultural change after a long and repressive dictatorship. At the same time, it provides legal education in Spain the chance to promote greater quality and the internationalization of Spanish law schools. Both aims—adapting to present conditions and achieving academic excellence—can be advanced through clinical legal education. The programs described in this chapter are good examples of how the Bologna Process can be viewed as not just one more bureaucratic demand, but as the means for the legal academic community to open up new paths for educating lawyers. These clinical programs do more than restructure the method of training future lawyers; they also open up new research opportunities and increase cooperation between law schools and other institutions, civil society, and the profession.

This is the true meaning of the Bologna Process and why clinical legal education can be so important to achieving its aims. It may not be easy; establishing clinical programs has introduced problems and difficulties for the people involved and has raised new tensions within the academy. But that is the challenge of Bologna: to break with traditions and habits in order to clear the path for a renewal of university work.

In this sense, cooperation and common interests have been a strategic link between the different professors from different universities in Spain. Clinical programs at Barcelona, Tarragona, and Valencia started closely together. Two seminars organized by Professor Maria Marques were milestones that have continued on with conferences and other opportunities to share ideas and experiences about innovations in law teaching and learning. The Carlos III clinical program has profited from close contacts in Latin America and the United States.

Help and assistance of Professor Felipe Gonzalez (from Diego Portales University in Chile) led to Professor Richard Wilson (from American University's Washington College of Law in the United States) to teach two workshops on clinical education for the Carlos III faculty that was open to other schools as well.

These are only a few examples of how clinical legal education can be used to pursue and realize the most important aims of the Bologna Process. As time passes, hopefully the success of these programs will motivate more law schools in Spain to introduce clinical programs into their curricula—thereby helping move forward the Bologna Process and its goal of European legal education reform.

LIST OF REFERENCES

ROBERT ALEXY, A THEORY OF LEGAL ARGUMENTATION: THE THEORY OF RATIONAL DISCOURSE AS THEORY OF LEGAL JUSTIFICATION (Ruth Adler & Neil MacComirck trans., Clarendon Press 1989).

Alfredo Gallego Anabitarte, *La Enseñanza del Derecho Público en España. Un Ensayo Crítico [The Teaching of Public Law in Spain. A Critical Essay]*, *in* MANUALES Y TEXTOS DE ENSEÑANZA EN LA UNIVERSIDAD LIBERAL 207 [Teaching Manuals & Books in the Liberal University] (Manuel A. Bermejo Castrillo ed. 2004).

Maria Marquès i Banqué, Rovira i Virgili University, La Asignatura Derecho Y Cárcel: Una Experiencia De Clinical Legal Education En El Ámbito Penitenciario [Legal Education in the Framework of the Bologna Process: The Prisoners Clinic: An Experience of Clinical Legal Education] (2005), *available at* http://www.sre.urv.es/web/aulafutura/php/fitxers/325.pdf.

MANLIO BELLOMO, L'EUROPA DEI DIRITTO COMMUNE [COMMON LAW'S EUROPE] (1996).

Andreas Bücker & William A. Woodruff, *The Bologna Process and German Legal Education: Developing Professional Competence through Clinical Experiences*, 9 GERMAN L.J. 575 (2008).

JAUMA CLARET, EL ATROZ DESMOCHE: LA DESTRUCCION DE LA UNIVERSIDAD ESPAÑOLA POR EL FRANQUISMO, 1936–1945 [The Atrocious Weeding Out: The Destruction of the Spanish University during the Franco Years, 1936–1945] (2006).

RONALD DWORKIN, TAKING RIGHTS SERIOUSLY (Harvard University Press 1978).

European Law Faculties Association, Statement Concerning the Bologna Declaration of the European Ministers of Education of 1999: For a European Space of Legal Education (May 31, 2002).

WOLFGANG GASTON FRIEDMANN, EL DERECHO EN UNA SOCIEDAD EN TRANSFORMACIÓN [LAW IN A CHANGING SOCIETY] (F. M. Torner trans., FCE México 1966).

ANTONIO SERRANO GONZÁLEZ, UN DIA EN LA VIDA DE JOSÉ CASTÁN TOBEÑAS [A DAY IN THE LIFE OF JOSÉ CASTÁN TOBEÑAS] (2000).

Ricardo Guastini, *Derecho dúctil, Derecho incierto* [*Pliant Law Uncertain Law*], 13 ANUARIO DE FILOSOFÍA DEL DERECHO [ANNUAL OF PHILOSOPHY OF LAW] 111 (1996).

Lusine Hovhannisian, *Clinical Legal Education and the Bologna Process, in* 2 PILI Papers 1 (2006), *available at* http://www.pili.org/dmdocuments/pili_papers_2_3.pdf.

Anna Cuxart Jardí & Clara Riba Romeva, Informe de Inserción Laboral de los titulados de DERECHO: *Proyecto de diseño de estudios de grado*. [*Report of Job Placement of Law Graduates: Design Project of Studies of Degree*] Agencia Nacional de Evaluación de la Calidad y Acreditación (ANECA) [National Agency of Quality Evaluation and Accreditation] (June 2004).

Angel M. López & Cecilia Gómez-Salvago Sánchez, *La enseñanza del derecho privado en la Universidad liberal* [*The Teaching of Private Law in the Liberal University*], *in* MANUALES Y TEXTOS DE ENSEÑANZA EN LA UNIVERSIDAD LIBERAL [TEACHING MANUALS & BOOKS IN THE LIBERAL UNIVERSITY] (Manuel A. Bermejo Castrillo ed. 2004).

JOHN HENRY MERRYMAN, THE CIVIL LAW TRADITION: AN INTRODUCTION TO THE LEGAL SYSTEMS OF WESTERN EUROPE AND LATIN AMERICA 2 (Stanford University Press 1969).

John Henry Merryman, *Legal Education There and Here: A Comparison,* 27 STANFORD L. REV. 859 (1974–1975).

Antonio Ruiz Miguel, *Del Dúctil, derecho y la virtuosa necesidad* [*From the Pliant Law and the Virtuos Need*], *in* 13 ANUARIO DE FILOSOFÍA DEL DERECHO [ANNUAL OF PHILOSOPHY OF LAW] 159 (1996).

ANECA, SOPP-Uc3m (Servicio de Orientación y Planificación Profesional Universidad Carlos III de Madrid [Professional Mentoring and Counseling Service of the Universidad Carlos III de Madrid]), Estudio sobre perfiles profesionales Licenciado en Derecho [Study Regarding Professional Profiles for Undergraduates in Law] (2003/2004).

Laurel S. Terry, *The Bologna Process and Its Impact in Europe: It's So Much More than Degree Changes*, 41 VAND. J. TRANSNAT'L L. 107 (2008).

Daniel Thürer, *Soft Law, in* MAX PLANCK ENCYCLOPEDIA OF PUBLIC INTERNATIONAL LAW 452 (Rudolf Bernhardt ed., Max Planck Institute 2000).

GUSTAVO ZAGREBELSKY, IL DIRITTO MITTE [THE MILD LAW] (Einaudi 1992).

9. BEYOND LEGAL IMPERIALISM
US Clinical Legal Education and the New Law and Development

RICHARD J. WILSON

> ... [S]imply because Americans say they do not "do" empire [doesn't mean] there
> cannot be such a thing as American imperialism. Niall Ferguson[1]
> ... American attitudes towards democracy itself... foster an unrealistic faith in
> political development assistance. Americans tend to view democracy as a natural
> political state; non-democratic systems are aberrations from a norm. Thomas Carothers[2]

INTRODUCTION

Clinical legal education[3] adopted by law schools outside of the United States—as
pedagogical method, as academic structure, indeed, as concept itself—is largely
an export from the United States, wherein lie its roots. There is little debate as to
those modern roots. After the early twentieth century, when clinics were discussed but hardly ever adopted in the United States, clinical programs arose from
social and protest movements of the 1960s and '70s. During that time, law school
clinics received an enormous boost from the Ford Foundation–funded Council
on Legal Education and Professional Responsibility (CLEPR), which served to
spread the gospel and deepen the presence of clinics in US law schools.[4] The first
law and development movement came into being in parallel with the growth of
clinics in the United States during those decades. The movement exported US legal
education models and methods to other countries, and eventually fell prey to a

---

1. NIALL FERGUSON, *Preface to the Paperback Edition,* in COLOSSUS: THE RISE AND FALL
OF THE AMERICAN EMPIRE xiii (Penguin Books, 2004)
2. Thomas Carothers, *The Resurgence of United States Political Development Assistance to
Latin America in the 1980s, in* THE INTERNATIONAL DIMENSIONS OF DEMOCRATIZATION
125, 143 (Lawrence Whitehead ed., 2001). Legal education reforms fall within the category
of political development assistance, as Carothers defines it.
3. I use the term "clinical legal education" here in its broadest sense, as any active
teaching method that involves experiential learning by students, including simulation,
externship, and/or in-house clinics providing legal services to real clients under close
faculty supervision.
4. The early years of modern clinical education in the United States are discussed in
Chapter 1, along with early developments in Canada, Australia, and the United
Kingdom.

devastating critique that brought it to a screeching halt, including, some argue appropriately, all legal education innovations exported from the United States.

James Gardner was perhaps the most vocal critic of the export of US law school teaching methods to Latin America during that period. (Gardner, 1980 at 14) Gardner's book, *Legal Imperialism*, has tenacious resonance, enshrined as the most-cited source on the imperial aspirations of US development assistance, whether in the commercial or political sphere. In fact, Gardner's work is the paradigmatic scholarly reference on legal imperialism, wherever, in whatever form, and seemingly by whatever government or group.

This chapter will, inter alia, attempt to determine the salience of Gardner's critique today, particularly as legal imperialism might be strongly associated with legal education methods in the United States. We might begin, however, by considering again the brief quotes that open this chapter. Both assume a certain naïve, self-referential, almost oblivious American view of its own imperialist aspirations today. The first is from the US-based Scottish historian Niall Ferguson, whose work includes extended reflections on both the British and American empires. (Ferguson, 2004 & 2003) In *Colossus*, he suggests that a more self-conscious American imperialism might be good for the world, but that such an option seems "highly unlikely," making American empire a real, if "somewhat dysfunctional entity." (Ferguson, 2004 at viii) Thomas Carothers, on the other hand, is the consummate insider, a prolific American writer on US development assistance and the rule of law, particularly in the years since the end of the Cold War. Both Ferguson and Carothers suggest that Americans are unself-conscious and insular, often unaware of the awesome, hegemonic power—military, political, economic, social, and cultural—asserted by their country throughout the world.

There is a thread of scholarly critique that maintains the legal imperialism critique of the United States. Duncan Kennedy cleverly asserts that the most recent wave of globalization has "a recognizable Unitedstatesean genealogy." (Kennedy, 2006 at 67). Some of that literature reveals anger and antipathy in titles that query, none too rhetorically, about "Lex Americana?" (de Lisle, 1999); allude to US law and its importers as a "Trojan Horse" (Stephenson, 2000); or suggest that the recipients of imported legal norms are seen by the exporting nations as "Savages." (Sajó, 1997; Mutua, 2001) But that literature is largely on big-sweep issues such as the rule of law, democracy, constitutionalism, civil society, and politics. (Kennedy, 2006 at Tables 1, 21) It does not address the much narrower issue of what might be called "clinical imperialism." There must be some question, in light of these critiques and those of Ferguson and Carothers, as to whether the export by US scholars of clinical legal education methods and philosophy within the institution of legal education today perpetuates clinical imperialism, perhaps simply because we are unaware or oblivious to the foreign perception of our actions.

The fact that the topic of clinical imperialism is so rarely raised today itself suggests that the issue has little traction, if any; the trickle of criticism itself suggests otherwise. If there were significant complaints about the imposition of clinics on unwilling recipients, they would have been made and heard more widely by now. Gardner makes clear that the imperialism critique of American legal education, and of its bearers, the American legal professoriate, was hardly polite or subtle during the first law and development movement:

> Some Third World lawyers–students in particular, and the more traditional law professors–rejected and were openly hostile to American legal assistance. This resistance was manifested in explicit statements of disinterest, in student strikes, indifferent or antagonistic receptions for visiting American law professors, or in requests (sometimes loud, usually quiet) to leave a country. (Gardner, 1980 at 9)

Moreover, this book itself is evidence of a vibrant worldwide movement toward adoption of US-based clinical legal education methods and philosophy. Nonetheless, there may be some nagging sense, perhaps related to that American lack of self-consciousness which the introductory passages suggest, that export of the clinical method, especially that which is funded by outside donors, is imperialistic. Perhaps, because funds for foreign law school clinics come from abroad, often from US-based donors, law school administrations and students in the developing or transitional receiving countries—always strapped for resources—do not bite the hand that feeds them, instead grumbling quietly to themselves about imposed Yankee largess.

This chapter explores the extent to which the export of clinical legal education from the United States today can legitimately be called imperialistic. I conclude that it cannot (except by those dyspeptic few who complain about all things American). Isolated instances of overzealous or ethnocentric export can unquestionably be found, but we have moved beyond clinical imperialism. I argue not only that its export is not now imperial, but that the original legal imperialism critique was as much a function of American hubris as it was real. In the next section, I set up a vocabulary to discuss legal imperialism, a brief reiteration of the accepted typology for the dissemination and reception of foreign law. I then explore the historical context of the legal imperialism critique, the three successive movements of law and development. Finally, I explore the central premises of the legal imperialism critique, as it relates to both the sweeping forced assimilation of entire legal cultures and the narrow issue of clinical legal education. Some of these premises are flawed, and some depend on the critic's perspective.

THE IMPORT AND EXPORT OF LAW: A BRIEF TYPOLOGY

The academic vocabulary that has grown up around the issue of the export and import of law is sometimes gentle and benign, sometimes aggressive. Perhaps the most classic articulation of the gentle and egalitarian exchange comes from comparative law, where one speaks of the "reception" of foreign law. (Wiegand, 1991 at 229) Gardner himself discusses the process of the sending and reception of foreign law under the rubric of "legal transfer." (Gardner, 1980 at 29) More recently, the terminology has taken on a botanical bent with "legal transplants." (Watson, 1976; Miller, 2003 at 839) Yet another relatively benign term for the movement and intermingling of law across borders is "legal pluralism" (Merry, 1988 at 869; Hooker, 1975), which can, however, take on a more aggressive sense to mean "[t]he imposed law, forged for industrial capitalism rather than an agrarian or pastoral way of life, embody[ing] very different principles and procedures." (Merry, 1988 at 869)

One is left with the sense that reception, transfer, transplant, and pluralism all are accomplished between countries or regions with the coequal power—at least within legal or other elites, according to some scholars—to send or receive the transmitted law or legal culture. Legal culture is exported with a mandate to knock before entering, and to be received or transplanted only where politely invited in by the receiving country. Somewhere between transfer and imperialism lies the notion of "legal development" (Friedman, 1969–1970), which implies a country that develops, as facilitated by one that is developed. There is neither the parity of transfer and transplant, nor the forced imposition implied by imperialism. Legal development, of course, took shape in various movements of law and development, three of which will be described below.

A slightly more nuanced approach to the denomination of the import and export of legal norms and methods is offered in the more extensive development of subcategories by some scholars. Under these etymologies, we see a blending of the two poles of the benign and the more coercive. Within the category of "transfer," Gardner includes imposed or uninvited transfer that clearly subsumes imperialism. Miller allows for an imperialist form of "externally-dictated transplant," an example of which he suggests occurred in "the post–World War II Japanese Constitution imposed by General Douglas McArthur." (Miller, 2003 at 847) While Miller's category seems to permit an element of will on the part of the receiving nation—it could reject the imported legal norms if it wished, but at high cost—the element of coercion remains a key element of the definition. Comparativists thus have abandoned the common-law-versus-civil-law paradigm in favor of broad factors of either prestige or efficiency as motivators on the part of the receiving countries, while imposition through colonialism or imperialism is the primary tool of the exporting countries. (Graziadei, 2006 at 455–61; Ajani, 1995 at 112–14)

"Legal imperialism" is, of course, the most freighted term associated with the import or export of law. The historically familiar context in which "legal imperialism" occurs is the global colonialization of the developing world by Europe during the age of exploration and conquest. Law was used overtly as an instrument of colonial rule. (Schmidhauser, 1989 at 871; Burman & Harrell-Bond, 1979) This is why Latin America's legal systems largely reflect Spanish, French, and Portuguese roots, why Africa is so heavily influenced by British or French legal structures, why the United States and Canada legal traditions take on largely British character.

The same was true of colonial influence on legal education. John Schmidhauser examines legal education in former colonies which have since become independent nations in the last century. He found that

115 (81 percent) of 142 such nations have indigenous law schools or their equivalent; but 74 (52 percent) have legal training programs similar to those of their former colonial nation; and 11 (8 percent) have their legal professionals trained in their former colonial nation, with London or Paris the most influential legal educational centers. Not surprisingly, 106 (74.6 percent) have adopted a legal system similar to that of their former colonial nation . . .. (Schmidhauser, 1997 at 345)

Noting that scholars researching former colonies disagree about how to investigate "the relative significance of various modes of legal education," Schmidhauser asserts that whether any teaching method is effective depends on whether law schools actually train lawyers for what lawyers do—a task hampered by the fact that there is precious little empirical information on the role of the legal profession in formerly colonial states. (*Id.*, at 345–46)

Legal imperialism today is only a bit more subtle; it can be accomplished through aggressive, indeed brutal trade and commerce regimes, as well as through armed conquest. Ugo Mattei is one of the leading exponents of a contemporary critique of rule of law programs, particularly the US hegemony in promotion of law and economics theory. Professor Mattei describes a "theory of imperial law" that "subordinates local legal arrangements world-wide . . . ." There, "[p]redatory economic globalization is the vehicle, the all-mighty ally, and the beneficiary of imperial law." (Mattei, 2003 at 383) Mattei and Laura Nader assert in a recent co-authored book that "the present dominance of the United States has been economic, military, and political first, and legal only recently, so that a ready explanation of legal hegemony can be found within a simple conception of law as a product of the economy." (Mattei & Nader, 2008 at 142)

In the typology of the import or export of law, legal imperialism is an epithet, never a compliment. It is hardly reflective of the gentle, bucolic scenes of reception, transfer, transplant, and pluralism, or even of legal development. Legal imperialism is accomplished by force or guile, by exploitation of the weak by the strong. Legal imperialism implies the intentional, and usually massive and complete, takeover of a legal system by an outside power. Governments or big foundations engage in transfer or transplant; they are *accused* of legal imperialism. These accusations have their analog in the foreign policies of US presidents: Monroe, Truman, Eisenhower, Nixon, and George W. Bush—by any other name, naked American imperialism.

THREE LAW AND DEVELOPMENT MOVEMENTS

The First Law and Development Movement

[I]n a Latin America whipped into a frenzy by the Fall of Arbenz, by the Stoning of Nixon, by the Guerrillas of the Sierra Madre, by the endless cynical maneuverings of the Yankee Pig Dogs—in a Latin America already a year and a half into the Decade of the Guerrilla—a student was something else altogether, an agent of change, a vibrating quantum string in the staid Newtonian universe.[5]

Indeed, during the decade of the 1960s and early 1970s, the time period of the first law and development movement, students throughout the developing world were "agents of change." One might say the same of the student movement in the United States, which challenged war (nuclear and Vietnam), racism, traditional sexual mores, economic privilege, and male chauvinism. And as the quotation above indicates, protestors nearly pulled Vice President Richard Nixon from his car in violent demonstrations in Caracas, Venezuela, in 1958. (LaFeber, 1993) The US government carried out a cynical foreign policy, a national security doctrine that promoted security at any price in the face of the perceived Soviet Communist threat. The US government cozied up to brutal and corrupt Latin American dictators like Anastasio Somoza of Nicaragua, and overthrew democratically elected leaders like Guatemalan president Jacobo Arbenz and Chilean president Salvador Allende, in CIA-inspired coups of 1954 and 1973, respectively. The   failed CIA-backed Bay of Pigs invasion of Cuba in 1961 made Fidel and Che even more infamous international heroes to the idealistic student left, symbols of anti-imperialist resistance. These are the Latin American students to whom American law professors of the day intended to bring the Socratic/case method. This is the raw, post-colonial world of the first law and development movement, a period of effort by the United States to bring developing countries within its sphere of influence before the Soviet Union gained a toehold in the great Cold War standoff.

The professors had strong backing. No lesser figures than President Dwight Eisenhower (Eisenhower, 1960), Chief Justice Earl Warren (Warren, 1963), and Justice William Douglas (Douglas, 1962) pitched development zealotry to US lawyers. Most of these appeals were calls to balance the potential influence of the Soviet Union by promoting liberty and freedom, with American law as the savior. Justice Douglas, for example, called on "teachers from the West by the hundreds and thousands" to give "underdeveloped nations . . . the benefit of our experiment in federalism." (Douglas, 1962 at 910)

Jerome Levinson and Juan de Onis wrote a scathing critique of the US Alliance for Progress, another of the foreign aid programs designed to prevent more

---

5. JONOT DIAZ, THE BRIEF WONDROUS LIFE OF OSCAR WAO, 110 (2007).

Cubas in the hemisphere. In their chapter called "Education: The Tinderbox," they note that "of all the Alliance targets, educational reform was the most strongly influenced by Castro's Cuba." (Levinson and de Onis, 1970 at 279) They point to two programs in the region, among others: the Cuban literacy campaign and the brilliant innovations of Brazilian educational theorist Paolo Freire. In his first year in power, Fidel Castro created "literacy brigades"—100,000 high school and university students who went into rural areas of Cuba and taught the elders how to read and write. In doing this, he sought to overcome the tradition that education was available "only to the core society." (*Id.*) In Brazil, Paolo Freire taught an even more volatile kind of literacy. This was the process of *conscientização*, or "critical consciousness," which promoted dialog between student and the basic literacy teacher in order to "help the ordinary man develop a sense of responsibility for his own fate." Castro and Freire were heroes to students, young and old, and their lean toward pedagogies of inclusivity of the poor probably contributed, in no small measure, to regional resistance to US innovations in legal education pedagogies.

The Second Law and Development Movement: Rule of Law, Democracy, and Good Governance

Thomas Carothers, who has dominated the scene in the reemergence of law and development, documents a second wave of law and development in Latin America and later worldwide. (Carothers, 1998 & 2001) Foreign assistance programs developed largely during the Reagan administration focused on democracy build-ing. Operating through the National Endow-ment for Democracy (NED), the US Information Agency (USIA), and the Agency for International Development (AID), these programs supported election reform and monitoring, administra-tion of justice, and democratic participation—grounded in the emerging field of human rights law, which had a faltering role in US foreign policy during the Carter administration. Broadly, Carothers concluded that the US assistance was a "positive initiative," but he cautioned that "there is no significant evidence . . . that the US democracy programmes had or are having a profound effect on any Latin American societies." (Carothers, 2001 at 142–43) He concluded that the US government had unrealistic expectations about the ease and speed of reform efforts, some of which are set out in an opening quote in this chapter.

Nonetheless, the second "rule of law and democracy" phase of law and devel-opment took root and thrived beginning in the late 1980s, taking off after the end of the Soviet Union in 1991. Because of the Cold War, the first law and develop-ment movement had been limited to countries within the sphere of influence of the United States, which consisted largely of Latin America and some of Africa, although some early work occurred in South Asia. The end of the Cold War opened up the world for development, and made accessible a large portion of the former Soviet Union as well as the last closed frontier: China, with its 1.3 billion people—a fifth of the world's population. New studies of Chinese legal education emerged as China began to permit outsiders in, and to reach out to the West for ideas. (Depei & Kanter, 1984 at 544) The early promoters of this second rule of law and democracy phase were highly self-conscious, both comparing themselves against the first movement and drawing from its lessons. Carothers, for example, notes reliance by a US government working group on Gardner's *Legal Imperialism*. (Carothers, 2001 at 145, n. 15) The early scholarship of this period is, not surprisingly, the most skeptical of the three stages of law and development. It seeks to reassure itself and the wider scholarly community that the Gardner critique is no longer viable. It largely concludes that this is a new and different kind of development assistance, and that it survives any criticism that it might be imperialistic. (Fowler & Bunck, 1991–1992; Rose, 1998; de Lisle, 1999; Stephenson, 2000; Widner, 2001 at 205 *et seq.*)

One of the most noteworthy aspects of the scholarship on the second wave of law and development is its identification of the growing legions of international donors, public and private, involved in legal exports. In Vietnam, for example, donors included the United Nations Development Program (UNDP), the World Bank, the Asian Development Bank, Denmark, Sweden, Canada, France, Japan, Australia, private foundations, universities, nongovernmental organizations (NGOs), private law firms, and the US government, which was represented there by USIS, NED, and AID. (Rose, 1998; de Lisle, 1999 at 184–212) This presence dwarfs any efforts undertaken in the first law and development movement, making it a truly international and cosmopolitan effort. Also noteworthy is the fact that legal education, and clinical education in particular, seldom appeared as donor priorities, with the possible exception of the American Bar Association's Central and Eastern European Law Initiative (CEELI). (de Lisle, 1999 at 258) Law schools in Vietnam continued to train lawyers as technocrats, focusing "too much on academic trends and not enough on practice." (Rose, 1998 at 133) The need for clinical education there is underscored by the failure of legal education to address issues of professional responsibility in legal training. (*Id.*, 134)

At bottom, though, the legal imperialism critique was fading, even in the second stage, and clinical imperialism was nowhere on the radar. As one article concludes, lawyers in the region studied "are much less concerned with cultural imperialism theories than with practical reforms that will help to deliver legal services to their citizens in an impartial and efficient manner." (Fowler & Bunck, 1991–1992 at 846) Bryant Garth, an astute and comprehensive scholar of law and development, concluded as follows: "A few naysayers complain about a repeat of legal imperialism, but they have trouble gaining adherents given the degree of enthusiasm for these programs in the south as well as the north and with the idealists as well as the realists." (Garth, 2002–2003 at 388)

A Third Stage of Law and Development: Globalization and Its Discontents

Scholars long involved in law and development have recently suggested the possibility of what they call a "third moment" in law and development. (Trubek

& Santos, 2006 at 7) Again, these scholars are analyzing law and development across the broad sweep of the interaction of law, economics, and institutions in development policy and practice. To the extent that a coherent picture of the third moment exists, it lies in the idea that "'development' means more than economic growth and must be redefined to include 'human freedom.'" (*Id.* at 8) Duncan Kennedy sees a central role for human rights in this latest stage. (Kennedy, 2006 at 65–66) Others see a new doctrine that "accepts the use of law not only to create and protect markets, but also to curb market excess, support the social, and protect direct relief to the poor." (Trubek & Santos, 2006 at 8) While the central role of judges and an independent judiciary are acknowledged as central components of development assistance, judges must not only protect property and contract rights, but "they also have to be sure to interpret regulatory law correctly, protect a wider range of human rights, and contribute to poverty reduction." (*Id.* at 9) The third moment acknowledges that "one size does not fit all." Actors in development programs must acknowledge that "they are willing to accommodate local conditions and national diversities." Perhaps most important of all, "in the current era, the concept of development has been expanded to include law reform as an end in itself," thus justifying the reform of law and legal institutions whether or not there is a direct link between those reforms and economic growth. (*Ibid.*)

This theoretical framework for the third moment is exactly apt for the adoption of reforms in legal education, and for the introduction of clinical legal education as an element of development policy. That opportunity is widely recognized in the most recent literature on the export of US legal education, particularly clinics, including my own writing on the topic. (Wilson, 2004; Wortham, 2006; Maisel, 2007–2008; Bloch, 2008; Barry et al., 2008; Moliterno, 2008) These scholars are not one-time visitors to other countries who spend two weeks of a summer break on a developing country adventure, but professors and practitioners who have devoted a significant part of their professional careers investing in their work throughout the world. The programs with which they work have long-term investments in the improvement of legal education, often part of a broader agenda of law reform (Note, 2007); clinical legal education becomes a cross-cutting theme that addresses many of the priorities of third moment development. Clinical legal education itself works against the grain of traditionally capitalist development policies, promoting care for the poor and marginal in the legal system, as well as greater attention to the ethical responsibilities of the legal profession, both within the attorney-client relationship and within society at large.

Lest support for this dawning of a new era in development policy become too breathless, let it be noted that there are still some who have been cautious and critical about the expansion of clinical legal education. James Moliterno, writing broadly on the export of US legal education, notes that what he calls "cultural imperialism" occurs among American and Western European scholars involved in such projects. "Too often, though, 'this is how we do it in the United States' is a one-line argument to which no engagement or rebuttal is permitted. It is as if the maker of such a statement is surprised and shocked by any further discussion of an issue after this simple assertion is made." (Moliterno, 2008 at 280) Again, these attitudes, to the extent that they exist, may be imperious, but they are not imperialistic. These are not the intentional and forced imposition of a particular view, with little or no resistance by the "savage" recipients; these statements are simply ignorant, and are easily (and often disdainfully) dismissed as such by those who hear them. Philip Genty aptly calls this "cultural blindness," and suggests that "we have 'oversold' US models of clinical education that are ill-suited to the civil law context." (Genty, 2008 at 146) Professor Genty goes to some length to challenge my own views, expressed more briefly elsewhere, that the US export of clinical legal education is not legal imperialism. (Genty, 2008 at 145–49, citing to Wilson, 2004) I could not agree with Professor Genty more as to the necessity that US exporters become more aware of the deep cultural differences between the civil and common law traditions. Again, however, "overselling" is not imperialism; it is shortsighted or narrow, but it lacks the intentionality of imperialist impulses. And like many comparative law scholars, I believe that issues are less about the differences between the common and civil law than about methods that empower the student not only to think like a lawyer, but to act like one in the highest traditions of the profession.

THE FALSE PREMISES OF THE LEGAL IMPERIALISM CRITIQUE

What is one to make of the legal imperialism critique of the United States and of Gardner's conclusion that the United States engaged in legal imperialism during a failed law and development movement, particularly as to the promotion of US legal education methods? And how does clinical legal education fit into Gardner's critique, if at all? There are several premises embedded in Gardner's assertions. This section will examine two of the most important: the premise about the nature and scope of Gardner's own legal imperialism critique, and the premise about the "demise" of the first law and development movement.

The first premise, then, is that the initial law and development movement engaged in legal imperialism at all. Where would clinical legal education fit into the broad synthesis of the conquest-driven, nation-altering legal imperialism of Schmidhauser or Mattei? Schmidhauser, I believe, would call legal education more an effect of legal imperialism than a cause; the statistical data above suggest as much. He notes that "assumptions about legal education in developing countries often reflects (sic) the interests of major powers, which historically were or are colonial powers." (Schmidhauser, 1997 at 345) Quoting another observer of legal education and development during the emergence of the law and development movement, he notes that the quality of legal education depends on "the competence of the instructor, the range of his curriculum and the adequacy of his course materials." (Hager, 1972 at 38) Although this is little information from which to draw any definitive conclusion, Schmidhauser seems unconcerned about the general thrust of legal education reforms as a form of imperialism. Similarly, Mattei's critique seems more focused on broad economic coercion through law, not the political assistance within which legal education falls.

As for James Gardner, one must put his critique itself into context. His thesis, at bottom, is very narrow. It focuses principally on Latin America, and within that region, only on the export of four American legal models: "methodological, educational, professional, and jurisprudential." He notes in fact, that the professional and jurisprudential models "encountered a measure of acceptance." (Gardner, 1980 at 14) He believed that only the educational and methodological models failed. "American case and Socratic methods of teaching law and the American legal education model did not find a receptive constituency in Latin America and elsewhere, with the result that these models did not take hold and are little used today." (Ibid.) The proponents of these reforms were mostly practicing lawyers and law professors, who "by training, intellectual tradition, and professional experience . . . were often poorly equipped for the tasks undertaken." American legal assistance was, he concluded, "inept, culturally unaware, and sociologically uninformed. It was also ethnocentric, perceiving and assisting the Third World in its own image." (Id. at 9)

Gardner's legal imperialism is hardly the muscular and aggressive brand of Schmidhauser or Mattei; it is, instead, a bumbling and inept, perhaps heavy-handed, failed attempt at export of a single method of legal education, the Socratic-case method. The method was roundly rejected by the recipients as inappropriate to their history, their culture, and the times. Moreover, Gardner's critique seems to suggest that the failure of export of the Socratic-case method was in part due to the internal lack of pedagogical breadth in the United States. He notes that the case method was an "atomistic and nearsighted pedagogy," and that US law schools at that time failed to offer "clinical and practical internship experience." (Id. at 253) Moreover, the case method "ignored parallel methodological explorations that were taking place in developing countries (e.g., clinical education [and] internships in law firms and in the public sector . . .)." (Gardner, 1980 at 249) I have noted elsewhere that Luís Bates, the founder of the clinical program at the Catholic University of Chile in 1970, did not obtain his first "foreign" funding from visiting law and development proponents. Ironically, the source of his funding was William Pincus, the president of CLEPR and great US innovator in clinical legal education. Pincus visited Bates in Chile in 1971 and provided encouragement and funding for him to visit the Jamaica Plain office of Harvard law professor Gary Bellow. The clinical program at the Catholic University continues to thrive today. (Wilson, 2002 at 543–544) These observations by Gardner suggest that the export of US law school pedagogies might not have failed, or been so misperceived, had they included a broader range of methodological or structural options, although one must acknowledge that clinical education was still in its infancy in the United States at that time.

A second implicit premise shared by the legal imperialism critique of law and development is that the movement was an unmitigated and *universal* failure. What may have been true for the *American* law and development movement, however, does not hold true for other developed and developing countries. This is where American hubris came to bear; we could not imagine a law and development movement without the United States at the center. An influential law review article by David Trubek and Marc Galanter (Trubek & Galanter, 1974), is said to have savaged the first law and development movement, assuring its demise. The article is entirely academic and entirely introspective of US experience. It focuses on the exporter of law, the United States, and its "liberal legal" paradigm, which I have summarized elsewhere. (Wilson, 1988–1989 at 397–98) While the Trubek and Galanter critique, together with Gardner's, were unquestionably devastating within the United States, the law and development movement hardly disappeared. Instead, it grew and thrived outside of the United States.

Perhaps the principal reason that law and development outside of the United States during the 1970s is so overlooked is that it was grounded in two areas that drew little attention from US scholars at the time: post-colonial economic exploitation and international law. Funding for law and development work continued apace during this period, but usually was funded by foreign sources. Professor James Paul, an early activist in African law and development work, noted that while the Ford Foundation–funded International Legal Center (ILC) died, a successor, the International Center for Law in Development, was begun with funds from Sweden. The new Center "rose from the ashes of the ILC, but it was a very different organization in terms of funding, underlying concerns, programme and strategies." (Paul, 1988 at 26) Other scholarly work, published in Europe or elsewhere, began to appear, grounding law and development in international law, and thus alienating American exceptionalists and legal scholars, who had largely ignored international law. (*e.g.,* Osgood Hall, 1973; Dias, 1981; Shanmugaratnam, 1984; De Waart, et al., 1988)

The reality, then, is that the original critique of law and development was grounded in the blind ignorance, at worst, of its proponents. Moreover, while the first law and development movement may have died in the United States, it grew and flourished in other parts of the world while progressive US scholars turned inward with the critical legal studies movement, firmly grounded in a kind of post-modern ennui.

CONCLUSION

I have, as the title of this chapter suggests, reached a firmer resolve as to the question of whether the US export of clinical legal education constitutes legal imperialism. Lest there be any doubt as to the role of clinical legal education as an agent of American imperialism, let me conclude with some humbling data.

One of the clearest ways to look at the issue of imperialism, legal or otherwise, is to examine how much is spent by the proponents of reform, and on what it is spent. In the economic analyses of writers such as John Schmidhauser or Ugo Mattei, corporate or government expenditures directed to subjugation are unlimited, and are often accompanied by an element of military force that incurs enormous additional costs. If measured by the extent of its investment in the enterprise, the US government is not seeking to mold the world into its image through its investments in law reform or legal education broadly, let alone the narrow subset of clinical education.

The international affairs budget of the US State Department for 2007 shows total expenditures of $38.7 billion in all, of which only just over $2 billion (roughly 5 percent) went to all bilateral development assistance, plus all funding for the Agency for International Development (AID). Funding for clinical legal education funds falls principally within the programs of the ABA Rule of Law Initiative, one of hundreds of programs funded by AID, and even there, part of much larger law reform and rule of law initiatives. In the grander scheme of US foreign policy goals, expenditures on *all rule of law initiatives*—let alone the export of *all* legal education reform within the rule of law programs—constitute a scintilla of all US foreign assistance expenditures. (US Department of State, 2008 at 1) While this calculation does not include the expenditures of other international development agencies or banks, or of foundation-funded programs, the total of those additional expenditures would reduce the proportionate expenditures on clinical legal education to an even lesser percentage of all investments in foreign assistance.

The US export of clinical legal education, in short, is not now and arguably never has been legal imperialism.

LIST OF REFERENCES

Gianmaria Ajani, *By Chance and Prestige: Legal Transplants in Russia and Eastern Europe*, 43 Am. J. Comp. L. 93 (1995).

Margaret Martin Barry et al., *Justice Education and the Evaluation Process: Crossing Borders*, 28 Wash. U. J.L. & Pol'y 195 (2008).

Frank S. Bloch, *Access to Justice and the Global Clinical Movement*, 28 Wash. U. J.L. & Pol'y 111 (2008).

The Imposition of Law (Sandra B. Burman & Barbara E. Harrell-Bond eds., New York Academic Press 1979).

Thomas Carothers, *The Resurgence of United States Political Development Assistance to Latin America in the 1980s, in* The International Dimensions of Democratization 125 (Lawrence Whitehead ed., Oxford University Press 2001).

Thomas Carothers, *The Rule of Law Revival*, 77 FOREIGN AFF. 95 (1998).

Jacques de Lisle, *Lex Americana?: United States Legal Assistance, American Legal Models, and Legal Change in the Post-Communist World and Beyond*, 20 U. PA. J. INT'L ECON. L. 179 (1999).

Han Depei and Stephen Kanter, *Legal Education in China*, 32 AM. J. COMP. L. 543 (1984).

INTERNATIONAL LAW AND DEVELOPMENT (PAUL DE WAART, PAUL PETERS, & ERIK DENTERS eds., Professional Books 1988)

CLARENCE J. DIAS, LAWYERS IN THE THIRD WORLD: COMPARATIVE AND DEVELOPMENTAL PERSPECTIVES (Africana Publishing Co. 1981).

William O. Douglas, *Lawyers of the Peace Corps*, 48 A.B.A. J. 909 (1962).

Dwight D. Eisenhower *The Role of Lawyers in Promoting the Rule of Law*, 46 A.B.A. J. 1095 (1960).

NIALL FERGUSON, COLOSSUS: THE RISE AND FALL OF THE AMERICAN EMPIRE (Penguin Books 2004).

NIALL FERGUSON, EMPIRE: THE RISE AND DEMISE OF THE BRITISH WORLD ORDER AND THE LESSONS FOR GLOBAL POWER (Penguin Books 2003).

Michael Ross Fowler & Julie M. Bunck, *Legal Imperialism or Disinterested Assistance? American Legal Aid in the Caribbean Basin*, 55 ALB. L. REV. 815 (1991–1992).

PAULO FREIRE, PEDAGOGY OF THE OPPRESSED (Continuum 1989).

Lawrence M. Friedman, *On Legal Development*, 24 RUTGERS L. REV. 11 (1969–1970).

JAMES A. GARDNER, LEGAL IMPERIALISM: AMERICAN LAWYERS AND FOREIGN AID IN LATIN AMERICA (University of Wisconsin Press 1980).

Bryant G. Garth, *Building Strong and Independent Judiciaries Through the New Law and Development: Behind the Paradox of Consensus Programs and Perpetually Disappointing Results*, 52 DEPAUL L. REV. 383 (2002–2003).

Philip M. Genty, *Overcoming Cultural Blindness in International Clinical Collaboration: The Divide between Civil and Common Law Cultures and Its Implications for Clinical Education*, 15 CLINICAL L. REV. 131 (2008–2009).

U.S. and Foreign Aid Assistance, GLOBAL ISSUES, Jan. 2, 2009, at http://www.globalissues.org/article/35/us-and-foreign-aid-assistance (last visited Feb. 9, 2009).

Michele Graziadei, *Comparative Law as the Study of Transplants and Receptions*, *in* THE OXFORD HANDBOOK OF COMPARATIVE LAW 441 (Mathias Reimann & Reinhard Zimmermann eds., Oxford University Press 2006).

L. Michael Hager, *The Role of Lawyers in Developing Countries*, 58 A.B.A. J. 33 (1972).

M. B. HOOKER, LEGAL PLURALISM: AN INTRODUCTION TO COLONIAL AND NON-COLONIAL LAW (Clarendon Press 1975).

Duncan Kennedy, *Three Globalizations of Law and Legal Thought: 1850–2000,* in THE NEW LAW AND ECONOMIC DEVELOPMENT: A CRITICAL APPRAISAL 19 (David M. Trubek & Alvaro Santos eds., Cambridge University Press 2006).

WALTER LaFEBER, INEVITABLE REVOLUTIONS: THE UNITED STATES IN CENTRAL AMERICA (W. W. Norton & Company 1993).

JEROME LEVINSON & JUAN DE ONIS, THE ALLIANCE THAT LOST ITS WAY: A CRITICAL REPORT ON THE ALLIANCE FOR PROGRESS (Quadrangle Books 1970).

Peggy Maisel, *The Role of U.S. Law Faculty in Developing Countries: Striving for Effective Cross-Cultural Collaboration,* 14 CLINICAL L. REV. 465 (2007–2008).

Ugo Mattei, *A Theory of Imperial Law: A Study on U.S. Hegemony and the Latin Resistance,* 10 IND. J. GLOBAL LEGAL STUD. 383 (2003).

UGO MATTEI & LAURA NADER, PLUNDER: WHEN THE RULE OF LAW IS ILLEGAL (Wiley-Blackwell 2008).

Sally Engle Merry, *Legal Pluralism,* 22 L. & SOC'Y REV. 869 (1988).

Jonathan M. Miller, *A Typology of Legal Transplants: Using Sociology, Legal History and Argentine Examples to Explain the Transplant Process,* 51 AM. J. COMP. L. 839 (2003).

James E. Moliterno, *Exporting American Legal Education,* 58 J. LEGAL. EDUC. 274 (2008).

Makau Mutua, *Savages, Victims and Saviors: The Metaphor of Human Rights,* 42 HARV. INT'L L.J. 201 (2001).

Note, *Adopting and Adapting: Clinical Legal Education and Access to Justice in China,* 120 HARV. L. REV. 2134 (2007).

OSGOOD HALL LAW SCHOOL. MATERIALS ON LAW AND DEVELOPMENT (2 vols.) (1973).

James C. N. Paul, *American Law Teachers and Africa: Some Historical Observations,* 31 J. AFR. L. 18 (1987).

Carol V. Rose, *The "New" Law and Development Movement in the Post—Cold War Era: A Vietnam Case Study,* 32 L. & SOC'Y REV. 93 (1998).

András Sajó, *Universal Rights, Missionaries, Converts, and "Local Savages,"* 6 E. EUR. CONST. REV. 44 (1997).

John R. Schmidhauser, *Legal Imperialism: Its Enduring Impact on Colonial and Post-Colonial Judicial Systems,* 13 INT'L POL. SCI. REV. 321 (1992).

John R. Schmidhauser, *The European Origins of Legal Imperialism and Its Legacy in Legal Education in Former Colonial Regions,* 18 INT'L POL. SCI. REV. 337 (1997).

John R. Schmidhauser, *Power, Legal Imperialism, and Dependency,* 23 LAW & SOC'Y REV. 857 (1989).

N. Shanmugaratnam, *International Center for Law and Development: Evaluation Report* (Swedish Agency for Research Cooperation with Developing Countries 1984).

Matthew C. Stephenson, *A Trojan Horse Behind Chinese Walls? Problems and Prospects of U.S.-Sponsored "Rule of Law" Reform Projects in the People's Republic of China,* 18 UCLA PAC. BASIN L.J. 64 (2000).

David M. Trubek & Marc Galanter, *Scholars in Self-Estrangement: Some Reflections on the Crisis in Law and Development Studies in the United States*, 1974 WIS. L. REV. 1062 (1974).

THE NEW LAW AND ECONOMIC DEVELOPMENT: A CRITICAL APPRAISAL (David M. Trubek & Alvaro Santos eds., Cambridge University Press 2006).

United States Department of State, Office of the Director of U.S. Foreign Assistance, Summary and Highlights: International Affairs Function 150, Fiscal Year 2009 Budget Request (2008).

Earl Warren, *Convocation Address*, 111 U. PA. L. REV. 913 (1963).

ALAN WATSON, LEGAL TRANSPLANTS: AN APPROACH TO COMPARATIVE LAW (University Press of Virginia 1976).

JENNIFER A. WIDNER, BUILDING THE RULE OF LAW: FRANCIS NYALALI AND THE ROAD TO JUDICIAL INDEPENDENCE IN AFRICA (W. W. Norton 2001).

Wolfgang Wiegand, *The Reception of American Law in Europe*, 39 AM. J. COMP. L. 229 (1991).

Richard J. Wilson, *The New Legal Education in North and South America*, 25 STAN. J. INT'L L. 375 (1988–1989).

Richard J. Wilson, *Three Law School Clinics in Chile, 1970–2000: Innovation, Resistance and Conformity in the Global South*, 8 CLINICAL L. REV. 515 (2002).

Richard J. Wilson, *Training for Justice: The Global Reach of Clinical Legal Education*, 22 PENN. ST. INT'L L. REV. 421 (2004).

Leah Wortham, *Aiding Clinics Abroad: What Can be Gained and the Learning Curve on How to Do So Effectively*, 12 CLINICAL L. REV. 615 (2006).

PART II

THE JUSTICE MISSION OF GLOBAL
CLINICAL EDUCATION

The chapters in this part examine the social justice mission of clinical programs and how that mission is carried out in various parts of the world. Each chapter focuses on a different aspect of the social justice component of clinical legal education, from broad ambitions to specific examples of social action projects. There are many more approaches to training lawyers for social justice than can be presented in these few chapters, although the chapters make mention of and cite references that cover a substantial representation of what is taking place around the world.

Chapter 10 explains the historical connection between the clinical and the access to justice movements in many parts of the world. The chapter includes descriptions of different models of legal aid clinics and shows how clinical education is enhanced when instruction is carried out while providing critically needed legal services. Chapter 11 follows up with an examination of community law clinics that offer students a different approach to lawyering as they seek to meet the needs of communities. The chapter draws on the experience of two different community clinic models, one in the United States and the other in Australia. Chapter 12 looks at one of the core educational goals of any clinical program, training law students in legal ethics and professionalism. The chapter analyzes the advantages of teaching these matters through various types of clinical methods, including real-client settings in which students come face to face with the ethical issues and professional values that arise in the actual practice of law.

The next two chapters discuss clinics that expose students to public interest and law reform practice. Chapter 13 analyzes the importance of emphasizing public interest law in legal education and the advantages of doing so through clinical programs. The chapter offers examples of two very different clinical approaches to public interest law training, one from Brazil and the other from Poland. Chapter 14 looks at the value of clinical instruction in law reform prac-tice, drawing on two examples from Australia. One is an internship program based at the Australian Law Reform Commission that offers students the oppor-tunity to learn while being integrated into the work of the commission; the other involves students in human rights advocacy projects being carried out by lawyers affiliated with a law reform nongovernmental organization (NGO).

This part continues with two chapters about clinics that introduce students to professional skills and values while engaging in different forms of community education. Chapter 15 is about Street Law, where law students study areas of law relevant to various groups that might not otherwise have access to legal assistance and then pass on what they learn to those groups. The chapter describes the methods used to prepare students to give Street Law "lessons" and the educational goals of Street Law clinics, based on experiences in the United States, South Africa, and the United Kingdom. Chapter 16 describes a similar type of clinical experience offered in some Indian law schools known as legal literacy campaigns. The chapter describes the general approach to legal literacy clinics in India and also discusses a project that used clinical teaching methods as part of a local good governance project.

The final chapter in this part looks at clinical programs that integrate alternative dispute resolution (ADR), including increasingly important non-litigation approaches to lawyering such as negotiation, conciliation, mediation, dialogue facilitation, consensus-building, and arbitration. The chapter examines programs in India, South Africa, and the United States, and shows how clinical instruction in these methods further the social justice goals of the global clinical movement.

10. LEGAL AID ORIGINS OF CLINICAL LEGAL EDUCATION

FRANK S. BLOCH AND MARY ANNE NOONE

INTRODUCTION

Clinical legal education is often associated with the provision of legal aid to the poor, marginalized, and disadvantaged in society. In this chapter we explore the connection between the provision of legal aid services—including legal representation, advice and assistance, community legal education, and law reform activities—and the development of clinical legal education in many countries of the world. We begin by outlining the development of modern legal aid schemes in the context of the access to justice movement of the 1960s and 1970s. We then detail the relationship between early clinical programs and legal aid services and analyze different models for delivering legal services in a law school legal aid clinic. Finally, we examine the transformative potential in legal aid-based clinical legal education programs relative to their two constituencies: the communities they serve and the students they teach.

THE ACCESS TO JUSTICE MOVEMENT

Equality before the law and the rule of law are fundamental concepts in liberalism, the ideology that underpins most industrialized democratic societies. The concern for improving access to justice that manifested in the 1960s and 1970s arose from the recognition that the liberal claim that the justice system ensured "equality before the law" was flawed. Progressive lawyers and academics realized that fundamentally this was merely a formal right, with little substance and limited practical effect. The reality was that most people rarely engaged with the legal system and those that did were often denied access to representation and advice because of financial reasons. At the same time, there was a growing awareness that it was not enough to have a formal right; there needed to be affirmative action to ensure the right was put into effect. (Cappelletti & Garth, 1978)

In many countries, government inquiries, reports, and academic research identified inequality in the justice system and significant areas of unmet legal need. (Sackville, 1975; American Bar Association, 1989) This often coincided with a renewed focus by governments on the issue of poverty, such as the "War on Poverty" declared by US President Lyndon Johnson in 1964. Many reports identified that law treated some groups of people less favorably than others, and that substantive areas of law of considerable importance to the everyday lives of poor people like residential tenancy, consumer credit, and social security were "heavily weighted against their interests." (Sackville, 1975 at 1) These inquiries often concluded that law regularly reinforces inequalities rather than redress them. (Government of India, 1977)

The developing awareness of the barriers facing those seeking access to justice was reinforced by socio-legal research. This research identified systemic barriers like race and gender, examined how and to whom the legal profession delivered legal services, and assessed the prevalence of unmet legal need in the community. It revealed that for most people there was no access to lawyers and legal advice, and that lawyers' work was predominantly in commercial and property-related matters. There was significant unmet legal need, much of which was seen as having been generated by an increase in the welfare state and new laws regulating the relationships of the poor. It was argued that this gave rise to the creation of "new rights" which could be enforced and defended. (Reich, 1964) There was growing concern that the legal needs of the poor were not being met by the traditional methods of delivering legal services.

Cappelletti and Garth identified three waves in the access to justice movement in a 1978 four-volume collection which surveyed the developments in access to justice across many Western industrialized countries in the preceding decade. This chapter is concerned primarily with the first wave, which addressed economic matters and sought to provide citizens with legal means to seek justice through legal aid schemes, although aspects of the second and third waves impacted on clinical legal education as well. The second wave focused on organizational matters that facilitated standing in a representative capacity, including class actions, in an effort to address the difficulty that individuals faced in vindicating their rights. With a growing awareness of new rights, many legal aid organizations adopted these new legal techniques—class action and test cases—to claim and enforce these new entitlements of the welfare state and poverty programs. The third wave developed alternatives for dispute resolution, recognizing that "in certain areas or kinds of controversies, the normal solution—the traditional contentious litigation in court—might not be the best possible way to provide effective vindication of rights." (Cappelletti, 1993 at 287) As a result, there was a "wave" of enthusiasm for developing alternative dispute resolution mechanisms in the 1970s and 1980s in many Western countries including Australia, the United States, and Canada.[1]

ACCESS TO JUSTICE AND LEGAL AID

The concept of lawyers providing free legal services to the poor dates at least back to the end of the fifteenth century when, in 1495, the English King Henry VII

---

1. The social justice implications of introducing ADR into the law school clinical curriculum are discussed in Chapter 17.

legislated to require a judge to assign a counsel (lawyer) to the poor when seeking justice. The *informa pauperis* procedure was adopted in many other parts of the world as part of the legacy of the British Colonial legal system, but it had very limited application. In the later part of the nineteenth century and the first half of the twentieth century, lawyers became more involved in various charitable organizations that provided legal assistance. Lawyers volunteered their time and in some countries, like Australia, there developed state-funded but professionally controlled legal aid schemes. (Noone and Tomsen, 2006)

In the second half of the twentieth century the emphasis shifted to ensuring legal assistance as a right. The critique of formal equality before the law and the focus on achieving substantive equality prompted the development of government-funded legal aid schemes around the globe. (Abel, 1985) These concerns were taken up particularly in the United States by the Office of Economic Opportunity (OEO), which was responsible for nearly all of the War on Poverty's best-known and most controversial programs, including legal aid. A key intent of these programs was involvement of the community in the actions and decisions being taken to assist them. The Equal Opportunity Act of 1964 thus required the "maximum feasible participation of the poor" with the goal of strengthening communities. The OEO recognized that the law and legal services had a role to play in eradicating poverty and accepted that the legal system could be an active contributor to improving social disadvantage. An array of legal services programs were funded by OEO through the early 1970s. These programs created a network of neighborhood law firms situated in poor areas that were staffed by salaried lawyers and paralegals who specialized in poverty law and took an active approach to informing people about their rights. (Cahn & Cahn, 1964; Johnson, 1974) Federal funding was taken over by the quasi-independent Legal Services Corporation in the mid-1970s following a political tug of war between federal and state authorities over the fate of a law reform-minded rural legal aid program in California. (Falk & Pollack, 1993) Although operating at times under significant restraints imposed by Congress, the basic model remains in place today.

The key concept underpinning neighborhood legal services was an approach to tackling legal aspects of poverty that went beyond individual cases. Legal services programs drew a distinction between "services" and "representation": lawyers offered individual assistance in individual legal matters (services), but also engaged in advocacy and major litigation directed to a wider goal (representation). The ultimate goal was to achieve systemic change for the benefit of the neighborhood, or an identifiable group within the community, and, in doing so, to develop "indigenous leadership" within the community. (Cahn & Cahn, 1964) This approach to the provision of legal services to the poor was replicated in a number of countries, including Canadian community legal clinics, UK law centers, and Australian community legal centers.

The neighborhood law office model was in stark contrast to the "judicare" model of legal aid developed in the UK pursuant to the Legal Aid and Advice Act of 1949. Under this approach, government pays private lawyers to provide traditional individual legal services in the areas of crime and family law. The judicare model, which does not seek to eliminate poverty, has been adopted in many countries and is a common approach to providing legal aid. Other models of legal aid include the establishment of a statutory body that employs lawyers to provide legal aid services, often described as a "salaried" service, or a "mixed" approach which includes both salaried lawyers and a judicare scheme. (Patterson, 1996)

CLINICAL LEGAL EDUCATION AND LEGAL AID PROGRAMS

As noted above, both the legal profession and the legal academy joined in the access to justice movement's efforts to address systemic inequality before the law. This shared concern of the profession and the academy is reflected in the regular and substantial links that exist between legal aid and clinical legal education throughout the world. It can be seen in the early history of clinical legal education in the United States—dating back to the first half of the last century—when most law school clinical programs were housed in "legal aid clinics" that served the local low-income population. (Bradway, 1930; Johnstone, 1951) Similarly, the earliest Australian university clinical programs established in the late 1970s were based in community legal centers. Typically, these clinical programs were founded on the belief that having law students work in a community legal service could have a positive influential role in the formal education of future lawyers as well the pragmatic reason that access to university resources would substantially improve the objectives of free legal aid and advice, community legal education, and law reform activities. (Noone, 1997; de Klerk, 2005; Wizner & Aiken, 2004)

In some instances, law school-based legal aid projects began before any serious thought was given to clinical legal education. Law school clinics—or sometimes law students acting on their own—took up the call for providing legal services to the poor as a matter of professional and public service, or as activists for social change. Some of these projects were more like externships, where the students worked at a local legal aid society under the supervision of a legal aid attorney.[2] Over time, many of these legal aid projects morphed into the law school's clinical program. Sometimes the link was formed from the other direction, where a law school first decided to start a clinical program and then, either at the outset or at some later point, structured the program at least in part around a legal aid office. Either way, the legal aid and the clinical education aspects of these programs were bound to influence each other. It does seem, however, that legal aid has

---

2. Externship programs are discussed in Chapter 22.

played a more substantial role in the clinical movement where clinical programs grew out of, or at least started up together with, law schools providing legal aid services. Under those circumstances, the legal aid dimension became somehow embedded in the clinical program and has had a pervasive influence on the clinical curriculum. When legal aid is introduced into a clinical program more pragmatically, as a way to provide students with a clinical learning experience, it can become an almost neutral vehicle for professional skills training.

In those countries where clinical legal education began as an offshoot of legal aid projects, initially there were few differences between a standard legal aid office—whatever form legal aid took in a particular country—and law school–based legal aid clinics. The services provided at the law school may have been more limited than those provided at a full-blown legal aid office, usually due to limitations on the types of cases that students could work on, but the essence of their mission was the same. Early law school legal aid clinics in the United States, for example, tended to handle a narrow range of cases that offered the best opportunity to contribute effectively to the legal aid movement. At law schools where students worked essentially on their own, they tended to identify particular settings, such a local jails, where they could provide reasonable competent counseling and advice. Where the students had access to lawyer supervision, often provided on a voluntary basis, they tended to concentrate on a relatively narrow range of cases that could realistically be monitored and overseen by the supervising attorneys. Prominent examples of early student-run "legal aid societies" in the United States include Yale University, the University of Southern California, and the University of Chicago. Typically, they were administered as extracurricular student associations with little or no faculty supervision. (Bradway, 1929; Holland, 1999) Early legal aid clinics in India, South Africa, and other countries were structured similarly in order to maximize the effectiveness of student participation in legal aid activity. (de Klerk, 2005; Bloch & Ishar, 1990)

Regardless of the precise form they took, these legal aid clinics incorporated the core mission of any legal aid office; that is, to serve the local community's legal needs. Thus, in spirit and in practice they were very much a part of the legal aid movement. Indeed, law school legal aid clinics have been touted at various times as a lower-cost means of providing legal aid services that otherwise would have to go unmet. This was the approach proposed in a series of government reports in India in the 1970s and is still in evidence today at many Indian law schools. Around the same time, the US Legal Services Corporation sought out law schools to accept legal aid funding; although few schools took up the offer, the idea resurfaced recently in efforts to increase funding for legal aid programs. (Government of India, 1977; Legal Services Corporation, 2000) Equally important with respect to their impact on clinical legal education, by their very nature these service-oriented legal aid clinics brought law students face-to-face with real people whose daily lives are affected by the power and limits of the law.

These types of law school legal aid initiatives are rare, however, and only a relatively small number of law schools have supported stand-alone legal aid clinics—even in those countries where law schools participate actively in the legal aid movement. For most law schools and in most countries, the trend ran in the other direction; the clinical legal education movement provided the motivation for setting up law school-based legal aid services. In South America, for example, law schools in Chile, Argentina, Peru, and Colombia formed the Inter-University Program on Public Interest Clinics to support access-to-justice initiatives through law school legal aid clinics. Law school legal aid clinics are key providers of legal aid in Africa as well. A prominent recent example of this trend is China, where improving access to justice is among the central aims of that country's rapidly growing clinical legal education movement. (Phan, 2005)

Often, the law school clinic–legal aid connection was established, at least initially, by funding organizations. This was the case with early Ford Foundation funding for legal aid-oriented clinical programs in many countries, including the United States, India, and South Africa, and continues with more recent Ford Foundation-funded clinical education projects in China. The American Bar Association has funded legal aid clinics throughout Eastern Europe and the countries of the former Soviet Union, as has the Open Society Institute. (de Klerk, 2005; Wilson, 2004)

These linkages to legal aid have had a profound effect on the direction of clinical legal education. Whether preceded by or developed together with legal aid projects, many law school clinical programs around the world have at the center of their educational mission exposing students to social issues and the role that the legal system can play in improving social justice. Clinical legal education aims to teach law students about professional values and the public responsibility that the law and lawyers have relative to the less powerful members of society, and it does so by placing students in a position where they can address real problems in the community as young professionals. And the place to do that is in a legal aid clinic.

MODELS AND FEATURES OF LEGAL AID CLINICS

These important linkages between the access to justice and clinical legal education movements have continued to influence the structure and operation of many law school legal aid clinics today, although not necessarily in the same way. Legal aid-oriented law school clinics typically fall into one of three different models, which can be classified according to how they incorporate legal aid practice into the curriculum. Many clinical programs that are concerned primarily with increasing individual access to legal services adopt an "individual service" model. This is an open-ended approach to legal aid, handling a variety of cases—and as many individual cases as possible—limited only by external considerations. A "specialization" model, by contrast, seeks to provide legal services in a particular area of the law, often to a specifically targeted group of clients. A "community" model is oriented toward a local community and utilizes a range of approaches—including organizing and community legal education—to address that community's legal needs, broadly defined. There are, of course, many other factors that go into structuring an educationally effective legal aid clinic, and therefore the operation of one clinic following one of these models can be quite different from another clinic following the same model. A critical feature that may or may not be tied to a particular model is the location of the clinic. A clinic physically based on campus, as opposed to being located in the community or within the office of an external legal aid organization, will have different types of clients and relationships. Nonetheless, each of these models presents students with particular types of cases and legal aid experiences, which in turn can affect profoundly the nature of their professional educational experience.

Individual Service Model

Individual service model legal aid clinics aim primarily to provide traditional legal services to the poor. This is necessarily the model for clinical programs that are funded specifically to provide general legal aid services, including those that are located in the statutory legal aid organization, or where support for clinical education is similarly conditioned by key institutional constituents such as local governments and professional licensing boards. They can also be the model of choice at law schools where the service mission of clinical education is paramount. This does not mean that service model clinics will always provide the same range of legal services as would a full-blown legal aid office. Typically that is not the case, since most law school clinics are limited in one way or another by their students' ability to handle complex or lengthy matters or to appear before various courts or agencies.

The educational goals of individual service model clinics tend to be more general than with community or specialty clinics. Rather than focusing on the legal needs of a particular community or on particular areas of the law, service model clinics can concentrate the students' attention on the core issues of law practice—what lawyers do—that come from the experience of working with a client on just about any type of case. As with the other legal aid clinic models, the students' clinical experience includes an important social justice component as well; with this model, it comes from engaging in a general legal aid practice and the exposure to the social issues and professional obligations that arise in that setting. (Brodie, 2009; Curran et al., 2005) Depending on the orientation of the supervising faculty, this aspect can be a substantial part of the individual service model clinical curriculum. There is, however, a difference with this model that can affect its professional training mission. As a result of their general service mission and the fact that the students are placed in what amounts to a general law practice, clinical programs following an individual service model tend to emphasize instruction in lawyering skills more than those with community or specialization model clinics.

Specialization Model

The legal aid mission of specialization model clinics is defined by a particular area of legal need, which may be identified by local communities—much like with community-based clinics. For example, many clinics located in urban areas specialize in housing law or public benefits matters, such as social security and welfare; clinics in communities with many immigrants may specialize in immigration law. Specialization clinics can also focus on particular types of legal matters in order to address broader national, or even international, concerns. Examples include clinics that specialize in domestic violence, employment discrimination, and international human rights. And some of these specialization model clinics focus on a particular area of the law for more parochial reasons, such as matching the supervising faculty member's interest and expertise or to secure support from a particular funding source. As this model of clinic concentrates on one particular area of the law, specialty clinics have the capacity to develop the expertise necessary to carry out a more targeted social justice agenda and to handle more complex cases. In this respect, they fit with the high-impact and law reform approach to legal aid practice typical of larger and more strategic legal aid programs.

The educational experience in a specialization model clinic is influenced not only by the particular area of the law that the clinic specializes in, but also by the fact that the students engage in a specialized legal aid practice. Students working in a specialty clinic can concentrate on relatively narrow legal issues framed by relatively limited substantive areas of the law, and are exposed repeatedly to those aspects of law practice dictated by the particular types of cases handled by the clinic. For example, students in a criminal defense clinic become immersed in the relevant jurisdiction's criminal laws and come face-to-face with the judges, lawyers, and all of the other actors who play a role in local criminal practice. The law and the nature of legal practice would be quite different, of course, in a clinic specializing in public benefits or international human rights. However the various lawyering skills and methods, such as law reform, community consultation and education, and major litigation, are often common across specialties. And regardless of their specialty, these types of clinics enhance the school's clinical curriculum by providing students the opportunity to engage in the concentrated study of a particular area of legal aid practice. Due to their focus on a particular area of law, special expertise is more important in specialty clinics and therefore clinical faculty tend to be more directly engaged with their students on the merits of the clinic's cases. Specialization model clinics can also provide an opportunity to expose students to a range of practice and ethical issues unique to a law-reform or high-impact legal aid practice. This can include involving students in a variety of projects in the particular field in which the clinic is providing service other than direct client representation. Examples of these special clinical experiences include scientific and survey research, as part of an environmental law clinic, and legislative lobbying and drafting in a public policy clinic. (Lopez, 2001)

Community Model

The key feature of community model legal aid clinics is their focus on geographic or other communities. They represent an important aspect of the neighborhood law office concept discussed earlier, in that they are guided by community priorities and are committed to working together with—and empowering—the communities that they serve. Two examples of these types of clinics are described in detail in Chapter 11: the Kingsford Legal Centre (KLC) at the University of New South Wales in Australia and the Community Enterprise Clinic (CEC) at Columbia University Law School in the United States. The approach typified by the KLC and other law school-based community legal centers in Australia and Canada sees the clinic as a resource for the community as a whole and looks to the community directly in determining how to allocate its services. (White, 1997) The legal work undertaken by the clinic can therefore vary considerably depending on how the community identifies its legal needs. One community may seek assistance with respect to particular problems, such as a lack of public services or widespread consumer fraud, while others may choose to address broader social agendas, such as promoting community economic development. Many community model clinics in the United States fall into the latter category. The CEC represents a somewhat different approach to community legal aid work. That clinic also works with communities and community leaders, but its focus is on providing legal services—often transactional work—and other types of support to organizations that serve the community.

By working directly with communities and having their legal aid agendas defined by community needs, these community model clinics provide a unique educational opportunity for their students. Typically, community model clinics are located away from the law school building or require students to go out to the communities that they serve. As a result, students working in these clinics are able to see firsthand the conditions that they are asked to address. Moreover, the very nature of the work requires that students try to understand community legal needs from the community's perspective. Another set of educational opportunities unique to community clinics result from students being placed in nontraditional lawyer roles—for example, when clinic faculty and students become involved in community organizing and promoting legal literacy. Street Law and legal literacy projects, common elements in many clinical programs around the world, can also be seen in this sense as community model clinics.[3] Finally, community model clinics can also open students up to considering different types of

---

3. These types of clinics and their approach to community education are described in Chapters 15 and 16.

law practice, such as "community" or "collaborative" lawyering. (Tokarz et al., 2008; Trubek & Farnham, 2000; White, 1997)

Tension between Service to Clients and Education of Students

Although the legal aid clinic models described above are not exclusive and can be modified, combined, and implemented in any number of ways, all legal aid clinics incorporate providing legal services into the clinical learning experience. Legal aid is therefore necessarily an integral part of what clinic students are taught and the context in which they learn. On a practical level, this means that legal aid clinics serve two purposes at the same time: providing services to clients and educating law students. This gives rise to a natural tension between meeting the service goals of the relevant legal aid setup and fulfilling the educational mission of the host law school. Most clinicians reject the idea that these purposes conflict, pointing to what are often described as the twin goals of clinical legal education: instructing students in professional skills and values and instilling in them an understanding of and commitment to public professional responsibility. Instructing students in not only skills but also in the public role of the profession to include pursuing social justice, is most effective and meaningful when it takes place in a setting where the law faces social needs; in other words, in a legal aid clinic. (Alfieri, 2004; Dickson, 2000)

Nonetheless, the tension persists. For instance, in South Africa law clinics had always provided legal advice and assistance to the poor. The focus on access to justice was accentuated, however, during the early 1990s when the Legal Aid Board increasingly relied on university law clinics to address the growing demand for legal assistance. Consequently, law clinics gained access to external funding, established specialty clinics, and developed significant expertise in poverty law. According to de Klerk, "the strength of the [South African] clinical movement today is therefore attributable to its role in access to justice and has little to do with the appreciation of clinical legal education by law schools." Moreover, he goes on to conclude that the important role of clinics in improving access to justice has "tainted their image as educational institutions." (de Klerk, 2005 at 941–42)

The challenge is to find a balance between the goals of service provision and educational opportunity to optimize the clinical learning experience. The three models presented above can establish that balance, each in its own way. These models can also be structured, depending on the situation in a particular country, to strengthen the role of clinical education in the access to justice movement and the broader mission of legal education reform. An individual client model clinic, for example, can be structured to provide students the opportunity for highly effective experiential learning in a broad range of traditional lawyering skills, while offering at the same time a significant volume of legal aid services. These types of clinics can also serve in a sort of partnership with other legal aid organizations, including the local bar. Specialization model clinics provide an ideal setting for advanced study in particular areas of the law, as well as more sophisticated aspects of law practice including impact litigation and law reform activities. Their service role can be extended beyond their own client base by offering assistance to other legal aid practitioners in their area of expertise, possibly in collaboration with nonclinical colleagues. Community clinics expose their students to innovative and progressive approaches to the practice of law while both assisting and empowering the communities they serve. They also tend to work across disciplines, thereby providing unique services to their clients while exposing their students to interdisciplinary practice and the importance of strengthening ties between lawyers and other professionals.

TRANSFORMATIVE POTENTIAL IN LEGAL AID–BASED CLINICAL LEGAL EDUCATION PROGRAMS

Legal aid-based clinics have enormous transformative potential for both legal aid and clinical legal education. Some indications of that potential have been cited already and others are noted below. The full extent of this potential is yet to be realized, however, and harnessing that potential for the benefit of social justice and legal education reform is among the most important opportunities and challenges of the global clinical movement. (Bloch, 2008; White, 1997)

As noted already, legal aid-based clinical programs increase the amount of legal aid services available to the poor, marginalized, and disadvantaged—but they can, and must, do more. At a time when there was (and still is) significant unmet legal need, putting academics and students in a clinical setting where they work together to solve social problems brought about by poverty and inequality can stimulate—not only in themselves but also in the profession—a stronger commitment and motivation to provide new and additional legal services to the poor and disadvantaged. Traditionally, neither legal educators nor legal practitioners have paid much attention to the legal problems of the poor, marginalized, and disadvantaged. With the development of legal aid clinics, new areas of expertise have developed in the field of poverty law, such as residential housing, welfare payments, domestic violence, and consumer credit. The development of special expertise in these and other areas is crucial to the long-term success of legal aid. Equally important are new approaches to raising and addressing legal issues that affect the low-income community, many of which—impact litigation, alternative dispute resolution, and community organizing—can be explored most effectively in a legal aid clinic. Clinicians have long advocated a client-centered approach to lawyering that enhances services to clients and communities, giving voice to their concerns. (Dinerstein, 1990)

The key to the future success of the legal aid movement rests, however, with the next generation—or generations—of lawyers. The legal aid clinic provides the opportunity for students to study the intersection between poverty and law in a uniquely profound way. Students who have no prior life experience of poverty often have a form of "culture shock" when providing services in the clinic. (Voyvodic, 2001) Providing legal services to the poor can have a transformative effect on students when they see firsthand the operation of the legal system and its imperfections and negative impact on certain sections of the population. They develop a deep understanding of how legal doctrine and theory actually functions—or not. The experience of "justice" in action brings life to what they learn in the classroom and provides a powerful forum for critique. Clinical programs based in legal aid clinics encourage students to examine how the legal system works to disempower certain groups and to become involved in law reform activities. (Curran, 2004; Trubek and Cooper, 1999)

The stereotypical images of lawyers held by students are often exposed when students work in legal aid clinics. They have the opportunity to observe alternative models of law practice, such as client-centered lawyering, and to work in a setting where the concern for justice is paramount. The professional attribute of service to the public is observed in practice, which brings real meaning to the social justice role of lawyering. (Curran et al., 2005) This is enhanced if the students are provided with readings on paradigms of lawyering and encouraged to discuss the professional role and responsibilities of lawyers. Many law students enter their studies with altruism but it fades with constant exposure to the existing law school culture and black-letter law. At legal aid clinics, they often rediscover why they wanted to study law. Students' experience of working in legal aid clinics can thus present them with alternative career paths and opportunities.

Clinical legal education cannot do it all alone. Legal aid clinical programs can—and must—impact the law curriculum as a whole. Even within a clinical course, a classroom component can add a great deal. It can enable the discussion and critique of a range of access to justice and social justice issues beyond those raised in a particular clinic case and the links between poverty, discrimination, and injustice encountered in the students' clinic practice can be explored in greater depth. The clinical experience often impacts on the students' learning in general and their participation in other subjects and studies. It can also engender research into issues confronted in the clinic and lead to the development of courses on issues of inequality and injustice. The involvement of clinical staff in teaching these units further enhances discussion, learning, and research related to legal aid, systemic barriers to access to justice, and the broader professional obligation to provide access to justice to the poor, marginalized, and disadvantaged in society.

CONCLUSION

The provision of legal aid services has been—and continues to be—integral to many clinical legal education programs around the world. We have outlined why this is so and put forward three models of how this is done. Specific ways these models may develop will vary from country to country, and their transformative potential on the legal aid and clinical movements is yet to be fully realized. For that reason alone, redressing injustice and furthering equality before the law must remain a consistent theme and overwhelming concern in legal aid clinics around the world.

LIST OF REFERENCES

American Bar Ass'n, National Survey of the Civil Legal Needs of the Poor (1989).

Richard L. Abel, *Law without Politics: Legal Aid under Advanced Capitalism*, 32 UCLA L. R. 474 (1985).

Anthony V. Alfieri, *Teaching Ethics/Doing Justice*, 73 FORDHAM L. REV. 851, 857 (2004)

Frank S. Bloch & Iqbal S. Ishar, *Legal Aid, Public Service and Clinical Legal Education: Future Directions From India and the United States*, 12 MICH. J. INT'L L. 92 (1990).

Frank S. Bloch, *Access to Justice and the Global Clinical Movement*, 28 WASH. U. J.L. & POL'Y 111 (2008).

John S. Bradway, *The Nature of A Legal Aid Clinic*, 3 S. CAL. L. REV. 173 (1930).

John S. Bradway, *The Beginning of the Legal Clinic of the University of Southern California*, 2 S. CAL L. REV. 252 (1929).

Juliet M. Brodie, *Little Cases on the Middle Ground: Teaching Social Justice Lawyering in Neighborhood-based Community Lawyering Clinics*, 15 CLINICAL L. REV. 333 (2009).

Edgar S. Cahn & Jean C. Cahn, *The War on Poverty: A Civilian Perspective*, 73 YALE L. J. 1317 (1964).

Mauro Cappelletti & Bryant Garth, *Access to Justice: the World-wide Movement to Make Rights Effective—A General Report*, in ACCESS TO JUSTICE: A WORLD SURVEY (Mauro Cappelletti & Bryant Garth, eds. 1978).

Mauro Cappelletti, *Alternative Dispute Resolution Process Within the Framework of the World-Wide Access-to-Justice Movement*, 56 MOD. L. REV. 282 (1993).

Liz Curran, *Responsive Law Reform Initiatives by Students on Clinical Placement at LaTrobe*, 7 THE FLINDERS J. L. REFORM 287 (2004).

Liz Curran, Judith Dickson, & Mary Anne Noone, *Pushing the Boundaries or Preserving the Status Quo? Designing Clinical Programs to Teach Law Students a Deep Understanding of Ethical Practice*, 8 INT'L J. CLINICAL LEGAL EDUC. 104 (2005).

Judith Dickson, *Clinical Legal Education in the 21st Century: Still Education for Service?* 1 INT'L J. CLINICAL LEGAL EDUC. 33 (2000).

Robert D. Dinerstein, *Client-Centered Counseling: Reappraisal and Refinement*, 32 ARIZ. L. REV. 501 (1990).

Willem de Klerk, *University Law Clinics in South Africa*, 122 S. AFRICAN L.J. 929 (2005).

Jerome B. Falk, Jr. & Stuart R. Pollak, *Political Interference with Publicly Funded Lawyers: The CRLA Controversy and the Future of Legal Services*, 24 HASTINGS L.J. 599 (1973).

Government of India, Ministry of Law, Justice and Company Affairs, Equal Justice-Social Justice: Report of the Juridicare Committee (1977).

Laura G. Holland, *Invading the Ivory Tower: The History of Clinical Education at Yale Law School*, 49 J. LEGAL EDUC. 504 (1999).

EARL JOHNSON, JR., JUSTICE AND REFORM: THE FORMATIVE YEARS OF THE OEO LEGAL SERVICES PROGRAM (Russell Sage Foundation 1974).

Quintin Johnstone, *Law School Legal Aid Clinics*, 3 J. LEGAL EDUC. 535, 541 (1951).

Legal Services Corporation, Serving the Civil Legal Needs of Low-Income Americans: A Special Report to Congress (2000).

Antoinette Sedillo Lopez, *Learning Through Service in a Clinical Setting: The Effect of Specialization on Social Justice and Skills Training*, 7 CLINICAL L. REV. 307 (2001).

Mary Anne Noone, *Australian Community Legal Centres—The University Connection, in* EDUCATING FOR JUSTICE: SOCIAL VALUES AND LEGAL EDUCATION (Jeremy Cooper & Louise G. Trubek eds., Ashgate / Dartmouth 1997).

MARY ANNE NOONE & STEPHEN TOMSEN, LAWYERS IN CONFLICT: AUSTRALIAN LAWYERS AND LEGAL AID (Federation Press 2006).

Alan Paterson, *Financing Legal Services: A Comparative Perspective, in* RESOURCING CIVIL JUSTICE (Alan Paterson & Tamara Goriely eds., Oxford University Press 1996).

Pamela N. Phan, *Clinical Legal Education in China: In Pursuit of a Culture of Law and a Mission of Social Justice*, 8 YALE HUM. RTS. & DEV. L.J. 117 (2005).

Charles Reich, *The New Property*, 73 YALE L.J. 733, 746 (1964).

RONALD SACKVILLE, LAW AND POVERTY IN AUSTRALIA: SECOND MAIN REPORT OF THE AUSTRALIAN GOVERNMENT COMMISSION OF INQUIRY INTO POVERTY (AGPS 1975).

Karen Tokarz et al., *Conversations on "Community Lawyering": The Newest (Oldest) Wave in Clinical Legal Education*, 28 WASH. U. J.L. & POL'Y 359 (2008).

Louise G. Trubek & Jeremy Cooper, *Rethinking Lawyering for the Underrepresented Around the World: An Introductory Essay, in* EDUCATING FOR JUSTICE AROUND THE WORLD (Louise G. Trubek & Jeremy Cooper eds. 1999).

Louise G. Trubek & Jennifer J. Farnham, *Social Justice Collaboratives: Multidisciplinary Practices for People*, 7 CLINICAL L.R. 227 (2000).

Rose Voyvodic, *"Considerable Promise and Troublesome Aspects": Theory and Methodology of Clinical Legal Education*, 20 WINDSOR Y.B. ACCESS JUST. 111 (2001).

Lucie White, *The Transformative Potential of Clinical Legal Education*, 35 OSGOODE HALL L. J. 603 (1997).

Richard Wilson, *Training for Justice: The Global Reach of Clinical Legal Education*, 22 PENN STATE INTERNATIONAL L. REV. 421 (2004).

Stephen Wizner & Jane Aiken, *Teaching and Doing: The Role of Law School Clinics in Enhancing Access To Justice*, 73 FORDHAM L. REV. 997 (2004).

11. COMMUNITY LAW CLINICS
Teaching Students, Working with Disadvantaged Communities

ANNA CODY AND BARBARA SCHATZ

Community law clinics take multiple forms. Some focus on the representation of community enterprises—nonprofit organizations and small businesses primarily serving low-income communities. Others are rooted in particular communities and handle a variety of matters, basing their caseloads on the needs that community members deem most urgent. Some focus on particular problems, such as land or housing issues, or on particular strategies, such as mobilizing communities through the building of coalitions designed to enhance the power of marginalized groups.

We will describe two different models of community law clinics in this chapter, the Kingsford Legal Centre of the University of New South Wales in Sydney, Australia (KLC) and the Community Enterprise Clinic at Columbia Law School in New York City (CEC), highlighting their similarities and differences and the benefits and challenges of each. Although these are only two models of many, they illustrate both the common features of community clinics and some of the choices and trade-offs they confront.

For reasons of history, geography, funding, community expectations, and approaches to pedagogy, these two clinics are quite different. KLC is both a teaching clinic and a community legal center, part of a larger movement of legal centers in Australia. As such, it is mandated by its funders to meet the varied legal needs of individuals in one community in Sydney while also doing statewide work on employment and discrimination issues. Students work under the supervision of full-time staff attorneys as well as faculty to handle a high-volume legal practice, often under considerable time pressure. The CEC is a law school-based clinic in which students, under faculty supervision, handle transactional matters for nonprofits and small businesses from all over New York City. The CEC is not limited to a particular community and is free to choose the clients and projects that it thinks will best meet the needs of students and disadvantaged communities.

Notwithstanding these differences, the CEC and the KLC share—along with other kinds of community clinics—some important characteristics. They expose students to the law as it impacts the disadvantaged and encourage students to think critically about the role of law in society and how it can be used to further social justice. They take a holistic, interdisciplinary approach, trying to understand clients' legal problems in context and often involving professionals ranging from social workers to business planners to help achieve client goals. They see clients and their communities as setting the agenda for the work, with lawyers serving as partners who can contribute expertise but do not have a monopoly on the knowledge and skills needed to solve problems. (Tokarz et al., 2008) They try to work in ways that build the capacity of communities and community organizations, emphasizing community legal education as a way of empowering clients to address their own problems. They see law reform as a key part of their mandate. These clinics exist in various forms throughout the world, from the Philippines, where students and faculty at Ateneo University in Manila partner with farmers on land rights issues, to countries of the former Soviet Union, where clinics strengthen civil society through their work with nonprofits.

All community clinics must resolve some basic questions. How should "community" be defined? Is a geographic focus important or can community refer to a client constituency, such as immigrants or low-wage workers, or to a set of institutions, like nonprofits? Is it essential that the clinic be based physically in the community that it serves? What kinds of clients will the clinic serve and how will they be chosen? Should the clinic be open to providing any kind of legal services needed or requested by the community or is it acceptable for clinics to limit their practices to certain areas? Is there a role for the lawyer's goals and priorities or is the "vision" the sole prerogative of the community? How does the clinic see itself as advancing social justice? And how does it balance two priorities—educating students and helping communities?

COLUMBIA LAW SCHOOL'S COMMUNITY ENTERPRISE CLINIC

Begun in 1985, at a time of cutbacks in federally funded legal services, the CEC tries to help low-income communities by assisting the nonprofit organizations and small businesses which provide services to those communities and help build assets within them. Its premise is that representing institutions rather than individuals—for example, helping organizations which develop affordable housing rather than representing individuals threatened with eviction because they cannot pay their rent—is an effective way of maximizing the benefits it provides. Based at Columbia Law School, the CEC serves disadvantaged communities from all over New York City, including Harlem, the neighborhood just north of the university, as well as organizations that work abroad.

Cases and Projects
Many of the CEC's nonprofit clients are young organizations seeking to build a structure through which to meet community needs. Most are service providers, ranging from literacy programs and food pantries to after-school programs for children and housing programs for recently released prisoners. Some focus on community organizing; for example, one client works with victims of predatory

lending, galvanizing them into action to protect their homes and alerting others to the problem. The CEC tries to get all of these organizations off to a healthy start, helping them not only to form a legal entity and qualify for tax benefits, but also to think carefully about the roles and responsibilities of stakeholders and to develop policies and practices for effective and responsible governance.

Other clients are mature nonprofits needing help with the legal aspects of implementing their programs, such as contracts, leases, governance and employment policies, protection of intellectual property, risk management, and issues relating to expansion or advocacy work. A particular clinic focus has been "social enterprise": helping nonprofits interested in developing businesses in order to provide jobs or job training for their constituents or to generate income to support their charitable programs. The clinic's small business clients seek to create jobs and to deliver services lacking in their neighborhoods and need help in creating workable legal and financing structures, as well as help with the legal aspects of conducting their businesses.

Clients apply for CEC services, and the clinic tries to take into account the needs of both the community and its students in choosing which clients to accept. It looks for organizations which are unable to afford legal services and which are making, or have the potential to make, important contributions to the welfare of their communities. It also tries to be responsive to changing community needs. For example, when the federal income support program for families ended automatic entitlement in favor of a requirement that beneficiaries work, the clinic, which previously represented only nonprofits, began to represent microenterprises that could contribute to the financial self-sufficiency of needy families. On the nonprofit side, the clinic expanded its services to groups working in disadvantaged communities abroad because these organizations had more difficulty in finding pro bono representation than did nonprofits serving New York City organizations.

The demands of pedagogy also play an important role in the clinic's caseload. The clinic's premise is that students learn the most when they have the primary relationship with—and responsibility for—their clients, not only for legal work but also for building and sustaining client relationships. One implication of this approach is a preference for relatively small and discrete matters which allow students to see their matters from beginning to end and to serve as the chief lawyers on their matters, rather than as assistants to the clinic supervisor. Although clients frequently request and receive services that go beyond their initial requests, the clinic typically does not undertake commitments to clients that are expected to exceed the two semesters that students spend in the Clinic. The students' caseloads are small in order to give them adequate time to plan and reflect (they work in teams of two and typically handle no more than six to nine matters in an academic year), but large enough to expose students to a range of legal skills in a variety of contexts and to enough community concerns and enough different kinds of people to "test . . . [their] assumptions—about poor people, about law practice, and about how they come together." (Brodie, 2009 at 337)

To give students a broader perspective on the ways they can use their legal training to promote social justice, they also participate in community education and law/regulatory reform. The legal education work—workshops and publications on legal topics for both community organizations and small businesses—requires students to think about how to make complex legal concepts comprehensible and to grapple with their assumptions about the role of the lawyer and the abilities of clients. Helping organizations to understand what they can do on their own, when they should consult a lawyer or other professional, and how they can work effectively with a lawyer challenges students to figure out how to build client capacity rather than monopolizing expertise. Students also help to identify problems that cut across client communities and to structure and participate in opportunities for organizations to engage in collective problem solving. Examples include a clinic conference on the barriers facing microentrepreneurs in New York City and the creation—together with Columbia's Business and Engineering Schools—of a "facilitated peer network" designed to help Harlem businesses develop solutions to common problems.

The CEC's law and regulatory reform work gives students a window into another route for promoting change. One of the clinic's recent projects sought solutions to New York's uniquely difficult process for forming nonprofit corporations. Students participated in meetings with officials of two key state agencies, prepared proposals for procedural reform, including proposals for revamping one agency's Web site, and wrote memoranda analyzing issues requiring statutory change.

Pedagogy

The CEC uses two main methods to help students make the transition from being students to being professionals: a weekly seminar and direct supervision of student casework. In the seminar, students learn the substantive law relating to nonprofits and small businesses, and study lawyering skills and professional responsibility in the special context of representing organizations rather than individuals. The classes on client counseling, for example, address whether the lawyer is responsible for ensuring a democratic decision-making process or whether respect for the client's autonomy requires leaving the decision-making process to the client. (Ellmann, 1992 at 1149–1153) The seminar introduces students to the economic, social, and political structure within which their nonprofit and small business clients operate and raises questions of efficacy and fairness: Who benefits and who is harmed by a regulatory system that makes it burdensome to establish a nonprofit or severely limits the ability of nonprofits to use the political system to accomplish their purposes? How can lawyers address the problems posed for start-up entrepreneurs by rules prohibiting the sale of goods made in home kitchens unless the kitchens are modified in ways that low-income entrepreneurs cannot afford? The seminar also introduces students to the kinds of non-legal issues with which their clients must grapple and to some of the other professionals (e.g., business planners, management consultants, community organizers) who may be helpful to their clients and with whom students and clients will need to develop effective working relationships. Students read the literature on lawyering for low-income communities and are asked to examine their own work with clients in light of the models proposed, as well as to critique the literature based on their own experiences. Seminar time is also used for class discussion of problems posed by particular cases and joint efforts to generate solutions.

Student pairs meet each week with the clinic supervisor to plan and review their work. To encourage them to be proactive in identifying issues and figuring out what help they need from the supervisor, students prepare agendas for these meetings and take responsibility for running them. The meetings are also an opportunity to discuss students' progress on "learning goals" that each student establishes at the beginning of the term. Sometimes the learning goals relate explicitly to social justice (for example, to learn about community needs and how lawyers can address them); sometimes they relate to personal or professional development (to learn to be a better collaborator or a better listener; to inspire confidence; to enjoy work more). The CEC takes both sorts seriously in the belief that lawyers who understand themselves and their motives are more likely to be effective lawyers for communities.

Working with Clients

The clinic works hard to further social justice values within the lawyer-client relationship, encouraging students to try to understand clients' perspectives, goals, and values and to find ways of working with organizations that further the clients' skills and contribute to their sense of efficacy and empowerment. With respect to decisions large and small, students think carefully about how to avoid hierarchical relationships and build collaborative ones. Should the initial meeting be at the clinic office or the client's premises? How should the obligations of each party be framed in the retainer agreement? How should the work be divided between students and client? What if the client prefers the students to make most of the decisions? What if the client—or a few representatives of the client—makes decisions that the students think may not serve the best interests of the organization or of the community? How should students deal with power imbalances among group members resulting from differences in English language proficiency or immigration status?

A frequent issue is whether and when the clinic should become involved in issues which are not strictly legal. When working with small businesses, how much responsibility should the students take on for making sure that the business model is likely to work? In representing organizations developing housing, how much responsibility should the students assume for the development process as a whole? How should the students respond to requests for help in building a board or developing a fund-raising program—or volunteering in the organization's programs? The clinic's basic approach is to try first to understand what the client needs and the role the client is hoping the clinic will play. Student preferences are also taken into account. Some students—like some lawyers—gravitate naturally to the "business" issues as well as the legal issues. Others—again like some lawyers—prefer to define their role more narrowly. Part of the clinic's role is to help students understand both their own preferences and the ways they can provide value to clients. When client and students both seek an expanded role, the clinic tries to ensure that students are competent in the nonlegal sphere (for example, by arranging a collaboration between the students and an organization which provides management consulting to small nonprofits). When student goals and capacities don't line up with client needs, students work hard to help clients find alternatives.

THE UNIVERSITY OF NEW SOUTH WALES LAW FACULTY'S KINGSFORD LEGAL CENTRE

Kingsford Legal Centre provides legal services to the population within the Randwick and Botany local council areas in Sydney. KLC is also part of an Australia-wide community legal center (CLC) network consisting of approximately 200 centers that operate within a social justice and social reform philosophy combining advice and casework, community legal education, and campaign/law reform work. KLC's funding comes from a variety of sources, including the state and federal legal aid services program, the university, local municipal government, and foundations; KLC also benefits from pro bono seconded solicitors from large corporate law firms. The funding through the legal aid services program means that staff at the center has ongoing advice and casework responsibilities in addition to teaching responsibilities. Only one of KLC's nine positions is an academic position.

The center provides free legal advice to anyone in the local area and, with respect to discrimination, to anyone in the state. In deciding whether to take on a case, the center looks at the specific circumstances of the client, including income, ethnicity, gender, age, and any disability. It also examines whether clients are able to advocate for themselves, what other sources of free legal help are available, and whether a case has the potential to change the law for the greater good. The center tends to take on cases in its areas of specialization—discrimination and employment—and sometimes will focus on a particular area of law such as pregnancy discrimination. In deciding whether to take on a community organizing or other project, KLC looks to repeat patterns emerging from its casework and to issues raised at interagency meetings and by governmental law reform inquiries.

KLC's clinical courses include a "generalist" clinic, an employment law clinic, and a family law clinic. The courses are offered as an elective subject to fourth- and fifth-year students and involve attendance at the center for one or one and a half eight-hour days per week. In each twelve-week semester, there are six students in each of the employment law and family law clinics and twenty-four in the generalist clinic. Up to 500 other law students interview clients at the center as part of a clinical component in their legal ethics course. There is also a course for first-year indigenous law students focusing on communication skills, interviewing, and the legal aid system. In 2010 a new clinic in conjunction with the Hong Kong Refugee Advice clinic begins, with students based in Hong Kong for eight weeks and representing clients seeking refugee status.

KLC's Definition of Community Lawyering

At Kingsford Legal Centre, community lawyering means working with communities to help disadvantaged people improve their lives by addressing individual problems, by dealing with underlying issues that affect the whole group, and by helping to empower community members to assert their rights. The approach is nonhierarchical and the methods are varied, going beyond legal advice and representation to include use of the media, education about rights, discussion with communities of the pros and cons of direct action, and encouragement to participate in law reform. Clients are encouraged to do as much as possible in their own cases. Collaboration with community organizations and nongovernmental organizations (NGOs) is an important part of the approach, as community organizing is an important part of what "community development" means in Australia, and both terms are used to refer to the same sorts of activities and approaches.

Teaching Students to Work in the Community

The meaning of "community" and how KLC works within the community is integral to its clinical curriculum. In the developed world it is sometimes difficult for students to think within the concept of community. Many students don't easily identify with a community themselves, and thus to unpack the concept is challenging. An additional challenge is helping students apply classroom learning to the real world. As recognized in the Australian Commonwealth review of community legal centers report, "The problems people face in their everyday lives are not 'well-structured.' They are quite messy and 'ill-structured.'" (Imai, 2003 at 202) This can be challenging for students who are used to analyzing case law in the context of a particular course or resolving neatly structured problems in an exam context. Real life is hardly ever so neatly delineated. Client contact at KLC is, for some students, the first exposure to "real law" since entering law school.

KLC utilizes a number of methods to teach and support students within a community lawyering framework, as well as to teach legal practice skills.

These include individual casework supervision, morning tutorials, and a seminar program, each of which is discussed below.

Each student is allocated between two and five casework files with a different clinical supervisor on each file. The cases generally involve discrimination law, employment, debt, traffic and other fines, victims' compensation, or housing. Students contact the client, draft letters and legal documents, and, in some cases, represent clients in negotiations or in conciliation hearings. Regular supervision sessions provide students an opportunity to analyze their client interactions critically, dealing with questions such as: why isn't the client returning our calls?, should we talk to the client's caseworker rather than the client?, what is the role of the client's partner and family in this case?, and how do we deal with the unrealistic expectations of the client? In discussing these questions, clinical supervisors encourage the student to understand more fully the life of the client—cultural background, health, employment, family—as well as to understand the client's issues from a broader social justice and community-based perspective.

Students work on more complex and generally longer discrimination cases, as well as on smaller matters; students have less responsibility in the more complex and longer cases but also learn important lessons. The center also takes on cases in minor criminal matters where the client is pleading guilty so that students can prepare and present the plea in the local court. But for the students, the center would not take on these cases.

Daily morning tutorials provide an additional opportunity for students to analyze their responses to clients in interviews and casework and to discuss collaboratively some of the issues faced by the clients and the issues raised for students and staff. For example, the legal process may be so slow as to not be a good option for a client; or, a student may think the center is wasting its time taking on a particular client's case.

Weekly two-hour seminar classes address topics relevant to community legal practice. Examples include a class on working with challenging clients that aims to encourage students to see the client as a whole person, not just a legal problem, and a class that addresses indigenous clients and communities that examines, through the voices of indigenous people, the experience of colonization and the law. The class on law reform and campaign work situates casework within the three-pronged approach of community legal centers described above. The legal skills classes are taught within the broader framework of asking "who are our clients?" and "who is our community?" The class on interviewing involves looking at the students' own identities and the impact they have on the students' interviewing. The seminars are presented in a workshop format with a lot of small group work, in line with the center's community lawyering style and with a view to imparting a collaborative approach of working with communities. (Imai, 2003)

Community Development/Community Organizing

Community development/organizing projects are another way KLC teaches students about community. These projects aim to enable disadvantaged people to advocate for themselves and their legal rights and to educate them about how the law can be used to assert those rights. A recent example of one such project illustrates student involvement in community development projects.

In 2004–2006 KLC, together with a range of other organizations, produced a statewide and Australia-wide report documenting the status of the human rights of women, which was presented to the Convention on the Elimination of All Forms of Discrimination Against Women (CEDAW) Committee in New York in 2006. The process was collaborative, and involved working with other NGOs around the country. The "community" in the context of this project comprised individual women as well as NGOs working with diverse communities of women. Students were involved in organizing various women's events that provided content for the report, including public consultations and an all-day national training event that included theater, storytelling, and small group work around rights themes. The students were then asked to write up sections of the report to reflect the women's voices from the events, and to do so in a concise way that would be appropriate for a UN body. The students were thus able to learn not only about diversity in community and what being responsive to community needs means on a statewide scale, but also about advocacy arising out of community needs.

BENEFITS, CHALLENGES, AND TRADE-OFFS

The CEC and KLC benefit students and clients in a number of important ways. Both clinics expose students to the law as it impacts disadvantaged clients and communities, encourage students to think critically about the role of law as a tool to promote social justice, and offer them the chance to deeply engage with lawyering in this context. Both help students to integrate law, ethics, and lawyering skills in ways that they see as critical to their legal education, often setting them on a new career path. Students in both clinics learn about communities and problems to which they have never been exposed and discover effective ways to be involved with disadvantaged communities throughout their careers, through representation, community education, law reform, and the joint problem-solving involved in bringing organizations and individuals together to explore common issues.

CEC students benefit particularly from the close supervision of full-time faculty, the opportunity to be the primary lawyer on their matters, the attention to their individual development as professionals, and the exposure to the world of community entrepreneurs. The students, some of whom themselves hope to create their own nonprofits or businesses, are inspired by clients who have the will to create and sustain institutions serving low-income and disadvantaged communities despite sometimes daunting obstacles. The CEC's clients appreciate the high-quality legal services they receive in the context of lawyer-client relationships that are respectful of their accomplishments and abilities and that keep them at the center of the struggle for social justice. The tangible evidence of their accomplishments, from new housing facilities to better outcomes for disadvantaged children, is a source of satisfaction to all. Many clinic graduates go on to represent nonprofits on a pro bono basis and to serve on their governing boards, sometimes continuing to work with the clients they first represented in the clinic. Providing young lawyers the skills and instilling in them the motivation to represent community enterprises in ways that empower their clients is an important aspect of the clinic's social justice impact.

KLC students benefit particularly from the opportunity to be part of a community law office and to see how the office handles a high-volume caseload of clients with critical and immediate needs. The exposure to poor or disadvantaged people's lives—the difficulties they face and the ways they deal with them—is eye-opening, inspiring, and often transformative in the ways that they later decide to use their legal skills. Students and clients also profit from KLC's strategic response to some of the longer term, entrenched issues which it sees in the communities it works with, particularly its community legal education initiatives, its law reform work, and its community organizing efforts. Students learn about the legal aid system and its limitations as well as seeing some of the limitations of the law and the legal system in dealing with disadvantaged people's issues.

Both programs also see challenges and trade-offs in their modes of operation. Like other clinics which work with communities in the pursuit of social justice outcomes, they face a multitude of questions ranging from the definition of the "community" to the appropriate role for the lawyer. Two particular challenges, both discussed below, are operating within a community framework and balancing the teaching and community service missions.

Challenges in Articulating and Adhering to a Community Empowerment/ Community Development Model

The use of a community organizing/development framework is a challenge for all Australian community legal centers, including KLC. The current challenge is less about teaching students to work within a community organizing/development model than about ensuring that the clinic/community legal center itself works from a community organizing/development model rather than an individual casework model.

In the most recent Australian Commonwealth review of community legal centers, the integral nature of community legal education and law reform to community legal centers was recognized by all stakeholders. The National Association of Community Legal Centres (NACLC) submitted:

> Law reform is a key element of the [community legal centre] service delivery model. It is an effective and efficient way to address the systemic problems facing some clients, complementing the important face-to-face individual client work. Law reform work can deliver far-reaching outcomes for clients,

resulting in improvements to laws, policies and practices. (National Association of Community Centres, 2007 at 63)

The emphasis of CLCs on this work is patchy however. Rich discusses these issues in a 2009 report, *Reclaiming Community Legal Centres*, in which she analyses the nature of most of the law reform work CLCs do—and thus teach—and concludes that it is ad hoc, reactive, unplanned, and not strategic. (Rich, 2009) This is a valid criticism; CLCs need to devote more time and resources to addressing the issue if they are serious about being effective community legal centers and teaching clinics.

It can be difficult to teach a different model if we don't know it ourselves. Ideally, KLC would respond to issues as framed by its community and attempt to make the law and legal system fairer as much through systemic work as through its individual client work. However, the center can be diverted too easily from this systemic and community work in favor of individual client work. Systemic law reform and community organizing are not what clinical teachers learned in law school and teaching it is thus a "learn-on-the-job" process. Working within a social justice model is not taught as the main aim of lawyers or as one of a lawyer's ethical duties. (Rand, 2006) It falls, therefore, upon community lawyering–oriented clinics and community legal centers to emphasize this aspect of the lawyer's role.

It can be a real challenge for KLC staff lawyers and students to truly work with community effectively. Not surprisingly, lawyers often are more naturally inclined to go for the "hot" case rather than engage in the hard slog that is involved in community building. The immediacy and tangible, measurable goals of individual casework make it much easier than longer term, less tangible community lawyering work. "Identifying and managing effective community projects and collaborations can be complicated and time-consuming, and even more so when that work must be balanced with different clinical activities." (Seielstad, 2002 at 494) Lawyers generally know how to run individual cases, not how to run campaigns or resource collective mobilizing efforts. While KLC works on community projects, this is an area where it could develop further and partner more effectively with other community organizations and community members. To this end, KLC tries to engage students in longer term projects such as the CEDAW shadow report and relationship-building with local communities.

The CEC works exclusively to build and sustain community organizations, and in that sense devotes 100 percent of its efforts to community development and community empowerment. There are challenges nonetheless, one of which is deciding which organizations to represent. The CEC has an eclectic vision of the kinds of organizations and services that promote social and economic justice and thus represents a huge variety of organizations from many different neighborhoods. The problem is that the request for the clinic's services exceeds its capacity, and it is not always easy to determine which of the many organizations that seek its help will, in the long run, make the most important contributions to their communities. The clinic's citywide scope, though advantageous in many ways, means that it does not have an intimate knowledge of any of the neighborhoods it serves and makes it difficult to identify individuals and organizations in each neighborhood able to provide good advice on unmet needs and the organizations best positioned to address them.

The larger question is whether the clinic would have greater impact if it identified some target problems or articulated some desired results, and then looked for clients who would contribute to a solution or otherwise advance its goals. Some community law clinics do take this approach, drawing on the views of Gary Bellow, one of the pioneers of clinical legal education in the United States, who believed that lawyers without a political and social vision of their own tend to serve the status quo. (Bellow, 1996) One contemporary clinical teacher writes of the importance of identifying a "defensible set of community goals," making sure that they align with the lawyer's own goals and then using these goals as a basis for deciding which clients to represent. (Diamond, 2000 at 115–18) Another argues that the job of lawyers is to stimulate "collective mobilization" and is critical of clinics that focus on the "microcosm" of the lawyer-client relationship; his clinic takes on cases for individuals only when they fit into a larger strategy for building power among low-wage workers. (Ashar, 2008) Figuring out whether the vision should come from the clients or from the clinic, and how the two mesh, is a major task for all community law clinics.

The issue of identifying the clients for whom a clinic works has a procedural dimension as well. The CEC asks clients to fill out a written request for assistance, and the requests are an efficient way of identifying organizations that seem to be addressing important needs and have issues that fit the clinic's pedagogical goals. Some community clinics use a very different approach, asking students to spend time at community meetings or community centers listening to the problems posed and trying to work out how their clinic might be helpful in addressing them. The question is whether this approach does more to keep a community law clinic focused on the types of problems that the community deems most urgent than CEC's approach, which basically sees community organizations as proxies for the communities they serve in terms of articulating community needs. Certainly one advantage for students of attending community meetings is the exposure to the unstructured problems with which lawyers often have to deal and which offer scope for creative and multipronged problem-solving. Another possible advantage is students' firsthand exposure to the sometimes painful realities that nonprofit clients address and from which the CEC's approach insulates them. The cost of this exposure would be less time spent on the concrete legal needs of community organizations. Clients unable to put their issues into a legal framework would benefit; the clinic's typical nonprofit and business clients would not. CEC is currently trying to strike a balance by encouraging students to be more proactive in identifying unmet legal needs—as they have done recently in working with the Harlem businesses in Columbia's facilitated peer network.

The broad question for CEC is whether changes or additions to its current practice—for example, additional efforts to understand and address some of the structural issues that lead to inequality or more complex development projects aimed at bringing new housing or commercial resources to low-income communities—would enable it to make a more effective contribution to community development. One factor for CEC and other community clinics to consider is the availability of other competent professional help. In New York City, it is no doubt easier to find pro bono representation for organizations needing transactional work than for community organizing efforts.

Balancing the Service and Teaching Missions

Like other kinds of clinics, community clinics need to manage the tension between the needs of students and the needs of the community. At KLC, the tension arises from its dual identity as both a community legal center and a teaching clinic. For example, KLC recently commenced an indigenous outreach legal service in response to community needs and as an initial step in improving the center's accessibility to indigenous clients. The center initially decided that bringing students to interview clients in the early stages of development of the service would be unwise because it could detract from, or interfere with, the process of building a relationship of trust within the community. Although KLC ultimately decided to include students so that they could have exposure to KLC's community development activities, the experience illustrates the tensions that can arise for a community-oriented teaching clinic.

Another tension can arise when, particularly at the beginning of a project, a clinical program doesn't want to risk the relationships it is building with community by relying solely on students with little experience and with only a short-term commitment. In this situation it may decide that the "face" in that relationship needs to be a permanent worker rather than a student. KLC experienced this tension recently in its work on an education program for high school students around domestic violence and sexual assault called the "Love Bites program." This was a joint community response to the high levels of violence in the community and involved KLC's commitment to offer a one-day "prevention" program to all local high school students. While they might come to a different decision with another project, in this instance KLC staff decided not to involve the clinical students in the program and instead trained for and delivered the program themselves.

Involving students in law reform poses additional difficulties. It is difficult to engage students when there is a short time-frame for submissions to law reform commissions and not all students are capable of the high-level writing required for this type of work. This means, in reality, that KLC's work with students in law reform can be patchy. But it can also be a particularly rewarding clinical experience.[1] For example, KLC made a submission in 2008 to the Productivity Commission on the need for paid parental leave. There was enough lead-time for a student to draft the first version of the submission. Together the student and clinical supervisor could then augment, edit, and finalize the submission, and both the student and the instructor appeared before the commission to give oral evidence.

A lot of the law reform work which KLC engages in is longer term, slow coalition building, and it is difficult to introduce students into this work when they are with the center for only twelve weeks. Another example where the center had mixed success was its participation in a recent federal human rights consultation and the preparation of a written submission. Students were active in gathering some case studies and organizing consultation sessions. But due to a short semester of twelve weeks, they could not actually run training sessions, and the submission drafting was done by clinical staff rather than students.

At one level, the CEC experiences little tension between student and community needs. There is high demand for the kinds of services the clinic provides and—judging by client surveys, unsolicited client comments, and student evaluations—both constituencies feel well served. As with KLC, however, issues arise when the clinic goes beyond its typical caseload to work on law reform issues or when matters for individual organizations become more complex than anticipated. These situations put the clinic supervisor rather than the student in "first chair" position, either because the project goes on for longer than the time students spend in the clinic, such as the multiyear effort to reform the way New York State regulatory agencies deal with nonprofits, or because a case expands or becomes too difficult for students without significant supervisor participation.

From a pedagogical point of view there are some advantages to having students work as junior lawyers on matters where the clinic supervisor has the primary client relationship. These types of matters give students opportunities to learn by observing the supervisor's lawyering, to work collaboratively with the supervisor, to see complex transactions close-up, and perhaps to acquire a deeper understanding of the goals and struggles of particular communities and community groups based on the supervisor's long-term involvement with them. The question is whether these benefits outweigh the often transformative experience of having real responsibility for the full lawyer-client relationship. In the end, the question is how student lawyers best serve or learn to serve social justice, and to this question there is no doubt not one right answer.

---

1. An externship program at the Australian Law Reform Commission is described in detail in Chapter 14.

CONCLUSION

The two clinics discussed in this chapter, Columbia Law School's Community Enterprise Clinic and the University of New South Wales Law School's Kingsford Legal Centre, are part of a growing number of community law clinics throughout the world. Like other such clinics, they seek both to meet community needs and to provide good learning experiences for students. Their choices as to how best to do so differ, however, in part because of their differing environments and differing mandates—one a community legal services office and one a law school–based clinic.

One of the keys issues for both KLC and CEC, as for other community law clinics, is identifying the best role for the lawyer in working with communities and community organizations. Community-oriented clinical teachers have proposed many different approaches: "collaborative" work that stresses the lawyer's intimate involvement in the community and the importance of drawing on clients' problem-solving abilities (Lopez, 1992); "facilitative" approaches in which lawyers leave the substantive work to clients and play a supportive and respectful but more traditional role (Marsico, 1995); "integrative" work in which the lawyer seeks to replicate the role of in-house counsel, advising on legal, programmatic and strategic issues in the course of a long-term relationship (Foster & Glick, 2007); and "activist" approaches in which the lawyer plays a key role in identifying, evaluating, and implementing strategies for building the power of low-income people. (Diamond, 2000) The best approach for a particular community clinic depends on a variety of factors unique to each clinic—the needs of the community and the availability of other legal resources, theories of how social change happens, ideas about the cases and projects that will best support student learning and about the lessons that it is most important for students to learn, mandates imposed by funders or law schools, and the strengths and preferences of clinical faculty.

Whatever the approach, one of the huge benefits from any community clinic is that students have the opportunity to work for, and with, some dynamic and strong clients who have clear ideas about how to improve their lives and their communities. This opportunity often transforms the ways students think about social justice and their role in achieving it.

LIST OF REFERENCES

Sameer Ashar, *Law Clinics and Collective Mobilization*, 14 CLINICAL L. REV. 355 (2008).

Gary Bellow, *Steady Work: A Practitioner's Reflections on Political Lawyering*, 31 HARV. CR.-C.L. L. REV. 297 (1996).

Juliet M. Brodie, *Little Cases on the Middle Ground: Teaching Social Justice Lawyering in Neighborhood-based Community Lawyering Clinics*, 15 CLINICAL L. REV. 333 (2009).

Michael Diamond, *Community Lawyering: Visiting the Old Neighborhood*, 32 COLUMBIA HUM. RTS. L. REV. 67 (2000).

Stephen Ellmann, *Client-Centeredness Multiplied: Individual Autonomy and Collective Mobilization in Public Interest Lawyers' Representation of Groups*, 78 VA. L. REV. 1103 (1992).

Sheila R. Foster and Brian Glick, *Integrative Lawyering: Navigating the Political Economy of Urban Redevelopment*, 95 CAL. L. REV. 1999 (2007).

Shin Imai, *A Counter-Pedagogy for Social Justice: Core Skills for Community-based Lawyering*, 9 CLINICAL L. REV. 195 (2002–2003).

GERALD P. LÓPEZ, REBELLIOUS LAWYERING: ONE CHICANO'S VISION OF PROGRESSIVE LAW PRACTICE (Westview Press 1992).

Richard Marsico, *Working for Social Change and Preserving Client Autonomy: Is There a Role for "Facilitative" Lawyering?*, 1 CLINICAL L. REV. 639 (1995).

Submission from the National Association of Community Legal Centres to the Commonwealth Attorney-General, Regarding the Internal Review of the Commonwealth Community Legal Services Program (March 2007), *available at* http://www.naclc.org.au/multiattachments/2327/DocumentName/NACLC_Review_Mar07.pdf.

Nicole Rich, Victoria Law Foundation, Reclaiming Community Legal Centres: Maximising Our Potential So We Can Help Our Clients Realise Theirs (April 2009), http://www.consumeraction.org.au/downloads/VLFCLCFellowship07-08reportWebFinal.pdf.

Spencer Rand, *Teaching Law Students to Practice Social Justice: An Interdisciplinary Search for Help Through Social Work's Empowerment Approach*, 13 CLINICAL L. REV. 459 (2006).

Andrea M. Seielstad, *Community Building as a Means of Teaching Creative, Cooperative and Complex Problem Solving in Clinical Education*, 8 CLINICAL L. REV. 445 (2002).

Karen Tokarz, Nancy L. Cook, Susan Brooks, & Brenda Bratton Blom, *Conversations on "Community Lawyering": The Newest (Oldest) Wave in Clinical Legal Education*, 28 WASH. U. J.L. & POL'Y 359 (2008).

12. ADDRESSING LAWYER COMPETENCE, ETHICS, AND PROFESSIONALISM

NIGEL DUNCAN AND SUSAN L. KAY

Education is the art of making human beings ethical.[1]

Training law students involves more than teaching them to think like lawyers, and more than teaching them the technical and doctrinal constituents of law practice. Law students must also be exposed to the ethical constructs and rules that confine the practice of law. Exploring and developing the ethical sensibilities of law students are among the most exciting and worthwhile aspects of law teaching. These ethical sensibilities help students to understand better the context of the other vectors of legal education: the sometimes technocratic vocational training and the vessel for intellectual development. They provide a foundation to help students maintain a principled approach when they enter practice.

Real understanding of legal ethics is best understood by students undertaking classes which expose them, in simulation or reality, to the actual practice of the law. Globally, the clinical legal education movement has been a powerful source of change for many law students and this chapter will address that phenomenon. It will survey the requirements for the teaching of professional ethics around the world and then focus on the particular ways in which clinical experience can fulfill the needs of ethical education. To this end, it will provide examples of learning methods from different jurisdictions that incorporate clinical methodology in unique and effective manners.

VARIETY IN HOW ETHICS AND PROFESSIONALISM ARE ADDRESSED

Chief among the responsibilities of legal education is the preparation of professionals for the practice of law. Nonetheless, many jurisdictions do not require ethical training as part of the required curriculum for law students. Even among those jurisdictions that do require ethics training, there is considerable variance in their chosen modes of teaching ethics and professionalism. This section will consider some of the reasons for this variety and explore the limited research into how educational establishments approach this important subject.

The responsibility for addressing professional ethics lies with different participants in different jurisdictions. For example, in the United States, where legal

---

1. G.W.F. Hegel, *Elements of the Philosophy of Right* §151.

education is entirely postgraduate, students may practice law with neither further training nor experience once they have completed their law degree (JD) and the appropriate state bar exam. One of the few compulsory elements of the JD curriculum is training in professional responsibility, including knowledge of the American Bar Association's (ABA) Model Rules of Professional Conduct,[2] a version of which has been adopted by a majority of the states. And all state bar examinations must include the Multistate Professional Responsibility Exam (MPRE), a multiple-choice test that covers the ABA's Model Rules.

In England and Wales, by contrast, students complete an academic law program (LLB) before going on to a professional program—the Legal Practice Course (LPC) for solicitors or the Bar Professional Training Course (BPTC) for barristers—and may not enter independent practice until they have completed an apprenticeship (the Training Contract for solicitors or Pupilage for barristers).

Most law degrees in Australia are completed in five years, but studies begin with a multidisciplinary education. Students must complete the material required for law practice during a five-year degree program and then attend a postgraduate course focused on the demands of legal practice. Consequently, Australian universities have a strong financial motivation to ensure that their degrees cover all the material that is required for practice, including the so-called "Priestley Eleven."[3]

Most jurisdictions have adopted a regime similar to either the United States, the United Kingdom, or Australia, and most of these regimes are enforced by the relevant licensing or supervisory authority within the jurisdiction. However, there are some examples (including Poland, Russia, and South Africa) where the regulation is by the state or a state agency, and other jurisdictions (including Kuwait) where there is no regulation. (Chandler & Duncan, 2007) Until recently, Japan had no regulation; however, new reforms introduced by the Justice System Reform Council have encouraged wide experimentation in curriculum design, and many Japanese law schools are very focused on addressing ethical issues. (Economides, 2007)

While there is diversity in the approaches for mandatory ethical training taken by the various jurisdictions, all seem to lack pedagogical creativity. In the United Kingdom, where there is a requirement to teach "professional ethics," the goals of the course are relatively narrow, largely focused on ensuring the recognition of formal ethical dilemmas and code compliance. There is no professional

---

2. This requirement is contained in Standard 302(a)(5) of the American Bar Association's Standards for the Approval of Law Schools.

3. The "Priestly Eleven" are: Tort Law, Criminal Law, Contract Law, Administrative Law, Company Law, Civil Procedure, Evidence, Equity and Trusts, Real and Personal Property Law, Federal and State Constitutional Law, and *Professional Conduct and Basic Trust Accounting* (our emphasis).

pressure to address ethical issues on the undergraduate degree. Likewise in the United States, many law schools satisfy the ABA requirements with a single, doctrinal course focused solely on learning the Model Rules of Professional Conduct. (Rhode, 2007) What is common, then, is a required curriculum which addresses relatively narrow goals. Formal requirements rarely demand a deeper or more reflective approach.

This is not to say that there is no pressure for a more educationally sound approach. The Australian Law Reform Commission, for example, has recommended the "development of . . . a deep appreciation of ethical standards and professional responsibility." (Australian Law Reform Commission, 2000 at Recommendation 2) In the United Kingdom, the Lord Chancellor's Advisory Committee on Legal Education and Conduct has recommended:

> Professional ethics and conduct should certainly form a central part in the extended education that we hope intending solicitors and barristers will receive in future. Students must be made aware of the values that legal solutions carry, and of the ethical and humanitarian dimensions of law as an instrument which affects the quality of life. (Lord Chancellor's Advisory Committee on Legal Education and Conduct, 1996 at para 1.19)

The Carnegie Foundation for the Advancement of Teaching has recommended that in the United States and Canada:

> . . . legal education needs to attend very seriously to its apprenticeship of professional identity. Professional education is highly formative. The challenge is to deploy this formative power in the authentic interests of the profession and the students as future professionals.
>
> . . .
>
> Further, the schools need to attend more systematically to the pedagogical practices that foster the formation of integrated, responsible lawyers. (Sullivan et al, 2007 at 128)

The academic community has responded to this growing interest in developing the quality of legal professional ethics in education with a regular International Legal Ethics conference and an international journal, *Legal Ethics*. University law schools have responded with a variety of new courses and teaching methods. Some of the most valuable and innovative of these courses have utilized the clinical methodology.

WHY CLINIC?

Though the relative efficacy of modes of teaching ethics has long been pondered, most law schools have ignored long-established principles of pedagogy and learning theory and continue to teach professional responsibility as a doctrinal, rules-oriented course. As Deborah Rhode has noted, "Many [professional ethics] courses, which focus primarily (and uncritically) on bar disciplinary rules, constitute the functional equivalent of 'legal ethics without the ethics' and leave future practitioners without the foundations for reflective judgment." (Rhode, 2003 at 340) Notwithstanding this practice, learning theory teaches us that several principles should animate the teaching and, more importantly, the learning of legal ethics in law schools.

First, as the Carnegie Report on Legal Education has posited, "[t]he experience of clinical-legal education . . . points toward actual experience with clients as an essential catalyst for the full development of ethical engagement." (Sullivan et al., 2007 at 160) The report relies on the well-established principle that learning is progressive. Students should first learn concepts and then utilize those concepts in more complex situations. Applying these principles, one should first learn the rules governing the profession, and then attempt to use these concepts in the complex and ambiguous context created by the practice of law.

Others have likewise proposed that students need to incorporate and utilize what they learn. "Most students learn better when they are engaged in 'active learning.' Through 'active learning' students are not merely 'passive receptacles' of information, but actively participate in the process of identifying, absorbing and understanding the material." (Lerner, 1999 at 116) Problem-solving is more efficacious than rote memorization. Allowing students to discover the problems, rather than having them spoon-fed, provides optimal learning. Drawing on the work of David Luban and Michael Millemann, Professor Rhode has noted that "moral decision-making involves more than knowledge of relevant rules and principles; it also demands a capacity to understand how those rules apply and which principles are most important in concrete settings." (Rhode, 2007 at 1052, citing Luban & Millemann, 2005)

Finally, as John Biggs has posited, learning requires both clear objectives and consistency between those objectives and the teaching methodology that is employed. Teachers should both understand and make clear to students the expected outcomes of the course. The learning process should be consistent with these objectives. (Biggs, 2003) If teachers of professional ethics truly want students to incorporate ethical behavior into their practice of law, they must create a learning environment that allows students the opportunity to do more than learn the applicable law. Students must be placed in a context in which they must balance the often-conflicting responsibilities contained in those rules.

Most courses designed to develop moral reasoning in students are based on the theories of Lawrence Kohlberg, in which he identified six stages of moral reasoning. There are two "preconventional" stages. The first is fundamentally punishment avoidance and accepts authoritarianism: might is right. The second is self-interestedly instrumental in that collaboration between others may be seen as desirable if it brings benefits. These two stages are seen as preconventional as they operate independently of the moral conventions of the culture within which the individual lives. Two "conventional" stages are based on those cultural conventions. Stage three involves conformity and establishing long-standing trusting relationships. People operating at this level tend to be highly concerned with approval by those close to them. Stage four involves a more conscious acceptance of the rules through which moral conventions are articulated. There is an acceptance of authority and recognition of the values of maintaining social order. Two "postconventional" stages are more concerned with principled moral reasoning. Stage five, which Kohlberg described as "social contract driven," engages the individual with fundamental moral principles such as justice and equality, involving a critical analysis of rules and recognition that there are competing values of individual rights and collective interests. Stage six involves reasoning based on universal ethical principles, and remains a very abstract concept. (Kohlberg, 1981)

The significance of Kohlberg's research for legal educators is that "[f]ormal education seems to be the most important factor in continued moral development. As people continue in school, they generally continue to progress toward the higher stages of moral reasoning, and, when they leave school, their progress stops." (Hartwell, 1994 at 511) This is both an indication of the need to continue to address ethics in our teaching and the basis of a guide to promoting students' moral development through experiential courses.

All of these theories lead inexorably to the conclusion that ethics and professionalism are best learned in the crucible of experience. While the classroom may be the appropriate venue for learning the words of rules and concepts underlying the rules, these principles of conduct can be absorbed fully only in context. To thoroughly understand and appreciate the conflicting obligations and responsibilities inherent in the actualization of the rules, students must utilize them in practice. Put differently, one can only understand the rules in theory if one has experienced them in practice. As Gary Bellow has observed: "Experience produces a qualitative change in the mode and content of knowing, which cannot be replicated by the transmission of information or the discussion of cases." (Bellow, 1973 at 391) Eleanor Myers finds this observation to be "particularly true of ideas about values, much of whose content is lost when understood in a purely intellectual way." (Myers, 1996 at 835)

Context thus makes the rules and the doctrine come alive to law students. It is through experiential education—a key element of the clinical methodology—that students "begin to internalize and make their own moral and ethical judgments." (*Id.*) All types of experiential education provide learning in context; the question remains as to which are best suited for teaching specific ethical problems and concepts to law students.

TEACHING LEGAL ETHICS AND PROFESSIONALISM EXPERIENTIALLY

There are three generally accepted methods for teaching legal ethics and professionalism experientially: simulation, externship, and live-client clinics. Simulation courses provide mock or simulated problems as the vehicle for learning; students learn in role and in context, but it is a context created by the faculty member specifically for the purpose of teaching particular skills or doctrine. Externship courses place students in real legal settings outside the law school. The materials of the course are the cases and problems on which the students work under the supervision of their site supervisors. Perspective and reflection is provided by the faculty supervisors who generally teach the students in the classroom component of the externship. Finally, in live-client clinics students represent clients under the supervision of law school faculty members. In these clinics, faculty select cases for their pedagogical value and students may engage in the full panoply of lawyering on behalf of their clients. Each of these types of experiential learning provides the context for discussion and resolution ethical questions. But surely each mode has its own benefits and detriments.

Simulation

The benefits of simulations are twofold: they are created by faculty members specifically to raise particularized issues or problems, and there are no live clients who are affected by the students' struggle with the issues. Faculty members can thus ensure that particular problems are addressed in particular ways. Real-life cases, on the other hand, are unpredictable and therefore one cannot be sure that any particular issue or problem will occur in a particular case or in a particular manner. Moreover, teachers are able to exercise considerable control over a simulated class. Thus, the experience is relatively safe, and it is relatively easy to plan seminar or tutorial work where students discuss the role-play. This didactic component can be directed by the teacher so that the ethical issues which have been designed into the simulation are fully addressed. Moreover, simulations provide students with the independence and the freedom to make mistakes that can help them formulate better ways to address the issues. Faculty can force the students to make hard—and even wrong—choices as a means of teaching the consequences of behavior, with no need for faculty intervention in the students' decision-making before the results accrue. This methodology cannot be utilized where clients are involved, as the faculty member has an independent responsibility to the client to ensure that the student does not make irreparable mistakes.

The limitations of simulation are straightforward. The students are acutely aware that they are working on a mock case. They cannot—and do not—feel the same kind of responsibility and imperative that they do when they are actually responsible for a client. Also, students can become jaded by overuse of simulations. Repeated role-play with fellow students can lose its effectiveness unless special effort is made to add a degree of realism. Using actors, practitioners, or members of the public may help, but often introduces costs which are unrealistic for many institutions. Professor Clark Cunningham has developed a simulation at Georgia State University in the United States which adds realism when students undertake modest individual empirical research, leading to an understanding of the ethical issues in the lawyer-client relationship.

Professor Cunningham asks students to find a member of the public who has been dissatisfied with the services of a lawyer and to ask that person to complete a questionnaire exploring the reasons for dissatisfaction. He then collates and analyzes the results and posts a set of the findings on his Web site. Through their active participation in this exercise, his students quickly discover the importance of effective communication with and respect for clients, providing an experiential opening into a consideration of lawyers' other duties to their clients and to the judicial process. The insights, freshly received from such an exercise, are also an excellent preparation for live-client clinical work, and, of course, for work as professional lawyers.

Externships

Externships allow students to work with lawyers and judges who are actively involved in practicing and making law.[4] Students work on whatever cases their supervisors may select, addressing those issues that actually arise at the work site. Students can have a multitude of experiences otherwise unavailable at the law school, by working with prosecutors, with nongovernmental organizations (NGOs), or with courts. Externship students also benefit from supervision by a faculty member, who can tease out the issues and allow the student to explore his or her options without being constrained by responsibility for a client. Of course, such freedom of teaching comes at a price.

> On the one hand, ensuring that students comprehend and execute appropriately all ethical constraints, including their duty of confidentiality, is a clear imperative. On the other, faculty also take their consultative role seriously and want to assist their students who are struggling with ethical dilemmas; they are constrained, though, in their ability to provide sage counsel by the need to respect the confidentiality of the externs' workplaces. (Anderson et al., 2004 at 485)

Because they are not part of the confidential relationship, faculty externship supervisors are not privy to information upon which the ethical problems arise. While they can thus discuss ethical issues without either defensiveness or loyalty to the client, they lack the information and thus cannot fully explicate the facts. Not only may faculty supervisors be protected from knowing the facts that underlie the ethical issues, they may not even know that ethical issues exist at the site. Obviously, externship programs make every effort to select only skillful, thoughtful, and ethical site supervisors. Nonetheless faculty supervisors have no way of assuring that their students are being instructed properly or that all relevant ethical

---

4. Externship programs are discussed in detail in Chapter 22.

issues are identified and addressed. The immediate difficulty is the faculty supervisor's relative lack of influence over the work that students undertake or the discussions that site supervisors have with the students. Indeed, if a student is placed in an environment where ethical practice is poor (or even if it is satisfactory, is unconsidered), the externship may be positively damaging.

Again, utilizing Biggs's analysis, externships are best where the faculty member wants to ensure that a student is exposed to issues in particular areas of practice that would otherwise be unavailable in the law school.

Live-Client Clinics

Finally, live-client clinics can provide some of the most direct training in professional responsibility. The students are able to feel, as well as learn, the concepts that govern ethical conduct. "Only by taking primary responsibility for clients may any law student fully experience the 'professional pulls and choices' and the 'balancing of loyalties and professional responsibilities' of being a lawyer." (Joy, 2004 at 837) The student confronts ethical issues under the supervision of a faculty member in a context where both student and teacher must address and resolve the issues, and both must do so as counsel to the client. The student thus feels the full responsibility of the representation, and the teacher can utilize the experience to provide the most full-bodied understanding of the tensions and balances within the rules.

The downsides are less clear. Because the faculty member is concurrently both teacher and lawyer, he or she cannot be as dispassionate as the externship faculty supervisor. This requires delicate balancing by live-client clinic supervisors, who "must resist the urge to exert so much control that they inhibit the student's learning process while still maintaining sufficient supervision that each student-lawyer is capable of performing at a level equal to or better than practitioners handling similar client matters." (Joy & Kuehn, 2002)

Some have queried the value of the conventional clinic for addressing professional ethics by suggesting that "moral questions . . . do not arise with the same frequency as they arise by design in a professional responsibility course." (Hartwell, 1994 at 535) Even if this is true (and it may be less valid if one takes a broader conception of professional ethics) there are methods of ensuring that students encounter ethical issues during their work in the clinic. One effective approach is that of the specialist ethics clinical course—Legal Practice and Conduct—at La Trobe University in Melbourne.

Like most clinical courses, Legal Practice and Content is an elective course. Students self-select, bringing a desire to "do good" to their decision. The title of the course and its stated objectives draw students' attention to the centrality of ethics, which is also reinforced by the reading materials and the design of the program. This latter aspect of the course is critical, for there is a risk that in a busy clinic the everyday demands of managing the caseload will overtake the need to draw attention to ethical issues as (and after) they arise. The course design also limits the number of client cases, thus ensuring time for regular team discussions and opportunities for one-to-one supervision. Students are required to maintain reflective journals to explore ethical issues further, which also provide supervisors with insight into the students' understanding of the issues. The circle is closed by requiring that assessments confirm the importance of ethical issues, including central concepts such as confidentiality and the development of a relationship of trust. (Curran et al., 2005)

The clinicians who teach this clinic take a broad view of legal ethics and "argue that ethical practice goes beyond mere adherence to rules and requires a lawyer to consider the implications of those rules for access to justice." (*Id.* at 119) They therefore encourage students to consider whether the issues arising in their casework expose a need for law reform or for public discussion. This enables them to go further in addressing issues of social justice than might be the situation with individual casework by undertaking research, preparing reports, and publicizing the results.

This approach provides a coherent way of ensuring that the ethical issues which are inherent in casework and those which arise from representing disadvantaged communities are brought to the fore and given the serious, reflective attention they should receive. Moreover, it is a model which may be adapted for many other types of clinical settings.

Other Approaches

What is common to all the examples of basic clinical methods described above is using an experiential approach. Whether using simulation, law school–based clinic, or externship, students are introduced to experiences through which they encounter (among other things) ethical dilemmas to which they must respond. This is a powerful development beyond a conventional class, where students are given case studies to which they must explain what they *would* do. In the clinical setting, they actually have to act.

Those seeking to introduce clinical teaching are often presented with objections based on its cost. A number of Indian law schools have developed opportunities for their students to go out to villages and other communities in order to learn by providing a variety of legal services through activities such as the "Legal Aid Cells" organized at V.M. Salgaocar College of Law.[5] As in the live-client clinics discussed above, the experience, however valuable, is not enough to ensure ethical learning. However, when incorporated into a clinical program, this method "provides distinctive opportunities for principled value-based teaching. Professors incorporate students' experiences, current events and community news through debates, discussions and case questions bringing their practical skills and ethics

---

5. Clinical programs in India are discussed in Chapter 3, covering South and Southeast Asia.

training in line with the substantive curriculum." (Bloch & Prasad, 2006, at 203)

Another example from India where students provide a service to members of the community who cannot afford to pay a lawyer is *lok adalats*, informal dispute mechanisms whereby students facilitate settlements between litigants in order to avoid full court hearings. Students act as advisers or mediators to the parties, which throws a number of ethical issues into high relief and provides a contrast to conventional legal practice. Provided students are able to discuss their experiences with their teachers and are able to realize the potential conflicts that may arise from these situations, there is enormous learning potential in these activities. Of course, the discussion must also include a comparison of the conflicts the students are facing with the conflicts inherent in traditional law practice, the development of conventional legal skills, and an awareness of social justice issues. (*Id.*)

Real experiences are inevitably rich in resources for learning about the ethics of legal practice, and careful design of programs that allow for discussion of—and reflection on—those experiences can provide the best learning. This learning will not only impact the students' life, but also their approach to the practice of law.

THE GLOBAL CLINICAL MOVEMENT AND ETHICS EDUCATION

The work of the global clinical movement has been well documented in other chapters of this book. However, it is appropriate to describe here briefly the particular contribution that various conferences of the Global Alliance for Justice Education (GAJE) have made to the development of ethical ideas.[6]

The first conference, held in India in 1999, included plenary sessions on research into the values of lawyers at various stages of their careers and whether their educational experiences had an impact on those values, and on cultural factors in attempting to apply the same research questions in a different legal culture and jurisdiction. There was also a postconference Train-the-Trainers workshop which focused on client interviewing, including considerable discussion of related ethical issues. From this workshop, participants developed training programs to deliver in the future.

The initial focus of the second conference, held in South Africa in 2001, was on ways of introducing justice as a central factor in the law school curriculum. This was developed further in the postconference Train-the-Trainers workshops, one of which centered on legal ethics. Another workshop, on training in trial advocacy, was led by the authors and Les McCrimmon and included addressing

---

6. GAJE is discussed more generally in Chapter 25.

the ethical issues which arise in that context. A further layer of ethical considerations came from an exercise in which the participants were asked to design sets
of materials (case papers) on which students were to work.

The third conference in Poland in 2004, included conference sessions
addressing teaching values to law students. Built around a theme of teaching
justice from scenes of injustice, the conference program included the powerful
experience of a visit by all of the delegates to Auschwitz together with plenary
session focused on teaching values to law students and a smaller session exploring how clinical programs can best prepare students for ethical challenges.
During the postconference workshops, the same team as in 2001 led a workshop
exploring the specific skills of client interviewing and advocacy on behalf of refugees, providing a further opportunity to consider ethical and social justice
issues.

At the fourth conference in Argentina in 2006, one of the five general themes
was "Professional Responsibility: Educating Lawyers in Social Justice." The
program included a series of interactive workshop sessions on teaching ethics
that explored such topics as extending clinic experiences to students who could
not share them, encouraging students to question their own views of professional values, and considering postqualification education and assessment in
ethical practice.

The most recent conference, held in the Philippines in 2008, had a stream of
sessions on "Justice Education and Professional Responsibility." This stream
included papers on how law schools might encourage public service as a core
value of the profession and a session combining presentations and workshops
on teaching legal ethics in a corrupt legal system, which challenged assumptions
about "justice" and "corruption" and developed practical work identifying the
sources of corruption in different jurisdictions.

A feature of an organization like GAJE is that it stimulates others to undertake valuable initiatives. For example, a number of GAJE members participated
in a stream on "The Legal Ethics Project in Legal Education" at the Third
International Legal Ethics Conference, held at Griffith University in 2008. More
recently, in July 2009, the Central European University and the Public Interest
Law Institute (PILI) organized a week-long course for international participants
in Hungary on "Teaching Law, Human Rights, and Ethics."

CONCLUSION

We have sought to indicate both why and how the use of clinical learning methods can be a powerful element in ensuring that proper attention is paid to ethics
and professional responsibility in legal education. We will conclude with a
reminder as to why this is important, in the words of the new president of the
United States.

The study of law can be disappointing at times, a matter of applying narrow rules and arcane procedure to an uncooperative reality; a sort of glorified accounting that serves to regulate the affairs of those who have power—and that all too often seeks to explain, to those who do not, the ultimate wisdom and justice of their condition.[7]

This reminds us of the need to ensure legal education which does not merely teach the rules and how to manipulate them, but which explores the ethical codes of the profession, the values which underpin those codes, and the questions of social justice inherent in any legal scheme.

LIST OF REFERENCES

Alexis Anderson et al., *Ethics in Externships: Confidentiality, Conflicts, and Competence Issues in the Field and in the Classroom*, 10 CLIN. L. REV. 473, 485 (2004).

Australian Law Reform Commission, *Managing Justice*, Report No. 89 (2000).

Gary Bellow, *On Teaching the Teachers: Some Preliminary Reflections on Clinical Education as Methodology*, in CLINICAL EDUCATION FOR THE LAW STUDENT (Council on Legal Education for Professional Responsibility ed. 1973).

Frank S. Bloch & M. R. K. Prasad, *Institutionalizing a Social Justice Mission for Clinical Legal Education: Cross-National Currents from India and the United States*, 13 CLIN. L. REV. 165, 203–06 (2006).

Sara Chandler & Nigel Duncan, International Survey on the Teaching of Ethics—A Preliminary Report, presented at Society of Legal Scholars Annual Conference (Durham University 2007).

Liz Curran et al., *Pushing Boundaries: Designing Clinical Programs to Teach Law Students an Understanding of Ethical Practice*, 8 INT'L J. CLIN. LEG. EDUC. 104 (2005).

Kim M. Economides, *Anglo-American Conceptions of Professional Responsibility and the Reform of Japanese Legal Education: Creating a Virtuous Circle?* 41(2) LAW TEACHER, 155 (2007).

Steven Hartwell, *Promoting Moral Development through Experiential Teaching*, 1 CLIN. L. REV 505 (1994).

Peter A. Joy & Robert A. Kuehn, *Conflict of Interest and Competency Issues in Law Clinic Practice*, 9 CLIN. L. REV. 493, 516 n. 86 (2002).

Peter A. Joy, *The Ethics of Law School Clinic Students as Student Lawyers*, 45 S. TEX. L. REV. 815, 837 (2004).

LAWRENCE KOHLBERG, THE PHILOSOPHY OF MORAL DEVELOPMENT (Harper & Row 1981).

---

7. Barack Obama, Dreams from my Father (2004).

Alan M. Lerner, *Law & Lawyering in the Work Place: Building Better Lawyers by Teaching Students to Exercise Critical Judgment as Creative Problem Solver*, 32 AKRON L. REV. 107, 116 (1999).

Lord Chancellor's Advisory Committee on Legal Education and Conduct, First Report on Legal Education and Training (1996).

David Luban & Michael Millemann, *Good Judgment: Ethics Teaching in Dark Times*, 9 GEO. J. LEGAL ETHICS 31 (1995).

Eleanor W. Myers, *Simple Truths About Moral Education*, 45 AM.U.L. REV. 823, 836 (1996).

Deborah L. Rhode, *Integrity in the Practice of Law: If Integrity Is the Answer, What Is the Question?*, 72 FORDHAM L. REV. 333 (2003).

Deborah L. Rhode, *Teaching Legal Ethics*, 51 ST. LOUIS. L. J. 1043 (2007).

WILLIAM M. SULLIVAN ET AL., EDUCATING LAWYERS: PREPARATION FOR THE PROFESSION OF LAW (Jossey Bass 2007).

13. THE IMPACT OF PUBLIC INTEREST LAW ON LEGAL EDUCATION

DANIELA IKAWA

The impact of public interest law on legal education—and, in particular, on clinical legal education—can be assessed by analyzing two main peculiarities of public interest law in relation to a more traditional perspective of the law: its special connection to reality and its connection to material justice. Understanding those peculiarities can in turn help address one of the main problems regarding modern legal education, its keenness to conformity.

This chapter begins with a brief discussion of the issue of conformity, followed by a discussion of public interest law's connection to reality and to material justice. Then, it analyzes the impact of those two peculiarities on legal education, drawing on two cases at two law school clinics: the case of community radios—cheap and easily accessible radio stations created by a particular community to discuss issues that have an impact on the daily life of the community members—at the Dom Evaristo Arns legal clinic in Brazil, and the Tysiąc case on access to abortions at the Warsaw University legal clinic in Poland.

THE PROBLEM: CONFORMITY IN LEGAL EDUCATION

Traditionally, law has been perceived as a means to preserve the status quo. It establishes and preserves rules, principles, and institutions that coordinate the relationship among individuals and the overall structure of a society. This conformist idea of law is often reflected in legal education. It is reflected in lectures about law that do not leave any room for discussion, in legal exams based solely on memorization, and in law school career offices that offer support only for certain legal careers. It is also reflected in students' and professors' belief in an inherently just character of the law and in their disregard of justice-related issues. Conformism is reflected in students' and professors' resistance against analyzing the actual impact of specific laws on society and in their insistence on perceiving progressive judicial decisions as the utmost indicator of social change (in the few cases when social change becomes a concern). As Sturm and Guinier put it:

> [L]aw schools breed a culture of . . . conformity, [which] exerts a constant pressure to make comparisons along a uniform axis. As a result, the requirement to conform will often trump the invitation to explore. . . . This culture is remarkably static, non-adaptive, and resistant to change, even in the face of strong pressure from significant constituents of legal education and evidence

that law schools are not fulfilling core aspects of their mission. . . . Indeed, the law school culture encourages the suspension of personal judgments, substituting an external reward system for students' internal moral or professional goals. (Sturm & Guinier, 2007 at 519–20, 539–40, and 544)

Along the same lines, Ashar explains that: "Reproduction, rather than social critique, forms the core mission of the vast majority of educational institutions. Functionality and efficiency, rather than individual expression and social integration, are the primary values that almost all of these public and private entities adhere to and advance." (Ashar, 2008 at 364–5)

Would it be possible, then, to use law to change society? In this chapter, I adopt the view that it is possible—as long as the gap between law and reality as well as between law and justice is narrowed. In this vein, public interest law has much to contribute to legal education. Its special connection to reality and to material justice inspires (future) legal professionals to think beyond the letter of the law in terms of what the law should be and of how the law should be implemented or reformed. And one of the means for this inspiration are law school clinics that work on public interest law cases, clinics where students can not only see what the law can be and do, but also can discuss and solve problems concerning the public interest.

TWO PECULIARITIES OF PUBLIC INTEREST LAW

Because legal education often adopts a conformist approach to law, there are many obstacles to change. These obstacles are not, however, insurmountable. The main ingredient for change is inspiring students to think critically beyond the letter of the law. Incorporating a public interest law perspective into teaching law is one means of doing that, as it will help in narrowing the gap between "law on the books" and "law on the ground," that is, between law and reality (Hershkoff, 2001 at 8–9), and narrowing the gap between law and material justice.

The Gap between Law and Reality
The gap between law and reality is narrowed when a public interest law perspective is incorporated into teaching law because public interest law is aimed at results. By starting legal analysis with the problem, or, more specifically, with the concern about how to solve the problem and how to change reality, those analyzing public interest law cases will need to develop problem-solving skills that go beyond the knowledge about the legal text. This problem-solving focus of public interest law is highlighted especially when public interest law is taught within a clinic. Clinics are the space where lessons start by addressing a particular social problem; they create the opportunity for students to understand the multifaceted implications of that problem and the place of law in solving it. More specifically,

they create the opportunity for students to "identify . . . and diagnos[e] the problem; generat[e] alternative solutions and strategies; develop . . . a plan of action; implement . . . the plan; and keep . . . the planning process open to new information and ideas." (American Bar Association, 1992) Clinics that take public interest law cases can work as powerful educational tools for bridging law and reality, as well as law and social change.

The idea of bridging law and reality is not a new idea. Legal realists proposed that connection in the last century, influencing legal education through the use of casebooks in American law schools in the 1940s and 1950s (Wentz, 1987) and the creation of legal clinics. (Rekosh, 2008) As Jerome Frank emphasized in the 1930s and the 1940s while proposing a new form of legal realism:

> [Constructive skepticism] is that attitude I would, if I could, inculcate in law students. Roughly speaking, it fuses these two elements: (1) an eagerness to contrive, or to make operable, social inventions which will improve the workings of our democratic society; [and] (2) an unceasing awareness of the difficulties of that undertaking (because of its complexity and inescapably guessy qualities) and of the consequent need ever to be tentative, experimental, in the formulation of ways and means. (Frank, 1947 at 1340)

Although problem-solving approaches that lead to the connection between law and reality are not new ideas, incorporating a public interest law perspective into teaching law adds to those approaches: first, by adding the idea of rational modifying principles; and second, by encompassing complex issues that must be addressed not only from a legal perspective, but also from moral, social, and political perspectives.

From a public interest law perspective, there is a connection between law and *rational principles*, principles which might serve as reasonably objective guides for legal interpretation and reform. Instead of the "legal realism's skepticism about the rational foundations of legal, moral, and political values" (Alexander, 2002, at 142–43), the public interest approach may rely on rationally justifying principles as a guidance for legal interpretation and reform. It can search and build such principles, which will not be atemporal but will not be grounded solely on prejudices and sympathies either, as advocated by Jerome Frank's legal realism. (Frank, 1947)

Such rational principles should be, however, grounded on reality. (Hare, 1952) Public interest law is prospective, experimental, and result-oriented. In its critical search for guidance in interpreting and modifying the law, public interest lawyers will not aim for abstract principles but for principles that are fed by context. In this vein, principles should be molded, specified, and reformed in accordance to reality.

A second element added by incorporating public interest law perspective into teaching law is the complexity of public interest law cases, illustrated by the cases analyzed later in this chapter. While assessing whether existing legislation fosters or inhibits equal implementation of rights, students working in a clinic can analyze what the realities of the clients are (as a group), which interests are served by existing laws, what justice and equality mean in each case, how law can be changed or interpreted to serve the interests of vulnerable groups, what the consequences of implementing (or not implementing) a particular right are with regard to a particular vulnerable group, whether or not it is feasible to fight for legal reform, and to which extent legal systems can respond to the group's demands. More specifically, students working in those cases have the opportunity to engage in discussions, such as whether a law that aims at combating media abuse can disproportionately inhibit access to information for the poor (Brazilian clinic) or whether a law that allows abortion in only a few cases is or is not a complete ban on abortion, leaving women's health unprotected (Polish clinic).

The complexity added to legal education by public interest law cases is related particularly to the goal inherent to public interest law: the goal to promote social change toward justice. This ambitious goal requires a broader and deeper perception of reality. More specifically, public interest lawyers must be concerned not only with the client herself, but also with the social and political issues that are essential for promoting social change. There are different ways to achieve that deeper perception of reality. As emphasized by Gerald López, when describing the "rebellious lawyer": "The great gap between the problem solving championed by the rebellious vision and that nurtured by the reigning approach can be described as revolving around knowledge: Which institutions and which groups of people do we regard as 'expert' sources of valuable knowledge? Which institutions and which groups of people do we believe need to be 'in the loop' about information?" (López, 2005 at 2043)

One way of getting a deeper perception about reality is by building a more horizontal relationship with clients themselves, where clients are regarded as "experts" (although not the only experts), where clients can share their priorities with their lawyers, and where lawyers can learn from their clients. But the complexity of public interest law cases goes beyond the need of achieving a deeper knowledge about reality. Complexity is also related to the degree of responsibility assumed by lawyers in public interest law cases. Public interest lawyers might extend their responsibility to adopt an approach similar to the social engineering approach held by legal realists in the past. According to Charles Houston, for instance, the "concept of 'social engineering' comprised a series of social obligations: (1) to pioneer the cause of group advancement; (2) to advocate for those in need of assistance and protection against moral injustice; (3) to work as peacemaker in the pursuit of social change; (4) to exploit the flexibility within the . . . legal regime and to use law as an instrument for social change; and (5) to advance a litigation strategy that establishes firm precedent while simultaneously generating favorable public opinion and grass-roots support." (Note, 1995 at 1621–22)

Public interest lawyers would then become what Carasik denominates an "activist-lawyer," with responsibilities that go beyond interpreting the text of the law and beyond the search for favorable judicial decisions to encompass the search for a deeper knowledge about reality—and for social change. This deeper responsibility would, therefore, foster a stronger connection between law and reality: the activist-lawyer does "not only interact . . . with the client on a non-hierarchical basis, but also participates with the client in the planning and implementation of strategies that are designed to build power for the client and allow the client to be a repeat player at the political bargaining table." (Carasik, 2006 at 49)

This deeper responsibility required of public interest lawyers—toward the achievement of a deeper knowledge about reality and social change—is also closely related to the second peculiarity of public interest law: its connection with material justice.

The Gap between Law and Material Justice

Teaching public interest law cases not only fosters the connection between law and reality, but also between law and justice; that is, between law and *material* justice. Besides, it adds a second layer of criticism to legal education. Beyond the critique grounded on the deeper connection with reality, it adds the critique grounded on values. As Trubek puts it: "[t]eaching law students to be effective in the world of practice . . . requires teaching values, skills, and substance." (Trubek, 2005 at 473) The latter cannot be, however, any values. Because of the connection between law and reality, values must be assessed with regard to reality. Values must lead not to an abstract concept of justice, but to a material concept of justice that would guide legal interpretation and legal reform.

In this sense, from a public interest law perspective, material justice is a set of values contained in directives to act that are constantly reassessed in light of a changing reality. And although those values will vary from one society to another, as well as in different points in time, the core of such values relies—from a public interest law perspective—on an equal implementation of rights for both vulnerable and nonvulnerable groups, for both empowered and disempowered groups. This equal implementation requires, therefore, a focus on those groups that face additional barriers to having their rights implemented, in order to make rights available in practice to all.

This is precisely why students at the Brazilian clinic, for instance, were interested in reforming the law and breaking with a previous principle of justice, a principle built during military dictatorship for the protection against abuses by the media. Students wanted to make the principle more flexible in order to assure that the right of access to information would be available to all in a context where deep economic inequalities and specific regulations made access to information available only to some.

The connection between law and reality, as well as the connection between law and material justice, has still another impact on legal education. Those connections foster the recognition that the legal interpreter is immersed in particular contexts. Therefore, the legal interpreter cannot perceive herself as detached from reality or as living in a realm of neutrality. In other words, the connection between law and reality and between law and justice imply the connection between law, justice, and the person who interprets the law, including here the law student. In this vein, a public interest law perspective gives a response to the often isolated character of traditional law school education: "law schools do their students a disservice by requiring them to completely dissociate their sense of justice and fair play from their legal persona, a practice encouraged by privileging and valuing a purely analytical perspective." (Carasik, 2006 at 41) Instead, and in Ashar's words, students should have in law school "the seed of legal and political judgment, an understanding of the long and unending struggle of social justice organizations, and a sense of how the rules of the profession empower and limit their ability to participate in that struggle. Law schools [should] be centers of social justice, rather than merely vocational schools for lawyers who deploy professional skills to endow those with wealth and power with more of the same." (Ashar, 2008, at 357) Incorporating public interest law perspective into teaching law can be used as a tool in achieving such a law school, a law school with the potential to engage students in real problems of injustice and with the potential to prepare students to address those problems.

More specifically, within law schools, clinics can be a catalyzing tool for breaking the gap between law and reality in a manner that is oriented toward material justice. By taking public interest law cases, clinics give students the opportunity not only to start their legal analysis on the ground, with regard to a particular problem, but also to start a discussion about the social change which they aim to achieve. Besides, as it will be analyzed below, students involved in public interest law discussions might easily break the gap between themselves (as interpreters of the law), reality, and justice. They have the opportunity to analyze principles of justice and to make them more specific; to make them better principles in ways that better guide application of the law toward a more egalitarian implementation of rights.

CASE STUDIES: THE IMPACT OF PUBLIC INTEREST LAW ON LEGAL EDUCATION IN BRAZIL AND POLAND

Two case studies presented below illustrate the impact of public interest law on legal education: the case of community radios developed by students of a Brazilian legal clinic and the case of abortion and maternal health, which inspired the coordinator of a Polish legal clinic to organize a moot court activity. The Brazilian case focused on the democratization of the media and the implementation of the right of access to information to all: not only the rich, but also the poor. The Polish case focused on women's rights and access to abortion, where this practice is significantly restricted by law.

These two case studies were selected for their successful use of public interest law in bridging law and reality as well as law and material justice. Both arose in clinics created as a result of the clinical movement in the 1990s.[1] Although the two clinics operated in different countries and under different legal and educational systems—and used different clinical methods—both managed successfully to engage students in issues of material justice aimed at changing law and social reality. Both clinics addressed the equal implementation of rights by disempowered, vulnerable groups: women and the poor. Both adopted a problem-solving approach that highlighted the complexity of the reality with which the lawyer, especially the public interest lawyer, has to deal.

The Brazilian Case: Community Radios and Access to Information

The legal clinic Dom Evaristo Arns was established in 1999 at the Catholic University of Sao Paulo, as a result of a 1994 resolution (*Portaria* n. 1886/1994) adopted by the Brazilian Ministry of Education and Culture. This resolution required law schools to foster practical education, by creating opportunities of supervised legal practice. (Ikawa, 2003) In spite of the 1994 resolution, however, there were only three legal clinics in the state of Sao Paulo by 2003: the legal assistance clinic at the Catholic University of Sao Paulo (established in 1999), the legal clinic Dom Evaristo Arns also at the Catholic University of Sao Paulo (established in 1999), and the legal clinic XI de Agosto at the State University of Sao Paulo (established already in 1919).

The Arns legal clinic mostly provides legal assistance for persons who cannot afford it otherwise, a service still much needed in Sao Paulo. The clinic was focused initially, as Ashar would put it, "on the relationship between the individual lawyer and the individual client . . .," a model that often disregards that "individual clients are a part of formal and informal movements of resistance." (Ashar, 2008, at 379–80) Recently, however, it has developed some innovative approaches to litigation in the cases of community radios that involved students in the community and required that they consider the context from which clients come. These cases, discussed in more detail below, placed the students in a position where they had to critique principles of justice encompassed by particular laws and construct a litigation strategy that aimed at achieving a social impact beyond the lives of the specific individual clients, in an attempt to produce social change.

---

1. The clinical movement in Latin America is covered in Chapter 5; the clinical movement in Central and Eastern Europe is discussed in Chapter 4.

The legal clinic, which counts on the involvement of students in the community, has worked with community radios since September 2003, when local associations requested the clinic to assist them. The students must maintain a balance between community demands and theoretical legal discussions in their working groups, where the situation of community radios and the existing law on the subject are analyzed from a critical perspective. They thus overcome the gap between law and reality, between "law on the books" and "law on the ground" by reaching out to the community where their clients live, engaging in an empowering dialogue with clients, and understanding their social demands. And they do so without forgetting the law on the books.

The Arns clinic works on a number of cases regarding community radios and access to information that focus mainly on the operation of community radios without the need of governmental authorization. While community members are often poor, community radios are a cheap and easily accessible source of information. The main aim of the clinic here is to guarantee access to information to those that would not have that access otherwise. The clinic first decided to address cases of community radios when asked by a not-for-profit organization to provide legal assistance for all community radios at Heliopolis, a poor neighborhood at the outskirts of the city of Sao Paulo. There were more than 500 pending cases at the time. However, students in the clinic do not refer to the community radio cases individually. They regard them as a tool to democratize the media in the country and to implement access to information to all.

Moreover, students are aware of the overall context in which their clients are immersed. And this awareness comes from a close contact between law students and the clients' community and from a resulting understanding of what community radios mean to the clients. As one student explained, "the main objective here is [to implement] the right to freedom of expression. . . . Community radios are a good (if not the best) means of communication available at the community. . . . It is accessible and cheap. Moreover, members of the community spend most part of their lives in their neighborhood. . . . Community radios have, therefore, a key relevance, as they address daily problems faced by community members." In the words of another student: "community radios exert considerable influence on the communities, [but because they oppose the 'big media'], those radios are criminalized in the country. . . . Community radios have an essential role in educating the Brazilian people, as they target local communities, by informing and responding to community demands." Students thus became aware that implementing laws as they had often been interpreted in the previous decades resulted not only in a small restriction against "saying something" in a particular moment, but also in a much broader restriction that would weaken the community and bar the construction of collective responses for the community's daily problems.

Restrictions to radio communications are found in the remnants of conservative regulations enacted during the *Estado Novo* (Getulio Vargas Regime) and the military dictatorship in Brazil. In 1931, a legal decree (Decree n. 20047/31) established that the electromagnetic spectrum would be controlled by the executive branch of the government. The Brazilian Constitutions of 1934, 1937, and 1946 followed this pattern, as did Act n. 4117, enacted in 1962 and still partially in force. The 1962 Act was amended in 1967 during military dictatorship. Then, Legal Decree n. 236 of 1967 revoked articles from the 1962 Act, increasing uncertainty and punishments. In 1973 (still during military dictatorship), a considerable number of radios were closed in Sao Paulo. Today, Article 70 of the 1962 Act continues to be used in order to justify the apprehension of equipments of community radios. The situation with regard to these radios has therefore not completely changed since military dictatorship. More specifically, the promulgation of the 1988 Constitution, which marked the transition to democracy in Brazil, has not yet changed the situation either. The new regulation (Act n. 9612/98 and Decree n. 2615/98) is still restrictive of community radios and the extent to which the strict regulation established by the Code of Telecommunications (Act n. 9472/97) should be applied to community radios remains controversial. Other provisions have been enacted, sometimes in favor of more freedom of expression (*Medida Provisoria* n. 214332/01) and sometimes in favor of restricting the work of community radios.

In most cases, the clinic's clients want to operate community radios without the need of governmental authorization. As the operation of community radios without such authorization is still often regarded as a criminal offense in Brazil, the Arns legal clinic has discussed two different alternatives for criminal responsibility: the practice should not be regarded as a legal offense at all, or it should be regarded as a mere administrative offense. The clinic has tried, therefore, to interpret the law as to detach radio communications from telecommunications, which is subject to especially strict regulation. It has also tried to enforce constitutional rights regarding access to information and freedom of expression, in spite of restrictive infraconstitutional laws. In this vein, the clinic has tried, according to Houston's view noted earlier, "to exploit the flexibility within the . . . legal regime and to use law as an instrument for social change." (Note, 1995 at 1621–22)

Besides conducting legal, political, and social research regarding community radios, writing legal documents (such as petitions), interviewing clients and other actors involved in radio communities, and participating in study groups on community radios, Arns clinical students usually visit the community and the community radios themselves. As a result, clinic students have adopted a more justice-oriented approach to the law that is not abstract in content. On the contrary, students' concept of justice is material for at least two reasons: they assess the broader reality faced by their clients and do not regard judicial decisions as marking the end of their role as "lawyers."

So, students' concept of justice is material because they seek to understand the broader reality faced by their clients. And to do that, they start by building a horizontal relationship with clients. Students at the clinic are encouraged to get involved with the community, by organizing trainings with the participation of those working in community radios. As one student explained, "we organize meetings with some of the radios to discuss what it means to be a community radio; we intend to generate a cultural movement in order to strengthen existing radios, to give them more visibility."

By further connecting with their clients, students are able better to understand the nuances of the right to information in the context of poor neighborhoods in Brazil. One student, for instance, emphasized the following: "my most remarkable experience was my first visit to the Heliopolis slum. Not only was I introduced to a completely new reality, but I also realized how important the community radios were for the community and how our work [could lead to] social change." As mentioned above, the students realized that community radios were a tool to strengthen the community and to respond collectively to the community's daily problems.

The students' concept of justice is material also in the sense that they see for themselves a role as lawyers beyond obtaining judicial decisions, to foster legal reform and ideally social change. They wish to promote access to information not only for the individual parties in a case, but also for the society at large. As one student put it, "the work on the community radio project [with community meetings and discussions] made me realize that the law can be used as a tool to expand rights." Another student phrased it in a more specific way: "our main goal is to protect the right to social communication in Brazil; [therefore], we fight for ignored rights, for certain laws which are not implemented, and for other laws not to be implemented. . . . Some of the legal norms regulating radio communication in Brazil are an example of . . . arbitrariness."

This material-justice-oriented approach to legal education adopted by the Brazilian clinic would not have been achieved either in a classroom where students are detached from concrete problems and social contexts or in a clinic focused solely on the parties in a case and unaware of the broader social picture regarding the equal implementation of rights.

The Polish Case: Access to Abortion and Maternal Health

The legal clinic at Warsaw University was established in 1998 with the support of the Ford Foundation. (Skrodzka et al., 2008) From 1997 to 2008, twenty-five legal clinics were created in Poland. The Warsaw University women's rights clinic focuses on cases regarding domestic violence, employment discrimination, and reproductive rights. Throughout the whole year, students attend three-hour weekly classes with the clinic coordinator. They meet with clients once a week and also attend supervised seminars, focused on interactive methodologies. The Warsaw clinic operates under a clinical model quite different from that discussed earlier at the Arns clinic in Sao Paulo. One of the main methodologies used by the clinic to integrate a public interest law perspective into legal education is simulation.

Using simulation over real cases has a few advantages in that it is an easier way to assure that students will work with *complex* public interest law cases and the only way to assure that students will work on a case until its very end. Real cases are sometimes only finally decided by courts after years of litigation, while simulated cases can last exactly one clinical semester. Simulation can also be especially valuable in countries like Poland, where law students cannot appear before courts.

A controversial real case is chosen each year by the clinic coordinator to serve as a basis for a hypothetical exercise. Students work through the hypothetical case and are allowed to ask the coordinator for answers only once they have presented at least one possible solution for the case. Students must analyze the case's strengths and weaknesses, as well as potential strategies and risks. They thus develop problem-solving skills as well as a critical, justice-oriented perspective regarding the legal issue before them. At the beginning of the second semester, students participate in a moot court based on the case.

The success of the Warsaw clinic's approach depends to a large extent on the particular case chosen for the simulation. A recent example is the case of *Tysiąc v. Poland*, regarding access to legal abortion in Poland. Alicja Tysiąc initially sought support from the Federation for Women and Family Planning, a not-for-profit organization based in Warsaw. The federation then asked the Warsaw University legal clinic to help the federation by providing legal assistance. The case eventually reached the European Court for Human Rights with further assistance from Interrights and the Center for Reproductive Rights, before being used as the basis for the simulation at the Warsaw University clinic.

Abortion has always been a crime in Poland. However, before the 1993 Act was adopted and the Supreme Court dismissed the possibility of abortion on social grounds in 1997, exceptions to the law were broadly interpreted. Currently, the four legally recognized exceptions (health of the mother, life of the mother, malformation, and rape) are not recognized in practice, resulting effectively in a full ban of abortions. As a consequence, women seek a legal abortion in Poland only when they do not have resources to pay for an underground abortion or when facing health problems.

In the particular case which inspired the Warsaw clinic's simulation, Alicja Tysiąc sought access to a legal abortion because her health was at risk. Three doctors stated that her sight would be put at risk if she continued the pregnancy. They did not agree, however, to write a statement that would allow Tysiąc to terminate her pregnancy. After noticing a worsening of her condition, Tysiąc scheduled an appointment with gynecologist R.D., who stated that there were no medical grounds to justify an abortion. By the time Tysiąc gave birth, her eyesight had deteriorated almost completely. Tysiąc presented a complaint before the European Court of Human Rights (ECHR), which decided that Poland had violated article 8 of the Convention for not fulfilling "its positive obligations regarding the effective respect of private life," a decision which was reaffirmed by the Court's Grand Chamber in 2007. (Bodnar, 2008 at 61)

The ECHR judgment in the Tysiąc case raised much debate in Poland. According to Adam Bodnar, the decision will have a long-term impact on providing women with access to legal abortion, even if it has not yet been implemented. It will "fill out the normative content of the regulations of Polish civil law in the spheres in which it would be difficult to obtain a specific decision of the legislator, and [it will raise] considerations of justice [in cases] of systematic violation of the rights of women." (Bodnar, 2008 at 64)

The ability to foster debate was a major reason why the coordinator of the Warsaw University legal clinic decided to develop a simulation inspired on this case. The clinic held special classes on international human rights law, with a focus on the European System of Human Rights. Students were divided into three groups: judges, plaintiffs, and the state. Each group developed the case from a particular perspective, and groups were responsible for organizing their own strategies. Debate within groups started from the problem and addressed moral and political issues that went beyond the letter of the law, breaking the gap between law books and law on the ground. Also, because the case dealt with an often discriminated group (women), students had the opportunity to discuss whose interests were being taken into account, what justice and equality meant in the particular case, and what the consequences of implementing the law were for women and other groups.

The public interest approach led to critical thinking also because the clinic had a group of students with varied ethical beliefs, including Catholic students. This diversity especially enriched discussions; within each small group, students quarreled on legal, moral, and political arguments. Students realized that the law did not forbid them from making decisions on moral values; instead it required them to do so. The discussion about law and values often raised in the clinic crossed the gap between law and justice, by overcoming the gap between law and those who interpret the law—in this case, law students. Students thus found a space where they could openly express their opinions: something not very common in Polish law schools.

In sum, the adoption of a public interest case by the clinic led to a justice-oriented perspective, not in the sense that one specific position is advanced, but in the sense that the question "what is just?" is posed and discussed by students. Moreover, the inclusion of international law in the discussion helped to improve students' critical analysis of the national law. Perceiving justice not as an absolute but as a set of modifying principles seemed to have been, therefore, one of the main achievements of this Polish clinic.

CONCLUSION

Public interest law has two main peculiarities in relation to a more traditional perspective of the law that have the potential to address legal education's keenness to conformity: its special connection to reality and its connection to material justice. Brazilian and Polish clinics have used those peculiarities by getting involved in the clients' community, drawing litigation strategies aimed at achieving a social impact beyond the lives of the specific individual clients, using law to expand rights and provoke social change, and debating a more material conception of justice, which implicates a more egalitarian implementation of rights, including for women and the poor.

By taking public interest law cases, those legal clinics also fostered a new perspective of what the law is. As a clinic coordinator has put it: "Law is not merely an instrument to maintain the status quo or to serve the interests of a particular social class. It can also be used as a tool for social change."

LIST OF REFERENCES

Gregory S. Alexander, *Comparing the Two Legal Realisms—American and Scandinavian,* 50 Am. J. Comp. L. 131 (2002).

American Bar Association, Report of the Task Force on Law Schools and the Profession: Narrowing the Gap (1992).

Sameer M. Ashar, *Law Clinics and Collective Mobilization,* 14 Clinical L. Rev. 355 (2008).

Adam Bodnar, *Case-law Concerning the Lack of Availability of Services for Terminating Pregnancy in Poland, in* Reproductive Rights in Poland— The Effects of the Anti-Abortion Law (Wanda Nowicka ed., Polish Federation for Women and Family Planning 2009).

Lauren Carasik, *Justice in the Balance: An Evaluation of One Clinic's Ability to Harmonize Teaching Practical Skills, Ethics and Professionalism with a Social Justice Mission,* 16 S. Cal. Rev. L. & Soc. Just. 23 (2006).

Scott L. Cummings, *After Public Interest Law,* 100 Nw. U. L. Rev. 1251 (2006).

Jerome Frank, *A Plea for Lawyer-Schools,* 56 Yale L.J. 1303 (1947).

Stephen Golub, *The Legal Empowerment Alternative, in* Promoting the Rule of Law Abroad: In Search of Knowledge (Thomas Carothers ed. 2006).

R. M. Hare, The Language of Morals (Oxford University Press 1952).

Helen Hershkoff, Public Interest Litigation: Selected Issues and Examples, *available at* http://www1.worldbank.org/publicsector/legal/ publicinterestlitigation.doc.

Daniela Ikawa, Ações Afirmativas em Universidades [Affirmative Action in Universities] (Lumen Iuris 2008).

Daniela Ikawa, *Hart, Dworkin e discricionariedade* [Hart, Dworkin, and Judicial Discretion], 61 Lua Nova 97 (2004).

Daniela Ikawa, Clinicas legais: descricao e propostas [Legal Clinics: Description and Proposals] (2003) (unpublished manuscript, on file with the author).

Legal Clinics Foundation, History and Activity of the Legal Clinics in Poland, http:// www.fupp.org.pl/index_eng.php?id=history (last accessed on Jan. 12 2009).

Note, *Legal Realism and the Race Question: Some Realism about Realism on Race Relations*, 108 HARV. L. REV. 1607 (1995).

Gerald P. López, *Keynote Address: Living and Lawyering Rebelliously*, 73 FORDHAM L. REV. 2041 (2003).

Edwin Rekosh, *Constructing Public Interest Law: Transnational Collaboration and Exchange in Central and Eastern Europe*, 13 UCLA J. INT'L L. & FOREIGN AFF. 55 (2008).

Marta Skrodzka et al., *The Next Step Forward—The Development of Clinical Legal Education in Poland Through a Clinical Pilot Program in Bialystok*, 2 COLUM. J. E. EUR. L. 56 (2008).

Hugo Slim, By What Authority? The Legitimacy and Accountability of Non-governmental Organisations, http://www.jha.ac/articles/a082.htm (last accessed on Aug. 12, 2009).

Susan Sturm & Lani Guinier, *The Law School Matrix: Reforming Legal Education in a Culture of Competition and Conformity*, 60 VAND. L. REV. 515 (2007).

Louise G. Trubek, *Crossing Boundaries: Legal Education and the Challenge of the "New Public Interest Law*,*"* 2005 WIS. L. REV. 455 (2005).

Karin M. Wentz, *Book Review*, 85 MICH. L. REV. 1105 (1987).

14. JUSTICE EDUCATION, LAW REFORM, AND THE CLINICAL METHOD

LES McCRIMMON AND EDWARD SANTOW

INTRODUCTION

A good lawyer must think critically about the law. A good lawyer will not only notice when the law produces injustice, but will also do something about it. At the heart of the term "justice education"—as distinguished from conventional legal education—is the notion that legal educators should see their role as something more than helping law students to become good technicians of the law. Instead, legal educators should instill in law students an understanding of, as well as a commitment to, justice and legal ethics.[1]

In this chapter we consider how law students can and should become involved in law reform. We also suggest how aspects of the method derived from clinical legal education can be adopted to foster a commitment in law students to justice, and not just the law.

JUSTICE EDUCATION AND LAW REFORM

To differentiate between law and justice is one of the first things a law student learns; to know that the plaintiff's success in a particular case does not necessarily mean that this was the just result. (Cook et al., 2006 at 6) As a matter of practical reality, one can only accept that the paths of law and justice sometimes diverge. Such divergence, however, is hugely destructive. It can cause enormous hardship for the individuals concerned. It also is more broadly corrosive of the legal system itself, and this provides an added reason for lawyers to combat injustice. That lawyers should be committed to the proper functioning of the legal system is a "natural law" in the sense used by Professor Lon Fuller when he talked about the "natural laws of carpentry"—namely "those laws respected by a carpenter who wants the house he builds to remain standing and serve the purpose of those who live in it." (Fuller, 1964 at 96)

Lawyers are, of course, far from powerless in combating injustice. There are two things in particular that lawyers can and should do to manifest their commitment to justice. First, lawyers must be personally committed to justice. To put it another way, lawyers must themselves act justly. This involves learning

---

1. Ethics and professionalism is the subject of Chapter 12.

about, and adhering to, established ethical standards. Secondly, and most importantly in the context of this chapter, lawyers have a responsibility to involve themselves in the overall operation of the law. This involves viewing the law—and its operation—through a critical lens, and offering their experience and expertise to minimize the divergence between law and justice. Where the law discriminates unfairly against a particular category of person or where the law trespasses on people's fundamental rights—in short, whenever the law gives rise to systemic injustice—lawyers have a legitimate role in counteracting this. In this sense, lawyers must be engaged deeply and actively with law reform.

If lawyers are to become more committed to achieving justice, legal educators must inculcate in law students an understanding of their twofold commitment—that is, a personal commitment to justice, by acting ethically, and also a broader commitment to achieving justice at the systemic level. While some laws are so fundamental to our system of government, or are so important in protecting people's human rights, that we should be careful not to disturb them, the law more generally does not fulfill its task of regulating people's interactions unless it responds to what the Hon. Michael Kirby AC CMG terms "the rapid and pervasive changes that are taking place in the society which the law serves." (Kirby, 1983 at 3) A lawyer who is only capable of applying the law leaves it in no better state than she or he found it.

One of the problems with legal education, as identified in a recent report on educating lawyers by the Carnegie Foundation, is that too often it focuses narrowly on the legal rule to be applied. While it is crucial for law students to learn how to identify and apply legal rules, this should not be the sum total of their skill set. The antidote, as the Carnegie report rightly points out, is to adopt a "highly self-conscious, reflexive" legal pedagogy, one that encourages students to learn more about the context of the law that they seek to apply. (Sullivan et al., 2007 at 32) Such a holistic approach—that is, one that seeks to take the law out of a contextual vacuum by seeing the law in its broader political and social framework—allows law students to engage more meaningfully with the law, because they are better able to see how and by whom it is formed and how it affects the community.

The remainder of this chapter discusses how these principles can be put into practice, using methods derived from clinical legal education.

LAW STUDENT INTERNSHIPS IN A LAW REFORM CONTEXT

The term "law reform" is "notoriously difficult to define. One reason is that it can refer, widely, to any beneficial change or proposed change in the law or, more narrowly, to the process by which such a change is attempted or accomplished." (Tilbury, 2005 at 3) In this chapter we focus on the narrow use of the term—involving law students in the formal processes by which the law is changed.

There are a number of ways in which law students can be exposed to the process of law reform. They may, for example, undertake a placement within a policy branch of government or a nongovernmental lobby group, or study the law reform process as a component of their substantive law subjects. If the student is exposed to quality work and on-site supervision, the best approach is to complete an internship with a law reform commission.

Institutional law reform commissions first made their appearance in the United Kingdom in 1965 and quickly spread to many countries throughout the world. Law reform commissions continue to be established, and are now a permanent feature of the legal landscape in a large number of countries. Thus, law reform commissions are now found in all but one of the Australian states and territories; New Zealand and the Pacific Islands; Canada; Hong Kong and South Asia (India, Pakistan, Sri Lanka, and Bangladesh); the Caribbean (Jamaica, and Trinidad and Tobago); Eastern and Southern Africa (South Africa, Namibia, Malawi, Lesotho, Kenya, Uganda, Tanzania, Zaire, and Zimbabwe); and Ireland. (Weisbrot, 2005 at 18) Further, in regions of the Commonwealth, associations of law reform commissions have been established to foster regional and interregional cooperation. These include the Commonwealth Association of Law Reform Agencies (CALRAs), the Association of Law Reform Agencies of Eastern and Southern Africa (ALRAESA), and the Australasian Law Reform Agencies Conference (ALRAC).

Law reform commissions are distinguished from other forms of institutionalized law reform—such as an ad hoc commission of inquiry or a policy branch of government—in that they are permanent, employing full-time legal and administrative staff. In addition, they are independent of government, in that the appointments to the commission are nonpolitical and free from conflicts of interest, and the commission's recommendations are made independent of interested stakeholders, including government. The core business of a law reform commission is the production of well-researched and authoritative scholarship on a given topic. (Weisbrot, 2005) It is to the fulfillment of this core function that law students contribute.

ESTABLISHING LINKS BETWEEN LAW REFORM COMMISSIONS, LAW SCHOOLS, AND LAW STUDENTS

Links between a law reform commission, a law school, and law students can arise in a number of ways: a commission may agree to become a placement site in the law school's externship program; a law school may contact the commission in a context unrelated to any clinical program to establish formal links with the commission for the placement of its students; a law student may contact the commission directly to arrange a placement; or a commission may contact a law school in the context of a particular reference to solicit the assistance of law students.

In the context of this chapter, it is the law reform commission as a placement site in a law school's externship program that warrants more detailed discussion. Examples of the other way law students may be involved in law reform commission internships are discussed in the first case study below.

LAW REFORM COMMISSION AS AN EXTERNSHIP PLACEMENT SITE

There is a perception among many legal academics and law students that an internship at a law reform commission provides students with little more than the opportunity to conduct in-depth research on a topic of interest to government. While legal research often is one of the student's primary tasks during the course of her or his placement, a well-organized law reform commission internship can offer the student much more. In particular, such a placement provides the student with a unique insight into the formulation of legal policy and the workings of government. In addition, students have an opportunity to increase their awareness of the law reform process and the factors that persuade legislators to choose one option over another, and to gain some understanding of the often complex legal and social issues being considered by the commission. It also provides a practical example of the importance of law reform in policy formulation, which, in turn, may augment other courses in the law school curriculum which focus on policy issues.

Working at a law reform commission allows students to engage practically with the policy choices facing legislators. For example, a reference into evidence law may address issues of cultural bias within the justice system, discrimination against same-sex partners, and protection of vulnerable witnesses.[2] A consideration of privacy law may involve an in-depth analysis of the impact of international human rights instruments on domestic law, and the balancing of competing human rights—such as the right to freedom of expression and the right to privacy.[3] For a law reform commission charged with the task of formulating recommendations for law reform, social justice considerations are an integral part of the commission's daily work. Thus, s 24(1) of the *Australian Law Reform Commission Act* (Cth) requires the Australian Law Reform Commission (ALRC) to aim to ensure that the laws, proposals, and recommendations that it reviews, considers, or makes do not trespass unduly on personal rights and liberties, and that they are, as far as practicable, consistent with the *International Covenant on Civil and Political Rights*.

---

2. For example, see Australian Law Reform Commission, New South Wales Law Reform Commission and Victorian Law Reform Commission, *Uniform Evidence Law*, ALRC 102, NSWLRC 112, VLRC FR (2006).

3. For example, see Australian Law Reform Commission, *For Your Information: Australian Privacy Law and Practice*, ALRC 108 (2008).

Students also will be exposed to a form of legal writing which, likely, will be different from that to which they have been exposed at law school. Law reform commission reports and consultation papers must be detailed enough to address the concerns of those with an in-depth knowledge of the area being considered, yet written in a style that can be understood easily by decision-makers and members of the public. Further, the student's research and writing relate to real, rather than hypothetical, issues and problems, and the student's work product, if of a sufficiently high standard, will be relied upon by the commission and may be incorporated into its publications.

Finally, and perhaps most importantly, students can engage in a practical way not only with what the law says, but also with what the law should say. As has been discussed above, this skill often is neglected in traditional legal education. Students must consider the law's effect on a diverse range of stakeholders and reflect on whether the desired outcomes are just. They gain an appreciation of the difficult choices facing law-makers, and the values inherent in the choices made.

STRUCTURING A LAW REFORM PLACEMENT: RESPONSIBILITIES OF RELEVANT PARTIES

The student, as an integral member of the commission's team working on a particular reference, often will have the opportunity to take part in team meetings (including those where recommendations for reform are discussed), be involved in consultations with stakeholders, and be exposed to the day-to-day workings of the commission. The law reform commission benefits from the student's skill in research and writing, and from having another team member working on a specific reference. For the placement to operate effectively, the responsibilities of the commission, the intern supervisor, and the student must be set out clearly and implemented efficiently.

Responsibilities of the Law Reform Commission

In accepting an intern for placement, the commission puts itself forward as a professional role model and agrees to facilitate the student's learning by providing proper supervision and mentoring. The commission must ensure that the student understands the nature of the commission's work, the various aspects of the commission's operations, and the institutional support available (for example, telephone and computer access, desk or office accommodation, and research support such as access to a library and online databases). The student should be made aware of various commission policies, such as those concerning occupational health and safety, the use of Internet and e-mail, and, most importantly, the obligation to keep confidential sensitive information obtained during the course of the internship.

The law reform commission must also monitor the quality of the internship experience. Someone within the commission—a commissioner, the executive director, or a senior legal officer (but not the intern's immediate supervisor)—should act as the placement coordinator with responsibility for ensuring that the placement operates effectively, both for the intern and the commission. The placement coordinator should be a point of contact for the intern in the event the immediate supervisor is not available, and should ensure that the intern/supervisor relationship operates smoothly and that any problems are identified early and dealt with quickly.

Responsibilities of the Intern Supervisor

It is the intern supervisor's role to supervise the intern on a daily basis and to serve as the intern's first point of contact with the law reform commission. It is the responsibility of the supervisor to ensure that the intern, upon each attendance at the commission, has adequate and appropriate work tasks and understands the nature and timeline for completing such tasks. The supervisor should ensure that the work tasks are tailored to the intern's particular skills, knowledge, and experience.

Upon the commencement of the internship, the intern should be provided with an overview of the commission's reference. This puts in perspective the work that has been assigned. The intern should be introduced to all team members and told which members of the team have expertise in the task assigned. This may be expertise in something as simple as arranging consultations, or as complex as researching and analyzing a particular area of law.

The primary objectives of an internship are to ensure that interns understand the process of law reform and gain some insight into how policy is formulated. Thus, interns should be provided with the opportunity to take part in team discussions and consultations with relevant stakeholders. Interns also should be exposed to the workings of the commission; for example, through attendance at management meetings and other commission activities. It is the supervisor's responsibility to ensure that such opportunities are made available to the intern.

Finally, it is the responsibility of the supervisor to ensure that the intern regularly receives constructive feedback on her or his performance. This enhances not only the intern's learning, but also provides an opportunity for the supervisor to monitor the intern's placement experience. If the intern is working with another member of the reference team, it is the supervisor's responsibility to ensure that the team member also provides constructive feedback to the intern.

Responsibilities of the Intern

Interns should familiarize themselves with, and adhere to, the policies and procedures of the law reform commission. As an integral part of the commission, interns should conduct themselves at all times in a professional manner.

For example, they should complete all assigned tasks on time and to the best of their ability, advise their supervisor or the placement coordinator promptly if they are experiencing any difficulties, and attend the commission as agreed. Finally, interns must keep confidential sensitive information to which they become privy during the course of their internship.

Potential Problems

Given the nature of a law reform commission's work—which usually is reference-based—problems can arise if the commission is used as an externship placement site. In particular, it is important to recognize that there may be little or no synchronicity between the law reform commission calendar and the law school calendar. For example, the commencement of the placement may fall at a time when a reference has progressed to the stage where there is little meaningful work for the student to do. As a result, the law reform commission may not be able to make a recurring commitment to be a placement site.

Further, the law reform commission may insist on having some say in the selection of students for placement. For example, the commission may want to interview the student selected by the law school's externship coordinator, with authority to accept or decline that student. This issue is most likely to arise if the commission selects interns from a wide range of law schools and the student selected by the externship coordinator does not meet the standard of other students seeking an internship placement. Such issues, while often not insurmountable, need to be considered and addressed—preferably at the time the law reform commission is approached to take part in the law school's externship program.

BUILDING NETWORKS THROUGH ESTABLISHED ORGANIZATIONS

In Australia, students usually establish a relationship with a law reform commission as a result of an existing link between the law reform commission and the law faculty, law students, or law student associations. Thus, law reform commissions commonly advertise their internship programs through notices placed on the commission's Web site, electronic and hardcopy notices provided to law schools and law student societies, notices placed in law student career handbooks produced by law student societies, attendance at student career fairs, and talks by members of the commission given to law faculties and groups of law students. An underutilized link, at least in an Australian context, is the formation of relationships between law reform commissions—either individually or through law reform associations, such as ALRAC, CALRAs, and ALRAESA—and associations containing a large number of legal clinicians, such as the Global Alliance for Justice Education (GAJE), the Australasian Clinical Legal Education Association, and the Clinical Legal Education Association in the United States.

A number of steps need to be taken to foster interaction and cooperation between law reform commissions and clinical legal educators. First, while perhaps self-evident, each group must be aware of the other. Secondly, a mutual understanding of the benefits flowing to each from a closer association must be acquired. This educative process could be facilitated in a number of ways, such as through invitations to speak at conferences and contributions to an organization's newsletter or web blog, and by keeping the office holders of each organization appraised of the other's activities. Finally, concrete linkages need to be established. Formal participation by a law reform commission in a law school's clinical program—for instance, as a placement site in the school's externship program—is an obvious example. Participation by law students in a law reform competition is perhaps a less obvious link.

LAW REFORM COMPETITIONS

In 1999 one of the authors attended the Inaugural GAJE conference held in Thiruvananthapuram, India. During one of the conference workshops, the National Community-based Law Reform Competition of India, sponsored by the National Law School of India University in Bangalore, was discussed. This innovative community-based law reform competition required students to formulate, over an eighteen-month period, proposals for law reform projects, based on facts and experience gathered from living and working in the community which was to benefit from the project. The proposals were judged by a panel of experts, and substantial monetary prizes were awarded to fund projects based on winning entries. This competition informed what has now become an annual law reform competition held in Australasia—the Kirby Cup Law Reform Competition (Kirby Cup Competition).[4]

The Kirby Cup Competition

ALRAC had, for a number of years, hosted the Kirby Cup Competition, which was designed to encourage law students to participate in a practical way in the process of law reform. While the format of the competition varied from conference to conference, its most recent incarnation prior to 2006 consisted of an undersubscribed student essay competition. In 2006, the ALRC hosted ALRAC. Using the National Community-based Law Reform Competition as its inspiration, the ALRC revamped the Kirby Cup Competition. Teams consisting of two law students were asked to develop, based on detailed guidelines, a proposal for law reform relevant to a current ALRC inquiry. Based on an assessment of the

---

4. The Kirby Cup was donated by the Honorable Michael Kirby AC CMG, a former Justice of the High Court of Australia and the first chairperson of the ALRC.

proposals submitted, three teams were selected to advance to an oral advocacy round and make oral submissions to a panel of five judges.

Following the success of the 2006 Kirby Cup Competition, the ALRC decided to run the competition annually in conjunction with the Australasian Law Students' Association (ALSA). In addition to having their names inscribed on the Kirby Cup, the winning entry is accepted as a submission to the ALRC reference to which the proposal related and a summary of the submission is published in the ALRC's journal, *Reform*.

The Kirby Cup Competition is only one example of the cross-fertilization of ideas that can occur when law reformers, legal educators, and law students share information. Institutionalized linkages among law reform commissions, commission associations, legal education—and in particular clinical legal education—bodies, and law student associations have the potential to be mutually beneficial to all concerned.

TWO CASE STUDIES

In this section, we consider two opportunities for students to engage in the "practice" of law reform. The first case study, the ALRC's internship program, allows students to participate in an organization that is responsible for a complete process of law reform—from liaison with government, to consultation with stakeholders, to research and advice to government. In the second case study, students are involved solely in the advocacy part of law reform: formulating submissions to persuade government decision-makers or advisers.

ALRC Legal Internship Program

An internship with the ALRC's Privacy Team certainly improved my research and writing skills. Far more importantly, it gave me an understanding of the complexity of the law reform process, and the skill and creativity of the Commission's work. It was a deeply fascinating—and fun—semester.[5]

The ALRC's internship program provides opportunities for law students to work as interns, on a voluntary basis, alongside commission staff. Interns work either one day a week for a university semester (approximately thirteen weeks), or full-time for a number of weeks (usually four to six weeks) during university vacations. Intern positions at the ALRC are competitive, and applicants must apply to the commission for a placement. The selection committee and interview panel usually consists of the executive director of the ALRC, the research manager,

---

5. Australian Law Reform Commission, Annual Report 2006–2007, 85. The quotation is taken from comments made by F. Roughley, 2006 ALRC intern from the University of Sydney.

and at least one staff member. The selection process is itself designed with an educational purpose in mind: "to provide applicants with practical experience in job applications and interviews, with a view to benefiting all who participate—not just those who are ultimately offered an internship." (Australian Law Reform Commission, 2007 at 82)

The ALRC offers internships to law students from Australia and other countries around the world. Internships for international students usually take place in July and August to coincide with the Northern Hemisphere university summer break. The ALRC has established formal relationships with two law schools in the United States—the University of Maryland School of Law and the American University Washington College of Law. Applications are also accepted from other overseas institutions (consisting of both academic institutions and law reform agencies), and in the past, internships have been taken up by individuals from institutions in Germany, Kenya, Malawi, Singapore, the United Kingdom, and the United States. International students, like their Australian counterparts, are expected to possess good research and writing skills, submit an application, and attend an interview (which, for international applicants, usually is conducted by telephone).

Upon taking up their internship, students are provided with detailed instruction on the ALRC's research resources and its office policies and procedures. After a detailed briefing they also are asked to read and sign a confidentiality agreement. Students are then introduced to their supervisor and other commission staff and commissioners.

Interns are assigned a research task commensurate with their knowledge and skills. All of the tasks assigned are those that would be done by a full-time legal officer. For example, a student may be asked to map legislative provisions relating to a particular topic both in Australia and internationally, consider and comment upon the judicial consideration of a piece of legislation, or assess the arguments put forward by stakeholders for or against a particular proposition. They also gain insight into writing an effective submission, and in particular how to formulate a persuasive argument. While these legal skills are generic, they are particularly valuable to those working in nongovernmental organizations with a social justice mission that engages in lobbying and advocacy. One such example is the Social Justice Advocacy Project, discussed in detail below.

During the course of the internship, the complexity of research tasks often increases, with many interns producing material that can be incorporated into an ALRC publication. As an integral member of a research team, interns are encouraged to attend team meetings, meetings of the reference advisory committee, and consultations.

Interns receive regular feedback on their work from their immediate supervisor, other team members, and the commissioner in charge of the reference to which they have been assigned. Further, at the end of the internship, students attend an "exit interview" with a senior manager who has not been involved directly in the supervision of the student. At the interview, the student has the opportunity to reflect on what he or she has learned from the internship, the strengths and weaknesses of the program, and improvements that could be made.

In recent years, the ALRC's internship program has proved to be an important pathway to permanent employment with the commission. Thus, three of six legal officers hired by the ALRC in 2005–2006 and 2006–2007 were former interns. Indeed, the ALRC has noted that since its internship program provides law students with "one of the few opportunities to undertake applied legal research in a public sector policy environment," an intern who applies for a job at the commission "does so with a clear understanding of the requirements of the role." (Australian Law Reform Commission, 2007 at 83) The ALRC, in turn, is able to assess the application for employment through the prism of the student's performance while an intern at the commission.

While internship programs require a substantial commitment of resources—in particular human resources—in the vast majority of cases the benefits to the commission substantially outweigh the disadvantages of establishing and running the program. This certainly applies to the ALRC's internship program. In addition to the written work produced by interns—the most valuable work product—commission staff are provided with the opportunity to employ and improve their supervision skills and establish collegial relationships with lawyers at the beginning of their legal career. Even if an intern does not pursue a career in legal policy and law reform, exposure to the work of the ALRC will provide her or him with an understanding of the mechanics, and the importance to society, of law reform.

Social Justice Advocacy Project

The Social Justice Advocacy Project (SJAP) is a joint venture between the University of New South Wales Faculty of Law, the student law society at that university, and Just Fair Treatment (JFT). JFT is a nongovernmental organization that brings together a number of lawyers from around the world, all of whom are involved in human rights advocacy. In this project, law students from the University of New South Wales work with practicing lawyers on real advocacy related to social justice or human rights.

Originally run as a pilot program in 2008, the students involved were not given course credit for the work that they had done. This ensured that only students who were genuinely interested in pursuing this work would apply, and it also allowed the project to be positioned as a stepping stone for more junior law students who might want subsequently to take more rigorous clinical courses offered later in their degree program.

The origins of this project lie in Cambridge University in 2004. This is, of course, an other-worldly institution, one in which students discuss human rights and global politics while they are served exotic dishes on fine bone china—all the while wearing a suit and tails. In this heady atmosphere, a group of postgraduate law students from around the world, including one of the authors of this chapter, decided to form a group to *do* human rights work. Under the unwieldy title, the International Human Rights Lawyers Working Group, the group held public forums on human rights issues and contributed submissions to public inquiries that related to human rights. From its first submission, the group's advocacy was cited with approval by a number of law reform bodies, such as the United Kingdom's only bicameral parliamentary committee, the Joint Committee on Human Rights.

Since 2004 the original student members have gone on to become practicing lawyers and academics in various countries, but have continued participating in the process of law reform. After renaming their organization Just Fair Treatment, the group searched for ways to help law students become involved in human rights work. A universal experience among the group's members was that they all had the opportunity, at some stage during their legal study, to work with practicing human rights lawyers. For each group member, this had been a transformative experience, and one that led to long-term, valuable mentoring.

With this in mind, the members of JFT were interested in pursuing the joint venture that led to the establishment of the SJAP because it provided an avenue to expose a new generation of law students to social justice advocacy. It also allowed them to extend to law students some of the opportunities that come from working in a close, mentoring relationship with practicing lawyers in a field of common interest. Moreover, they realized that the paralegal and research assistance of law students would be of real benefit to the human rights work of the organization.

At the date of publication of this book, the SJAP was being run as a pilot program. In its initial year, the SJAP was planned and run by a working party comprising a member of faculty, who happened also to be a member of JFT, and two representatives of the university's law student society. The working party was responsible for disseminating information about the project to law students, and fielding questions about its operation. It also developed selection criteria for students wishing to participate in the SJAP, in the knowledge that there would be more applicants than places available.

The criteria for selection included a demonstrated commitment to social justice and a strong academic record—both of which are common requirements for social justice projects. In addition, however, the working party also sought to obtain a diverse range of participants—with diversity measured in terms of gender, ethnic origin, and also experience. The rationale for seeking a diverse range of experience was to encourage law students who had not previously been involved in social justice work to expand their horizons. In the event, the selection of participants occurred by consensus among the working party members.

Once selected, the students were introduced into the actual work of the project. That involved two parts. First, the students were given an intensive half-day workshop on the basic principles of human rights law and on written advocacy. The students were taught in a seminar format, with examples and exercises. The students were later given a briefing on the project that JFT had decided to undertake—a submission to the Australian Human Rights Commission's inquiry on freedom of religion and belief. The students were divided into groups of two or three, and they were each given a set of questions to research and to which they should draft responses. Each group was assigned a mentor, who in each case was a human rights lawyer and member of JFT. The students met regularly with their mentor—either in person, or using online telephony. A faculty member oversaw this process.

In the research and drafting process, the students were able to discuss their work with their mentor. They began by developing with their mentor a draft policy position which would provide the direction for their advocacy. They also discussed how to approach the research and writing. Next, through the iterative stages of legal writing in which the students submitted drafts and redrafts that were annotated by their mentor, the students were able to learn how to refine their written advocacy to the stage of finality. This back-and-forth process, though a common experience for junior lawyers, is almost unheard of in law school where a piece of work usually has a very short trajectory: from the student to their lecturer and back again, without the student having the chance to respond to feedback and improve their own writing.

The third element of the project was an opportunity for the students to come back as a group and reflect on what they had learned, and how it might affect their career choices and opportunities. They also were given the opportunity to comment on how the pilot program could be improved.

CONCLUSION

Studying to be a lawyer should involve something more than merely learning the law and the basic skills needed for legal practice. In particular, it should involve learning *about* the law: what the law is intended to achieve and where lie the law's deficiencies. That knowledge is interesting and useful in itself, and certainly allows practicing lawyers to identify loopholes that can be exploited for the benefit of their clients. However, in preparing law students for entry into a profession—one based on lofty ideals to achieve justice—law students also should learn how to use this knowledge to *reform* the law, making it more responsive to the needs of the community that lawyers serve.

This chapter has considered, in the context of institutional law reform and direct social justice advocacy, why law students should become involved in law reform. In particular, we consider two examples of law-reform-oriented projects—the internship program at the Australian Law Reform Commission and the Social Justice Advocacy Project. They are significant because each adopts elements of the clinical method to inculcate in law students a broader understanding of the role of practicing lawyers to achieve systemic justice.

LIST OF REFERENCES

Australian Law Reform Commission, Annual Report 2006–2007 (2007).

CATRIONA COOK, ROBIN CREYKE, ROBERT GEDDES, & DAVID HAMER, LAYING DOWN THE LAW (6th ed., LexisNexis Butterworths 2005).

LON FULLER, THE MORALITY OF LAW (Yale University Press 1964).

MICHAEL KIRBY, REFORM THE LAW: ESSAYS ON THE RENEWAL OF THE AUSTRALIAN LEGAL SYSTEM (Oxford University Press 1983).

WILLIAM L. SULLIVAN et al., EDUCATING LAWYERS: PREPARATION FOR THE PROFESSION OF LAW (Jossey Bass 2007).

Michael Tilbury, *A History of Law Reform in Australia, in* THE PROMISE OF LAW REFORM (Brian Opeskin & David Weisbrot eds. 2005).

David Weisbrot, *The Future for Institutional Law Reform, in* THE PROMISE OF LAW REFORM (Brian Opeskin & David Weisbrot eds. 2005).

15. STREET LAW AND SOCIAL JUSTICE EDUCATION

RICHARD GRIMES, DAVID McQUOID-MASON,

ED O'BRIEN, AND JUDY ZIMMER

INTRODUCTION

"Street Law was the best thing I did in law school" is an often-heard evaluation of the Street Law experience. Ed O'Brien had the same reaction in 1972, when, as a law student, he taught the first Street Law class at an inner-city high school in Washington, DC. Shortly after that, he cofounded Street Law, Inc., which supports and encourages the development of legal literacy programs in the United States and further afield. Law students, high school students, and many other community groups have since voted with their feet and the program spread from Washington, DC to law schools, school districts, and many other institutions across the country and around the world. Today more than one hundred law schools worldwide have established Street Law programs. Many thousands of Street Law sessions have been delivered in schools, prisons, and other community settings and with a range of different groups—often with specific needs and frequently suffering from clear social disadvantage. (Miller, 2008)

In essence, Street Law is a vehicle through which the public can be made more aware of their rights and responsibilities. While the sessions can be led by experienced experts—law teachers and practicing lawyers—they are often most effective when done by law students whose task is to learn the material themselves before helping others to understand it. Law students often strike an immediate rapport when working with school pupils, in part because they may not be many years senior to their target audience. At the same time, the law students learn a great deal more than the law that they teach—about the communities they serve and the role that the law and lawyers can have in addressing the legal needs of the public. Of course, if students are leading Street Law sessions, their work must be supervised by lawyers to ensure that the content meets professionally required standards.

This chapter examines various approaches to Street Law programs worldwide, by focusing on their mission and goals and their contribution to justice education, drawing in particular on the authors' experience in the United States, South Africa, and the United Kingdom. It also looks at various practical issues for law schools running Street Law modules, including the training of students, the assessment of their work, and the question of whether Street Law programs should be conducted for credit or offered more as a pro bono service. The chapter also discusses the rationale for teaching law using the Street Law methodology and looks at how Street Law can be structured and delivered, highlighting the models used and the principles of best practice employed in effective Street Law programs. It also offers some specific examples of successful Street Law initiatives. Finally, the authors draw their conclusions and the lessons to be learned in terms of future and sustainable development.

The experience in the United States is valuable not only for showing what the Street Law method is—an interactive and participatory approach to study for teacher and student alike—but also for demonstrating how sound pedagogic principles can be transferred usefully from one jurisdiction to another. This basic technique has been taken and adapted to suit many other countries; when sensitive to cultural context and perceived needs, the Street Law approach to raising awareness of rights and responsibilities appears to work in a variety of practically effective and socially relevant ways. For example, in the United Kingdom, law students are often involved in Street Law sessions, making one-off presentations or providing short courses on specific legal topics, which may then be backed up with support services such as advice or representation. The law students and their teachers may also meet with members of a community group to discuss and customize the teaching to meet the group's specific needs. Insights from the South African experience show how improved levels of legal literacy can be a powerful tool for social change, promoting greater awareness of civic rights and encouraging participation in the democratic process. Much of the success of Street Law in South Africa occurred at a time when the country was attempting to shake off the shackles of the apartheid era.

STREET LAW'S MISSION AND GOALS: STREET LAW AS A MOVEMENT FOR SOCIAL CHANGE

The 1960s and 70s were a time of social change and reflection in the United States. While the civil rights and women's rights movements focused on the promise of equal opportunity, there was a slowly dawning realization that in order to get your constitutional rights you really had to know about them and claim them. (Alexander, 1993) Law was complicated and written in a language that made average people feel left out. This historical backdrop provided some of the inspiration for the launch of the first Street Law program. (O'Brien, 1978) The name "Street Law" was used from the beginning; it was catchy and meant to portray the teaching of practical law to nonlawyers, so that it would be useful in their everyday lives "on the street."

The original course provided information about how to avoid legal problems and what to do when problems arose. The following year Georgetown University expanded the program and offered law students the opportunity to teach Street Law in tandem with high school teachers in high schools across Washington, DC. (Miller, 2008; McQuoid-Mason, 2003) The origins of Street Law in the United Kingdom can be traced to a pilot project that took place in 1997 at the University of Derby, in which a team of law students guided fifteen-year-olds in an inner-city school through a realistic criminal case. The pupils reacted by saying that they better understood the role of law and the courts as a result, with some stressing that they now had no intention of ever ending up in court themselves unless it was as a lawyer! (Grimes, 2003) The Street Law program was introduced in South Africa in the mid-1980s when the country was subjected to brutal repression by the apartheid regime. The first Street Law workshop in South Africa occurred on the day the first state of emergency was imposed in that country. (Maisel, 2007; McQuoid-Mason, 2003; McQuoid-Mason, 2000)

From the beginning young people seemed to readily understand the power of Street Law and the impact it could have on their lives. Engagement in Street Law means participation, not listening to lectures. Law student "teachers" are encouraged to use interactive techniques in the classroom including role-plays, small groups, case studies, and mock trials. High school students and others tend to respond positively to these methods as well as appreciating the practical content.

But there is no prescribed community for Street Law. Street Law projects have involved such varied groups as school pupils and their teachers, adult prisoners, juvenile offenders, foster children, prison officers, tenants' associations, social welfare claimants' groups, victims of domestic violence, residents in homeless persons hostels, patients on drink and drug dependency programs, people with mental health problems, citizenship teachers and trainees, volunteers in not-for-profit organizations, and managers in health care trusts. (Miller, 2008)

Whatever the form or content, it is important to work closely with any partner group to make sure that the material covered is relevant to local needs. Depending on resources and individual requirements, Street Law courses can range from one-off presentations (for example, an outline of domestic or international human rights legislation and its implications) to short courses on consumer law, remedies in cases of domestic violence, environmental protection, housing rights, or social welfare entitlements. Street Law can also be offered as a full semester or year-long course covering many legal topics.

The essence of Street Law is public or community-based legal education. Discussions with the community do not just happen. For a variety of reasons the public may be unfamiliar with and possibly uncomfortable in taking a lead role in determining what the Street Law sessions should cover. They may also be hesitant in playing an active part in the planned presentations. With a degree of sensitivity and with genuine respect for cultural and social diversity, experience suggests that the community can become readily and willingly involved—and indeed soon welcomes that involvement. Other factors may come into play as well. Thus, Street Law has been readily welcomed in schools and colleges in the United Kingdom, due in part to the government's emphasis on citizenship (since 2002, a part of the National Curriculum in schools) and attendant resource implications.

A stark example of the scope, adaptability, and power of Street Law can be seen in the South African context. During the period of increased repression and repeated states of emergency it was important to indicate to people that certain laws—despite the apartheid legal system—could still protect them. The Street Law program sought to educate ordinary people about the law and how they could seek help if they required it. At the same time the program aimed to encourage citizens, especially young adults and schoolchildren, to think about the type of legal system they would like in the future. (Miller, 2008; Maisel, 2007) This became particularly important once apartheid began to crumble in the early 1990s. During the negotiations for a new constitution, there was widespread consultation with the public about what a future constitution would look like. As a result Street Law introduced a series of annual "Space Colony" camps (later known as "Youth Parliaments") to enable young people from different racial and economic backgrounds to meet and debate constitutional issues. (McQuoid-Mason, 2003)

The Street Law program helped to break down the apartheid racial barriers between young people by enabling Black and White schoolchildren to share experiences and debate important societal issues with each other at integrated weekend workshops and Street Law sessions. It also provided law students with an opportunity to interact with schoolchildren from different racial and socio-economic backgrounds, and exposed them to the legal needs and aspirations of local communities. In some instances, students found themselves actively involved in assisting with community development and capacity building in the neighborhoods where the schools were located.

Street Law thus used a number of creative methods to subvert the apartheid system by projecting the program as politically neutral and working with strategic partners, such as the university law faculties, the legal profession, the judiciary, and government education departments. Clearly, the Street Law mission in South Africa was to promote and facilitate social change.

Street Law is but one form of clinic that can be used as a conduit through which social justice issues can be directly and effectively addressed. It shares many of the features of other clinical legal education programs in that it carries a dual benefit of hands-on education for law students while at the same time providing a legal service, usually for those who may be unable to access a lawyer through more conventional means. It differs from the other clinics in that it is primarily about raising awareness of legal rights and responsibilities (rather than tackling individual problems) through a community-based service.[1] As will be seen below, however, it can also be carried out in a hybrid format that offers both improved levels of legal literacy and customized help.

---

1. Legal literacy programs in India, discussed in Chapter 16, follow a similar approach.

The rest of this chapter focuses on Street Law programs that are led by law schools, for two reasons: first, most Street Law initiatives are law school–based; and secondly, Street Law programs appear to be most effective when organized and delivered by a law school. The Street Law approach to learning forms a bridge between social action and justice education. For the law student, Street Law is an alternative but complementary way in which the knowledge, skills, and values implicit in the practice of law and in justice education can be studied to practical effect. It provides a setting in which students can address not only the letter of the law, but also the professional and ethical considerations of legal practice and the obligations on—and expectations of—legal practitioners.

STREET LAW CLINICS IN ACTION: PRACTICING SOCIAL JUSTICE EDUCATION

The primary rationale for the law school in running Street Law clinics is that they provide law students with a powerful professional development opportunity. By improving the level of the public's legal literacy, the students come to realize—from the Street Law experience—that they increase the possibility of more-informed choice for the community as a whole and for the individual as and when he or she encounters legal difficulties.

As in any clinical program, Street Law gives students the opportunity to become actively involved in their learning by providing a practical setting in which students can address the professional and ethical issues relevant to law practice and legal practitioners. Street Law clinics also directly address various lawyering skills, most notably research, problem-solving, communication, drafting, and teamwork. Study in this way reinforces learning through application and reflection; supporting student learning elsewhere in the law curriculum through exposure to a multitude of practical, and often overlapping, legal issues. (Pinder, 1998)

Street Law clinics around the world are, of course, by no means identical in form or content. The emphasis in individual schemes will focus on specific outcomes according to the aims of that particular program and the needs of the client group with whom the law school and its students are working. Nonetheless, there are a set of common features that have perceived advantages over more traditional forms of legal education. In particular Street Law programs focus on the specific and often unmet legal needs of the community and can support otherwise "hard-to-reach" groups. They forge links between the law school and the wider community and provide an opportunity for academics, practitioners, students, and members of the local community to work in partnership to increase understanding of law and the legal process. (Pinder, 1998) This form of clinical education promotes pro bono involvement on the part of practicing lawyers through their participation as supervisors and mentors and through follow-up work generated by Street Law presentations.

A further feature of Street Law is that it may complement moves to address active citizenship and social inclusion in a wider educational context. In the United Kingdom, for example, the government introduced a compulsory component in the curriculum in 2002 for all eleven- to sixteen-year-olds in state schools. Pupils are now required to study a range of civic issues, many of which might appear in a Street Law program, such as the workings of the courts, the differences between criminal and civil law, and the operation of the democratic process. In any event, a well-targeted Street Law scheme should increase awareness of rights and responsibilities for both students and targeted community groups, as well as generate wider community involvement through the identification of projects for further work (which may or may not involve the law school)—a practical manifestation of community empowerment.

There are several Street Law models that have evolved in the United States and in other jurisdictions to match the needs of the law school and the community. These models have stood the test of time and are robust in terms of educational and legal practice. Each is described briefly below.

The credit-bearing or integrated model is usually a law clinic run by the law school as part of its overall curriculum. It normally includes a structured training and induction program, a weekly seminar, a detailed schedule for delivery of the Street Law sessions, and a transparent assessment process. Law students not only learn the relevant substantive law and related procedures, but also address innovative teaching strategies to prepare, develop, and deliver their Street Law classes. This model can also build a foundation from which students can progress in working in other, live-client, clinics; for example, an advice or representation clinic. This is the case with many Street Law programs in the United Kingdom.

The nonclinical, pro bono model is typically organized by either an enthusiast within the law school or someone working for a nongovernmental organization (NGO) or other type of not-for-profit or voluntary sector body. (Caplow, 2006) Training and technical assistance may be provided, but in essence this model works to satisfy a public interest requirement and is not designed for the legal education, foundational training, or professional development of the law student. A variant on this model can become overtly clinical if the law student returns to the law school and is then given the opportunity of deconstructing the experience and reflecting on what happened and why. This is akin to placement or externship clinics discussed in Chapter 22.

The law student organizations model is a common one started and implemented by a law student group. In the United States, the Black Law Students Association and the Public Interest Law Group are two examples of student organizations that have started Street Law programs based on this model. It can accommodate large numbers of law students, but sustainability can be challenging because it often depends on a small group of committed law students who turn over from year to year. It is not itself a clinical model, as the faculty does not normally support it. It is, however, often a lead-in to the credit-bearing or integrated model described above. (Kovach, 1998)

There are, of course, pros and cons to each of the models. However, the greatest value in terms of educational benefit for law students—and, quite possibly, the community alike—comes from the credit-bearing or integrated model. This is simply because the learning experience is a structured one for law students and the community, where outcomes are clear and the reflective process is an integral part of the learning. It is one thing to have a hands-on experience but another to discuss and appreciate the value of it.

No matter which model is chosen, one of the keys to Street Law program sustainability is to build the program with the support of law faculties, local schools, district, regional, state, federal, and national governments, the legal profession, industry, and the wider community. Connecting the Street Law program with the law school mission or diversity statement and outlining the ways which it helps the law school accomplish its mission is an important starting point. Successful programs also reach out and invite key people to participate in the activities of the Street Law classes. Stakeholders needed for the ongoing support of the program include leading lawyers and judges, law school management, and frontline teachers from the school district and/or community sites where law students will be teaching. The more people are exposed to the power of this type of educational experience, the more they are likely to understand and support the program. The cooperation of all interested parties can also have significant tactical advantages; for example, in South Africa the involvement of the judiciary and practicing lawyers lent legitimacy to the program which might otherwise have been banned under the restrictions imposed by the apartheid regime.

The South African Street Law experience is in many ways unique, given the historical point at which it rose to prominence. It is worth pointing out, however, that although it was born out of a particular political and social context, it was still based on a clear and proven methodology. One aspect of this is the use of training and teaching manuals. These valuable materials were first produced in 1975 through Street Law, Inc. in the United States and are now in their eighth edition. (Arbetman & O'Brien, 2010) They cover a range of legal issues and topics from criminal law to consumer rights and from constitutional matters to family law. The manuals are used across all states in the United States and have been adapted for use in many countries worldwide.

BEST PRACTICE

All models, to be effective, require a structured training program so that all participants understand what is expected of them and how the program is to work. This discipline is also good professional practice and illustrates for the law student the nature and extent of professional requirements and expectations. Most, if not all, Street Law programs use a manual or textbook that is written in simple language, often produced in two versions—one for the target group, for example, school pupils, and the other complete with notes of guidance for law students and their teachers and supervisors. An interesting slant on this occurs in some jurisdictions where the law students, under professionally qualified supervisors, produce the manuals and other learning materials which become valuable teaching resources. The Street Law book produced by Street Law, Inc. and which later influenced a South African edition is a rich resource and fine example of what can be achieved. The South African book, which is highly user-friendly with engaging cartoons and case studies, contains clear operational instructions and student-centered exercises. (McQuoid-Mason, 2003; McQuoid-Mason, 2000) It covers an introduction to South African law and the legal system, criminal law and juvenile justice, consumer law, family law, socio-economic rights, and labor law. Other manuals on human rights and democracy for all were developed jointly by Street Law South Africa and Street Law, Inc. Most universities and colleges offering Street Law in the United Kingdom utilize a manual that gives guidance on setup and management as well as providing core resource materials. (McQuoid-Mason, 2000)

Best practice must begin with quality. The manual and handbooks referred to above are a good starting point, but quality assurance can be achieved and maintained only through robust supervision and ongoing monitoring. Therefore, when law students deliver Street Law sessions, law teachers and/or law practitioners must be able to follow the students' research and preparation and view the product before and after it is delivered.

Another important aspect of best practice in Street Law is interactivity, both when preparing law students to teach and when the law students are teaching. The more you engage the audience the more likely they are to take on board what it is you are trying to get across. Because the Street Law approach emphasizes both content and methodology, the preparation must actively engage the law students. Similarly, the most effective classes teach lessons that provide a sufficient quality and quantity of relevant information using interactive strategies. High school classes that involve students in examining all sides of complex issues help them use analytical and decision-making skills. The best seminars build on the existing knowledge of the law students and provide multiple opportunities to practice and debrief the experiences. Thus, the highest quality law student preparation should mirror the style of teaching that law students are expected to use in school or community settings.

As well as being interactive, the Street Law program needs to have clear goals and outcomes and one (some might say essential) way of achieving this is through the use of lesson plans. In effective Street Law programs, law student "teachers" prepare detailed lesson plans that specify what is to be covered, what the audience is expected to get out of a particular session, and how the session will be conducted (including the various activities and their timings). The actual process of preparation focuses the law students' minds on the "what," the "why," and the "how" of their sessions.

Street Law classes help both law students and target audiences understand what the law is, why it works the way it does, and how it can be made better. This integrated and holistic approach to learning involves teaching both content and skills. For law students, clarity of outcomes and the use of interactivity through mock trials, legislative hearings, role-plays, and simulated negotiations provide in-depth knowledge of law and legal procedures and—at the same time— enhances their capacity to organize thoughts and communicate effectively.

Another aspect of best practice is to ensure community engagement in the Street Law program from the very outset. For example, in the UK Street Law programs—normally termed *Streetlaw*—a community group is contacted (or perhaps contacts the law school) and discussions take place between members of the community group and law school staff and students on what the group would like to learn in terms of content. The students then agree with their law teachers about what needs to be researched and how the presentation will be structured. The research is carried out, and the law teachers ensure that their findings are legally accurate and that the proposed presentation is appropriate for the audience. In accordance with good teaching practice, most if not all of the Streetlaw programs in the United Kingdom make the presentations highly interactive, encouraging participation from the target audience. If the principle of hands-on learning applies to the students then surely it is the same for the community group concerned?

Once the form and content of the presentation has been agreed upon with the community, the students deliver the session(s). The student performance may well carry academic credit, in which case the law teachers must assess and grade the student work. Assessment may be by grading oral presentations, assessing preparatory work, evaluating a reflective journal or more conventional essay, by examination (although using the latter has limitations in terms of providing a formative means of assessment), or by a combination of these methods. In UK law schools, Streetlaw may be offered as extracurricula activity or may be a credit-bearing compulsory or elective module. It is typically delivered over one semester. Whichever approach is used, community feedback is essential to value the worth of the session(s) and the quality of the law student performance. The engagement of the community therefore runs from initial contact through to final feedback. It is almost as if a lawyer-client relationship had been created—a relationship founded on professionalism and mutual respect.

In brief, the following "best practice" points can be made.

Quantity vs. quality—It is important to focus on quality of instruction rather than quantity: set realistic goals for the number of classes law students will teach. Law students may seem extremely eager to teach several times a week, but come exam time, this eagerness may be tempered by assessment-induced anxiety

Materials—Students should be encouraged to use existing materials (for example, from Street Law, Inc. or other tested curricula.) This allows students to focus on structure, content, and methodology and spend less time creating teaching resources from scratch

Preparation—Peer teaching can be an important and valuable part of law student preparation. This takes the form of a law student teaching a mock class to other law students. It will provide law students with an opportunity to try out a lesson with a friendly audience, learn the substantive law, receive feedback on their teaching style, and demonstrate a particular teaching strategy. By creating a supportive and constructive environment in this way, the law students can become learning resources and constructive critics for each other

Reflection—To enable full participation in the reflective process law students should be given the opportunity to analyze their experiences. This process is often termed "debriefing" by the Street Law community. Street Law injects the human element into a law school education. Law students learn from their Street Law audiences about how laws impact on people and the strengths and weaknesses of the legal system in practice. This insight sensitizes the law students to crucial public policy issues and concerns, which can encourage law students to pursue a career path aimed at combating social injustices. Some programs ask law students to keep journals built around their classroom experiences. The journals enhance the reflection process and document the progress of the law student throughout the class

Lesson plans—We cannot emphasize enough the importance of working with relevant, realistic, and deliverable lesson plans. The creation of the plan itself is an important stage in the learning process, but the following-through of the plan gives structure to the proposed Street Law session and provides a basis for feedback and reflection on the part of all participants. It should also give confidence to the law students when delivering the Street Law session as they have a planned structure to follow and a rationale to explain to their target audience. Well-developed Street Law programs hold preparatory seminars where law students are taken through sample lesson plans exposing them to a wide variety of teaching techniques and subjects taken from the Street Law manuals and other texts. In South Africa, for example, the curriculum typically covers introduction to law, criminal law and juvenile justice, consumer law, family law, socio-economic rights, and labor law, as well as human rights, gender and racial sensitivity, democracy, and HIV/AIDS. Law students are then required to devise or adapt lesson plans to suit the proposed delivery.

For both the law student and the community participants, Street Law provides the chance to look at the substantive law, legal, and related skills (e.g., communication) and lawyering values (e.g., professionalism) in the light of the outcomes or objectives set in the lesson plan for particular Street Law sessions. The outcomes therefore can cover not just what the law says, but also the skills and values involved.

Interaction—Successful Street Law sessions depend on active participation. Those responsible for managing Street Law programs should insist that the bulk of the delivery time is devoted to interactive study; "chalk and talk" is not enough! Students must be taught how to use interactive teaching methods such as brainstorming, small group discussions, debates, moots, and case studies. These and other techniques are set out in South African Street Law teaching manuals (McQuoid-Mason, 2008). Street Law students must also learn how to structure an effective lesson and how to prepare lesson plans to ensure interactivity (Pinder, 1998 at 214–15). One particularly powerful form of interactive teaching is role-play. In South Africa students are taken, step-by-step, through the preparation and presentation of a mock trial involving up to twenty-four participants. They experience a mock trial for themselves as a class and are then required to compile and conduct their own mock trial at a high school, in prison, or with a community group. Mock trials have become so popular in the United States that there are over 40 state-wide competitions held annually. Many other countries, including the United Kingdom, have also adopted this "competition" model.

Time and credit—Before leaving best practice, it may be worth looking briefly at the time factor. The amount of contact hours allocated to Street Law varies from university to university depending on whether or not it is an accredited course and what weight is attached to the module. Where Street Law is a credit course, it is usually offered for the same number of hours as other clinical courses and often is treated as any other elective or optional subject. In some universities, the courses run for one semester while in others they continue for the whole academic year. For instance, the Street Law course at the University of KwaZulu-Natal, in Durban, South Africa (UKZN), is a full-credit course offered over two semesters, which requires two contact hours per week plus community service throughout the year. The time allocated to Street Law by the law school timetable, however, tells only part of the story. In part because of the social responsibility involved, but also, we suspect, because of the interest generated and the positive experience encountered, law students frequently spend many more hours engaged in the Street Law module than they do in other parts of the curriculum. While this may be laudable—who does not want law students to work hard?—the expectations and demands of study in this way must be carefully handled to ensure a balanced and manageable learning experience. Student enthusiasm must not be allowed to prejudice study elsewhere on their programs.

EXAMPLES

Let's peek into a typical Street Law classroom . . .

"So… is it in the "best interests" of Kimberly to stay with her mother?"

There's the law student watching as the high school class works in small groups trying to decide if it is in the "best interests of the child" for Kimberly to remain with her mother. Kimberly's mother is in a drug rehabilitation program and sometimes her apartment is used as a shooting gallery. What is the responsibility of the state in this case? The school pupils are analyzing the facts, discussing the issues, and for-mulating an opinion. They all seem to have a view. Yes, the child should be taken into the care of the Council. No, the mother and child should not be separated. What needs to happen is the mother wants help and support. But she is an addict, say some—how can she have care of her child?

This example, from a Street Law program at a high school in the United States, is not only typical but shows the sort of approach and the relevant and contem-porary nature of a good Street Law session. It happens to be about parental and child rights and the role of the state in protecting the vulnerable. It could easily have been about how laws are made or changed, about housing rights, or about what happens if you go to court. There are many other examples of Street Law sessions taking place around the world that demonstrate the breadth and flexibility of the concept as a clinical teaching and learning method. Specific examples have raised some interesting issues:

The "diversity pipeline"—In the United States (and many other countries, we suspect) ethnic minority participation in law school is low, often less than 10 percent. Some Street Law programs in the United States, in partnership with the Law School Admissions Council, integrate strategies especially designed to reach out to young people of color while they are still in high school. School pupils take part in these Street Law sessions, learn about careers in the law, and raise the possibility of going to law school and becoming a lawyer.

Credit or not?—Street Law programs in South Africa vary between optional credit courses and pro bono voluntary classes where law students receive no academic credit for their work. As noted above, UKZN in South Africa has an optional two-semester, full-credit Street Law course. The academic component of the course requires students to attend training seminars; prepare lessons to present lessons in high schools, prisons, or other organizations; keep a reflective diary of their lessons; write an examination; and prepare a mock trial package. Conversely, the Street Law program at Nelson Mandela Metropolitan University (Port Elizabeth, South Africa) is not a credit course, yet the training program to prepare law students to present lessons in high schools, prisons, and commu-nity groups is similar to that at UKZN.

Making changes to rules and policy—Street Law sessions can lead on to a bigger project. This happened at a session in a rundown area of northern England where local residents were experiencing a variety of problems in their area including antisocial behavior, drugs-related activity, prostitution, and a high police presence. Much of this seemed to stem from the gradual decline of social conditions including the deterioration of housing stock. Many of the houses had been abandoned and were now used for illicit purposes. Residents did not want to come down hard on the (mainly) young people abusing the area; they just wanted to see the situation improve for everyone. A local law school did a Street Law presentation on the powers of the Council to compel landowners to improve the condition of their houses. Armed with this information, the residents asked the law students and teachers to help them discuss with the Council what could be done. As a result of the meetings, the Council changed its policy on intervention and agreed to take action in specific cases. What began as a lesson on the law turned out to be an exercise in using the law as a lever or persuasive device. This showed not only the empowerment of the community but how law was not just a long-winded and expensive instrument focused on litigation. The end result was improved housing stock and many of the problems previously experienced abated. No one had to be sued or prosecuted.

Streetlaw "Plus"—The Streetlaw program at The College of Law in England has been developed to go beyond an initial information stage typical of Street Law sessions, in response to a specific need for help with letter-writing and form-filling. The "Plus" component is follow-up legal help. Law students do a session, for example, on social welfare benefit entitlement, and then run a clinic at which clients can get assistance with filling in the often-demanding forms needed to claim benefits. Discussions around rights and responsibilities in the classic Street Law approach have led to other specific services, such as providing individual clients with help in putting their concerns into writing (and sending them to the appropriate person or body responsible) and assisting clients in completing various types of paperwork. This variant of Street Law group work sees law students raising awareness of entitlements on both a collective and individual basis. The letter-writing and form-filing clinics—known respectively as "*Say it write*" and "*On-form*"—are held in a community setting that is accessible to members of the public. College of Law students have carried out these services, for example, at a law centre, in a public library, with an ethnic minority organization, and at a school.

Assessing law students—The UKZN Street Law program in South Africa requires students to write a practical examination (50 percent), produce a reflective journal (30 percent), and develop a mock trial package (20 percent). The examination requires students to prepare unseen lesson plans for designated aspects of the law, human rights, or democracy. They are also asked to analyze a mock trial package with a view to choosing a side and then describing how they would deal with the case, including the questions they would ask in direct and cross-examination. The reflective journal includes the lesson plans for each of the twenty-five lessons prepared, a brief school report for each of the lessons signed by a teacher, and a short reflective essay on each of the lessons presented. Finally, each student is required to prepare an original mock trial package that may be based on a real or hypothetical case.

Training the trainers—Particular attention has been paid in the United States to training teachers in issues of law and the legal process. Using the Street Law textbook and other materials, schoolteachers attend classes sometimes run by law schools and on other occasions led by Street Law, Inc. staff. This in turn builds confidence and capacity, enabling the teachers to return to their classrooms better equipped to address issues of law, human rights, and democracy. Variants on this theme exist in other Street Law programs, notably in the "developing" world where the "training of trainers" model is followed. Street Law–type seminars to train high school teachers were conducted at different universities in South Africa during the late 1980s and early 1990s, when there was abundant funding for democracy education. However, as funding for NGOs became more difficult and funding for the Street law programs was taken over by the universities themselves, more emphasis was placed on training law students than teachers. At present teacher training in aspects of Street Law is occasionally done under the auspices of the different provincial education departments with assistance from the national and provincial Street Law coordinator. Some law schools in the United Kingdom have designed short courses capable of carrying credit for members of the community who have completed the *Streetlaw* program successfully. This fits not only with the educational objectives of the university or college, but also with the government's stated commitment to continuing adult education and capacity building.

CONCLUSIONS AND LESSONS LEARNED

In any country, and notably a developing country like South Africa, it is important that law students be encouraged to participate in community service and be given academic credit for their efforts. In our experience, a properly integrated academic and community service Street Law program provides law students with an opportunity to experience social justice in the real world, while rendering a service to society and obtaining valuable insights into their own potential as future lawyers. Here is a chance to apply knowledge, develop skills, and begin to grasp what it means to behave professionally. If properly supervised, it provides the community with a valuable addition to existing legal services and a flexible and appropriate tool through which wider social justice issues can be addressed. In other words, everyone is a winner—the law student who learns more effectively, the public who are better informed, the law school that is able to serve a community mission, the legal profession that inherits more socially aware and skilled lawyers, and the government which (presumably) supports greater social inclusion.

Understandably, students often have limited experience of teaching and may need considerable support in the initial stages of preparation. Experience suggests that they are usually both dedicated and professional in their approach, and soon come up with effective and innovative means of delivery. The work involved in Street Law is considerable and, although students are invariably delighted to have been selected, there can be complaints when the deadlines for preparation and delivery approach. Obvious times to avoid are assessment pressure points.

Working with the community can present particular challenges. Students come face-to-face with law in the real world, and with that the implicit need for a professional standard of delivery. Sensitive issues can be at stake and care must be taken to deliver what is needed in a clear and nonpatronizing way. A very effective device is to involve the community—at the earliest possible stage—in discussion over what is required. In some of the schemes referred to above, a steering group is formed that represents residents of the area and other stakeholders and can oversee projects.

Perhaps the biggest challenge is managing expectations of both the community and the students. Street Law programs are generally oversubscribed and failure to get a place can cause disappointment. Once stimulated by participation, community groups often ask for more, and the expectation on how much can be done needs careful management if quality is to be maintained and everyone kept happy. A good program should make clear at the outset that Street Law is awareness-raising of rights and responsibilities and not (at least initially) individual advice. Where people do need individual assistance, this can be done by active referral to other sources of help, mainly through the pro bono services of lawyers, the use of the law school's other clinics, or existing legal aid and NGO resources. Expectations of both student instructors and the target audience are also directly addressed with a structured induction and training program and a Street Law manual which sets out the program's form, content, ethos, and assessment methods.

At the beginning of the twenty-first century, our world faces many new challenges. Educating citizens about law, democracy, and human rights through law school–based Street Law programs is one effective strategy for creating a reservoir of people who understand and treasure the values of a constitutional democracy—and can both claim and respect their rights and the rights of others.

In conclusion, let us leave you with these apposite words from both sides of the Street Law experience:

A law student said recently, summing up the value of experiential learning in general and Street Law in particular:

> *This was the best thing I did in my time at law school. Problems come to you as real, everyday difficulties—not neatly packaged as "contract" or "tort." I learnt to take the questions apart, to identify the legal issues, to research the law and to come up with practical solutions. That is what learning should really be all about.*

Following a Street Law presentation at a secondary school, an eleven-year-old was heard to say:

> *I understand that it's important to get involved but how can you if you don't know your rights?*

We rest our case.

LIST OF REFERENCES

Mark C. Alexander, *Law-Related Education: Hope for Today's Students*, 20 OHIO N.U. L. REV. 57 (1993).

LEE ARBETMAN & ED O'BRIEN, STREET LAW: A COURSE IN PRACTICAL LAW (8th ed., McGraw-Hill 2010).

Alexandra Ashbrook, Street Law: Putting Your Legal Education to Work, *available at* http://www.streetlaw.org.

Stacy Caplow, Comment, *Clinical Legal Education in Hong Kong: A Time to Move Forward*, 36 HONG KONG L. J. 229 (2006).

Lamar Cravens, *A Lesson in Street Law*, 60 TEX. B.J. 264 (1997).

Richard Grimes, *Legal Literacy, Community Empowerment and Law Schools—Some Lessons from a Working Model in the UK*, 37 LAW TEACHER 273 (2003).

Kimberlee K. Kovach, *The Lawyer as Teacher: The Role of Education in Lawyering*, 4 CLINICAL L. REV. 359 (1998).

Peggy Maisel, *Expanding and Sustaining Clinical Legal Education in Developing Countries: What We Can Learn from South Africa*, 30 FORDHAM INT'L L.J. 374 (2007).

STREET LAW: PRACTICAL LAW FOR SOUTH AFRICAN STUDENTS: BOOK 1 INTRODUCTION TO SOUTH AFRICAN LAW AND THE LEGAL SYSTEM (David J. McQuoid-Mason ed., 2nd ed., Juta and Co. 2005).

David J. McQuoid-Mason, *The Delivery of Civil Legal Aid Services in South Africa*, 24 FORDHAM INT'L L.J. S111 (2000).

David J. McQuoid-Mason, *Teaching Human Rights in a Hostile Environment: A Lesson from South Africa*, 22 WINDSOR Y.B. ACCESS TO JUST. 213 (2003).

David J. McQuoid-Mason, *Street Law South African Experience with Particular Reference to the University of KwaZulu Natal*, 17 GRIFFITH LAW REVIEW, 27 (2008).

Adam Miller, *Street Law Uses Legal Education to Empower Underprivileged Youth*, 13 PUB. INT. L. REP. 38 (2008).

Edward L. O'Brien & Lee P. Arbetman, *A New Clinical Curriculum: Teaching Practical Law to High School Students and Inmates*, 29 J. LEG. EDUC. 568 (1978).

Kamina Pinder, *Street Law: Twenty-Five Years and Counting*, 27 J. LEG. & EDUC. 211 (1998).

16. LEGAL LITERACY PROJECTS
Clinical Experience of Empowering the Poor in India

AJAY PANDEY AND SHEENA SHUKKUR

Legal literacy may be defined narrowly as educating the common populace on various provisions of law affecting their everyday well-being. It can also be defined more broadly as an effort to empower members of the community and secure their participation in bringing about social justice, including good governance. Legal literacy is particularly important in India because while there are many laws and regulations aimed at securing a just and fair society, their effective implementation will always remain incomplete if the common population does not have adequate information about these provisions. Good governance is linked to legal literacy in India because the state has a larger mandate to ensure justice and equity, but this too means little in practice due to a lack of effective implementation.

Legal literacy projects, when conceived in the narrow sense set out above, are in many ways similar to Street Law projects discussed in Chapter 15. When conceived in the broader sense, they can still serve as the "clinical experience" for a Street Law-like clinical course—but they can also serve as a vehicle for extending the scope and impact of a law school's social justice mission. This chapter explores the use of legal literacy projects and their role in the clinical legal education movement in India in both of these respects. After this brief introduction, the chapter continues with a description of the goals and methods of law school-based legal literacy clinics as they have existed in India for many years. The next section describes a novel legal literacy project aimed at empowering villagers in rural areas to work toward good governance, which can be a model for enhancing the social justice mission of legal literacy clinics in India.

A number of different entities undertake legal literacy projects in India, including government, nongovernment organizations (NGOs), and law schools. All these projects, no matter who conceives and implements them and irrespective of their duration, reach, and effectiveness, have the common objectives of creating legal awareness and helping further the cause of rule of law in society. They are particularly helpful in mobilizing communities and protecting and promoting rights of people by ensuring effective implementation of law. Projects undertaken by the government generally have larger mandates, more resources, a larger audience, and the benefit of continuity. A prime example of the Government of India's involvement in this work is the National Legal Literacy Mission (2005–2010) launched by the prime minister in March 2005 with the goal of empowering citizens and securing the rule of law. Projects undertaken by NGOs are generally of a temporary nature, but some of them are very effective as compared to government projects. Law schools have a great potential to steer legal literacy projects in India; however, the traditional legal education structure has not been encouraging law schools to undertake such initiatives.[1] As set out in the remainder of this chapter, with greater flexibility to experiment with new methods of learning, law school clinical programs can play a critical role in shaping legal literacy projects to achieve their desired goals.

LAW SCHOOL LEGAL LITERACY CLINICS

Where law is the means to secure and maintain justice for all, the legal profession and everyone associated with the field of law have an extraordinary duty to ensure that masses of people are not excluded from its processes and services. It is important that the values associated with this intent are instilled in lawyers and legal professionals at the very time they begin their study of law. Law school legal literacy clinics can serve to achieve these objectives and also to provide law students the opportunity to develop lawyering skills. This section describes some of the key aspects of law school legal literacy clinics currently operating in India.

Dual Objectives of Law School Legal Literacy Clinics

Law school legal literacy clinics in India have two particular objectives shared by most clinical programs around the world: to have clinical law students serve and support the school's social justice mission, thereby instilling in them a sense of lawyers' public responsibility; and to provide instruction in the practical skills young future lawyers will need to carry out their professional responsibility. (Quigley, 1995) Clinical legal education is largely about the role of lawyers and the legal system as a vehicle for change and a philosophy which builds up faith in the legal system as a means of reform. It provides context for testing legal theories against the problems that people face in the "real world" and sensitizes law students to the ethical and moral responsibilities of performing pro bono legal work. Pragmatically, modern legal education needs to be humanistic so as to enhance and enrich human sensibility in the law and the profession. In addition to developing their skills and competence, law students need to learn to identify social problems and seek solutions to eradicate corruption, injustice, nepotism, and poverty from the global society. Law schools in India have been initiating legal literacy projects with these considerations in place.

In legal literacy clinics, students learn that working toward social justice in legal practice is both good and possible. It may seem attractive to law students to

---

1. The current state of clinical legal education in India is discussed in Chapter 3, which covers South and Southeast Asia.

leave law school believing that they can practice law for individual clients who have money and power and not have to negotiate the law for people with few resources, or no resources and no power. But it is important to remind students that it is impossible to practice law without looking into its consequences. As noted earlier, legal literacy projects bring law and the legal system to life for poor and legally disenfranchised members of society; law students doing this work are shown that extending the reach of the law to all is part of their moral responsibility as lawyers and it enhances the nobility of the profession. Legal literacy clinics, thus, teach law students to value the lives and perspectives of their clients and to understand—through experience—that social justice can be advanced by their actions—in this case by empowering the citizens who would be essentially powerless if left ignorant about the law.

Empowerment, in this context, means providing information and knowledge pertaining to law and the legal system to persons or groups that help them make their own decisions. It is giving power to the powerless, legally enriching the poor and the ignorant. Legal literacy for empowerment educates communities about their rights so that they may exercise these rights themselves. Law reform and access to justice rely on the presence of lawyers because lawyers see things in legal terms, or, more precisely, in their own perception of legal terms. A problem becomes a legal problem not because it can be legally resolved, but because lawyers transform it into something that they themselves can deal with. To be resolved by a lawyer, any problem must be transformed into a legal problem which becomes more complex when the lawyers and the public speak two separate languages. Engaging law students in this empowerment endeavor enables them to help others understand the language of their case—and helps them understand the role that they can play in overcoming limitations inherent in the legal system's capacity to provide justice for all.

Legal Literacy Clinics in Operation

The task of achieving empowerment through legal literacy is achieved primarily by producing legal literacy materials and conducting legal literacy workshops and mass legal literacy campaigns. Legal literacy clinic law students work with and in groups and communities of different regions, religions, and classes to reduce the power imbalances among the individuals, between the individuals and society, and between the society to which they belong and the government. In this context, the students must understand that some laws aim to empower the poor alone, but there are laws meant to empower the poor along with all others.

Care is taken in preparing the materials to simplify the laws as much as possible and to use as many tools as can be devised for effective communication—including books, pamphlets, manuals, posters, films, and radio plays. Basic laws are translated and expressed in the way they are applied in court, and the possible result of a cause in a particular situation is described with examples. Materials are generally prepared in local languages, despite the fact that many laws are written in English, so that the target audience can understand. Examples of laws that have been explained in a lucid manner for use by legal literacy clinics include the Minimum Wages Act, the Equal Remuneration Act, the Maternity Benefit Act, and the Workmen's Compensation Act. In addition, materials have been prepared on Hindu, Muslim, and Christian laws on marriage, divorce, maintenance, adoption, custody of children, and property rights. Other areas covered in legal literacy material range from criminal law provisions on dowry, rape, and citizen rights vis-à-vis police to laws on child marriage, the Medical Termination of Pregnancy Act, the Pre-Natal Diagnostic Techniques Act, the Consumer Protection Act, the Right to Information Act, and the Protection of Civil Rights Act.

Mass legal literacy campaigns and legal workshops are usually organized by various volunteer groups and registered organizations. Apart from offering classes and engaging in discussions and answering questions, these campaigns and workshops prepare and use many other educational tools to connect with the community. Examples include legal films with numerous songs, action, and high drama in the story line, and audio cassettes based on the films. Law students play a very important role in these initiatives. They organize public events by involving lawyers, judges, police officers, and other relevant people to make the initiatives more effective. They also participate directly in the classes and other information sessions by imparting knowledge about the law. In addition, sometimes they address important matters not covered adequately by the law, such as access to health service, protection for the handicapped, poor nutrition, lack of potable water, and inadequate social security measures.

Legal literacy clinics can also operate in collaboration with a law school-based National Service Scheme (NSS). The activities of NSS, which involve all segments of a university, are designed to instill concern for the community and to provide care for the underprivileged. A large number of students and teachers are brought together in an organized form to address frequently raised issues of exploitation, discrimination, unemployment, poverty, and many other areas of concern. NSS volunteers for legal literacy campaigns are given training before they are engaged in the campaigns, and law students are given particular training to impart legal literacy. The volunteers prepare training modules on important themes like citizen's rights and police, consumer rights, the structure of courts in a particular area, and on legal aid and legal services. Workshops aimed at developing training skills, material development, and curriculum design are organized as well.

It is not easy, however, for the students to gain the citizens' trust and bring them to the venue of a legal literacy campaign. Therefore, they first make a preliminary study of the nature of the problems faced by the people belonging to that particular area and prepare themselves to explain the easiest, most expeditious, and least expensive ways to resolve the problems. NSS volunteers work in nearby villages to clean the streets and organize public functions; later, the law students transform themselves into speakers to steer these events toward legal empowerment. The law students are taken to slums, villages, and tribal areas to promote legal literacy and awareness. They visit selected villages to conduct legal surveys to learn about various kinds of cases, some of which may then be referred to the state-run District Legal Aid Authority for proper legal aid and advice. In order to sharpen the students' skills and make their efforts more effective, group meetings among the law students and professors may be organized as a supplement to legal surveys, training, workshops, and seminars. Working in this manner, under suitable guidance and supervision by their teachers, these legal literacy clinic students bring "Law to the People." (Baxi, 1975–1977 at 27, 30; Baxi, 1976)

A COMMUNITY-BASED, RESULT-ORIENTED LEGAL LITERACY PROJECT

Participation of people is critical in ensuring rule of law, good governance, and human rights. This section describes the efforts undertaken by the Policy, Governance, and Advocacy Centre (PGA Centre) of the Institute of Rural Research and Development (IRRAD) in effecting good governance in some select villages of the Mewat district of Haryana, India—and, in doing so, underscores the relevance of clinical legal education and law school legal literacy clinics to these efforts. It also proposes this project as a model for enhancing the social justice mission of law school clinical programs in India.

IRRAD's Good Governance Project

IRRAD works in villages of one of India's most backward districts, the Mewat district of Haryana, with an overall mandate to empower rural India and reduce rural poverty. It works with a multidimensional approach called the "Integrated Sustainable Village Development Model" (ISVD). The PGA Centre was established at IRRAD with a mandate to work for good rural governance and effective rural policies. One of the major concerns for the center was to bring sustainability to IRRAD's initiatives under the ISVD.

In its efforts to effect good rural governance and keeping in view the goal of sustainability, the PGA Centre launched a targeted project for a select group of villagers to prepare them as effective participants in the affairs of local governance. The center looked at making people aware of their rights and entitlements and then, through this awareness, enabling them to participate and bring about good rural governance. It wanted the project to deliver three specific results: villagers' effective participation in public affairs; good rural governance; and sustainability to the initiatives of the ISVD model. Empowerment of villagers was to play the key role in achieving these objectives, which meant two things: access to information, and participation with the help of that information.

This is how the center conceptualized a project on legal literacy and training, and for a project like this, the most effective model would be that used in a legal literacy clinic.

The Project's Clinical Methodology

Using the methodology of clinical legal education in the center's legal literacy and training project had two objectives. The first objective was to use the clinical methodology to develop an effective model of legal literacy for the rural populace in India. The second objective was to create a model for law school legal literacy clinics—as part of a socially relevant clinical program for the benefit of the poor and illiterate rural masses.

The project was based heavily on clinical education's most critical aspect of "learning by doing." (Frank, 1933; Wizner, 2002) The duration of the entire project was one year. In a month of literacy and training activities, only four half-day sessions were allocated for classroom learning and planning. For the rest of the time, the villagers participating in the project were required to do practical work based on the information that was imparted to them in the classroom. As with a law school clinic, when the villagers worked with the information received in the classroom, they learned by doing—and in doing so, they effected good governance in their villages. Yet another objective that the project achieved through the methodology was developing the villagers' belief and confidence in the learning. They could use the information received in the classroom easily, thereby realizing that it worked and that there is no disconnect between theory and practical reality. The results that the villagers achieved through their work increased their confidence and kept them motivated and interested in the project—because the project relied on experiential learning.

Another clinical education component of the project was its being client oriented. The project aimed at effecting good rural governance particularly with respect to villagers' entitlements on the right to food, the right to education, the right to health, and the right to social security. In addition, since the project looked at peoples' participation as the kernel of all the efforts aimed at achieving good governance, the right to information formed an integral part of the project to cut across all the other entitlements of citizens. In the same vein, other incidental areas that the project covered were the law relating to consumer protection and the entitlement to free legal aid and advice.

All these areas of law, policy, and governance were chosen for three reasons. The first reason was the project's objective to target the delivery of services relating to some of the most fundamental aspects of the life of a citizen: food, education, health, shelter, and social security. Secondly, the project looked at the effectiveness of citizens' participation and, therefore, included the legal regime relating to the right to information and consumer protection. Thirdly, the project sought to work in areas of law where ordinary citizens could participate without a lawyer. This was particularly important from the point of view of involving law students as a part of a legal literacy clinic. Full-time law teachers are not allowed to practice law, which is regarded as a major hurdle in developing effective clinical legal education in India. And there are no provisions authorizing law students to practice law in a legal clinic. Therefore, it was important for the project to show a clinical model where law students and law teachers could engage in substantial legal work without breaching the rules barring them from practicing law.

The project aimed at preparing rural citizens to participate effectively in all spheres of rural governance. Thus, it worked on a model that had the potential to serve a very large spectrum of clients. The first step in identifying the clients was taken in the very first session of the project. The participating villagers in the project were informed of the entitlement of the poorest of the poor and those below poverty line under the Public Distribution System (PDS). After the session, the participants were given the tasks to make a list of all the people who were below poverty line and those who were identified by the government as the poorest of the poor in the villages covered by the project. The participants were also required to convene a meeting with the beneficiaries of the PDS and discuss their problems. Through this process, the participants—while learning some skills—identified some problem areas and the clients in relation to the PDS. Since there were serious anomalies in the implementation of the PDS, all the people below the poverty line and those identified as the poorest of the poor were the clients.

In the next week, the participants assembled for the second classroom session and discussed their experience with the entire group of participants and the team of instructors. Through the discussion in the session, the participants decided to make complaints to the district authorities against the anomalies in the PDS. They also decided that the point of view of the ration distributors under the PDS should be heard. With this intent, and with the idea to involve other stakeholders in addressing the problems, the participants were required to convene a meeting with the ration distributors to know from them what ails the PDS. The ration distributors came up with problems that needed research, wider debate, and policy intervention. Thus, the tasks of the participant trainees required them to take up research and investigation into the problems afflicting the most basic component of the right to food in India, the PDS. At the same time, the participants were also exposed to the need for advocating some policy change vis-à-vis implementation of the PDS.

The project included two other very important components of the right to food, the Mid-Day Meal (MDM) program and the provision of supplementary nutrition under the Integrated Child Development Services (ICDS). Through the MDM program, children attending primary school are given a freshly cooked meal in all the government-run schools in India. The program is sponsored with two objectives: to ensure that the children get at least one healthy and nutritious meal in a day, and to ensure that the children attend the school to at least complete their elementary education. In India, it is a fundamental right of every child of six to fourteen years of age to receive free and compulsory elementary education. Children below six years of age, lactating mothers, and pregnant mothers are entitled to supplementary nutrition under the ICDS. Several other provisions of the ICDS relate to health and education of the targeted beneficiaries. Thus, these programs cut across various components of the right to food, the right to health, and the right to education. As regards the tasks relating to the MDM and ICDS, the project adopted the same methodology as it did in regard to PDS. The participants were informed in the classroom session of the provisions of the MDM and ICDS, including the mechanism and procedure for redressing grievances pertaining to their implementation, and were required to accomplish certain tasks. The preliminary tasks, for example, in the case of the MDM and ICDS, involved meeting and discussion with the beneficiaries and then meeting and discussion with the people directly involved in disbursing the provisions.

When the beneficiaries of the MDM and ICDS reported to the participants that these programs were largely nonfunctional, the participants organized a meeting with the cooks who were responsible for cooking and serving food to the beneficiaries. They then prepared a multipronged approach to serve the clients based on the information that the participants received from the beneficiaries of the MDM and ICDS and the problems that were reported to them by the cooks. This approach included writing complaints; using the right to information to know the status of the complaints and the action taken on them; invoking appropriate jurisdictions of consumer forums, quasi-judicial bodies, and other forums for redressing grievances; and organizing panel discussions with senior government officers and policy-makers to discuss issues requiring larger debate and policy intervention. This methodology and pattern was used throughout the project in all the areas of intervention that it included.

The Outcome and the Way Forward

Through the project, the villagers participated in effecting good governance in their villages. In addition to many fascinating success stories, the project has generated two booklets and a poster to further consolidate and strengthen the efforts of villagers to effect good rural governance. The project also came up with a slogan—"Good Governance Now"—and initiated efforts on good governance that are continuing under this slogan. Bringing about "good governance now" is critical as "[n]ow that we have the vote, we should all be in a hurry." (Gupta, 2009 at 9) Out of the targeted group participating in the year-long training and literacy effort, eight were selected and further trained to become trainers or resource persons to work on similar projects. These trainers have chosen about one hundred villagers from fifteen villages in the Mewat district to participate in a similar year-long literacy and training project. The trainers, along with the hundred villagers participating in the project, are working directly to bring about good governance in fifteen project villages—with an objective to make Mewat a good governance district through persistently strengthening these efforts. The larger objective of the project is to create and congeal a culture of good rural governance in the villages in Mewat district and to project this model for its replication in other parts of India.

The clinical program at the Jindal Global Law School (JGLS) is working toward supporting the efforts of these villagers to achieve their above-stated objectives. JGLS students, working in a clinic under the supervision of professors, would do the following: organize specialized legal literacy classes for the community with a view to empowering the poor; develop and support the preparation and publication of legal literacy material in local languages; identify the legal solutions to day-to-day problems of poor governance at the community level with the participation of the people in the local community; help the community in pursuing those solutions consistently to their logical conclusion; raise the concerns of the community at appropriate forums; work in collaboration with the institutions and officials at the local levels; and replicate IRRAD's model of effecting good rural governance in villages of Sonipat (Haryana) where the law school exists. As a beginning, ten students have participated in a month-long internship program with IRRAD and have worked on some of the above-stated objectives. Through these initiatives, the law school will achieve some of clinical legal education's main objectives: developing students' lawyering skills, instilling in them the need to work for social justice, and discharging the law school's public service responsibility. The most important skill that law students acquire through legal literacy clinics is the ability to empathize with the poor and other underprivileged sections of society. In this respect, components of the literacy project discussed above relate to features of proposed for law school human rights clinics in India. (Pandey, 2006–2007). The students also become engaged in what can be seen as "social change lawyering" (Johnson, 1999), "community lawyering" (Villazor, 2004–2005), and "empowerment lawyering" (Quigley, 1994). Thus, legal literacy projects have the potential to not only achieve the objectives of clinical legal education, but also to formalize and revolutionize it in India.

It is sincerely hoped that these efforts to develop a clinical model based on the IRRAD project will bolster community participation in effecting good governance and making it more authoritative and effective. IRRAD and JGLS can, subsequently, explore ways to motivate other law schools to adopt, replicate, and further develop this model to achieve the desired goals. This would also contribute to the Indian clinical movement's effort to implement legal education's transformational or revolutionary role.

CONCLUSION

Empowerment and inclusion of people and their effective participation in public affairs are critical factors for a democracy's well-being. The "disconnect" between promises of law and how law serves the common population poses a serious threat to the rule of law and the state of harmony in society. Law and legal processes do not help the everyday well-being of the majority of people in India. There is also a stark and startling disconnect between the larger promise of law to secure a dignified life to every Indian citizen and its reality. People generally do not have faith and confidence in processes of law, which further restricts their already circumscribed access to justice. This disconnect is analogous to what Deborah Rhode describes of the scenario in the United States: "'Equal justice under law' is one of America's most proudly proclaimed and widely violated legal principles." (Rhode, 2004 at 3) The situation is even grimmer in India, where access to justice has a much wider spectrum and "includes access to education, means for meeting basic needs and other human rights." (Schukoske, 2009 at 251) The global clinical movement has the potential to improve access to justice around the world. (Bloch, 2008) India's system of legal education must address the above stated challenges. Law school-initiated legal literacy projects can play a very important role in achieving the many aspirations of law and legal education, and the clinical methodology can be utilized to carry out effective, result-oriented legal literacy projects.

Law schools need to experiment with new ways to work with communities both to secure social justice and to educate lawyers for social justice. What is unique about the project initiated by IRRAD is its mandate to go beyond just legal literacy and to show to the target audience that theory and practice are not different. The project was successful largely due to this reason alone. The villagers could realize that whatever information they received in the classroom also worked in the practical realm, and thus resulted in better governance and delivery of services. This aspect was a great motivational force for them. All this was achieved because the project used the clinical methodology in identifying clients and serving them until a successful conclusion to their quest was reached. Law schools can support IRRAD's model and explore other ways to strengthen legal literacy in India. The Bar Council of India and other authorities responsible for deciding the course of legal education and the legal profession in India must pay attention to more socially relevant requirements of law schools. It is in the greater interest of society to make legal education more socially relevant, and the way to do that is to integrate socially responsive clinical programs into the law school curriculum.

LIST OF REFERENCES

Upendra Baxi, *Notes Towards a Socially Relevant Legal Education*, 5 J. B. COUNCIL INDIA 23–55 (1976).

Upendra Baxi, *Notes Towards a Socially Relevant Legal Education: A Working Paper for the UGC Regional Workshops in Law 1975–1977*, in A CONSOLIDATED REPORT OF THE UNIVERSITY GRANT COMMISSION'S WORKSHOP ON MODERNIZATION OF LEGAL EDUCATION 1, *available at* http://www.ugc.ac.in.

Frank S. Bloch & Iqbal S. Ishar, *Legal Aid, Public Service and Clinical Legal Education: Future Directions from India and the United States*, 12 MICH. J. INT'L L. 92 (1990).

Frank S. Bloch, *Access to Justice and the Global Clinical Movement*, 28 WASH. U. J.L. & POL'Y 111 (2008).

Jerome Frank, *Why Not a Clinical Lawyer-School?*, 81 U. PA. L. REV. 907 (1933).

DIPANKAR GUPTA, THE CAGED PHOENIX: CAN INDIA FLY (Penguin Viking 2009).

Kevin R. Johnson, *Lawyering for Social Change: What's a Lawyer to Do?*, 5 MICH. J. RACE & L. 201 (1999).

Ved Kumari, *Clinical Legal Education—Issues of Justice*, 24 DELHI L. REV. 78 (2002).

CLINICAL LEGAL EDUCATION: CONCEPT AND CONCERNS, A HANDBOOK ON CLINICAL LEGAL EDUCATION (N. R. Madhava Menon ed., Eastern Book Company 1998).

S. MURLIDHAR, LAW, POVERTY AND LEGAL AID—ACCESS TO CRIMINAL JUSTICE (Lexis Nexis Butterworths 2004).

Ajay Pandey, *Promoting Human Rights in India through Law School Human Rights Clinics*, XXVIII–XXIX DELHI L. REV. 67 (2006–2007).

William P. Quigley, *Introduction to the Clinical Teaching for the New Law Professor: A View from the First Floor*, 28 AKRON L. REV. 463 (1995).

William P. Quigley, *Reflections of Community Organizers: Lawyering for Empowerment of Community Organizations*, 21 OHIO N.U. L. REV. 455 (1994).

DEBORAH L. RHODE, ACCESS TO JUSTICE (Oxford University Press 2004).

Jane Schukoske, *Legal Education Reform in India: Dialogue Among Indian Law Teachers*, 1 JINDAL GLOBAL L. REV. 251 (2009).

Richard J. Wilson, *Training for Justice: The Global Reach of Clinical Legal Education*, 22 PENN ST. INT'L L. REV. 421 (2004).

Rose Cuison Villazor, *Community Lawyering: An Approach to Addressing Inequalities in Access to Health Care for Poor, of Color and Immigrant Communities*, 8 N.Y.U. J. LEGIS. & PUB. POL'Y 35 (2004–2005).

Stephen Wizner, *The Law School Clinic: Legal Education in the Interests of Justice*, 70 FORDHAM L. REV. 1929 (2002).

17. ADVANCING SOCIAL JUSTICE THROUGH ADR AND CLINICAL LEGAL EDUCATION IN INDIA, SOUTH AFRICA, AND THE UNITED STATES

KAREN TOKARZ AND V. NAGARAJ

As the story goes, Shah Jahangir (whose son Shah Jehan built the Taj Mahal in Agra, India) created a Chain of Justice made of pure gold with sixty bells that ran from Agra Fort, located near the Taj, across to a stone post on the Yamuna riverbank. He reportedly built the Chain of Justice as a symbol of his readiness to hear complaints from his subjects, "so that if those engaged in the administration of justice should delay or practice hypocrisy in the matter of those seeking justice, the oppressed might come to this chain and shake it so that its noise might attract attention." (Darling, 2002) Regardless of their class, those who felt they were not being given fair, timely, and effective resolution of their disputes could shake the chain for access to justice—by the ruler, outside of the courts.

Shah Jahangir appears to have been an early practitioner and advocate of alternative dispute resolution (ADR), who understood and embraced its crucial role in providing social justice, or what some call "people's justice." There are many other examples of the use of ADR throughout history, from King Solomon's creative mediation of a maternity dispute to the African tradition of "justice under a tree," or *kgotla*, aptly reflected in the architecture and logo of the new South African Constitutional Court building on Constitution Hill in Johannesburg. Well-known ADR advocates from India, South Africa, and the United States include Mahatma Gandhi, Nelson Mandela, and Sandra Day O'Connor, all of whom practiced alternative approaches to conflict resolution and inspired social justice movements across the world.

Today, ADR—an umbrella term for a range of dispute resolution processes outside the courts that includes negotiation, conciliation, mediation, dialogue facilitation, consensus-building, and arbitration—has emerged as a principal mode of legal practice in virtually every legal field and in virtually every country in the world. Adversarial legal practice is no longer perceived as the most desirable or effective approach and litigation is no longer the preferred, likely, or even readily available avenue for the resolution of legal disputes, given the current widespread clogging of the courts. Some of the aspects of ADR that distinguish it from litigation include value creating, norm creating, informal, accessible, flexible, voluntary, consensual, situational, individualized, interest-based, consensus-driven, person-centered, relationship-oriented, future-focused, and transformative. (Boulle, 1996; Macfarlane, 1997)

There is a growing consensus that ADR expertise increases the capabilities of lawyers to engage effectively in creative problem-solving, strategic decision-making, and peacemaking in legal practice and in society. (Macfarlane, 2008) There is also an increasing belief that ADR expertise is a crucial tool for social justice advocates.

Because ADR and clinical education share overlapping goals of advancing the interests of parties and addressing deficiencies in access to justice, ADR education and clinical legal education are slowly integrating and advancing beyond the teaching and practice of basic negotiation skills that have been included in the clinical curriculum for many years. This chapter examines the impact that the integration of ADR into the clinical curriculum has had or might have in law schools in India, South Africa, and the United States. It argues that clinical programs that teach and practice ADR can inform, improve, and reform not only legal education, but also—over time—the practice of law and the legal profession as well, thereby furthering the social justice goals of the global clinical movement.

ADR AND THE GLOBAL CLINICAL MOVEMENT

The role of lawyers, the role of legal dispute resolution, and the role of legal education in addressing social justice are all in flux, to one degree or another, in many countries of the world including India, South Africa, and the United States. Many legal educators in these countries and beyond believe that ADR is crucial to the education of law students, the preparation of competent law graduates, and the development of relevant legal education. (Macfarlane, 1997) Others argue specifically that clinical legal education needs to incorporate ADR to heighten the development of a social justice consciousness in law students and to counteract "the risks of acculturation to adversarial modes of thinking" that might develop through litigation-focused law school clinics. (Osborne, 1996 at 101) But, while law schools have been adding ADR courses to the curriculum over the past three decades, ADR is a long way from being part of mainstream legal education or clinical legal education.

ADR clinics and community lawyering clinics that strongly embrace ADR skills and values are slowly growing in number, scope, and variety in law schools around the world. In their recent article on community lawyering clinics, Karen Tokarz, Nancy Cook, Susan Brooks, and Brenda Blum suggest that this new direction in clinical legal education, in part, reflects recognition that ADR is an essential lawyering tool in the quest for social justice.

> Perhaps [the growth in these new types of clinics] is because the problems of the 'un' and 'under' represented are growing in new directions, requiring more complex models of response. Perhaps this is because of prior misconceptions that social and economic problems could be solved with individual legal strategies, and because of new insights about the integrative nature of

social and economic injustice. *Perhaps this is because of an increased recognition of the need for collaborative problem solving and dispute resolution as lawyering strategies, and new perspectives on the capacities of law clinics to teach these modes of practice. Perhaps this is because of a renewed investment on the part of law schools to teach social justice lawyering.* (Tokarz et al., 2008 at 401) *(emphasis added)*

India, South Africa, and the United States share some parallels and exhibit some differences in the development of ADR and the development of ADR clinical education. India and South Africa have strong tribal and cultural commitments to conflict resolution processes that foster reconciliation of the parties, seek to restore and maintain relationships, and endorse compromise and settlement. This is quite the opposite of the pervasive, modern litigation model in the United States that embraces a rights-based, winner-take-all, adversarial form of dispute resolution that rejects face-to-face dispute resolution—although, perhaps, akin to the communal ethics and practice of both Native Americans and early English settlers. (Chase, 2005) Indians and South Africans committed to social justice are struggling to hang onto their alternative dispute resolution roots as their legal systems become more formalized and adversarial. People from the United States, on the other hand, are seeking new, alternative approaches to litigation to achieve social justice. Whether because of a commitment to social rights, community, or counter culturalism, or an effort to address problems like overcrowded courts, law teachers in all these countries are endeavoring to better prepare law graduates for their new professional roles as conflict resolvers. ADR clinical legal education plays a key role in this endeavor.

We must acknowledge certain constraints before engaging in a comparative analysis of ADR clinical legal education. First, dispute resolution processes "assume different meanings depending on the context" and culture, and the examination of "any ADR scheme needs careful study of the social conditions in which it may operate." (Nader & Grande, 2002 at 589–90) Indigenous dispute resolution methods, modern ADR approaches, and law inevitably interact differently in different countries. Second, different countries may respond differently to ADR in light of the economics and politics of local law practice. ADR clinical legal education, like all legal practice, is nuanced and site-specific as well. Third, modern ADR is relatively new terrain with little empirical data on its long-reaching social justice consequences. (Milner, 2002) There is still much to be learned from examining ADR clinical education, questioning its underlying assumptions, and exploring both its strengths and weaknesses—especially as to its role in advancing social justice as part of the global clinical movement.

ADR AND CLINICAL LEGAL EDUCATION IN INDIA

While clinical education faces serious institutional challenges in India, ADR is one area where clinical programs have had some success. Neither full-time faculty nor law students can represent clients in court under the Bar Council of India mandates; there are few trained clinical instructors and stringent law teacher qualifications that discourage advocates from becoming clinic teachers; there are few trained ADR instructors in the academy; ADR education is seen as largely extracurricular; and law schools have little extra money for experiential education. In addition, India has a vast multilingual and multiethnic population that requires clinic faculty and students to have knowledge about many languages, local cultures, living conditions, ethnic problems, and urban/rural differences. (Bloch & Prasad, 2006)

Yet under these conditions, where clinical education involving litigation advocacy may not be possible, several law schools in India have developed ADR clinical programs in which law students assist in organizing and setting up *lok adalats* (people's courts).[1] The Bar Council of India, the regulatory body for legal education, mandates the establishment of legal service clinics in law schools to promote clinical legal education; it prescribes public interest lawyering, legal aid, and paralegal services as one of the four compulsory "practical papers" for all law students, which includes providing legal literacy programs, organizing *lok adalats*, and paralegal training. Thus, the *lok adalat* movement, which started in 1982 in the Indian state of Gujarat as an informal and voluntary dispute settlement process operating outside the court system, has become greatly intertwined with law schools throughout the country. In *lok adalats*, many of which are facilitated by law students, parties receive conciliation and mediation assistance to help them settle their disputes outside of court, often in a faster, less expensive, and more equitable manner than through traditional trials.

With the passage of the Legal Services Authorities Act of 1994, *lok adalat* settlement is no longer purely voluntary dispute resolution; *lok adalats* have become legally recognized and "court-annexed." The Act creates authorities—such as law schools—to organize *lok adalats* composed of a sitting or retired judicial officer and other persons of repute as may be prescribed by the state government in consultation with the Chief Justice of the State High Court. Cases can be referred by consent of both parties to the disputes, if the court is satisfied that the matter is appropriate for consideration by the *lok adalat*. Although *lok adalats* have become a major source of resolving legal disputes and reducing litigation in India, some commentators have raised concerns about the social justice ramifications. (Galanter & Krishnan, 2004; Whitson, 1992) Some critics believe that state authorization has undermined the informality, flexibility, and voluntary nature of *lok adalats*. Justice V. K. Krishna Iyer, one of the founders of the movement, later became an ardent critic. In his book, *Legal Services Authorities Act—A Critique*, he calls *lok adalats* "clumsy imitations of Courts, not social mobilization

---

1. Clinical legal education in India and elsewhere in South and Southeast Asia is the subject of Chapter 3.

schemes." (Iyer, 1988 at 47) He reproaches the Act for monopolizing the dispute resolution functions of *lok adalats* and marginalizing the "considerable credibility, creativity, and experience" of the formerly voluntary bodies. (Whitson, 1992 at 415–16)

The Legal Services Authorities Act of 1987, amended in 1994 and 2002, also supports ADR clinical legal education in India. The Legal Services Authority is mandated to organize legal aid cells to educate the weaker sections of the society as to their rights and to encourage the settlement of disputes through *lok adalats*, negotiation, arbitration, and conciliation. Most, if not all, law schools have established such legal aid cells where law students provide community legal education and other services for local communities. Some cells guide people in identifying their problems, educate them about available remedies, and assist them in informal negotiation and mediation of disputes. These cells in Indian law schools parallel, in some ways, the clinical education experience provided law students in mediation and community lawyering clinics in North America, and those beginning to be provided to law students in South Africa.

Noted Indian legal educator Dr. N. R. Madhava Menon endorses the development of law school ADR clinical efforts. He has shown that participation of law students in *lok adalats* and other forms of dispute resolution enables them to acquire essential professional skills and values, and to develop a necessary and critical understanding of the role of law, lawyers, and the legal system in advancing social justice (or not) in India. (Menon, 1998; Menon, 1985) The National Law School of India University in Bangalore, V. M. Salgaocar College of Law in Goa, and the Menon Institute of Advocacy Skills in Trivandrum are among the legal education institutions beginning to develop training programs to educate teachers in clinical and ADR legal education. The Hidayatullah National Law University and other law schools have introduced training in interviewing, counseling, and negotiation "to better prepare students for socially relevant legal practice." (Sivakumar, 2003 at 245)

Frank Bloch and M. R. K. Prasad suggest that law students could work with villages to conduct needs assessments, arrange public fora, and engage in dialogue facilitation, community consensus-building, and dispute resolution. They endeavor to provide a roadmap for Indian law school curricular reform that implicitly calls for the development of ADR clinics, arguing that the roster of professional skills and values identified in the American Bar Association's MacCrate Report—often touted as a template for reforming legal education in India, as well as in the United States—should be reordered and supplemented for Indian law schools. They identify three key fundamental values for legal education in India (and elsewhere): provision of fair and effective resolution of disputes; striving for social justice; and the promotion of alternate lawyer roles, such as the traditional lawyer roles of counselor, negotiator, mediator, conciliator, and public policy-maker. Chief among their list of key fundamental skills needed for Indian lawyers that should be developed in law schools are innovative, alternative problem-solving techniques, skills to invent new options beyond established norms, and mass communication skills. Not surprisingly, Bloch and Prasad argue that ADR skills and values, like most fundamental lawyering skills and values, are best taught to future practitioners through clinical education. (Bloch & Prasad, 2006)

ADR AND CLINICAL EDUCATION IN SOUTH AFRICA

According to R. B. G. Choudree, "the use of alternative methods of conflict resolution by the traditional societies of South Africa is deeply rooted in the customs and traditions of its various tribes," ranging from "fairly rudimentary processes of the Khoisan of the remote Northern Cape to the sophisticated traditional courts of the Zulu in KwaZulu-Natal." (Choudree, 1999 at 10) The *kgotla* is a public meeting, community council, or traditional village court—usually headed by the village chief or headman—in which community decisions are arrived at by consensus. Anyone is allowed to speak and no one may interrupt while the speakers are "having their say." In the exercise of their roles as mediators and conciliators, "the courts of chiefs and headmen in South Africa are similar to the lok adalats and panchayats of India." (Choudree, 1999 at 12)

The traditional village courts have been largely, although not wholly, replaced by commissioners and, more recently, by magistrates. Many believe that the modern courts greatly diminish accessibility for disputants. "Traditional courts have a major advantage in comparison with other types of courts in that their processes are substantially informal and less intimidating, with the people who utilise these courts being more at ease in an environment that is not foreboding." (Choudree, 1999 at 12) According to Richard Abel, "[t]he introduction of [modern courts] into the [traditional courts] leads to a decline in tribal litigation. Tribal litigation is integrative; it preserves and even strengthens those relationships. If courts are modernised, one forum for tribal litigation is removed. Furthermore, the mere availability of modern courts seems to undermine tribal dispute processing elsewhere in the society." (Abel, 1991 at 84) Although the new constitution of South Africa provides for the recognition of traditional authorities and indigenous law, the future of traditional leaders and customary and indigenous law is in question.

Alan Rycroft, noted South African educator and ADR specialist, argues that some of the traditional values of ADR have reemerged in South Africa today. He cites the establishment in 1983 of the Independent Mediation Services of South Africa (Imssa) as "pivotal in transforming both public and state attitudes toward mediation and arbitration" in modern-day South Africa. (Rycroft, 2009) Despite initial skepticism from trade union leaders, Imssa eventually achieved the privatization of labor disputes and also moved consumer disputes toward mediation and arbitration. Rycroft suggests that the conciliation/mediation/arbitration model, popularized by Imssa, led to the successful establishment of the new Commission for Conciliation, and asserts that this movement has had normative influences on post-apartheid legislation and policy in South Africa. He notes that many of the key drafters of the constitution were Imssa panelists or key users of its services, and asserts that "constitutional negotiations in the early 1990's provided the opportunity for politicians and policy makers to re-imagine more progressive mechanisms for resolving constitutional, institutional, societal and personal disputes." (Rycroft, 2009)

Rycroft cites instances of post-apartheid legislation that embrace ADR. Perhaps most notably, after the transition from apartheid, President Nelson Mandela authorized a Truth and Reconciliation Commission empowered to utilize mediation to facilitate reconciliation and redress for victims. The commission was seen by many as a crucial component of the transition to a full and free democracy in South Africa. Despite some flaws, it is generally (although not universally) thought to have facilitated a successful and peaceful social and legal transformation. New South African institutions such as the Human Rights Commission and the Gender Commission may intervene in disputes at an early stage and engage in mediation, conciliation, or negotiation to resolve any dispute involving a violation of human rights. ADR is prominent in many other key South African institutions as well: the constitution gives the Public Protector the power to resolve disputes by mediation, conciliation, or negotiation; the Independent Electoral Commission requires the Chief Director of Monitoring to mediate disputes arising in the course of an election; and the Pan South African Language Board requires mediation, conciliation, and negotiation for dispute resolution. (Rycroft 2009)

All of this suggests that ADR education and ADR clinical education are essential for the preparation of competent new law graduates, as well as practicing lawyers, in South Africa. And indeed, the law school ADR curriculum in South Africa is slowly evolving through the efforts of academics such as Professor Rycroft. But there is a long way to go. The University of KwaZulu-Natal (UKZN) law faculty was the first in South Africa to introduce a course on dispute resolution for law students. Dispute Resolution is an elective course in the UKZN LLB degree program that has been taught in various incarnations over the past decade to approximately thirty students per year. On the other hand, the Labor Law LLM curriculum is the only one among an impressive array of UKZN LLM degree programs that offers a discrete dispute resolution module, Labor Dispute Resolution.

UKZN also was a frontrunner in clinical legal education, establishing the first law school clinic in South Africa in 1973. The clinic at UKZN and others in South Africa, like their counterparts in the United States and India, started as legal aid clinics.[2] In recent years, some South African law school clinics have

---

2. Clinics at UKZN and other universities in South Africa are described in Chapter 2, which covers clinical legal education in Africa.

begun to engage in ADR practice in areas such as land dispute mediation. And, some clinics have begun to include community court practice and mediations in the clinical curriculum.

Other South African law faculties are gradually developing more sophisticated ADR legal curricula that one day might include clinical training. For example, Stellenbosch University Business School in Cape Town is home to the African Centre for Dispute Settlement. The center focuses on dispute practices that affect individuals and organizations, with a particular focus on Africa to ensure that African heritage and values are incorporated in the development of solutions that suit African conditions. The business school has collaborated with the law school in the field of commercial and international arbitration, which are both electives in the LLB and LLM degree programs. The University of Cape Town's Centre for Conflict Resolution is an independent nonprofit organization that has developed an international reputation for its training, mediation, and policy research and development. The organization's expertise places particular emphasis on capacity-building in conflict prevention, management, and resolution—and, to this end, works closely with continental and regional organizations and programs across the African continent. Only in recent years has the center's work begun to inform the law school curriculum.

ADR AND CLINICAL LEGAL EDUCATION IN THE UNITED STATES

Many law schools in the United States offer ADR courses, with a few law schools requiring students to take at least one ADR course. A growing number of schools have developed mediation and arbitration clinics over the past three decades, and some law schools now offer community lawyering clinics that include ADR components. And some law schools—like many in South Africa—also offer Street Law programs in which law students provide peer mediation and conflict resolution training for grade school and high school students.[3]

Approximately forty US law schools offer ADR clinics. In many of these clinics, students assist in the mediation of community, landlord-tenant, consumer, and small claims disputes. In others, clinic students assist in juvenile victim-offender dialogues, employment mediations, and consumer arbitrations. Frequently, these clinics are loosely or formally connected to court programs where litigants are offered an ADR option in lieu of a formal court trial. There is also a recent growth of community lawyering clinics that utilize ADR among other lawyering strategies in collaboration with client communities and community groups to

---

3. Street Law clinics are discussed in Chapter 15.

empower communities, promote social justice, and foster systemic social and economic change.[4] (Tokarz et al., 2008)

In her acclaimed new book, *The New Lawyer: How Settlement Is Transforming the Practice of Law*, Julie Macfarlane examines in depth law practice and legal education in the United States and Canada over the past thirty years. She concludes unequivocally that there is an urgent need for lawyers to modify and evolve their professional role from adversarial "pit bull" to creative conflict resolver, that there is pressure from many quarters for civil justice reform, and that the widespread development of court-connected and private mediation is testament to serious concerns and delays in justice. She criticizes law schools for being "in thrall to the traditional models of lawyering" and argues for dramatic overhaul of legal education to prepare new graduates for the negotiation and dispute resolution challenges they will face in practice and for their new roles and new identities as "conflict resolvers" in society. She asks, "If lawyers do not represent conflict resolution in our public culture, then what is their function?" (Macfarlane, 2009 at 1)

THE INTEGRATION OF ADR AND CLINICAL EDUCATION: DOES IT ADVANCE SOCIAL JUSTICE?

While many argue that clinical education must incorporate ADR skills and values, a number of critics and commentators raise cautionary notes about the increased use and diffusion of ADR, especially ADR on behalf of poor and less-powerful individuals. Despite the success and growth of ADR on a worldwide scale, some are concerned whether it is a form of lesser justice for the poor—and, thus, whether it truly provides access to justice. (Galanter & Krishnan, 2004) Thankfully, there are a growing number of legal anthropologists and others examining ADR, questioning its underlying assumptions, and exploring its role in advancing social justice.

American law professor Tina Grillo issued an early warning about gender inequality in American ADR and the disadvantages of the ADR process for less-powerful disputants, particularly for women in domestic disputes with men. (Grillo, 1991) Professors Laura Nader and Elisabetta Grande have written extensively and critically about the use of American ADR approaches for managing conflict in African and other communities. They argue that "the imposition of American ADR as a condition of foreign aid or capital investment is problematic," in large part because it denies the effects of inequality of money and power on conflict resolution. (Nader & Grande, 2002 at 573) Professor Neal Milner is

---

4. Two different types of community clinics, one in the United States and one in Australia, are described in Chapter 11.

less convinced that ADR has "a shadowy villain quality—shady, opaque, scary, seductive, alien, too suspicious to get near, something to steer clear of," but he insightfully highlights that we know little empirically of long-reaching social justice consequences of ADR beyond simplistic measures of "success," "satisfaction," and time and cost savings. (Milner, 2002 at 623, 627) He suggests that ADR practitioners and academics (and we would add, ADR clinicians) must recognize and resist the temptation to "idealize" and "romanticize" ADR processes, to "make false dichotomies between ADR and law," and to endorse uncritically ADR over all other processes. (*Id.* at 627)

CONCLUSION

ADR has always been an important element of legal dispute resolution. But, according to commentators such as Mauro Cappelletti, what is new is "that modern societies have developed new reasons to prefer such alternatives," including access to justice: "the fact that the judicial process now is, or should be, open to larger and larger segments of the population, indeed in theory to the entire population. This is, of course, the cost of access to justice, which is the cost of democracy itself; a cost that advanced societies must be ready and happy to bear." (Cappelletti, 1993 at 287)

As Professors Bloch and Prasad point out, "[c]linical legal education has always had a broader goal—to teach law students about what lawyers do and to understand lawyers' professional role in the legal system . . . in the context of having students provide various forms of legal aid services." (Bloch & Prasad, 2006 at 166) In ADR clinics and clinics that embrace ADR, law students develop their professional identity and fundamental lawyering skills and values as problem-solvers, conciliators, mediators, and peacemakers. For these reasons, we believe that ADR has a unique contribution to make to clinical legal education around the world—as a richer way to teach and advance social justice.

LIST OF REFERENCES

Richard L. Abel, *The Imposition of Law, in* T. W. BENNETT, A SOURCEBOOK OF AFRICAN CUSTOMARY LAW IN SOUTHERN AFRICA (Juta and Co. 1991).

Frank S. Bloch & M. R. K. Prasad, *Institutionalizing a Social Justice Mission for Clinical Legal Education: Cross-National Currents from India and the United States*, 13 CLINICAL L. REV. 165 (2006).

Laurence Boulle, *Law and Mediation: Conflict or Coalescence?* 2 COMM. DISP. RESOL. J. 167 (1996).

Sandra Burman & Wilfried Scharf, *Creating People's Justice: Street Committees and People's Courts in a South African City*, 24 L. & SOC'Y REV. 693 (1990).

Mauro Cappelletti, *Alternative Dispute Resolution Processes Within the Framework of the World-Wide Access-to-Justice Movement*, 56 MODERN L. REV. 282 (1993).

OSCAR G. CHASE, LAW, CULTURE, AND RITUAL: DISPUTING SYSTEMS IN CROSS-CULTURAL CONTEXT (New York University Press 2005).

R. B. G. Choudree, *Traditions of Conflict Resolution in South Africa*, 1 AFR. J. CONFLICT IN RESOL. 9 (1999).

Linda T. Darling, *Do Justice, Do Justice, For That Is Paradise: Middle Eastern Advice for Indian Muslim Rulers*, 22 COMP. STUD. OF S. ASIA, AFR. & THE MIDDLE EAST 3 (2002).

Marc Galanter & Jayanth K. Krishnan, *"Bread for the Poor": Access to Justice and the Rights of the Needy in India*, 55 HASTINGS L. J. 789 (2004).

Trina Grillo, *The Mediation Alternative: Process Dangers to Women*, 100 YALE L. J. 1545 (1991).

V. R. KRISHNA IYER, LEGAL SERVICES AUTHORITIES ACT—A CRITIQUE (Society for Community Organization Trust 1988).

Julie Macfarlane, *The Challenge of ADR and Alternative Paradigms of Dispute Resolution: How Should the Law School Respond?* 31 INT'L J. LEGAL ED. 13 (1997).

JULIE MACFARLANE, THE NEW LAWYER: HOW SETTLEMENT IS TRANSFORMING THE PRACTICE OF LAW (UBC Press 2009).

CLINICAL LEGAL EDUCATION: CONCEPT AND CONCERNS, A HANDBOOK ON CLINICAL LEGAL EDUCATION (N.R. Madhava Menon ed., Eastern Book Company 1998).

N. R. Madhava Menon, Lok Adalat in Delhi: A Report from a Legal Education Perspective (1985).

Neil Milner, Commentary, *Illusions and Delusions about Conflict Management in Africa and Elsewhere*, 27 LAW & SOC. INQUIRY 621 (2002).

Laura Nader & Elisabetta Grande, *Current Illusions and Delusions about Conflict Management – in Africa and Elsewhere*, 27 LAW & SOC. INQUIRY 573 (2002).

Matthew Osborne, *Alternative Dispute Resolution and Clinical Legal Education in Australian Law Schools: Convergent, Antagonistic, or Running in Parallel?* 14 J. PROF. LEGAL EDUC. 97 (1996).

Alan J. Rycroft, *"The Problems of Process Pluralism, or Why Are We Resolving Our Disputes So Badly?"* (Inaugural Lecture, University of Cape Town 2009).

PENAL REFORM INTERNATIONAL, ACCESS TO JUSTICE IN SUB-SAHARAN AFRICA: THE ROLE OF TRADITIONAL AND INFORMAL JUSTICE SYSTEMS (Wilfried Scharfe ed. 2000).

S. Sivakumar, *Access to Justice: Some Innovative Experiments in India*, 22 WINDSOR Y.B. ACCESS JUST. 239 (2003).

Adam Stapleton, *Introduction and Overview of Legal Aid in Africa*, in ACCESS TO JUSTICE IN AFRICA AND BEYOND: MAKING THE RULE OF LAW A REALITY 3 (PRI/Bluhm/NITA 2007).

Karen Tokarz, Nancy L. Cook, Susan Brooks & Brenda Bratton Blom, *Conversations on "Community Lawyering": The Newest (Oldest) Wave in Clinical Legal Education*, 28 WASH. U. J. L. & POL'Y 359 (2008).

EDUCATING FOR JUSTICE AROUND THE WORLD: LEGAL EDUCATION, LEGAL PRACTICE AND THE COMMUNITY (Louis Trubek & Jeremy Cooper eds., Ashgate/Dartmouth 1999).

Sarah Leah Whitson, *"Neither Fish, Nor Flesh, Nor Good Red Herring" Lok Adalats: An Experiment in Informal Dispute Resolution in India*, 15 HASTINGS INT'L & COMP. L. REV. 391 (1992).

PART III

THE GLOBAL CLINICAL MOVEMENT AND EDUCATING LAWYERS FOR SOCIAL JUSTICE

This part looks at global clinical legal education as a movement, with particular reference to its objective of educating lawyers for social justice. It includes chapters that examine the nature of a global clinical movement, its agenda, and how its agenda is carried out. It also includes chapters that focus on ways that the global movement has enhanced clinical legal education's influence around the world through the work of various national and regional organizations and the Global Alliance for Justice Education (GAJE).

The part begins with Chapter 18, which examines the motivation and objectives of a global clinical movement. It identifies essential elements of clinical legal education that are shared by clinical legal educators around the world and argues that common educational goals and professional values can bring a diverse worldwide community of clinicians together in a movement aimed at transforming legal education into justice education. Chapter 19 follows with a discussion of national and regional clinical organizations that have helped create the global movement and shows how they contribute to its future growth. It includes descriptions of clinical organizations in Africa, Australia, China, Europe, Southeast Asia, and the United States.

Chapter 20 examines ways in which various aspects of clinical legal education, including its emphasis on professional skills and values and its use of experiential teaching methods, have influenced broader projects of legal education reform around the world. It also examines the contributions that clinical teachers and their students have made to the overall law school experience by highlighting the importance of client interests, social justice, and professional values. Chapter 21 focuses on clinical scholarship, defined as scholarship grounded in or directed at clinical practice that addresses clinic-related issues, such as professional skills training, experiential learning, and the teaching of professional responsibility and social justice. The chapter identifies topics that tend to dominate clinical writing, notes that they are often approached from an unnecessarily local perspective, and argues for greater global relevance and impact. Chapter 22 looks specifically at externships and how that form of clinical education fits within the global clinical movement. The chapter analyzes the externship experience and argues that externship placements, when properly selected and supervised, can play a key role in carrying out the social justice mission of the global clinical movement.

Chapter 23 proposes an agenda for the global clinical movement framed by three goals widely shared by clinicians around the world: increasing access to justice, training future lawyers in professional skills and values, and promoting a more diverse, skilled legal profession committed to serving social needs. The chapter also identifies structures and resources necessary for the movement to implement its agenda and sustain its work. Chapter 24 seeks to promote the delivery of justice education by offering a set of self-assessment criteria that focus on education in the social responsibility of the law and the legal profession. The chapter concludes with four instruments that measure indicators of justice education, including specific components of legal ethics and social responsibility instruction, clinical and pro bono programs, and criteria for staff selection. Finally, Chapter 25 presents a brief history of the Global Alliance for Justice Education (GAJE), including a description of some of its key projects that have helped advance justice education around the world. The chapter also analyzes GAJE's past and future role in the global clinical movement.

18. THE GLOBAL CLINICAL MOVEMENT

FRANK S. BLOCH AND N. R. MADHAVA MENON

INTRODUCTION

Not too long ago, the very idea of a global clinical movement would have seemed farfetched. While clinical legal education had gained enough of a foothold in a number of countries by the 1970s and early 1980s to encourage talk of "clinical movements" in various parts of the world, those developments were almost exclusively local in their outlook and ambition. Clinical law teachers' plates were full with local challenges as they sought to introduce new clinical teaching methods and social justice-oriented curriculum reform at traditionally conservative legal education institutions. With so much to do at home, most clinicians who ventured across borders to learn about developments in clinical education in foreign lands did so for the benefit of their own—or perhaps their host's—national clinical movement. (Grossman, 2001) Cross-national exchanges among clinical law teachers began to pick up in the late 1980s and early 1990s, enough so that talk about common goals and shared experiences began to surface among clinicians around the world, along with calls for collaboration in areas of mutual interest and concern. (Wortham, 2006; Maisel, 2008) A key manifestation of this developing international perspective on clinical legal education was the founding of the Global Alliance for Justice Education (GAJE) in the late-1990s.[1]

Today, the existence of a global clinical movement is no longer in doubt. Through the activities of a number of national and international organizations, including GAJE, there is a growing global network of clinical law teachers and others committed to building and strengthening clinical legal education around the world. These activities are supported by funding institutions that in the past might have concentrated on promoting clinical programs in one country or region.[2] Although not specified in any formal sense, the clinicians who participate in global clinical activities are motivated by certain shared basic concerns about professional legal education, including its lack of social relevance and indifference to the demands for equal access to competent legal services. By working together at conferences, in workshops, and on specific clinical projects, this global network of clinicians has developed into an emerging global clinical movement with the capacity to stimulate support for and interest in clinical legal

---

1. GAJE is the subject of Chapter 25.

2. Many of these clinical organizations and funding institutions are described in Chapter 19.

education far beyond the capacity of any group of individual clinicians. It acknowledges the impact of globalization on law, legal education, and the legal profession, and supports the spread of rights awareness around the world. (Bloch, 2008) On the other hand, what drives this new global clinical movement—its *raison d'être*—is not so clear. Is there a global perspective on clinical education that can inform and influence legal educators in different parts of the world? What can a global movement contribute to the cause of justice education beyond what can be done by various national and regional clinical organizations?

This goal of this chapter is to identify the key elements of the global clinical movement that demonstrate not only its existence and viability, but also its richness and strength. First, it posits three defining qualities of clinical legal education that amount to a set of goals and ambitions that are shared, to one degree or another, by clinical legal educators around the word. Next, it shows how these common goals and purposes are maintained despite the wide diversity of contexts and particular challenges that exist in different countries and regions. Finally, it argues that there are fundamental shared educational and professional aspirations that rise out of this diversity and serve to support and reinforce a worldwide community of clinicians to transform legal education into justice education.

Of course, like any movement the global clinical movement must do more than aspire. It must set for itself an agenda that will carry its goals forward to fruition. To be effective, an agenda for the global clinical movement must present coherent goals in the context of great diversity and must be realistic in the face of varying resources and ambitions. This chapter does not suggest any particular agenda; rather, it seeks to define the essence of the movement that such an agenda would serve.[3]

THE DEFINING QUALITIES OF CLINICAL LEGAL EDUCATION

There cannot be a global clinical movement without a clear sense of what makes the movement a *clinical* movement. In other words, there must be some core qualities of clinical legal education recognized around the world that give the movement its substantive focus—that serve to identify what the clinical modifier of the movement means. Three such defining qualities come to mind.

The first quality goes directly to its professional educational mission. Clinical legal education around the world focuses on two curricular goals aimed at preparing students for practicing law not otherwise emphasized sufficiently in the traditional law school curriculum: providing professional skills training and

---

3. An agenda for the global clinical movement is the subject of Chapter 23.

instilling professional values of public responsibility and social justice. A second quality relates to its methodology. At the core of the clinical teaching mission is a commitment to experiential learning. Clinical training in professional skills and values takes place while students are in professional roles—real or simulated— and not in a traditional classroom setting, where law is taught through one-way lectures or from cases and material presented exclusively in printed texts. Finally, clinical legal education is committed to reforming legal education by reorienting it toward educating lawyers for social justice. This follows naturally, even necessarily, from its role in expanding the professional values and public responsibility curriculum and its dedication to promoting the use of innovative methods for teaching law.

These three defining qualities, each of which is discussed in more detail below, did not arise in a vacuum. At the same time, as seen in the chapters in Part I of this book, the contexts in which clinical legal education developed—the state of legal education, the status of the legal profession, the political and economic condition of the nation—vary considerably across countries and regions of the world. A major factor in the emergence of clinical education in many countries was the sense that the existing system of apprenticeships or practical training after completing the law degree, if it existed at all, was inadequate, and that the law schools had to take some responsibility for imparting professional skills. In this respect, it is no coincidence that the term "clinical" has been borrowed from medical education. Another common factor, although one that has been implemented with even greater differences among countries, was the felt need for changes in the core curriculum to acknowledge an increasingly active role that lawyers were taking, or should take, in addressing social problems. The relative scope and intensity of these concerns in one country or another is then reflected in the different ways that clinical education operates and how clinical programs implement the common shared qualities of providing professional skills and values training though the use of clinical methods in an effort to promote legal education reform.

Professional Skills and Values

In a sense, clinical education's curricular ambitions—providing training in professional skills and values—cannot be separated from its methodology. A clinical curriculum seeks to educate future lawyers for not only more competent but also more professionally responsible law practice. The clinical methodology is the means for implementing the clinical curriculum, but it also has a profound influence on its content. Nonetheless, there are some essential points about clinical legal education's focus on professional skills and values that stand on their own.

Combined training in professional skills and values is a fundamental quality of the clinical curriculum. Professional skills training is designed to improve the lawyering skills of the practicing bar; values training seeks to incorporate an understanding of—and commitment to—strong professional values, including lawyers' public responsibilities. Together they carry out clinical legal education's goal of educating future lawyers for more competent and professionally responsible law practice. It is the core curricular ambition of "socially relevant legal education," a term often used to describe the essence of clinical legal education in India. (Menon, 1996; University Grants Commission, 1975–1977) Of course, experiential learning is not new to legal education. Indeed, in many countries where clinical legal education is considered an innovation lawyers had been trained traditionally through apprenticeships or other forms of supervised law practice. What is new is the context in which experiential learning takes place. In a structured clinical program, training in professional skills and values is informed by lawyering theory, social context, and ethical standards—a very different "learning by doing" than what took place in the past.

To be sure, the particular skills taught in a clinical course—traditional skills, or new skills needed to address new models of law practice—will vary depending on the type of legal system in place in a particular country. But by preparing future lawyers for the practice of law through a structured skills curriculum that looks beyond the narrow confines of day-to-day practice, clinical legal education addresses a worldwide need for more than just-competent lawyers. Professional values training must also take into account differences in national and legal cultures, but the need to inculcate in students a sense of ethical and professional responsibility—sometimes referred to as clinical education's "social justice mission"—exists throughout the world. By drawing law students' attention not only to the ethical obligations and responsibilities of the profession, but also to the powerful influence that law and lawyers have in society, clinical legal education inspires new generations of lawyers to engage in social action and empowers them to make a difference in the world.

The clinical curriculum begins to spill over to the clinical methodology when the professional values component is directed at the public role of lawyers and the profession, and in particular to the professional obligation to provide legal services to the poor, marginalized, and disadvantaged. While some clinical programs operate without an articulated social justice mission, most programs—and almost all "live" client clinics—focus rather significantly on social justice issues, as seen in the chapters in Part II of this book. As discussed more fully below, the students' clinical experience is thus not just part of the teaching method; when presented in the context of providing legal aid services, it also provides much of the substance of what they learn.

Clinical Methodology

The heart of the clinical methodology is experiential learning, or learning by doing. The clinical method is the obvious choice for implementing the clinical curriculum discussed above; that is, training in professional skills and values. But the greatest impact of the clinical methodology is tied to the type of experience involved. Simulated experience using a problem file constructed on the basis of a realistic scenario can be quite effective for clinical programs that focus on teaching professional skills, especially if they concentrate on particular skills. Skills training takes on an entirely different dimension, however, when experiential learning occurs in the real world. By bringing real-world experience to law students as the "material" through which they learn what lawyers do—through a legal aid clinic or some other type of "live" clinical experience—the clinical methodology is able to fill the gap that so many lawyers feel between what they were taught in law school and what they do in practice.

What binds most clinicians around the world together, however, is more than a common method of teaching law. The broader scope of clinical training in skills and values discussed above—its ambition of carrying out a socially relevant clinical curriculum—requires a clinical methodology that brings students face-to-face with persons or communities in need of services that they, as law students about to become lawyers, can provide. It may be a legal aid clinic in the United States or South Africa, a community legal center in Australia, or a legal literacy project in India. (Wilson, 2004) The clinical methodology builds on clinical experiences that offer students a unique opportunity to learn, under supervision, not only about the professional skills used by lawyers but also about many other aspects of the law and the legal system that are essential for preparing law students to think and act like a lawyer. Experiences gained through clinical work can thus enable law students to understand and assimilate their responsibilities as members of a public profession in the administration of the law, in the reform of the law, in the equitable distribution of legal services in society, in the protection of individual rights and public interests, and in upholding the basic elements of "professionalism."

Just as the clinical curriculum can spill over to the clinical methodology, carrying out a clinical curriculum through the clinical methodology inevitably implicates broader legal education reform. A key element of clinical legal education is its commitment to shifting the focus of student learning from the classroom to the real world, particularly when students are required to deal with real-life situations in a legal aid clinic. In this context, clinical legal education goes far beyond learning the law, or even about the legal process. Interests are cultivated, attitudes are developed, skills are imparted, value clarification is provided, ethical decisions are made, and confidence and responsibility are experienced. This strength of the clinical methodology is coming to be recognized elsewhere in the legal profession as well, including judicial education and other forms of in-service training for judges.

Legal Education Reform

Finally, clinicians around the world are united in their commitment to legal education reform. As noted above, this is, at least in part, simply a reflection of their work as clinical legal educators. Thus, developments in clinical legal education are cited regularly with reference to their contributions to legal education reform. (Mao, 2007; Jessup, 2002) Perhaps as a result of their experience introducing a new clinical curriculum with a new clinical methodology, clinical faculty tend to be far more engaged in exploring the professional curriculum and in developing new methods for educating lawyers than is typical of law faculties in general.[4] This can be seen in the rapidly expanding body "clinical scholarship," much of which is devoted to topics relevant to legal education reform.[5]

In terms of curricular content, clinical legal education is responsible for introducing instruction in the lawyering process. Broadly conceived and applicable throughout the world, the lawyering process is what lawyers can and should do as members of a public profession. Specific courses on particular skills that originated in clinical programs appear regularly in the curriculum, varying according to the skills needed to practice law in one country or another. Clinical legal education also seeks to take at least part of the law school curriculum out of the classroom and place law students and law teachers face-to-face with the society that the law serves, including most importantly that segment of society systematically underserved yet most in need of legal services. Clinical practice in this context often requires the creation of new alliances with other disciplines and professions, which can lead to a broader social understanding of often complex socio-legal problems. With real problems to solve, common and counterproductive barriers to interdisciplinary solutions—for example between lawyers and doctors—are not acceptable. Clinical legal education thus offers opportunities for the legal academy to extend the boundaries of legal knowledge. Its capacity to expand notions of law practice further strengthens the global clinical movement, as many of these types of new understandings about interdisciplinary law practice can easily cross borders as well.

Perhaps the most dramatic change in legal education attributable to the rise of clinical legal education has been a gradual acceptance by legal education institutions in many parts of the world that the legal academy itself—through its faculty, its students, its curriculum—shares the profession's obligations to the community. Clinical legal education is characterized as "justice education" or "socially relevant legal education" because its primary goal is to educate future lawyers for the benefit of both the profession and society. The curricular goals of clinical legal education are always multifaceted; a clinical curriculum approaches each and every aspect of the lawyering process from a theoretical, practical, and public/social perspective. It seeks to train lawyers who will not only serve society, but will also help improve society for all. Clinical legal education's interest in legal education reform must be understood, therefore, as more than seeking a place for a clinical curriculum; it seeks to integrate clinical reforms across the entire law school curriculum.

---

4. The role that clinical legal education plays in broader legal education reform is the subject of Chapter 20.

5. Clinical scholarship and its impact on the global clinical movement is the topic of Chapter 21.

UPHOLDING THE CORE QUALITIES OF CLINICAL LEGAL EDUCATION AROUND THE WORLD

Global adherence to these core qualities of clinical education cannot be expected to be uniform, given the many differences that exist in legal education institutions (how lawyers are trained) and in legal systems (how law is practiced) in various countries and regions of the world. Certain fundamental differences in the structure of legal education can have a profound influence on how clinical legal education develops in a particular country, such as whether the basic law course is taught at the undergraduate or graduate level. The same can be said about differences in local political and economic conditions. A clinical curriculum built around preparing lawyers to address systemic wealth inequality in a major industrialized country will look very different than a clinical curriculum aimed at preparing lawyers to promote and enforce the rule of law in transitional societies. Even the most common aspects of clinical education may not be implemented in the same way from country to country.

Despite these inevitable differences, the same core qualities of clinical legal education listed above—experientially based training in professional skills and values together with a commitment to reorienting legal education toward educating lawyers for social justice—are found in clinical programs throughout the world. Professional skills training through clinical methods is probably the most common feature of global clinical education, although the contexts in which skills are taught run the gamut from formal credit-bearing courses on particular skills to teaching high school students about their rights in a Street Law program. Prominent examples are the related skills of interviewing and counseling. Until clinicians began teaching these skills as necessary tools for their students' clinical practice, they had no place in the law school curriculum. Today, instruction in those skills is found not only in classrooms and clinics, but also in sessions preparing students to participate in an international client counseling competition.

Clinicians seek to train lawyers in skills and values not because they have a unified theory of law practice, but because they want to prepare their students for the practice of law. This places clinical education at the forefront of legal system reform, as countries around the world question existing models for resolving legal disputes and look to native and indigenous mechanisms for solutions. These types of innovations in legal process and law practice—sometimes referred to as "alternative" dispute resolution, or ADR—are tested and implemented regularly in clinical programs around the world.[6] The fact that law is practiced differently in different parts of the world does not detract from the global relevance

---

6. ADR clinics are described in Chapter 17.

of clinical education; its global relevance stems from the fact that experience-based clinical skills training is the only way to address increasingly impatient calls for not just "socially relevant" but also "vocationally relevant" legal education reform.

The clinical methodology is practiced as a means of instilling professional values of public responsibility and social justice most commonly through the establishment of various types of law school "legal aid clinics" that have been the mainstay of clinical education in many countries since the 1960s and 1970s. While they may exist in many different forms, they share the fundamental clinical value of providing law students a learning experience that not only offers them the opportunity for skills training, but also deepens their understanding of the role of law in society through direct and meaningful personal experience of addressing pressing local social needs. Common features of legal aid-based clinical programs can be seen in many parts of the world, from Australia to China, from India to the United States.[7]

Clinical programs focus student attention on values and justice in many other ways, often in collaboration with nongovernmental organizations (NGOs) and other agencies concerned with social justice around the world. International human rights clinics involve collaborations among students and faculty across borders; depending on their capacities and the resources available to them, students can play any number of roles alongside faculty or cooperating practitioners in documenting and prosecuting human rights violations. Moreover, clinical programs have the capacity to adapt to immediate social needs and to lead students to look critically at the functioning of existing legal institutions. Examples include the emergence of clinical legal education in South Africa during the apartheid regime and in Central and Eastern Europe after the collapse of the Soviet Union.

A GLOBAL CLINICAL MOVEMENT

The illustrations set out above and many others documented in this book confirm the worldwide relevance and applicability of the core aspects of clinical legal education. Clinical programs around the world dedicated to professional skills and values training though the use of clinical methods have built a base for the global clinical movement, from which clinical legal education can continue to pursue its goal of opening up the social action role of legally trained persons. The Indian context is instructive in this regard, as the legal profession in India offers great challenges and great opportunities. It is a dynamic, changing profession;

---

7. Chapter 10 chronicles the legal aid origins of clinical legal education around the world.

it is also a controversial profession in much need of reform. Apart from litigation-oriented activities, lawyers are involved at the professional level in the social, political, and economic life of the country. They influence the course of developments and, in turn, become influenced by them. Students have to be exposed to the complexity and dynamics of this situation to make their own professional choices in an informed and intelligent manner. Moreover, for legal education to be responsive to the current deficiencies in the legal profession, law students must be provided with at least a basic level of professional skills and a basic understanding of the foundations of professional responsibility.

Global Clinical Legal Education: Richness in Diversity

It may seem, therefore, that clinical legal education is best approached from a purely national perspective—not only to achieve particular national goals, but also given its orientation toward professional skills training and its emphasis on preparing lawyers for the practice of law. It is certainly true that clinical legal education cannot be synthesized into a single, uniform approach applicable in every country. But clinical legal educators around the world are preparing future lawyers for high-quality, ethical law practice grounded in a legal profession dedicated to social justice by focusing on the importance of what local lawyers do. The fact that they do so in many different ways does not dilute the importance of what they share. The global clinical movement draws its strength not just from its global reach, but also from the richness found in its diversity.

We must be mindful that clinical legal education has to remain as diverse as the societies in which lawyers and their clients live—and the legal systems in which they practice. As a practical matter, then, the first order of business for any clinical program is to pursue the goals of the global clinical movement at the local level. By orienting clinical training in that way, a law school clinical program can have a direct impact not only on local society but on the local legal profession as well. Up to this point, the global clinical movement has emerged from the bottom up; groupings of local programs come together to start a national movement, programs scattered around the world come together to start a global movement. Over time, a vibrant and effective global movement could surface that way.

The reality, however, is that wherever clinical education has been introduced— wherever one now finds a clinical component in a law school's curriculum—it got there with a struggle. With its focus on new areas of study, its links to social action, and its dramatically different teaching methods, clinical education has never been an easy sell. Creating a successful clinical program in one part of a country or in one corner of the world is a notable achievement, but the future growth and development of clinical legal education depends on something more than harnessing the collective strength of clinician legal educators worldwide. It depends on the support of a different type of collective framework: a global clinical movement.

The "Value Added" of a Global Clinical Movement

We must return, then, to the question of what value does a global clinical movement add to the cause of justice education. The most important added value of a global clinical movement is its global quality; however much national and regional organizations have contributed to the clinical movement, they cannot signal the truly global presence of clinical legal education today. This is not to detract from their work. There can be no doubt that the efforts of these organizations have served to enhance clinical education's global movement status. Moreover, they continue to reach out to the global clinical community as part of their efforts to develop clinical programs in their respective jurisdictions and with respect to their particular areas of concern.

We have shown how the global clinical movement can define itself. Building on a set of core qualities that promise a future of socially relevant legal education, the global movement must now stimulate new ideas and encourages new ways of thinking about global clinical education through collaborations and syntheses that come about only in a global context. A global clinical movement can thereby offer a global perspective that will benefit the targets of clinical legal education's reform agenda—students, the profession, the communities the profession serves—on a global scale. The ambition of the global clinical movement is not to replace or downplay local movements. Certainly it must not head toward some sort of "clinical imperialism" by championing one national model, or even a globally modified national model, over all others.[8] Indeed, perhaps the greatest value of a global clinical movement is the special credibility and support it can provide national and regional developments in a way not possible through local movements and organizations.

CONCLUSION

There is no apt conclusion for this chapter as the global clinical movement is truly a work in progress. But it is a work in progress that can—indeed must—set far-reaching and ambitious goals. Clinical legal education operates in the sphere of legal aid, social justice, sustainable development, and good governance, where individuals' attitudes and approaches make a difference. Clinical education techniques—some still waiting to be discovered—take law education above the cognitive level to the emotional and affective domains, where attitudes are shaped and ethics of actions are questioned. This can be seen around the world where clinical law students become involved in community law reform projects, disaster management projects, migration issues, and a wide variety of activities aimed at

---

8. The concerns of clinical imperialism are discussed in Chapter 9 in the context of the debate over legal imperialism and the law and development movement.

alleviating poverty. A new jurisprudence on social justice is evolving out of clinical experiences, one that enhances the social relevance of legal education and offers great opportunities for the global clinical movement.

The power of clinical legal education is that it seeks to impart justice education, which can affect not only how future lawyers see the law but also how they serve the law. And how lawyers serve the law can change the way that law is perceived by the society at large. Looking forward, the challenge for the global clinical movement is to establish itself as an effective vehicle for stimulating new ideas and encouraging new ways of thinking about clinical legal education that can arise only in a global context. And that means not just new ideas and new ways of thinking about clinical legal education, but also about how clinically trained lawyers can address social justice at home and around the world. The aim of the global clinical movement is, therefore, not simply global clinical education. The aim of the global movement is to develop and support clinical legal education for the benefit of legal institutions and the societies they serve—everywhere in the world.

LIST OF REFERENCES

Upendra Baxi, *Notes Towards a Socially Relevant Legal Education*, 5 J. B. COUNCIL INDIA 23–55 (1976).

Frank S. Bloch, *Access to Justice and the Global Clinical Movement*, 28 WASH. U. J.L. & POL'Y 111, 130 (2008).

Frank S. Bloch & Iqbal S. Ishar, *Legal Aid, Public Service and Clinical Legal Education: Future Directions From India and the United States,* 12 MICH. J. INT'L. 92 (1990).

Lawrence M. Grosberg, *Clinical Education in Russia: "Da and Nyet,"* 7 CLINICAL L. REV. 469 (2001).

Grady Jessup, *Symbiotic Relations: Clinical Methodology—Fostering New Paradigms in African Legal Education*, 8 CLINICAL L. REV. 377 (2002).

N. R. Madhava Menon, In Defense of Socially Relevant Legal Education (1996), *available at* http://www.gaje.org.

Peggy Maisel, *The Role of U.S. Law Faculty in Developing Countries: Striving for Effective Cross-Cultural Collaboration*, 14 CLINICAL L. REV. 465 (2008).

Mao Ling, *Clinical Legal Education and the Reform of the Higher Legal Education System in China*, 30 FORDHAM INT'L. L.J. 421, 432 (2007).

University Grants Commission, Towards a Socially Relevant Legal Education (1975–1977) (report based on a working paper prepared by Prof. Upendra Baxi).

Richard J. Wilson, *Training for Justice: The Global Reach of Clinical Legal Education*, 22 PENN. ST. INT'L L. REV. 421, 428 (2004).

Leah Wortham, *Aiding Clinical Education Abroad: What Can Be Gained and the Learning Curve on How to Do So Effectively*, 12 CLINICAL L. REV. 615 (2006).

19. THE ROLE OF NATIONAL AND REGIONAL CLINICAL ORGANIZATIONS IN THE GLOBAL CLINICAL MOVEMENT

MARGARET MARTIN BARRY, FILIP CZERNICKI, IZABELA KRAŚNICKA, AND MAO LING

INTRODUCTION

The everyday work of legal clinics around the world fulfills both of the main goals of clinical legal education: to educate socially sensitive lawyers and to provide free legal services to indigent members of the community. To make such work possible, various national and regional clinical organizations have been formed to support clinics and to help provide the resources needed to develop clinical programs on the national, regional, and international level. Whether formed as an association, foundation, organization, or committee, these clinical organizations have also developed and supported strong national and regional networks. Moreover, through their national and regional projects—including conferences, meetings, seminars, and workshops, as well as exchanges of experience and practical knowledge through publications and Web sites—these organizations have helped spawn the global clinical movement.

Clinical organizations have been established in all parts of the world, a number of which—in Europe, Africa, Southeast Asia, China, the United States, and Australia—are described later in this chapter. Though established on different continents and operating under different circumstances, these organizations attempt to achieve essentially the same goals using similar methods and performing similar tasks. Moreover, newer organizations learn from more established ones and then pass on their experience to others. For example, the Polish clinical movement began with engagement and support from the United States, and the Polish national clinical organization is based on the African experience. Later, the Russian, Ukraine, and Czech clinics and clinical organizations profited from the Polish experience.

This chapter describes selected major national and regional clinical organizations and their various approaches to supporting and sustaining clinical legal education in their respective countries and regions. It also discusses their major goals and initiatives, as well as their contributions to the global clinical movement. Following a brief overview outlining the basic components of these clinical organizations, the chapter focuses on particular organizations in the United States, Africa, China, Central and Eastern Europe, the United Kingdom, Australia, and Southeast Asia. The chapter concludes with the observation that these organizations, individually and collectively, have played an important role in enabling clinical legal education to advance as a global movement.

OVERVIEW

The core mission of all clinical organizations contains three major elements: support, development, and promotion of clinical education programs. In addition, most organizations seek to integrate the activities of the legal clinics in their area by becoming a forum for common initiatives. Membership in these organizations can include law teachers (for example, the Russian Clinical Legal Education Foundation (CLEF) and the British Clinical Legal Education Organization (CLEO)), law schools (for example, the Polish Legal Clinics Foundation (FUPP) and the Committee of Chinese Clinical Legal Educators (CCCLE)), both individuals and legal entities (for example, the Association for Moldovan Legal Clinics (APCJM)), legal clinics (for example, the Ukrainian Association of Legal Clinics (UALC) and the South African Association of University Legal Aid Institutions (AULAI)), or any clinician who wishes to join (for example, the US-based Clinical Legal Education Association (CLEA)).

Fund-raising strategies also vary widely because support may be provided based on two very different institutional goals: financing the establishment of particular clinics or financing the establishment and operation of clinical organizations. Major institutions providing one or both of these types of support include the Ford Foundation, the Open Society Institute (OSI), the American Bar Association Central and East European Law Initiative (ABA CEELI), now known as the Rule of Law Initiative (ROLI), and the Swedish Section of the International Commission of Jurists. Other organizations provide assistance in searching for sponsors and gaining financial support, such as the Public Interest Law Institute (PILI) and the Open Society Justice Initiative (OSJI). Since clinical organizations are intended to support legal clinics, most understand fund-raising to be a major task in achieving their goals. Thus, fund-raising is included in the statutes of the Nigerian Network of University Legal Aid Institutions (NULAI), the Chinese CCCLE, the South African AULAI, and many others. On the other hand, the two major clinical organizations in the United States, the Clinical Section of the Association of American Law Schools (AALS) and CLEA, do not engage in fund-raising. This task may not be central to the operational goals of these organizations because legal clinics in the United States are financed for the most part from university budgets or grants. (Binford, 2009)

Whether national associations should create standards for legal clinics has been widely discussed and represents one of the major differences between national clinical organizations. Some have created a list of standards for clinical education and for providing legal services that their clinics are required to follow. Thus, the Polish FUPP provides financial support only for the clinics it accredits based on proper implementation of FUPP's standards. The Ukrainian UALC created standards and model regulations for Ukrainian legal clinics, which led to the Ministry of Education and Science adopting an order, On Standardized Provisions on Legal Clinics at Higher Schools in Ukraine. Pursuing a different approach, CLEA has advocated successfully for the inclusion of certain criteria in the American Bar Association's law school accreditation standards that have been helpful to clinical programs in the United States. (Stuckey, 1996) More recently, CLEA supported a project to establish "best practices" for legal education, including clinical programs. (Stuckey and Others, 2007)

Other organizations have decided to provide only basic requirements or recommended standards for clinics, such as the Model Rules of Organization and Conduct of Legal Clinics established by the Russian CLEF. The British CLEO's Model Standards for Live-Client Clinics provide a benchmark for institutions active in or setting up clinics, and reflect the experience of those already operating clinics both in the United Kingdom and abroad. (Clinical Legal Education Organization, 2007) The Moldovan APCJM also prepared Minimal Standards for Organization and Activities of Legal Clinics in Moldova, which provides direction for creating and managing legal clinics' activities.

Those organizations whose mission is only to provide assistance and guidance to clinics typically do not recommend or require stringent standards. The Chinese CCCLE, for example, does not have any rules concerning clinical work. The South African AULAI supplies manuals to clinics proposing some basic solutions for their organization and management. Following the example of AULAI, the Nigerian NULAI created a Clinical Legal Education Curriculum for Nigerian Universities' Law Faculties, which can be used as a model for clinical education programs around the country.

All clinical organizations declare in their statutes that improving the quality of clinical legal education in their countries is their highest priority. As a consequence, they sponsor a wide variety of activities on both the national and the international level to help achieve this goal. Nationally, these include organizing trainings, conferences, and workshops; publishing newsletters, manuals, journals, and books distributed to the clinics; and creating Web sites or e-mail lists. Internationally, this is achieved mainly through international and global conferences, as well as extensive use of the Internet to share ideas and material and to promote the development of clinical education in every part of the world. National conferences or other meetings usually focus on the organization and proper management of clinics (institutional development) and the improvement of clinical teaching methods (educational development). For example, the Russian CLEF conducts an organizational development program consisting of, among other things, in-service training for staff searching for new managers, while the Polish FUPP co-organizes national clinical conferences twice a year dedicated to different topics on clinical organization and teaching.

A number of clinical organizations engage in various publishing activities. CLEA and the Clinical Section of the AALS—together with New York University Law School—publish the *Clinical Law Review*, a semi-annual peer-edited journal devoted to issues of lawyering theory and clinical legal education. The *Clinical Law Review* published a special issue in 2005 consisting of a major annotated bibliography of articles on clinical legal education,[1] and CLEA publishes a handbook for new clinical teachers that is available on its website. The Polish FUPP has published several books dedicated to clinics and clinical teaching methods, as well as *Klinika*, a biannual journal open to all Polish clinicians. Some organizations, including the CCCLE and the NULAI, publish internal materials and most have Web sites that are used to share knowledge and promote clinical education on national and international levels. Many send out newsletters and sponsor online discussions using e-mail electronic mailing lists.

The largest global meeting dedicated to clinical issues is the biannual worldwide conference of the Global Alliance for Justice Education (GAJE).[2] Another prominent clinical forum is the international meeting of the *International Journal of Clinical Legal Education*, which is often held in collaboration with a national clinical organization. With the initiative and support of the Open Society Justice Initiative, the Polish FUPP hosted the Legal Clinics Organizations Roundtable Meeting in 2007, which allowed clinical organizations from around the world to compare their achievements and goals. As part of that project, a manual titled *The Legal Clinic: The Idea, Organization, Methodology*, was translated from Polish into English and can be downloaded from the FUPP Web site.

EXAMPLES OF NATIONAL AND REGIONAL CLINICAL ORGANIZATIONS AND THEIR GLOBAL ACTIVITIES AND ACHIEVEMENTS

This section presents examples of national and regional clinical organizations selected on the basis of geographical representation and scope of global activities and achievements. The section begins with two major organizations in the United States followed by two in Africa and the official organization in China. Then comes a selection of organizations from Central and Eastern Europe, United Kingdom, and Australia, followed by an overview of a unique organization that works across boundaries in Southeast Asia.

Two Clinical Organizations in the United States

Two organizations have led the development of the clinical legal education movement in the United States: the Section on Clinical Legal Education of the Association of American Law Schools (AALS) and the Clinical Legal Education Association (CLEA). The AALS Clinical Section was the exclusive

---

1. J. P. Ogilvy & Karen Czapanskiy, *Clinical Legal Education: An Annotated Bibliography* (3d ed.), 1 CLINICAL L. REV. (Special Issue) 1 (Fall 2005).

2. GAJE conferences and other GAJE initiatives are discussed in detail in Chapter 25.

clinical organization in the United States until the early 1990s, when CLEA was established to provide an independent voice for clinical legal education. This was necessary since the AALS is a law school membership organization with rules that limit advocacy to policies and procedures approved by the organization. Today, the two organizations work both cooperatively and independently to support and advocate for clinical legal education and clinical teachers in the United States. The AALS Clinical Section is open to faculty members at AALS member law schools, while CLEA membership is open to all clinical teachers, both within the United States and outside of the country. Both organizations receive funds from membership dues and registrations fees for workshops and conferences, but most accomplishments come from the volunteer efforts of their members. A third organization supportive of clinical legal education is the Society of American Law Teachers (SALT), membership in which is open to all law faculty in the United States, including clinical faculty.

Probably the most important activity of the AALS Clinical Section is its sponsorship of workshops and conferences, which facilitate the development and sharing of clinical teaching methods. These include a major clinical conference held once a year, a program and luncheon at each annual AALS meeting, and a biannual workshop for new clinicians. The Clinical Section has also provided financial support for regional conferences across the country. Together with other informal means of exchanging ideas and information, including a national electronic mailing list ("lawclinic"), the Section has helped build a strong and supportive network of clinicians in the United States.

Clinical Section members have also looked beyond the United States in building this network. One of the first efforts by the Section to reach out to clinicians from outside the United States was the 1996 AALS Clinical Section Conference in Miami. Law professors from India, Australia, and South America were invited to attend and it was during that conference that the first meetings were held that led to the creation of the Global Alliance for Justice Education (GAJE).[3] Since then, clinicians from abroad have attended AALS clinical programs—although not in significant numbers. The Section also has an International Clinical Legal Education Committee that seeks to promote greater international communication and collaboration among clinical teachers and students.

Like the AALS Clinical Section, CLEA has also supported regional faculty development conferences. Indeed, CLEA initiated and still conducts workshops for new clinicians held in alternate years to the program sponsored by AALS and in connection with the annual AALS clinical conference. Perhaps more importantly, CLEA has been a major voice in asserting the need for security of position and participation in law schools governance for clinical faculty. For example, CLEA has written briefs and issued statements in support of protecting the

---

3. This meeting and the others that followed are described in Chapter 25.

academic freedom and fair treatment of clinical faculty when they have been attacked for representing controversial clients and has advocated within the American Bar Association for accreditation standards that treat clinicians fairly. In 2007, the organization published a widely cited book, BEST PRACTICES FOR LEGAL EDUCATION, which addresses many of the fundamental concerns of the clinical movement in the broader context of general legal education reform. (Stuckey and Others, 2007)

Together with New York University School of Law, the AALS Clinical Section and CLEA sponsor the *Clinical Law Review*, a peer-reviewed journal that has become a major vehicle for clinical faculty development. It provides an outlet for clinical scholarship that explores a wide range of substantive law and issues of practice and pedagogy connected with clinical programs, including a number of articles that discuss developments in the global clinical legal education movement. Through its editorial board, composed of clinical faculty elected by the board or appointed by the sponsors, the *Review* actively promotes clinical scholarship by working closely with authors and by sponsoring workshops for clinicians working on articles that they hope to have published.[4]

As noted earlier, CLEA has advocated actively within the American Bar Association for changes to law school accreditation standards. Certain key provisions in the ABA Standards for Approval of Law Schools highlight some of the issues that have been of concern to clinical programs, reflecting both support for and constraints on their role in the academy. Standard 301(a), for example, provides that law schools must prepare students "for admission to the bar, and effective and responsible participation in the legal profession." Standard 302 specifies that the curriculum must cover professional skills, most of which are associated traditionally with clinical legal education. It also requires "substantial opportunities" for "live-client and other real-life practice experiences." Standard 305 establishes externship course requirements that essentially track those developed over the years by clinical faculty. Standard 701 requires adequate physical facilities, including suitable space for conducting clinical programs. (American Bar Association, 2009–2010)

Another key standard of interest to clinical programs is Standard 405(c), which addresses the status of clinical faculty. Efforts to strengthen this standard have been an important part of the clinical movement agenda in the United States, as faculty status plays an important role in assuring the integrity of clinical programs. In its present form, Standard 405(c) provides for some security of position and a limited role in law school governance for most clinical faculty, but this is significantly less than the tenure track traditionally extended to doctrinal faculty.

---

4. The role of clinical scholarship in the global clinical movement is the subject of Chapter 21.

Two Examples from Africa

Two African countries have taken the lead in establishing national clinical organizations in the region: the Association of University Legal Aid Institutions (AULAI), a voluntary association established in the early 1980s to create a forum for all university-based law clinics in South Africa to share experiences, to establish and develop clinical programs, and to provide free legal services to indigent communities; and the Network of University Legal Aid Institutions in Nigeria (NULAI Nigeria), which was established in 2003 as an association of university law clinics promoting clinical legal education, legal aid, and access to justice.

The first law clinic in South Africa was established in the early 1970s. Only in the late 1980s, however, were university legal clinics formalized.[5] In its early years, AULAI merely had meetings during law teacher conferences during which the members discussed aspects of common interest. A key development in AULAI's history was the establishment of the AULAI Trust in 1998 to provide more stable financial support for South Africa's legal aid clinics. Since then the trust has provided financial support for the establishment and expansion of clinical programs throughout South Africa. Through the mid-1990s, AULAI also focused on addressing national and regional iniquities and inequalities through access to justice programs.

More recently, AULAI has become more involved in the growing international clinical movement. In 2003, AULAI hosted the First All Africa Colloquium on Clinical Legal Education in collaboration with the Open Society Justice Initiative (OSJI) and the University of Natal, which brought together clinicians from established clinics in South Africa and other African countries to share experiences and learn how to strengthen clinical education on the continent. In addition, the colloquium generated several specific initiatives, including plans to develop clinics in a number of other African countries, especially in West Africa. Training courses for clinicians in Africa and exchange programs between clinics in African nations and other developing countries were carried out, as well as the production of resource materials for law clinics in the region. AULAI subsequently played a significant role in the establishment of the Nigerian network of law clinics, now called the Nigerian Association of University Legal Aid Institutions (NULAI).

Finally, AULAI has supported the linking of clinical legal education to strong access to justice outreach programs. It has done so via the establishment of Access to Justice Clusters, a cooperative body of university law clinics, justice centers, private practitioners, and other organizations jointly managed by representatives of all stakeholders. Through its law clinics and the paralegal advice offices with which it cooperates, AULAI extends legal services to the poor and

---

5. The development of clinical legal education in South Africa and other countries on the continent are discussed in Chapter 2.

marginalized in South African society. Its member university-based legal aid institutions have developed unique relationships with the Legal Aid Board, national paralegal organizations, and local governments—and have become key service providers in the field.

Since its establishment, NULAI has advocated vigorously for the reform, development, and institutionalization of clinical legal education in Nigeria. Currently, NULAI has a network of six university-based law clinics that were established in collaboration with the Open Society Institute (OSI) and OSJI. Support from the MacArthur Foundation has allowed NULAI to expand its membership to include four additional law clinics, which would bring clinical legal education programs to about one-third of the law student population in Nigeria. NULAI also draws resources from other international programs to facilitate its capacity-building programs for law teachers, including regular clinical teacher training workshops.

Furthermore, NULAI followed the lead of AULAI by sponsoring a number of national and regional conferences on clinical legal education. In 2004 and 2008, with the support of OSJI/OSI and the MacArthur Foundation respectively, NULAI hosted the First and Second All Nigeria Clinical Legal Education Colloquium in Abuja. In 2005, it hosted, again with the support of OSJI/OSI, the Second All Africa Colloquium on Clinical Legal Education in Abuja. NULAI has also promoted curriculum reform; in 2006, it published the Clinical Legal Education Curriculum for Nigerian Universities/Law Clinics. Other activities of the organization include a nationwide legal clinics competition and the National Client Interviewing and Counseling Skills competition for Nigerian law schools and law faculties.

China's Committee of Chinese Clinical Legal Educators

The Committee of Chinese Clinical Legal Educators (CCCLE) has led the development of the clinical legal education movement in China since it was established in 2002, with the approval of the China Law Society Legal Education Studies. As discussed in more detail in Chapter 6, the Ford Foundation, which had supported the early years of clinical education in China, shifted its policy with the establishment of CCCLE to fund CCCLE instead of giving funds directly to individual law schools.

CCCLE is a nonprofit national academic organization made up of two kinds of members: individual members and school members. Any clinical teacher who applies will be accepted as an individual member. However, CCCLE does provide standards for approving the school members. Its mission is to launch all possible initiatives to promote the spread and development of clinical legal education in China. The organization's executive body is the secretariat, which is responsible for implementing the decisions of a thirteen-member standing committee and carrying out all other administrative matters. According to its constitution, the standing committee of CCCLE is elected by all school members and only teachers from the member schools can be elected to the standing committee. The most important activities of CCCLE include organizing an annual conference each year, organizing workshops on different topics, preparing publications, and running a Web site aimed at facilitating the development and sharing of clinical teaching methods among Chinese clinicians. (Zhen, 2005)

In addition to its national activities, CCCLE has attempted to develop projects and initiatives on the international level. Indeed, one of the duties imposed on CCCLE in its constitution is to develop international or global activities that promote the development of clinical education in China and elsewhere in the world. Accordingly, the organization has a three-step strategy to promote international collaboration that includes learning from the experience of other countries, going abroad and seeking input from other countries, and conducting cooperative programs with other countries. Just as it played a leading role in furthering various activities to develop clinical legal education throughout China, the Ford Foundation has promoted CCCLE's efforts to encourage Chinese clinicians to engage in the global clinical movement. (Note, 2007)

The first attempt by CCCLE to engage in the global clinical movement was to work with clinical teachers and organizations outside of China to train Chinese clinical teachers. CCCLE and the Ford Foundation thus decided to fund eight pilot law schools to have sister-partners in the United States to help them build clinics and train clinical teachers. This partner-initiated cooperation model focused on the mutual exchange of visitors for teaching and learning. From 2000 to 2007, five groups consisting of thirty-six Chinese clinical teachers made field visits to the United States during which they visited legal clinics, attended clinical classes, and shared their experiences in curriculum setup, classroom teaching, individual instruction, teaching methodology, class and student evaluation, clinic management, and other organizational matters. The Ford Foundation also provided funds to send faculty from the US partner schools to China. (Phan, 2005)

Another important effort of CCCLE at the global level has been to host national and international conferences in order to improve research and academic exchanges on clinical education. CCCLE is required by its constitution to prepare a plan for Chinese clinical legal education to promote the development of community legal education (CLE) in China. According to this plan, CCCLE should hold two clinical conferences per year. In order to seek opportunities for expanding international exchange and cooperation, foreign clinical experts have been invited to attend CCCLE workshops and conferences in different parts of the country. In addition, CCCLE sponsors participation by its members at major international clinical conferences, such as the worldwide meetings of GAJE. Other organizations with which CCCLE has collaborated internationally include International Bridges to Justice (IBJ), the Beijing and Mongolian office of the Council of Europe, the Culture and Education Committee of Great Britain, the Sino-Canada Cooperative Service Office, the Public Interest Law Institute (PILI), the Open Society Institute (OSI), the Asian Foundation, and the Asian Legal Resources Center. Most recently, CCCLE joined a project funded by the US Agency for International Development (USAID) partnering two law schools from the United States and three Chinese law schools with the aim of enhancing clinical legal education and professional skills training in China through experiential teaching methods.

CCCLE has also played a prominent role in obtaining resources—and gaining attention and recognition—from important institutions in China, including legal education administration organs, legal aid bodies, lawyers associations, and the law society. For instance, CCCLE works with PILI and the Beijing Public Interest Law Firm to fund twenty-six volunteers working as public interest lawyers at twelve public interest institutions in China. Among the more than one hundred school members of CCCLE, almost half are funded by the Ford Foundation and CCCLE; the others are directly funded by their university's budget or have established some cooperative relationships with law firms or social organizations. In 2002, CCCLE created its own Web site for clinical educators to share information, publicize clinical legal education activities, and promote international cooperation. The organization is responsible for sending news to individual members and university members, publishing activities and any important decisions made by CCCLE, issuing training materials, and publicizing the latest developments of every clinic. In 2004, two pages were added to the Web site, one on foreign clinics and the other for sharing resources.

Clinical Organizations in Central and Eastern Europe

National clinical organizations have played an important role in the development of clinical legal education in Central and Eastern Europe. These organizations were established over a relatively short period and, for the most part, have similar goals. Over the years they have cooperated among themselves and with other like-minded organizations, both within and outside the region, thereby creating a network that has played an important role in the global clinical movement.[6] (Rekosh, 2008) Five such organizations, in Poland, Russia, Moldova, the Czech Republic, and Ukraine, are discussed below.

Clinical legal education developed quickly in Poland, with twenty-five clinics established over a ten-year period beginning in the late 1990s. Legal clinics are now present at every public and most private law schools in the country. An important element of this success was the decision to establish the Legal Clinics Foundation (FUPP). In December 2001, three representatives of Polish legal clinics were invited to visit the Republic of South Africa to learn from the AULAI's experience. The visit was financed by the Ford Foundation and designed and organized by the Public Interest Law Initiative, affiliated at that time with the Columbia

---

6. Clinical movements in a number of countries in Central and Eastern Europe are discussed in Chapter 4

University in New York and now the Public Interest Law Institute (PILI). The trip resulted in the creation of a strategy for the development of Polish legal clinic programs based on the experience of South Africa. Consequently, FUPP was established with the mission of strengthening the structure of clinical education in Poland and constructing a platform for cooperation in shaping its future.

FUPP's objectives included not only ensuring the financial stability of the clinical movement, but also constituting a forum that would bring together efforts to enhance the clinics' position in the academic and legal communities. One of the foundation's first projects—undertaken together with PILI and the Open Society Justice Initiative (OSJI)—was to organize the Fifth Regional Conference of Clinical Law Teaching, which was held in 2002 in Warsaw. The main topics of the conference were the prospects for the development of clinical programs in the region and devising a strategy for the future. Approximately seventy people participated, representing more than twenty countries. A few years later, in 2007, FUPP convened a "roundtable meeting of national legal clinics organizations" jointly with OSJI. The meeting brought together representatives of national clinical organizations from all over the world, including China, Nigeria, Poland, Russia, South Africa, Ukraine, the United Kingdom, and the United States. The objectives of the meeting were to survey the activities and missions of existing clinical organizations, exchange experiences in organizing and standardizing or institutionalizing university-based legal clinics, and explore possible international networking and capacity-building initiatives.

As Polish clinical programs are at present among the leading programs in the region, FUPP and its members have sought to share their experience and to assist in the creation of new clinics by inviting guests from other countries of Central and Eastern Europe to participate in training, courses, and study visits. Thus, FUPP has hosted visitors from Montenegro, Czech Republic, Hungary, Slovakia, Ukraine, Belarus, Russia, Uzbekistan, Kazakhstan, and Georgia, as well as Japan, China, and the United States. FUPP has also been involved in the creation and support of clinical organizations in Ukraine, Russia, and China. Representatives of the foundation and other Polish clinicians take part in international clinic-related conferences, play an active role in international projects, and have been members of GAJE since its establishment.

Law clinics first appeared in Russia in the late 1990s, stemming from collaborations between Russian law schools, international donors, and law schools in the United States. (Grosberg, 2001) Russian clinicians were also influenced by a 1999 conference for Street Law clinics in St. Petersburg that sparked a very rapid growth of such programs, not just in Russia but in other countries of the former Soviet Union as well.[7] Around the same time, from 1998 to 2002, clinical teach-

---

7. Street Law programs and their contribution to clinical legal education are the subject of Chapter 15.

ers and students from the former Soviet republics participated in summer and winter schools hosted by several Russian law schools—most notably Tver University Law School and the Oldenburgsky Institute. Some of these teachers and students also came for longer internships and training programs. Eventually, the Oldenburgsky Institute evolved as a leader and resource center for clinics in Russia and other countries in the region. The Clinical Legal Education Center was organized by the institute's team to continue performing this role.

One of the center's global projects, instituted jointly with PILI in 2004, involved creating—and further developing—a network of law clinics specializing in serving nonprofit organizations. Among other things, this resulted in the creation of an independent interschool law clinic, the Open St. Petersburg Law Clinic. Over the next two years, the center and PILI initiated the creation of a new national organization, the Clinical Legal Education Foundation (CLEF). They also organized a process of consultation and strategic planning among Russian clinicians, sponsored the participation of delegates at the 2004 GAJE conference in Krakow, and facilitated the exchange of experiences and insights with the Polish Legal Clinics Foundation (FUPP). Funded by the Ford and MacArthur foundations, CLEF is currently implementing and supporting a number of innovative projects related to clinical legal education and human rights in Russia.

The Association for Moldovan Legal Clinics (APCJM) was established in 2005 with support from a variety of organizations, including the American Bar Association's Rule of Law Initiative (ABA ROLI) and OSJI, in order to consolidate and improve the management capacities and sustainability of legal clinics in Moldova. APCJM offers professional, innovative, result-oriented assistance to Moldovan legal clinics in their daily activities, as well in their efforts to strengthen their internal capacity and external role in local communities. It organizes an annual forum that provides a platform for discussion of various dimensions of clinical legal education and free legal assistance to the disadvantaged categories of the population, and has created a Web site that includes a discussion forum for students and other members of the legal community. In 2006, APCJM implemented a complex program designed to improve the management and action capacity of legal clinics. It consisted of training seminars on sustainability and organizational development, volunteer management, and communication.

Another of APCJM's activities is to engage in continuous advocacy with the Ministry of Education and the Ministry of Justice to institutionalize the curriculum on clinical legal education and to include clinics in the national system of providing free legal aid to the needy. Due to APCJM's interventions, Moldovan legal clinics are part of an anticorruption alliance and are involved in a program of preventing and fighting corruption at the national level. As part of a strategy to strengthen its cooperation with regional and international counterparts, the APCJM attended the roundtable meeting of national clinical organizations in Warsaw organized by FUPP. This activity marked the beginning for sharing practical knowledge and experience with counterparts from China, Nigeria, Poland, Russia, South Africa, Ukraine, the United Kingdom, and the United States.

Since the establishment of the first legal clinic in 1996 at the Faculty of Law of the Palacký University, Olomouc (FLPU), the implementation of clinical legal education in the Czech Republic has always been closely connected with international cooperation. FLPU's clinical program was transformed and enriched in 2006 through a project supported by the European Social Fund and the state budget of the Czech Republic. The transformation was strongly inspired by FUPP's Polish Legal Clinics Foundation Standards and intensive cooperation of clinical teachers from FLPU with FUPP. Czech clinicians have established contacts for future international cooperation by participating in various international conferences. Understanding the importance of international cooperation was one of the main impulses that led FLPU to organize an international conference on "Practical forms of education" in 2008, with participation of clinical teachers from the United States, the United Kingdom, Poland, and, of course, the Czech Republic.

The legal clinics program in Ukraine was launched in 2000 to provide legal aid and assistance to low-income citizens, and also to meet the need for training young lawyers in new approaches and principles of practice that reflect an understanding of social and public needs as well as facilitating and supporting their activities in the future. In order to preserve and provide for the further development of clinical programs, the existing network of legal clinics was transformed in 2004 into an informal union known as the Ukrainian Legal Clinics Association. Then, in 2007, legal clinics from fourteen Ukrainian regions created the Ukrainian Legal Clinics Foundation (ULCF), a central coordinating and supporting body that works to increase the efficiency of Ukrainian clinics, and also supports and advocates for the values and goals of the clinical movement at the national level.

The ULCF has considerably strengthened the position of clinical legal education in Ukraine. Today, there are more than forty-five legal clinics operating in twenty-one regions of the country. Through the work of the ULFC and its members, there are now a number of approved programmatic documents regulating activities of legal clinics in Ukraine, including Ukrainian Legal Clinics Standards, Model Regulations for Ukrainian Legal Clinics, and Ethical Code of Ukrainian Legal Clinics. These documents have also identified specific objectives to be included in a standardized curriculum of a course entitled, Fundamental Principles of Legal Clinical Practice. A professional periodical designed to cover the nature and character of clinical legal education as well as the problems and perspectives of its further development, the *Newsletter of Ukrainian Legal Clinics Program*, began in 2006. Another measure of the institutional success of the Ukrainian clinical movement is that key government agencies, including the Ministry of Education and the Ministry of Justice, now realize the value of clinical programs. For example, in 2006, the Ministry of Education adopted an order titled, On Standardized Provisions on Legal Clinics at Higher Schools in Ukraine.

The involvement of Ukrainian clinicians at the international level has had a very positive professional impact. Since its establishment, the ULCF has been supported by OSJI, which helps organize international exchanges, conferences, and trainings. Ukrainian clinical teachers have thus participated regularly in activities of the FUPP and have attended many international clinical conferences.

United Kingdom and Australia

The United Kingdom and Australia are both countries with long-standing and vibrant clinical legal education programs. Their national clinical organizations have adopted less formal means of promoting and supporting their respective clinical movements.[8] Thus, the Australian Clinical Legal Education Association has been overshadowed by various activities of individual law school programs. The British Clinical Legal Education Organization (CLEO) functions quite well as an informal organization of academics, most notably with annual conferences that gather clinical representatives from around the country. Cross-ocean cooperation between these two countries exists in the form of strong links and exchange ventures, especially at the annual conferences sponsored by the *International Journal of Clinical Legal Education.*

Clinical methods were first developed in the United Kingdom during the 1970s at Warwick, Kent, and South Bank, but very few programs used them until the 1990s, when a number of universities developed in-house clinics. CLEO was established in 1994 to promote clinical methods through conferences and publications, including the first book on the subject in the United Kingdom, published in 1998. CLEO is also responsible for publishing the Model Standards for Live Client Clinics and for organizing annual clinical conferences. Clinicians from the United Kingdom were among the founding members of GAJE in 1996, and there has been a regular UK presence at GAJE conferences and on the steering committee ever since.

Three particular initiatives are worth mentioning in terms of the United Kingdom's contribution to the global clinical movement. The first is the work of The College of Law, which has developed more clinical programs than any other law school and has provided advice and support to developing programs in many countries. Another is the work of Northumbria University, whose Student Law Office is the most developed of any in the United Kingdom. In 2000, they introduced the *International Journal of Clinical Legal Education*, which has published

---

8. The early years of clinical legal education in both the United Kingdom and Australia are discussed in Chapter 1.

articles on clinical education from a number of jurisdictions and supports an annual conference, often in collaboration with cosponsors elsewhere in the world. Thirdly, the UK Centre for Legal Education is a government-funded body which supports both academic and professional legal education by funding research and providing training and resources. Its Web site contains valuable information about clinical legal education and practical advice on developing new clinics and related programs. It also hosts the Model Standards developed by CLEO.

Australian clinics developed out of the Community Legal Centre movement of the 1970s and benefited from energetic contributions from students eager to make their law studies more relevant. While some early Australian clinical teachers looked to the United States and England for insights and examples, informal local networks were the key to promoting clinical teaching and supporting clinicians. The Australian clinical movement has benefited every few years since the late 1980s from increasingly international clinic-specific conferences, thereby benefiting from the insights of clinical teachers from far and wide. (Zariski, 1992)

A national clinical organization, the Australian Clinical Legal Education Association, was established in Adelaide in 1996, but found itself overtaken by already-existing informal networks of Australian clinicians. For example, the clinical program at the University of New South Wales (UNSW) supports a clinical electronic mailing list and also publishes a biennial guide to Australian clinical programs. A Clinical Legal Education Interest Group has convened regularly at the annual Australasian Law Teachers Association conference, and there are regular clinic discussions at meetings of the National Association of Community Legal Centres.

A group of Australian clinicians have recently collaborated on efforts designed to foster clinical legal education across the country by consolidating existing programs and providing encouragement and support to law schools interested in establishing new programs and reinvigorating dormant ones. The Australian Clinical Legal Education Network was established in 2009 and is likely to facilitate law school efforts to obtain additional government support for Australian clinical programs. If funding is secured, it may result in greater formalization of the structures used to promote the interests of the Australian clinical movement.

Australian clinicians have made a range of contributions to international clinical activities. Several contributed to the establishment of GAJE, and a GAJE regional conference was hosted by UNSW and Sydney University in 2002. Clinic staff members from Newcastle University and UNSW have been involved in separate projects in Timor Leste; Murdoch Law School clinicians have worked with international refugee agencies on immigration issues; and other Australian schools have worked closely on projects with law schools in the South Pacific (Monash & Griffith), China (UNSW), and Nigeria (Griffith). The UNSW clinical program has also contributed extensively to the work of the United Nations Committee on the Convention on the elimination of All Forms of Discrimination Against Women (CEDAW). Finally, Australian clinical scholars have been active contributors to the *International Journal of Clinical Legal Education*, with a range of articles written by clinicians and students from programs at La Trobe, Griffith, Monash, Newcastle, and UNSW.

Southeast Asia's Cross-Border Clinical Initiatives

Clinical legal education is relatively new to Southeast Asia. While India and the Philippines have had clinics for quite some time, most other clinic-type programs existing in the region had little to no jurisprudential pedagogy and operated without a specific focus of working with marginalized and vulnerable communities.[9] There has been some international support for legal education reform in the region; however, this aid was centered on more traditional legal education models and not on clinical education. This began to change during the early 2000s with the development of clinical programs in Cambodia and Indonesia with the help of the OSJI and Bridges Across Borders Southeast Asia (BABSEA), now known as Bridges Across Borders Southeast Asia Community Legal Education Initiative (BABSEA CLE), and, more recently, in Vietnam, where the United Nations Development Program has been exploring ways to promote and support clinical education initiatives.

Relying on lessons learned and models of successful clinic programs and networks, BABSEA CLE's Community Legal Education Initiatives Program is currently active in Thailand, Cambodia, Vietnam, Laos, Malaysia, the Philippines, and Singapore. It has established working partnerships with a number of universities and governmental, nongovernmental, and community-based organizations throughout the region, and it is working actively to encourage cooperation between those programs as well as among the larger legal community in Southeast Asia. BABSEA CLE points to a number of advancements and successes in its cooperative efforts to expand clinical legal education in Southeast Asia. These include running community legal education programs attended by professors and students alike, organizing thematic regional clinical education workshops and conferences, sponsoring regional strategic program planning development sessions, and sharing curriculum, lesson plans, manuals, and other resources between partners, both nationally and regionally. It can also point to continued enrollment and participation in its annual International Legal Studies Internship Program, which has been attended by students, professors, and other legal educators from countries throughout the region and other parts of the world.

---

9. Background and analysis of clinical programs in this region are discussed in Chapter 3.

CONCLUSION

The story of the global clinical movement is a story of many people around the world involved in different institutions and organizations, all taking up the mission to educate lawyers and provide professional assistance. The key elements for a global perspective of clinical legal education are that in every corner of the world lawyers need to be better—and more ethically—trained and poor people need legal advice. Each country described in this chapter found its own way of engaging in clinical legal education and consequently established institutions or organizations to support their clinical programs. It is the force of the idea and the potential of those involved that make the global clinical movement effective.

LIST OF REFERENCES

ABA Standards for Approval of Law Schools 301(a) (2009–2010),
  available at http://www.abanet.org.
Association for the Promotion of Moldovan Legal Clinics, APCJM Development
  Strategy for 2007–2009 (2006).
Margaret Martin Barry, Jon C. Dubin, & Peter A. Joy, *Clinical Legal Education for
  This Millennium: The Third Wave*, 7 CLIN. L. REV. 1 (2000).
W. Warren H. Binford, *Reconstructing a Clinic*, 15 CLINICAL L. REV. 283 (2009).
Clinical Legal Education Organisation, Model Standards for Live-Client Clinics,
  June 2007, *available at* http://www.ukcle.ac.uk.
Stephen Ellman, Isabelle R. Gunning, & Randy Hertz, *Foreword, Why Not a
  Clinical Lawyer-Journal?*, 1 CLINICAL L. REV. 1 (1994).
Lawrence M. Grosberg, *Clinical Education in Russia: "Da and Nyet,"*
  7 CLINICAL L. REV. 469 (2001).
Peter A. Joy & Robert R. Kuehn, *The Evolution of ABA Standards for Clinical
  Faculty*, 75 TENN. L. REV. 183 (2008)
Bruce A. Lasky, The Expansion of CLE Initiatives Throughout SE Asia and the
  Role of Bridges Across Borders, *available at* http://www.babsea.org.
The Legal Clinics Foundation (FUPP), The Legal Clinics: The Idea,
  Organization, Methodology (2005), *available at* http://www.fupp.org.pl.
Note, *Adopting and Adapting: Clinical Legal Education and Access to Justice in
  China*, 120 HARV. L. REV. 2134 (2007).
Phan, Note from the Field, *Clinical Legal Education in China: In Pursuit of a Culture
  of Law and a Mission of Social Justice*, 8 YALE HUM. RTS. & DEV. L.J. 117 (2005).
Public Interest Law Institute, Clinical Legal Education Foundation Established
  in Russia, *available at* http://www.pili.org.
Edwin Rekosh, *Constructing Public Interest Law: Transnational Collaboration and
  Exchange in Central and Eastern Europe*, 13 UCLA J. INT'L L. & FOREIGN AFF. 55
  (2008).

Roy Stuckey, *Report on Changes in the ABA Accreditation Standards,* 5 CLINICAL LEGAL EDUCATION ASSOCIATION NEWSLETTER 10 (1996).

ROY T. STUCKEY AND OTHERS, Best Practices for Legal Education (Clinical Legal Education Association 2007).

Archie Zariski, *Roll Over Socrates: Reflections on the Conference on Clinical Legal Education and Some Implications for Law at Murdoch,* 9 J. PROF. LEGAL EDUC. 155 (1992).

Zhen Zhen, The Present Situation and Prosperous Future of China Clinical Legal Education (Oct. 7, 2005), *available at* http://www.law.ucla.edu/docs/zhen__zhen_prosporous_future_of_chinese_clinical_educatio_.pdf.

20. BRIDGING DIFFERENT INTERESTS
The Contributions of Clinics to Legal Education

JEFF GIDDINGS AND JENNIFER LYMAN

Clinics play a distinctive bridging role in legal education, bringing together groups who otherwise are at best passing acquaintances—law schools and the practicing profession, law students and the profession, law schools and their local communities. Clinics also can link law schools with their alumni. This chapter examines five overlapping elements of clinical legal education for their impact on the broader project of legal education: clinics as components of the curriculum; clinicians (or clinical teachers); clinical teaching methods; clinical social justice values; and clinic students. Each of these elements plays its own role in affecting legal education more generally.

Recognizing that diverse regional contexts lead to variations in emphasis among these different elements, the chapter does not try to quantify the impact of clinical programs across many regions. Rather, it presents ideas for spreading the influence of clinics based on concrete examples and the authors' exposure to clinical teachers from various parts of the world. We also acknowledge that a great many variables influence clinical education's impact on traditional legal education, including: the degree to which governments (ministries of justice or education) control curriculum in higher education; the extent of any further professional training required before law graduates can commence practicing law; the related availability of private legal education institutions and their ability to innovate; the rate of change in the structure of the legal profession and the manner of delivering legal services, particularly legal aid services; the number and age of law students, and the extent of their previous education and work experience; and the presence of larger forces for educational reform (international or domestic) and an openness to ideas from outside, whether as a result of change within the system or new sources of professional interaction. The experience in one system therefore never repeats exactly in another.[1] Nevertheless, we attempt to identify common threads and themes that may transfer across legal and educational cultures.

CLINICS IN THE CURRICULUM

Clinics make their initial impact on legal education simply by getting accepted as legitimate curricular activity—but the process of getting accepted usually is far

---

1. This point is taken up relative to the law and development movement in Chapter 9.

from simple. One reason for this is that often clinical activities begin in volunteer work conducted by students, although sometimes with the assistance of volunteers from the faculty.[2] To gain recognition as a course deserving academic credit, clinics need persuasive advocates within the academy and a source of funds that lasts long enough to develop an internal constituency in the law school. To exert a noticeable influence on general legal education, they must touch a significant number of students and become recognized for their unique contributions to legal education. Thus, modern clinical legal education came into its own in the United States in the 1970s with extended Ford Foundation funding engineered to gradually transfer funding responsibility to the law schools.

The influence of clinics on law school curricula goes beyond the existence of clinical programs to the introduction of subjects such as interviewing and counseling, negotiation, and alternative dispute resolution (ADR). Indeed, the very idea of studying "lawyering" as a dynamic process gained traction in legal curricula through texts authored by clinical teachers (e.g., Bellow & Moulton, 1978; Binder & Price, 1977; Sherr, 1986; Brayne & Grimes, 1994) and lawyers practice manuals produced in various Australian jurisdictions and in South Africa (e.g., Springvale Legal Service, 1985; SCALES Community Legal Centre, 2004; de Klerk et al., 2006). In some instances, law faculties have recognized the special appropriateness of practical or clinical methods for teaching professional ethics. Where the profession has codified ethics rules, some schools have moved ethics education out of the arid environment of a rules-based lecture format into either simulated or real experience-based teaching that sets ethical decision-making in context.[3]

In more subtle ways, students' clinical experiences have challenged law schools to pay more attention to factors previously neglected in academic legal education. Depending on the particular model of clinic chosen, clinics draw attention to the significance of clients, to questions about access to justice and the distribution of legal services, to the contexts in which ethical decisions take place, and to the uncertain or contingent nature of legal problems that add complexity to the real practice of law. Peter Joy has thus argued that "skills training is not sound or good skills education unless it teaches law students not only how to be technically adept at lawyering skills, but also how to understand and develop the values necessary for a lawyer to represent clients in a professionally responsible manner." (Joy, 1996 at 386)

Moreover, clinical teaching methodologies are responsive enough to enable particular types of student learning to be emphasized. Different clinical models

---

2. This phenomenon is discussed in Chapter 1 relative to the United States, Canada, the United Kingdom, and Australia.

3. Clinical approaches to teaching ethics and professionalism are the topic of Chapter 12.

can be used in sequence to support students as they develop their understanding of the various dimensions of legal reasoning and the practice of law. Externships, for example, can be particularly well-suited to students engaging in critique of legal institutions and practice, as well as of the roles played by lawyers. Involvement in legal environments outside the law school through externship placements may generate institutional or systemic insights and provide opportunities for cross-disciplinary research and applied legal scholarship. (Condlin, 1986; Smith, 1999) *Best Practices in Legal Education*, published recently by the US-based Clinical Legal Education Association, refers to externships as enabling students to develop their "understanding of professional values and commitment to those values, including seeking justice, fostering respect for the rule of law, and dealing sensitively with diverse clients and colleagues." (Stuckey and Others, 2007 at 208) A well-structured externship program promotes student reflection on—and critique of—their experience, which can affect other classroom discussions as students learn to link the practical, theoretical, and doctrinal dimensions of their legal education.[4]

A live-client or in-house clinic model highlights the role of clients, who are otherwise largely ignored in legal education. (Shalleck, 1993) Work with real clients in collaboration with a supervisor involves sharing responsibility for identifying and addressing the legal issues facing those clients, and provides students with an intense learning opportunity that brings home the immediacy of the lawyer's impact. Students who have the opportunity to hear clients' stories examine the ways the law and legal processes affect everyday people. The real-client clinic emphasizes the value of supervision accompanied by detailed critique of students' actions, often a more intensive form of reflection than accompanies an externship. As with externship students, students who represent real clients bring their new-found perspectives into doctrinal classroom discussions as well.

Operating a real-client clinic also provides a law school with the opportunity to make a community service contribution through the provision of legal advice and representation. This has a curricular dimension as well. Grimes refers to clinic participation leading to student assumption of responsibility, organization of time and resources, the gradual growth of confidence in oneself and other students, and the engendering of a better understanding of the substance and processes of the law. (Grimes, 1995) He notes, in addition, that "[t]he client base provides a ready resource for legal research and socio-legal study, and generates related legal research, policy and reform initiatives." (*Id.* at 174) Many writers have emphasized the importance of justice education for law students and real-client work is uniquely suited to such learning. (Quigley, 1995; Aiken & Wizner, 2004)

---

4. Externship programs are discussed in Chapter 22.

Where clinical legal education is well-established, clinicians have argued persuasively for integrating experiential learning across the curriculum—using a developmental progression that begins with simplified or simulated lawyering and builds to more complex activities in externships or internal live-client settings. This point is central to an "integrative model" for legal education in the United States that would encompass practical experience with lawyering and professional values, urged in a recent Carnegie Foundation report. (Sullivan et al., 2007) The argument for integration recognizes the educational benefit gained from connecting students' learning in doctrinal courses more closely with their clinical experiences. (Maranville, 2000) This approach to law teaching can weave together a wide range of insights implicating ethics, theory, culture, and thereby maximizing the contribution of clinical programs to legal education more broadly.

Integration emphasizes the client focus that is so important to both clinical learning and legal practice. The law and legal processes can be examined, analyzed, and critiqued with the client's concerns and interests in mind. General practice clinics, with a strong emphasis on community service, involve students in providing advice to clients across the wide range of issues that prompt clients to seek help. Besides developing their appreciation of the dynamics of lawyering, students can be exposed to a diversity of client issues. They also learn that legal issues do not necessarily come in neatly defined or segregated course topics. Such exposure may help students who are unclear as to where they want to focus a future practice, and gives them a broader repertoire of possibilities. On the other hand, a specialized clinic can provide a useful contrast to the abstract nature of some law school hypotheticals. Specialist clinics can usefully focus on an area of substantive law in which a law school has significant strength. As these students extend and intensify their attention to key legal concepts in the clinic, they may feed their experiences back into the doctrinal classroom.

Clinic integration has been promoted also as assisting students to develop appropriate professional values and the ability to reflect critically on their own work. Munger argues that without the use of clinical teaching methods, "students have no model for sequencing steps in the handling of a case or for integrating facts, law, personal doubts, client pressures and values." (Munger, 1980 at 726) Clinical integration can also alleviate the monotony and mental fatigue which can develop in any course governed by a single teaching methodology. (Vaughn, 1995) The various clinical and nonclinical models should be viewed as complementary, as they often work best in combination to foster incremental development of student understanding and skills. Clinical experiences involving real clients can focus the student on responding to uncertainty, as well as on applying the understandings they have earlier developed.

There remain, however, significant barriers to realizing clinical legal education's full impact on the law school curriculum. Even when clinics are well-ensconced, it takes a long time to influence the rest of legal education.

Critiques of mainstream legal education in the United States have had some influence in legitimizing clinical methodology for use in regular classroom settings, such as the American Bar Association–sponsored MacCrate Report that emphasized the need for legal education to address both "skills" and "values" (American Bar Association, 1992) and the Carnegie Report's support for integrating practical experience with teaching lawyering and professional values. These calls for curricular and methodological overhaul without any enforcement or incentive structure backing them up have not produced a rush to curricular reform. In countries where the legal and educational systems have been undergoing rapid change, there also has been growing recognition of the need to reform legal education to develop and practice critical thinking. At the same time, there tends to be more talk about encouraging critical thinking and introducing interactive methods than action that produces those results.

Chief barriers to curricular reform in the United States and elsewhere include: higher costs of individualized supervision needed for live-client clinics; resistance to retraining of doctrine-focused faculty in interactive methods (especially where law faculty are not formally trained as teachers in the first place), coupled with a lack of practice experience among many academic faculty; lack of central governance in law schools for making big/complex changes; the power of the status quo and anxiety over the possibility of losing academic/scholarly status by teaching practical skills; and—in some institutions—an association of the clinical methodology with disfavored or controversial political views. In countries where most law teaching is done by adjuncts, they may not have time to participate in methodological changes. Overall, faculties tend to return quickly to their default approach to teaching unless they are actively encouraged to persevere with new approaches. The Nigerian example is an interesting one, where Ernest Ojukwu very astutely focused on building the local capacity for sustaining a new clinic-focused curriculum.[5] Even so, the efforts to transform the vocational phase of Nigerian legal education and foster active learning approaches have faced a considerable challenge.

In many instances cultural barriers add to the natural resistance of senior faculty to seeing themselves in the role as a participant with students in a clinical course, or even in role as the student (of a new teaching method). Where tradition sees the teacher as the Authority in possession of the Right Answer—for example, in many East Asian cultures—it may be especially difficult for distinguished faculty to embrace the uncertainty and contingent outcomes of interactive teaching methods. The civil law tradition reinforces these cultural forces, with an emphasis on the learned interpretation of the code.[6] Finally, government

---

5. The development of clinical education in Nigeria and other countries in Africa is discussed in Chapter 2.

6. This phenomenon is discussed in Chapter 8 in the context of promoting clinical legal education in Spain.

ministries that set the law curriculum can pose a significant impediment to flexibility and adoption of clinically inspired curriculum.

CLINICAL TEACHERS AND CLINICAL TEACHING METHODS: INFLUENCE ON METHODOLOGY IN THE MAINSTREAM CLASSROOM

Clinical teachers and their methods have different kinds of influence on mainstream law teaching, depending on whether the teachers move from a doctrinal classroom into the clinic or come into a law school clinic from practice. In this sense, their influence links with issues of clinical faculty status. Where clinical teachers come from the ranks of already well-established and influential legal educators, they can have a big impact by sponsoring a move toward interactive methods. In Poland and China, for example, some renowned legal educators helped start clinics at prestigious universities such as Jagellonian University in Poland and Beijing, Tsinghua, and Wuhan Universities in China. In England, clinical pioneers Avrom Sherr and Roger Burridge implemented prominent initiatives to advance legal education at Warwick University Law School, which is also the home of the United Kingdom Centre for Legal Education. In Scotland, Paul Maharg and his colleagues at the Glasgow Graduate School of Law have been very prominent in harnessing technology to enhance the use of simulations in legal education. In India, the development of clinical legal education benefited greatly from the leadership of N.R. Madhava Menon, the founding director of both the National Law School of India University in Bangalore and the National University of Juridical Sciences in Kolkata. Where clinical teachers come from practice, on the other hand, it may take longer for them to gain recognition and influence within the legal academy.

The pace at which clinical teachers and their methods gain acceptance and are incorporated into mainstream teaching can be affected by cultural factors in the legal profession (and the particular law faculty)—especially when professional cultures are in transition. Clinical teachers can serve as a resource for helping other teachers learn interactive methodology during efforts to introduce more flexibility or more critical thinking among students. In Chile, in Japan, and to some degree in China, educators have recognized the need to reform teaching methods to meet the needs of students entering increasingly dynamic and diverse legal systems. In this respect, mainstream legal education in the United States may lack a sense of urgency that sets the stage for influence from clinics because it is so dominated by variations on the Socratic method—despite potent critiques from the profession.

Cultural and policy choices within a law faculty affect the influence of clinical teachers and adoption of clinical methods more directly. For example, cross-fertilization increases where clinical teachers enjoy equal status with doctrinal faculty and clinical programs share space with mainstream classroom programs.

A faculty culture that supports collaborations between clinical and nonclinical faculty can lead to the introduction of clinical teaching methods to doctrinal teachers, and also relieve clinicians' stress from long-term supervision in live-client clinics. A supportive dean can encourage such partnerships; Georgetown University Law School's highly regarded clinical program "hosted" mainstream faculty for particular semesters, and two of its clinical faculty alternate through a single clinic, each spending every other semester in doctrinal teaching. The well-integrated clinical faculty at American University, which also has a top-quality clinical program, has gained influence through formal and intellectual leadership—in the broader clinical teaching field and at the law school itself.

Clinical faculties also have gained influence at schools that focus on clinical programs as a way to gain stature and distinguish themselves from competing institutions. Northwest University Law School in Xi'an, China, took the initiative to join the Ford Foundation's initial group of clinics and undertook ambitious programs for practical teaching that involved both clinical and regular faculty, which brought increased international recognition to that regional law school. New York University (NYU) integrated clinical methodology into the full three years of its law school curriculum and enhanced live-client clinical opportunities, which has had a significant positive impact on its standing among law schools in the United States. Griffith Law School in Australia has taken a similar approach to utilizing clinical insights across its curriculum. An extensive and systematic curriculum review in 2004 and 2005 resulted in the development of a suite of six "Vertical Subjects," three of which—Legal Skills, Ethics, and Groupwork and Leadership—drew on insights from clinical teaching.

Clinical teachers have been particularly influential through their pioneering use of simulations to teach lawyering skills and problem-solving. In many ways this educational "technology" has transferred most readily to mainstream legal education. Simulations allow the teacher some control over the content and the timing of the students' experience—and they provide a safe environment for learning in which no client suffers and confidentiality concerns do not complicate the teacher's plans. In another variation, clinic supervisors at the University of Northumbria in England developed Problem-Based Learning (PBL) by looking to a medical education model to enhance the realism with which students undertook simulations. Students are divided into small groups and presented with a problem situation and asked to identify resources for learning how to solve it. They then pursue those resources independently and apply them to address the problem. The instructor facilitates this process of learning how to learn. (Burridge, 2002; Sylvester et al., 2004)

Mainstream law teachers in the United States increasingly have adopted other clinical methods, such as small-group activities and role-plays, in large classes. They also use problem-focused methods to supplement or replace case study. Rather than cover all the material through reading and discussing appellate decisions in completed cases, the teacher assigns students to work on legal problems of varying complexity. Some doctrinal teachers also have incorporated outside placements related to the course subject-matter, following the examples (and sometimes the contacts) generated by externships. Besides potentially exposing students to master practitioners, who may have lawyering skills beyond those of law school faculty, such placement experiences can enrich the classroom discussion with examples from the "real world." Substantial resistance remains, however, due in part to the unscripted quality of interactive teaching methods that challenges classroom teachers who want to control what happens in the course.

Clinical teachers can also contribute to the academic teaching environment by bringing cross-disciplinary perspectives into the insular world of the law school. In an effort to solve problems or understand the behavior of clients in live-client clinics, clinicians turn to collaborations with psychologists, social workers, and medical personnel. Clinics focused on small business assistance may collaborate with business students, and those with an international focus turn to outside experts in culture and language. The effects on mainstream legal education may be subtle, but over time these collaborations expand the capacity of both students and faculty.

Besides influencing methods for delivering legal education, clinical teachers have contributed insights to the development of law school assessment practices. The provision of regular feedback to the learner is a hallmark of clinical education, and the experiences of clinic supervisors appear to have heightened awareness of the benefits of feedback at developmental stages during a course, rather than as a summation by way of an examination at the end. (Stuckey and Others, 2007; Chavkin, 1998) Students' performance in clinics can serve as a form of assessment for their classroom education to that point. The effectiveness of a standard introductory legal-writing course or a traditional course on family law can be measured, for example, by whether students who took those courses can craft basic legal documents or prepare a strategic plan for a child custody matter in a live-client clinic.

Clinical teachers may also influence teaching methods and choices indirectly, through connections to the legal profession. In many instances, they enjoy closer connections and higher standing with members of the profession than within the academy. They are well positioned, in that case, to mediate the academy's relationship with the profession, and to inform critiques of legal education mounted from outside. The clinical community exerts considerable effort to sustain and expand the influence of clinical methods throughout the curriculum through its network of clinical organizations and dissemination of clinical scholarship, much of which is devoted to topics relating to legal education reform.[7]

---

7. This aspect of the work of clinical organizations is discussed in chapters 19 (national and regional organizations), 23 (on the agenda for the global clinical movement), and 25 (on the Global Alliance for Justice Education). Clinical scholarship is the topic of Chapter 21.

SOCIAL JUSTICE VALUES

Clinical legal education plays a major role in promoting and implementing a social justice mission for legal education. Clinical programs in many parts of the world began as legal aid offices, and many programs today feature an ongoing commitment to community service.[8] Sustained community links require genuine and continuing effort on the part of law school leadership, which tends to be fostered by input from clinicians.

The history of Australian clinical legal education shows the success of the early programs—Monash, La Trobe, and the University of New South Wales—in serving local communities while providing students with a distinctive learning experience. The 1990s saw the development of further programs, most notably at Newcastle, Murdoch, and Griffith, which have also emphasized the importance of community links. The sustainability of these programs suggests that clinics can provide an effective hub for fostering law school community engagement. In much the same way, the early clinical movement in the United States—in the 1960s—took up the cause of practical professional training in the context of efforts to bring social justice values into legal education and to bring law-student resources into legal services for poor people.

Some clinics have adopted community development models with a view to involving their clients and others in addressing issues of community concern. While such models utilize noncasework approaches, they are obviously informed by casework and linked to other community agencies. Working in the La Trobe clinical program, Liz Curran has emphasized the importance of involving clinic students in law reform work as this exposes them "to the broader role they may wish to play in public life when they are fully fledged lawyers encouraging their participation in their law association and to be unafraid in speaking out against injustice." (Curran, 2004 at 174) The Monash clinical program has utilized the community development process articulated by Brazilian educator Paulo Friere to enable students and clients together to move beyond "individual reflection to group reflection upon the underlying social injustices which diminish an equitable society." (Evans, 1999 at 179) Because of these and similar links to legal aid and community service in clinical programs around the world, clinic students are able to address complex issues of group representation and identification of community concerns.

Clinics and clinicians have played significant roles in fostering pro bono contributions from law schools and their students. Exposing students to their first clients in the context of representing poor clients influences their outlook on other courses. There is substantial anecdotal evidence that clinics are significant in encouraging their graduates to maintain a pro bono and public service ethos

---

8. The legal aid origins of clinical education are documented in Chapter 10.

while in practice. At Monash, Adrian Evans has been involved in ongoing research designed to determine how the values which appear to characterize the mass of Australian lawyers in their early careers might best be influenced by the various dimensions of legal education. (Evans & Palermo, 2006) Australian clinicians Alison Vivian and Anna Copeland have written about the importance of encouraging clinic students to view their work in the clinic as being related to human rights issues. They emphasize the value of clinic teachers highlighting for students the potential human rights dimensions of clinical casework, stating "[w]e propose that a starting point for our emerging conceptualisation of human rights might be that the practice of human rights can be defined as the *ordinary work of clinics.*" (Vivian & Copeland, 2007 at 37) (emphasis in the original)

The professional culture in the United States has traditionally accepted (even if it did not fully implement) the idea that professional responsibility includes helping improve access to justice. In a sense, many clinical teachers in the United States have seen themselves as struggling to hold the line and keep this element in the profession, to counter its being eroded by mega-firm detachment from that vision of the profession. Where private law practice itself is new (e.g., former Soviet countries, China), it has been even harder to bring the access-to-justice obligation into the professional mindset. Clinics have had some success in that direction, although their influence on legal education and the profession in this regard may be even more attenuated where it is associated with political viewpoints outside the mainstream.

CLINICAL STUDENTS

Student enthusiasm for clinics is almost universal, with students often the driving force behind getting clinical teaching started. Early clinical programs often developed out of volunteer programs in which students worked on cases without receiving academic credit. This phenomenon of student investment in the establishment of a clinical component in legal education was a significant factor in the development of clinical education in many parts of the world. For much of the twentieth century, students at law schools across the United States operated volunteer legal aid services until for-credit programs were developed in the 1970s. (Holland, 1999) In Australia, both the Monash and La Trobe programs were commenced with very substantial student volunteer input. The clinic at what is now the University of KwaZulu-Natal in Durban, South Africa, started on a voluntary basis for both students and academics, and it was six years before students were granted credit for their work. Student-initiated volunteer projects sprang up in Russia and China as well, as students identified justice issues in their communities and were anxious to address them before the end of their brief student careers.

This history indicates that new clinical programs may develop from current law school pro bono initiatives, with volunteer programs being a stepping-stone to the establishment of for-credit clinics that have a strong focus on both student learning and community service. Students have been, and can continue to be, good and forceful advocates for legal education reform—and for leading that reform through clinical programs and clinical methods.

Students' enthusiasm for clinical learning correlates with the fact that clinics focus more directly on students than do other forms of legal education. In cultures where education traditionally has focused on the teacher, this involves a more dramatic shift of attention than in cultures that are traditionally student-centered. Rather than emphasizing the law, clinical methodology focuses on the student's individual capacity to apply the law to a client's problems. It attends to how students develop their understanding of spontaneity and uncertainty, and their ability to work effectively with others. Most students find the experience more intense and engaging than other law school coursework.

As a result, clinic alumni may influence mainstream legal education even more than do current law students. Alumni also are in a position to tell mainstream legal educators about the value of their clinic experiences in equipping them for work in the profession. Australian clinic students have been prominent in efforts to encourage the practicing legal profession to engage more effectively in the provision of pro bono services. There has also been increasing government interest in fostering the development of pro bono legal services. (Giddings, 2008) Clinical programs now have close links with the three Public Interest Law Clearing Houses in Eastern Australia, each of which hosts for-credit clinics as well as making extensive use of volunteer student contributions. The alumni of clinical programs have also been very prominent in promoting pro bono activities to their firms.

CONCLUSION

Clinical programs, their academics, and their students have made a range of contributions to the law school experience that place client interests, social justice, and professional values at the center of legal education. These clinical contributions are best made when insights from the work of the clinic are effectively integrated within the law school. The capacity to promote links among the various groups interested in the outcomes of legal education suggests clinics should be viewed by law schools as a bridge for community and professional engagement. Sustained engagement requires substantial effort on the part of law school leadership to appreciate and acknowledge the contributions others should make to the legal education project. Valuable contributions can be made by community and government agencies, the practicing profession as well as current students and, importantly, alumni.

LIST OF REFERENCES

Jane H. Aiken & Stephen Wizner, *Teaching and Doing: The Role of Law School Clinics in Enhancing Access to Justice*, 73 FORDHAM L. REV. 997 (2004).

GARY BELLOW & BEA MOULTON, THE LAWYERING PROCESS: MATERIALS FOR CLINICAL INSTRUCTION IN ADVOCACY (Foundation Press 1978).

DAVID BINDER & SUSAN PRICE, LEGAL INTERVIEWING AND COUNSELLING: A CLIENT-CENTERED APPROACH (West 1977).

DAVID BINDER, ET AL., LAWYERS AS COUNSELORS: A CLIENT-CENTERED APPROACH (2nd ed., West 2004).

HUGH BRAYNE & RICHARD GRIMES, THE LEGAL SKILLS BOOK: A STUDENT'S GUIDE TO PROFESSIONAL SKILLS (Butterworths 1994).

ROGER BURRIDGE, LEARNING LAW AND LEGAL EXPERTISE BY EXPERIENCE, IN EFFECTIVE LEARNING AND TEACHING IN LAW (Roger Burridge et al., eds., Kogan Page 2002).

SUSAN CAMPBELL & SPRINGVALE LEGAL SERVICE CO-OPERATIVE, LAWYERS PRACTICE MANUAL (Victoria 1985).

David Chavkin, *Am I My Client's Lawyer?: Role Definition and the Clinical Supervisor*, 51 SMU L. REV. 1507 (1998).

Robert Condlin, *"Tastes Great, Less Filling": The Law School Clinic and Political Critique*, 36 J. LEGAL EDUC. 45 (1986).

Liz Curran, *Innovations in an Australian Clinical Program: Students Making a Difference in Generating Positive Change*, 4 INT'L J. CLINICAL LEGAL EDUC. 162 (2004).

WILLEM DE KLERK ET AL., CLINICAL LAW IN SOUTH AFRICA (Lexis-Nexis Butterworths 2006).

Adrian Evans, *Client Group Activism and Student Moral Development in Clinical Legal Education*, 10 LEGAL EDUC. REV. 179 (1999).

Adrian Evans & Josephine Palermo, *Preparing Australia's Future Lawyers: An Exposition of Changing Values Over Time in the Context of Teaching About Ethical Dilemmas*, 11 DEAKIN L. REV. 1 (2006).

Jeff Giddings, *Contemplating the Future of Clinical Legal Education*, 17 GRIFFITH L. REV. 1 (2008).

Richard Grimes, *Reflections on Clinical Legal Education*, 29 LAW TEACHER 169 (1995).

Laura Holland, *Invading the Ivory Tower: The History of Clinical Education at Yale Law School*, 49 J. LEGAL EDUC. 504 (1999).

Peter Joy, *Clinical Scholarship: Improving the Practice of Law*, 2 CLINICAL L. REV. 385 (1996).

Deborah Maranville, *Passion, Context, and Lawyering Skills: Choosing Among Simulated and Real Client Experiences*, 7 CLINICAL L. REV. 123 (2000).

Michael Meltsner & Philip Schrag, *Report from a CLEPR Colony*, 76 COLUMBIA L. REV. 581 (1976).

Frank Munger, *Clinical Legal Education: The Case Against Separatism*, 29 CLEV. ST. L. REV. 715 (1980).

Fran Quigley, *Seizing the Disorienting Moment: Adult Learning Theory and the Teaching of Social Justice in Law School Clinics*, 2 CLINICAL L. REV. 37 (1995).

SCALES COMMUNITY LEGAL CENTRE, LAWYERS PRACTICE MANUAL (Western Australia 2004).

Ann Shalleck, *Constructions of the Client Within Legal Education*, 45 STANFORD L. REV. 1731 (1993).

AVROM SHERR, CLIENT INTERVIEWING FOR LAWYERS: AN ANALYSIS AND GUIDE (Sweet & Maxwell 1986).

Linda Smith, *Designing an Extern Clinical Program: Or as You Sow, so Shall You Reap*, 5 CLINICAL L. REV. 527 (1999).

ROY STUCKEY AND OTHERS, BEST PRACTICES FOR LEGAL EDUCATION: A VISION AND A ROAD MAP (Clinical Legal Education Association 2007).

WILLIAM SULLIVAN ET AL., EDUCATING LAWYERS: PREPARATION FOR THE PROFESSION OF LAW (Jossey Bass 2007).

Cath Sylvester et al., *Problem-based Learning and Clinical Legal Education: What Can Clinical Educators Learn from PBL?* 4 INT'L J. CLINICAL LEGAL EDUC. 39 (2004).

Robert Vaughn, *Use of Simulation in a First-Year Civil Procedure Class*, 45 J. LEGAL EDUC. 480 (1995).

Alison Vivian & Anna Copeland, *Human Rights as the Ordinary Work of Clinics*, *in* INNOVATION IN CLINICAL LEGAL EDUCATION: EDUCATING LAWYERS FOR THE FUTURE (Bronwyn Naylor & Ross Hyams eds., Legal Service Bulletin Cooperative 2007).

21. CLINICAL SCHOLARSHIP AND THE DEVELOPMENT OF THE GLOBAL CLINICAL MOVEMENT

NEIL GOLD AND PHILIP PLOWDEN

This chapter seeks to do two things: first, it briefly examines the nature and shape of clinical scholarship, its aims, its discernible outcomes, and its unspoken agendas; second, and perhaps more importantly, it asks what such scholarship can and should contribute to the global clinical movement and, through it, to clinical legal education practice everywhere.

Let's begin by saying a few words about what we mean by clinical legal scholarship. Traditional legal scholarship takes many shapes. For the most part it is analytical, positivist, and rules-oriented. Frequently, it is also theoretical, observational, or comparative work focused upon doctrine and developments in the law. In the last generation there has been a movement toward empirical and interdisciplinary work. Clinical legal scholarship, by contrast, is scholarship undertaken by students, supervising lawyers, and law professors that is observational, empirical, or theoretical and focused on professional skills training, experiential learning, and the teaching of professional responsibility and social justice. Perhaps it can be put another way: Gary Bellow said many years ago that clinical education begins with the student taking on a formal role within the legal system and proceeds to examine the student's work and experience through the complete circle of knowledge and understanding around that work and experience. (Bellow, 1973) In a word, clinical scholarship is the study of that educational mode.

THE INITIAL DEVELOPMENT OF CLINICAL SCHOLARSHIP

Clinical scholarship has grown exponentially in the last four decades. A search using HeinOnline, a US-oriented online law journal library, for the keyword "clinical" for the decade 1960–1970 returns 41 articles with "clinical" in the title; by contrast, for the ten years between 1995 and 2005, the figure is 330. Similarly, a search for the word "clinic" for the same two decades produces an increase from 17 title references to 148—but possibly more tellingly, whereas the majority of uses of the word "clinic" in the 1960s referred to medical or psychiatric projects, in the more recent period the term referred almost exclusively to clinical legal education projects.

However, writing about clinical legal education predates these developments by almost fifty years. Published in 1917, William V. Rowe's "Legal Clinics and Better Trained Lawyers—A Necessity" (Rowe, 1917) is almost two decades earlier than Jerome Frank's more famous question and law review article, "Why Not a Clinical Lawyer School?" (Frank, 1917; *see also* Bradway, 1929; Bradway, 1930) It is an article that establishes from the start the core concern of much clinical writing—namely, laying the claim to a place for a clinic in the highly academic law school curriculum.

Rowe's argument for the necessity of clinical teaching as an integral and substantial part of legal education is fourfold: law schools need to be more in touch with wider society and to draw on the best practices of other professions, among which is clinical teaching; a clinic will open up access to justice, which is central to making the "boast of freedom" real; lawyers will always be the "governing class" and must therefore engage the common law as a living instrument for good; and a clinic is the only way in which law students can get experience with law because new technologies (at that point, the telephone, typewriters, and copying devices) would mean that there would not longer be opportunities for work-based learning as clerks in legal offices. (Rowe, 1917) As an American law professor, Rowe wrote with a focus on what he perceived as the particular importance of lawyers as essential components in the political life of his nation. However, his central concerns—more effective education, producing better lawyers, and meeting unmet needs for legal services—remain the core concerns that underpin much clinical writing today. This in turn raises the issue of the extent to which American clinical writing does, or can, represent wider global concerns.

Thus, for example, many of Rowe's educational concerns arise from the fact that his students will enter directly into practice from law school, which remains the case in almost every state in the United States. As Frank the legal realist put it, writing of the newly qualified lawyer:

> With the practical working of the law he has little or no familiarity. He may come to the bar almost ignorant of how the law should be applied and is applied in daily life. It is, therefore, not unusual to find the brightest student the most helpless practitioner, and the most learned surpassed in the profession by one who does not know half as much. (Frank, 1917 at 919, quoting Judge Crane of the New York Court of Appeals)

Rowe, like Frank, is therefore concerned about the impact on lawyering of the exclusion of law students from law offices. In his book, *Law School*, Robert Stevens shows how American legal education abandoned supervised practice learning opportunities for residential, university-based post-degree education. (Stevens, 1983) Rowe worried that technological development would deny aspiring lawyers the clerkships of the past and, like him, Frank and others were certain that American lawyers needed practical training that clinics could provide.

It is this imperative that continues to drive the development of clinical legal education in American law schools, as the continuing debate around the American Bar Association requirements in this area bears out. Yet many other jurisdictions—particularly those drawing on the traditional English model of some form of "articles of clerkship" or "pupilage"—will have an intervening apprenticeship or work-based learning stage, prior to qualification, which is intended to bridge the reality gap between the classroom and practice. This is not to say that there is no role for clinical teaching in such jurisdictions, but there is less focus on the "practice gap" as a driver for clinical expansion. For example, in Canada, a jurisdiction derived from the traditional English model, each of the fifteen common-law schools operates or works in partnership with a local clinic to provide students with clinical learning opportunities.

There is a not dissimilar point to be made about Rowe's concerns with access to justice. Professors Philip Schrag and Michael Meltsner make a strong case for the argument that clinical legal education in the United States "was born in the social ferment of the 1960s," grown out of the expansion in legal rights and the consequent recognition of the inability of many to access legal services to enforce those rights—and the desire of law students and their schools to contribute to the redistribution of such goods. (Schrag & Meltsner, 1998 at 3) Through a spin-off called the Council on Legal Education and Professional Responsibility (CLEPR), the Ford Foundation may have been almost single-handedly responsible for the early proliferation of clinical legal education in the United States and, to a lesser extent, Canada. For CLEPR, professional responsibility required knowledgeable and skilled lawyers who cared about those whose lot deprived them of social goods. Some jurisdictions have had—at least until relatively recently—provision for relatively comprehensive public funding for lawyer-delivered legal services. To be sure, the social justice imperative is not removed; there will always be unmet need, and there will also be powerful pedagogic rationales for seeking to engage students in work where social justice concerns will be at the forefront of the cases. (Dickson, 2000) But the obvious "justice gap" as a rationale for clinic is not always as striking, though no doubt claims of complete legal services coverage will almost always be exaggerated. Social justice clinics beyond the traditional "poverty law" focus have indeed proliferated at American law schools, so much so that each school hosts an average of six clinics focusing on the familiar landlord-tenant, immigration, and criminal defense matters, to the less-common environmental, constitutional, and veterans benefits matters. (CSALE, 2008 at 9)

THE PAROCHIAL CONCERNS OF CLINICAL SCHOLARSHIP

Much traditional academic legal writing is parochial, rooted in an examination of the particular issues thrown up by national legal systems. The justification for the tendency of clinical scholarship to have a similarly narrow national focus is at first less apparent. On the one hand, if much of clinical writing is produced by American clinicians, then it is to be expected that they should focus on issues relevant to their own clinical contexts. On the other hand, it is perhaps surprising that clinical writing has had relatively little ambition in addressing the issue of whether it is pedagogy with a cross-jurisdictional, global implication. This is all the more surprising given the nearly worldwide acceptance of clinical legal education. (Wilson, 2009)

In the most recent of their annotated bibliographies of clinical legal education (the 2005 revision) Ogilvy with Czapanskiy provide an essential overview not only of the range of journals that host clinical writing, but also the weight of the contributors' concerns. (Ogilvy & Czapanskiy, 2005) In creating the bibliography, Ogilvy and Czapanskiy consulted a wide range of general and specialized electronic and print sources for both clinical legal articles and articles dealing with "poverty law." Their findings—which we summarize grossly with a page count of the initial part of the bibliography where they list the titles of articles covering different categories of topics—bear out the assertion that the concerns raised in the early clinical writings of Rowe and Frank remain dominant in contemporary clinical scholarship.

1) Clinical Legal Education (history, methodology, critiques, non-US programs, the future): 15 pages
2) Clinical Teaching (design, administration, supervision, assessment, externships, simulation): 12 pages
3) Theoretical Backdrop of Clinical Legal Education (cognitive theory, feminist theory, lawyering theory and practice): 7 pages
4) Reflections and Critique of Scholarship (including student experiences): 3 pages
5) Lawyering Skills: 11 pages Professional Responsibility (ethics, lawyer-client relationships, values): 11 pages
6) Difference/Diversity: 2 pages
7) Poverty Law/Political Context of Clinical Legal Education: 11 pages

The picture is of a community of writing that is firmly inclined toward the pragmatic: how to set up and run different forms of clinic; how to teach particular legal skills; the teaching of ethics and values, with a powerful, but secondary, focus on examination of the contexts in which a clinic is taught—its history and methodology, its political contexts. The debate between the two types of clinical scholarship, lawyering skills and writings that concentrate on law and social change—sometimes summarized as the skills vs. values debate—has been regarded as "a proxy for a debate over the heart and soul of the clinical movement when understood in the context of broader questions concerning the ultimate value of clinical scholarship." (Bloch, 2004 at 11) It is perhaps the sign of a relatively young discipline that there is less focus on the theoretical, whether in the context of pedagogic or cultural theories, or reflections on the scholarship itself. To characterize clinical scholarship in this way is not to cast doubt on its value, but an attempt to establish why a practice with its roots in concerns about social justice should have remained so largely blind to issues around global justice.

It is not enough, however, to categorize existing clinical scholarship purely on the basis of its subjects; it also necessary to attempt to analyze something of the purpose of the writings. Much of the practical writing makes clear its overt agenda of sharing practice (encouraging others) and occasionally sharing best practice (exhortatory). There is limited writing about the relationship between clinic and educational theory, but as clinicians find less need to justify the value of their pedagogic practice ("It *does* work"), it may be that there will be more scope for moving to the more interesting issue of *why* it works or what would make it work better. There is a strong strand of writing that seeks to link clinic practice to its political and social agendas, although again a substantial element of this is justificatory—"it works"—as well as practical.

However, the sharing of ideas and practices within the community may be only the visible driver for clinical publications. It is hard to avoid the suspicion that much clinical writing is also motivated by the desire, whether recognized or unconscious, to show that clinical teachers have a direct equivalence to their traditional black-letter counterparts: if a professor of contract law is characterized by the quality of her publications, then a member of clinical faculty can help to establish herself by achieving a measure of published equivalence. We write because that's what legal academics do—or, as John Elson puts it:

> The importance of scholarship to the careers of law teachers is difficult to overestimate. Hiring, promotion, pay, collegial recognition, societal prominence, and intellectual satisfaction is mainly a function of the production of scholarship. (Elson, 1989 at 354)

This is found in the context of an article that argues strongly that traditional legal scholarship is often created at the expense of delivering a meaningful education for practice competence. A 1966 *New Yorker* cartoon captures the position nicely: *Two professors watch as a third is about to be executed by a firing squad: "It's publish or perish, and he hasn't published."*

To examine the topics of clinical writing is not therefore a form of narcissism, it is a necessary element of what should be an anxious and critical self-examination for clinicians, an examination which must have at its heart a question as to what clinical scholarship is, and what it can be. Is clinical scholarship merely writings that are produced by clinicians? Bloch argues that clinical scholarship needs to have at its heart an intense focus on the clinical experience and on the goals of the clinical movement—but then argues against "false compartmentalization":

> Clinical law teachers have a duty to write about the academic side of their work, whether on the lawyering process, law and society, or legal education

reform. Indeed, having both the responsibility for and the opportunity to write clinical scholarship is a key to establishing clinical legal education's rightful place in the legal academy. (Bloch, 2004 at 17)

The reality is that if clinical scholarship is defined by its focus on the clinical experience, then it will be as broad and varied as that experience is: a springboard for a wide range of discussions and analyses. It will include, as Ogilvy and Czapanskiy's bibliography evidences, writings about the teaching process (sometimes grounded in theories of education, sometimes more purely observational), about the reality of particular aspects of the law in practice, and about societal contexts and political imperatives. But above all, clinical scholarship faces in two directions: it is both a developmental conversation with other clinicians, and it is the making of a case to the traditional legal academy that clinical teaching is worthy of equal respect.

The difficulty with this approach is that there is still a privileging of a certain type of academic legal writing, a tendency to associate the abstract with the scholarly—and an accompanying tendency to treat writing which focuses on the practice of lawyering as lower value. (Bok, 1983 at 3) The continued strength of this attitude can be seen in the United Kingdom, where the most recent Research Assessment Exercise (the grading process which determines the distribution of government research grants to universities) maintained its antipathy to practice-based and pedagogic materials in law.

If one driver for clinical writing is the esteem of the academy, then will clinicians embrace this move toward abstraction? And if so, do they risk falling into the irrelevance that Elson sees in the doctrinal academy? Does the conversation become a monologue?

> In fact, clinical scholarship has fallen into two broad categories: doctrine or jurisprudence, and the work of clinicians. The scholarship is either mainstream or work that more broadly comments on the legal system or legal education. It is written for a particular audience—the academic audience of tenure, namely the review committee that considers the clinician for renewal, tenure, or hire. Ironically, clinical scholarship is rarely written for those actively engaged in the practice of law or those actively working on behalf of the underrepresented. (Boswell, 1992 at 1190)

CLINICAL SCHOLARSHIP AND THE GLOBAL CLINICAL MOVEMENT

Up to this point, this chapter has argued that clinical writing largely continues to reflect the imperatives for clinical teaching in American law schools that were first expressed by Rowe and Frank. It has argued that there is, however, an additional agenda beyond the desire to reflect and to communicate, *viz.*, the desire to adopt the practices of the "mainstream" academy and to achieve peer recognition from nonclinical teachers by engaging with a recognized tradition of academic writing. The adoption of at least some of the expectations of the traditional academy has not been without its benefits. Clinical writing has moved remarkably fast from the earlier heavily descriptive "how to" or "about" pieces to a wider analytic writing that—at its strongest—draws on a multiplicity of sources and disciplines, reconnecting legal writing with the wider societal contexts. However, what it has not shed, and what perhaps has been reinforced by the parochial nature of traditional legal scholarship, is its localized focus.

Whether in its social justice focus, or in its more theoretical social, political, and pedagogic reflection, or in its specific skills focus pieces, clinical writing should have supranational relevance. Is then there any good reason for the lack of this wider development?

The first and most obvious obstacle to the development of a global perspective is the tendency to identify difference—to see what separates the structures for legal education in different countries rather than what they have in common. Thus, an American legal educator will be immediately struck by the formalized split legal professions of England and Wales, by the provision of law as an undergraduate rather than post-graduate discipline, and of course by its structured postschoolwork-based learning stage. An English clinician looking, for example, at the Japanese context will be struck by the unique relationship between law schools and central government, and the extent to which issues such as law school pass rates and indeed the law school curriculum will be governed by a series of formal and informal *dictats* laid down by the central government. A visitor to South Africa will note the ways in which clinics (and law schools generally) are developing to meet the needs of the postapartheid state, and in particular to close a massive justice gap that has led to increased pressures on law schools to provide sufficient numbers of trained lawyers. Maxim Tomaszech wonders, in setting up a clinical program at the Pavalacky University in the Czech Republic, whether clinical education could operate successfully only in common law contexts and might not be viable in a civil law jurisdiction. (Bryxová et al., 2006)

Yet, in the face of what could be an endless list of differences, it is worth looking again at the Ogilvy and Czapanskiy bibliography and the list of legal skills which it uses to categorize the various lawyering skills articles: interviewing, counseling, trial advocacy, mediation, negotiation, problem-solving, and collaboration among professionals. None of these is likely to be controversial for any jurisdiction. Not all jurisdictions would teach all of these skills—collaboration among professionals, for example—but there can be little argument that these are significant elements of a lawyer's skills. What is interesting to a non-American is the omission of certain skills from this list, *viz.*, research, writing, drafting, an omission that presumably reflects the fact that these skills are taught as part of the usual law school curriculum in the United States. But if the argument remains valid, add these skills to the list and we still have a list of core skills for lawyers in a global context.

Is this argument for shared experience equally valid in the context of the other major strand of American clinical writing, the "values" context? A glance at this section of the bibliography shows writings about such shared experiences as seeking to ensure that tenants' voices are heard in housing courts (Bezdek, 1992), the debate between allocating resources to the needy individual or the high-impact representative case (Margulies, 1996), and the question whether exposure to social justice issues in law school leads to a longer-term commitment to pro bono lawyering (Chaifetz, 1993). These random examples are all from American writings, drawn from the experience of the American clinicians; but each is illustrative of an issue—one narrow, one broader, one which goes to the whole question of the longer-term value of clinic—that is relevant to clinicians in every jurisdiction.

So should it then be said that since the issues in so much of clinical writing are often of relevance in the global context that it is immaterial that so much of the scholarship is grounded in the American experience? To this the answer must be "no"; it does matter. The American model of clinical legal education has been adopted across the world, often as part of projects designed to improve rule of law issues in the recipient countries. In other cases the adoption occurs simply because the US model has stimulated local adoption by local clinical champions who can see the pedagogic advantages of the clinical method. Whether these local models of the clinic have their roots in the projects or are more spontaneous growths, clinical scholarship makes clear that each jurisdiction has needed to adopt and adapt the clinical model to meet the exigencies of its own system. An American clinical scholarship that looks only at its own local practice limits itself because it can often make unwarranted assumptions: it assumes, for example, that the teaching of writing and drafting is not an issue for clinicians; and it assumes that every student enters into practice without an apprenticeship period. The assumptions make clear that the conversation is one that is intended to take place only with other American clinicians, which tends to make the non-US reader feel that this is a conversation to which she is not invited or that she is reading about something truly foreign to her.

So must all clinical writing be "global" in its scope? The answer again must be "no." How can it always take a global view? How can this be asked of each clinician? It is impossible for any of us to have that complete knowledge and understanding of every national legal context. Moreover, clinical writing is at its best where it is rooted in the detail of the context of the specific clinical experience, talking about how the particular and local can lead to a discussion of the impact on the general and even the universal. What is required is that clinical scholarship must be global in its sensitivity. It must acknowledge the reach of the global clinical movement and acknowledge that in our clinical writing we should aim to speak more broadly than simply to our known colleagues.

Clinicians are entitled to protest that simply to exhort sensitivity to the global agenda is insufficient. We must at least give some indication of how this is to be achieved. One answer lies in the limited quantity and developing nature of international clinical scholarship: how can we write with sensitivity to one another when we know so little about each other? One model for making good this deficiency is found in the "views from abroad" articles—often the product of American clinicians who have been on overseas projects, supporting the growth and development of clinical models overseas, such as Richard J. Wilson's long-term study of clinical legal education in Chile (Wilson, 2002), and Peggy Maisel's examination of clinical legal education in South Africa (Maisel, 2007), and sometimes the collaborative product of the visiting clinician and their host—for example, the study of the development of clinical education in Poland by Skrodzka, Chia, and Bruce-Jones. (Skrodzka, Chia, & Bruce-Jones, 2008) There is some space in American clinical journals for articles by clinicians from abroad. However, the obvious remedy is for clinicians to be more prepared to engage with global justice issues in their writing or to focus on the uniqueness of the context in which their clinical experience arises and to find general analytical tools and criteria for the assessment of experience in context, thus enabling the discussion of jurisdictional differences on the part of the reader. If clinical scholarship has already developed from description about local practice to a scholarship which seeks to ask why and how it operates both as a pedagogic instrument and as a tool of social justice, then the next major development must be for clinical scholarship to engage more often with justice in its broadest and most fundamental context, that of global justice There may be growing opportunities to do this with the development of clinics based in one jurisdiction dealing with the needs of another. The example of the clinic at the University of Michigan, Ann Arbor, on microbanking for developing nation populations comes to mind.

If we already write about the impact of our individual clinical projects on our students and on our clients and on our local communities, why as clinicians do we seem so reluctant to ask what wider lessons can be learned? If it is right that there is a "growing introspection over legal scholarship and the dissonance between legal scholarship and the legal profession" (Joy, 1996 at 388), an observation that certainly is equally applicable to legal scholarship in the United Kingdom as it is in the United States, it is a shame that clinicians, who are best placed in the academy to produce a scholarship that is grounded in the realities of legal practice, seem to have failed as yet to create a global scholarship which might so effectively counter this introspection.

It is not only precisely because clinical scholarship is able to draw on the habits of reflection and scholarship associated with the academy, enhanced by clinical pedagogy, that our writings should be able to lay claim to a wider relevance than the purely local. It is also because clinical scholarship is informed by direct contact with the reality of law as it is practiced in our communities, as it impacts on the individual and upon the wider society. If we recognize that as clinicians we are part of a global educational and justice-oriented movement, then we can also begin to recognize the potential of our scholarship to achieve global relevance and impact.

CONCLUSION

We have argued that the concerns that dominate clinical writing—the effectiveness of the clinical pedagogy and its contributions to justice—are not concerns that are unique to any one jurisdiction. They are global concerns. We have also argued that clinical writing is surprisingly local in its focus and limited in its ambitions, given this potential for a global engagement.

If clinical scholarship is to remain part of a larger conversation with an engaged community of law teachers, then clinicians may need to consider more carefully with whom they intend to converse. Clinical scholarship, because it is a writing grounded in the reality of legal practice and legal teaching, can be a scholarship that engages across borders regardless of jurisdictions. To do this, however, it needs to be scholarship that is sensitive to cultural and national difference. It needs to recognize that alongside the shared experience of clinicians, we are also distinguished by fundamental differences—in education structures, in the levels of resourcing, and in the societal and political pressures that may be brought to bear on law schools and law students. There will always be a place for writing that is tightly focused on the specific, if only as an opportunity for generalized learning or to meet local needs. That same writing will also demonstrate that so much of our core experience as clinical teachers is shared; as a result, an opportunity is lost when we fail to open up that experience to the wider discussion within and for the global clinical community.

LIST OF REFERENCES

Gary Bellow, *On Teaching the Teachers: Some Preliminary Reflections on Clinical Education as a Methodology*, in CLINICAL EDUCATION FOR LAW STUDENTS (Council on Legal Education for Professional Responsibility ed. 1973).

Barbara Bezdek, *Silence in the Court: Participation and Subordination of Poor Tenants' Voices in Legal Process*, 20 HOFSTRA L. REV. 533 (1992).

Frank S. Bloch, *The Case for Clinical Scholarship*, 4 INT'L J. CLINICAL LEGAL EDUC. 7 (2004).

DEREK BOK, HIGHER LEARNING (Harvard University Press 1983).

Richard Boswell, *Keeping the Practice in Clinical Education and Scholarship*, 43 HASTINGS L.J. 1187 (1992).

John S. Bradway, *The Beginning of the Legal Clinic of the University of Southern California*, 2 S. CAL. L. REV. 252 (1929).

John S. Bradway, *The Nature of a Legal Aid Clinic*, 3 S. CAL. L. REV. 173 (1930).

Vendula Bryxová, Maxim Tomasczech, & Veronika Vlčková, *Introducing Legal Clinics in Olomouc, Czech Republic*, 9 INT'L J. CLINICAL LEGAL EDUC. 149 (2006).

Ctr. for the Study of Applied Legal Educ., Report on the 2007–2008 Survey (2008), http://www.csale.org/CSALE.07-08.Survey.Report.pdf.

Jill Chaifetz, *The Value of Public Service: A Model for Instilling a Pro Bono Ethic in Law School*, 45 STAN. L. REV. 1695 (1993).

Judith Dickson, *Legal Education in the 21st Century: Still Educating for Service*, 1 INT'L J. CLINICAL LEGAL EDUC. 33 (2000).

John S. Elson, *The Case Against Legal Scholarship, or If the Professor Must Publish, Must the Profession Perish?*, 39 J. LEGAL EDUC. 343 (1989).

Jerome Frank, *Why Not a Clinical Lawyer School?*, 81 U. PA. L. REV 907 (1933).

Peter Joy, *Clinical Scholarship: Improving the Practice of Law*, 2 CLINICAL L. REV. 385 (1996).

Peggy Maisel, *Expanding and Sustaining Clinical Legal Education in Developing Countries: What We Can Learn From South Africa*, 30 FORDHAM INT'L L.J. 374 (2007).

Peter Margulies, *Political Lawyering, One Person at a Time: The Challenge of Legal Work Against Domestic Violence for the Impact Litigation/Client Service Debate*, 3 MICH. J. GENDER & L. 493 (1996).

J. P. Ogilvy & Karen Czapanskiy, Clinical Legal Education: An Annotated Bibliography (Revised 2005), http://faculty.cua.edu/ogilvy/Biblio05clr.pdf.

William V. Rowe, *Legal Clinics and Better Trained Lawyers—A Necessity*, 11 ILL. L. REV. 591 (1917).

PHILIP G. SCHRAG & MICHAEL MELTSNER, REFLECTIONS ON CLINICAL LEGAL EDUCATION (Northeastern University Press 1998).

Marta Skrodzka, Joy Chia, & Eddie Bruce-Jones, *The Next Step Forward—The Development of Clinical Legal Education in Poland Through a Clinical Pilot Program in Bialystok*, 2 COLUM. J. E. EUR. L. 56 (2008).

ROBERT STEVENS, LAW SCHOOL: LEGAL EDUCATION IN AMERICA FROM THE 1850S TO THE 1980S (University of North Carolina Press 1983).

Richard J. Wilson, *Three Law School Clinics in Chile, –: Innovation, Resistance and Conformity in the Global South*, 8 CLINICAL L. REV. 515 (2002).

Richard J. Wilson, *Western Europe: Last Holdout in the Worldwide Acceptance of Clinical Legal Education*, 10 GERMAN L.J. No. 7, 823 (2009).

22. EXTERNSHIPS
A Special Focus to Help Understand and Advance Social Justice

LIZ RYAN COLE

> I would not trade ANY experience or any class I have had in law school for the experience and training I received.
>
> I cannot reiterate enough that I enjoyed going to work every day with people who shared a common goal. I am sad to close this chapter of law school, but I am excited for what lies ahead as a result of this opportunity.

The students who made these comments were writing about their experience in an externship. Most of this book is about what are commonly called *legal clinics*, or *law clinics*, a specialized form of apprenticeship that constitutes the core element of many law school clinical programs. When a law school runs a law clinic, it means the job responsibility of the lawyers in the clinic includes teaching the students who practice in the clinic. This chapter, however, is about another type of apprenticeship, one in which law students earn academic credit as they apprentice with lawyers and judges who neither work for nor are paid by a law school. These supervising lawyers and judges owe their primary professional responsibility to their clients or the public, rather than to their students. These experiences are coming to be called *externships*.

People learn by watching, imitating, reflecting, practicing, and watching again, cycle after cycle. Sometimes this practice is unstructured. In other circumstances people have found it valuable to develop structured methods to learn from observation—developing standards and articulating levels of expertise, which allows novices to develop mastery. The structured practice of watching and learning from the work of masters is an "apprenticeship," a method of teaching found in fields from baking to silver making, through building design and the healing arts to learning how to work with and within legal systems.

The role legal apprenticeships play in training lawyers around the world varies tremendously, both in countries with common law systems and in those with civil law systems. The German system provides for a multiyear period of apprenticeship. In England, legal apprenticeship is an integral component of preparation for practice through the Inns of Court (for barristers) and the Law Society (for solicitors). Most former British colonies originally adopted some version of an Inns of Court model, while others have modified the apprenticeship model or have abandoned practicum-based learning entirely. In North America, it was not until the turn of the twentieth century that apprenticeships lost their primacy in favor of classroom-based teaching. In much of Spain and Latin American there is currently no established role for supervised legal experience for academic credit.

EXTERNSHIP DEFINED

As legal education is changing, so is the language we use to describe it. Forty years ago, law students in North America generally talked about *jobs* when they were paid for their experience, *clerkships* when the experience was post graduate (especially with a judge), and *internships* for most other experiences that could be considered part of their professional education. The term *externship* was introduced in the 1980s to clarify the distinction between credit worthy practice experience internal to the law school (ordinarily an "internal clinic" such as a legal aid clinic or an immigration clinic) and credit worthy practice experience external to the law school—an externship. While students can learn about and make contributions to advancing social justice in many practice settings, externships offer great promise for allowing law schools to support an effective and pervasive focus on social justice. Externships already play an important part of the global clinical movement and have the potential to play an ever more significant role.

There are some who do not consider externships when they think about the global clinical movement because they do not consider externships to be part of a clinical program. Others see externships as an affiliated activity that can supplement—but may also compete with—internal clinics. (Backman, 2006) If we are to address social justice as effectively as possible—for students and those they serve—we limit ourselves if we fail to include externships.

The English word *clinic* comes from the Greek word for bed and applies generically to a place a patient (client) gets medical (legal) assistance. When care-givers/problem-solvers (doctors or lawyers) are actually helping people in need (patients or clients), they are providing a clinical service. What is important about an externship—for purposes of defining what is clinical—is whether the student is actively engaged in providing a legal service to a client. As long as the student in an externship is providing supervised legal service in a lawyer's role (rather than as a researcher removed from any specific legal problem and client), then that externship is clinical. Well-structured, clinically informed externships can enhance a clinical program and advance social justice.

An externship has three essential components: the student's actual experience, the student's reflection guided by the externship supervisor, and the law school's supportive and evaluative involvement. In the first component, the student's primary experience is external to the law school and provides the content of the course. The student observes and participates in the work of a supervising attorney or judge. The second component is the tutorial and reflective activity at the practicum site. In this component—also external to the law school—the supervising attorney or judge guides the student's practice and reflection. The third component is analysis, reflection, and evaluation with a faculty member or other person responsible for overseeing the educational goals of the externship. This is ordinarily the function of the law school.

Just as giving a student a question to research on a legal matter is not the same thing as providing clinical legal education, simply going out from the classroom into the world and having a legal experience is not an externship. What distinguishes an externship from an otherwise valuable legal experience—whether called job, clerkship, or internship (as internal to the lawyer's work site)—is the structured opportunity to reflect upon the experience under the direction of an independent expert, ordinarily a member of a law faculty. One measure for determining whether the field experience qualifies as an externship is whether the law school is sufficiently involved in structuring and implementing the external experience that it awards academic credit.

There are two reasons why having an external source of oversight and responsibility is essential. The first reason is that observation and practice without reflection guided by experienced independent teachers may lead to the unintentional development of poor habits and sloppy practice. In the crush of a busy practice or judicial chambers, it is too easy for students to reach erroneous conclusions about the nature of certain clients, ways to approach decision-making, or the substantive law underlying a particular approach to resolving a problem. An experienced and independent teacher is in a position to—and has the ability and the responsibility to—help students understand what they are seeing and doing, and to help them build on that experience. Consider the following scenario:

> A group of student externs were talking in their externship seminar. Some students were apprenticing with lawyers in the state prosecutor's office; others were apprenticing with justices of the supreme court of that same state. The students were discussing the state prosecutor's practice of citing a large number of similar cases in a row ("string cites"). One student who worked at the prosecutor's office commented on how "silly" it was for the law school faculty to teach that string citing is not good practice. Another student working in the same office agreed, adding that he used string cites "all the time." Because the students were in an externship seminar, the teacher had an opportunity to ask whether anyone working at the state supreme court had any comments to share, whereupon the students working at the court smiled at each other and said, ". . . and you should see what the judges think of those string cites."

Without the opportunity for prompted independent reflection, the students at the state prosecutor's office would have drawn a lesson from their experience that would have ill-served them in practice.

Reflection can be directed in certain educationally valuable ways by combining materials prepared specially for externship students with their field experience. Using a chapter from Learning From Practice (Ogilvy et al., 2007) students were asked to examine the role differences can play in the legal profession. In the course of a discussion about bias and how women could be excluded when conversational topics in an office setting might exclude them, a male student noted the following: "The fact that recreational sports-playing, or professional sports-watching is frequently the easiest way to get 'face time' with some firm partners is surely the result, as the book suggests, of a male-dominated profession. I guess I really didn't think about it until now."

The second reason is that it is difficult for the student—and indeed for the supervisor—to maintain the distance essential for reflection on practice while balancing the demands a busy lawyer faces. Unless one person or institution is invested in and responsible for independent reflection, then reflective practice will likely fall to the pressures of daily professional obligations.

What happens when there is insufficient support? The experience of pro bono programs may provide a opportunity for comparison. Many law schools in the United States require students to participate in a pro bono program, in which students provide uncompensated law-related services in the "public interest." Among the goals of these programs is to instill in students a sense of the lawyer's obligation to provide pro bono services. A pro bono coordinator—not a faculty member—usually administers these pro bono programs, and the students, by design and definition, do not earn academic credit. In most pro bono programs, law school support for students is very thin. Students are often energized when they return to the classroom from a pro bono experience, but they too often also return with many misunderstandings from practice. Consider this scenario:

> After volunteering with a church-based immigration group in a required pro bono program, a student reported that she would never feel sorry for "those people" again as she could now see how illegal immigrants brought most of their problems on themselves. Specifically, she was disappointed in her interaction with two clients, describing them as lazy and dishonest. When she asked her supervising attorney to explain her client's behavior, the supervisor's only response was that poor people were all God's children and that lawyers needed to show more understanding.

It was not the pro bono coordinator's responsibility, nor did she have the resources, to help the student develop an independent analysis. The student missed the opportunity to understand enough about her clients and their lives to leave the experience committed to improving access to justice. She had the opposite experience. She concluded the people who came looking for help with immigration issues were lazy and not worth her time. She concluded not only that a pro bono requirement was not important for law students, but also that it was not something she would support as a practicing lawyer.

A different lesson about support and oversight comes from contrasting experiences in Canada and the United States. Canada has a post-undergraduate legal education model similar to that in the United States, but which follows a different path when calling lawyers to the bar. Rather than spending a few days answering written questions, prospective Canadian lawyers participate in a simulation- and practicum-based bar qualification process (which varies from province to province). Part of what makes the process successful is that each province has created a separate entity to directly oversee and evaluate the process. The now-abandoned apprenticeship practice in the United States was quite different. At the turn of the twentieth century, when every state had some form of preadmission practice requirement, experienced practitioners who understood the value of the apprenticeship oversaw apprentice lawyers. Eventually, however, this practice changed. Lawyers delegated oversight of apprenticeships to administrators with little motivation to devote scarce resources to making the system work well. The system deteriorated and ultimately disappeared. Canada's success with practice based admission in contrast with the United State's change to paper and pencil testing suggests that whatever entity oversees apprenticeships must develop a carefully structured and well-resourced process to support independent reflection and oversight. While law schools are in the best position to provide the external structure and support required in an externship, a bar association, state court, or other entity can assume these responsibilities as well.

Externships are not perfect. They are less manageable and predictable than internal clinics (just as internal clinics are less predictable than simulation-based classes). It is sometimes also the case that more traditional members of law school faculties do not appreciate the teaching and learning that occurs in externships. As a result, they do not support devoting resources to externships as an integral part of the law school curriculum. There is also a temptation on the part of many administrators to collect tuition dollars from students in externships without offering teaching commensurate with what is offered in the classroom. The legal education community can address these pressures in a number of ways. One of the most effective is to have accreditation standards that make clear that sufficient instructional resources must be devoted to make externships high-quality educational experiences. (Joy, 2004)

EXTERNSHIPS AND SOCIAL JUSTICE

There are three fonts that drive the social justice mission of the global clinical movement. First, many people experience the need for social justice on a daily basis. Second, most law students enter law school open to the idea that part of being a lawyer is serving the public good. (Abel, 2002; Nguyen, 2008) Third is the view held by most lawyers, law teachers, and law schools that a lawyer's role is defined, at least in part, by his or her obligation to serve the public and work toward social justice. Law students must, however, balance their desire to serve the public good against a variety of obstacles. Too often it seems almost impossible to further the cause of developing and practicing social justice because it is too time-consuming or too expensive, seems not to be valued by professors and other role models, or because it raises too many conflicts with potential employers. There are a number of reasons why externships can help students and lawyers address the obstacles to working toward social justice.

First, where externships are an option, more students become involved in the practice setting and more financial and human resources are available to students and supervisors. The end result is a significant increase in the number of students involved in social justice work.

Second, it is well accepted among those who study cognition that student motivation is higher when they exercise initiative in their choice of study. Student motivation plays a large role in how open students are to learning new material and how much effort they are willing to exert. That effort leads in turn to more effective study, improved retention, and improved ability to access and build on what has been learned. (Maharg, 2007) Many students miss the opportunity to learn in a clinical setting because they think that on-campus or internal clinics are just for those who want to practice "poverty law" or "family law," and do not understand the significant carryover value from internal clinic experience to their developing expertise as lawyers. Even some of those students who do enroll in internal clinics do not fully engage, and therefore do not get the most out of the experience, because they cannot see the connection to practice. Contrast this with the interest that a student who imagines she will be protecting the environment once she enters into practice might bring to learning about enforcement of environmental regulations. Her high motivation will help her learn more effectively.

Third, externships can be established with practitioners in a broad variety of types of practice. When a law school offers an internal clinic, ordinarily it is focused on a particular practice area (immigration law, housing law, health law, etc.) and—at least in the United States—client-focused within the court system. Occasionally, a clinic will be process-focused, as in a business transactions clinic. Overall, however, law school clinical programs, no matter where in the world they exist, operate within a relatively narrow range of practice and service. Moreover, there must be sufficient faculty and student interest in the clinic's area of practice or service to support the expenditure necessary to operate the clinic. On the other hand, with an externship there are as many types of experience available as there are types of practice with lawyers interested in serving as externship supervisors. As just one example, a student who thought she might want to carry her interest in pro bono in practice said: "I thought it would be interesting to see how public interest work is done outside of the nonprofit arena—to have the greater resources available in a private firm, but also to learn about how to generate money for pro bono work within a private firm." She was able to find a firm with a commitment to pro bono work and completed an apprenticeship within a firm.

Fourth, externships offer geographic variety. This is true both locally and globally. There are, of course, limits on international site locations imposed by world politics, the ability of students and schools to afford the programs, and the availability of trainer-lawyers. Nonetheless, today one can find apprentices from India to Argentina to Alaska.

Fifth, students in externships are able to help build bridges between the law school and lawyers in practice. Practitioners often view law teachers as part of the "ivory tower." Their potential contribution and perspective are often dismissed or devalued by the profession. This can lead to dissonance between what a student learns in school and what a student comes to value in practice. When the law school is integrated into practice through an externship program, students can serve as a bridge between the academy and the profession. For the purposes of social justice education, this can mean involving law teachers in specific social justice initiatives, providing opportunities for combined academic and practice-related discussion about legal strategies and outcomes. Externship students reach out to classmates back on campus for resources for people in the client community, including food, toys, and books, and also to their law school itself for access to libraries, librarians, and other support to carry out their legal work at their placement site.

> The defendant was deaf. The rural and remote public defender's office was understaffed. An extern asked if the client should have a translator. This idea, new to the supervising lawyers, was one the student was encouraged to explore. She used the resources available to the public defender's office and then reached out to her home law school for support. She ultimately wrote and argued a motion for the appointment of a publicly funded translator. The motion was granted and the defendant had a very different voice in court than he would have had without the student extern.

Finally, externships offer opportunities for students to be exposed to lawyers who regularly address social justice issues in their own practices. When their role models are lawyers who are actually living their commitment to social justice while also supporting themselves, it is easier to persuade students of the value and practicality of social justice work. Not all students will elect social justice work in their externships and it is sometimes hard for lawyers involved in social justice work to accept that not every student will do the same. Nevertheless, exposure to social justice-related practice can have a positive effect; while more empirical work needs to be done, it appears that significant numbers of students select social justice work when given a choice. (Stover, 1989) Externships can create and reinforce lessons about social justice that will carry on into the rest of the student's professional life. After the close of an externship with a public defender in the immigrant community from which the student came, he wrote:

> I have come to realize that this is my chosen career path and is what I was meant to do. I have learned that "criminals" are not "born" but are oftentimes

the results of life's harsh and unfortunate circumstances. While here, I confirmed what I already suspected, that the poor, uneducated and downtrodden amongst us, and those suffering from mental illness or drug or alcohol dependencies are disproportionately represented in the criminal justice system . . . As I reflect on my internship, I realize that I walk away with a deeper more profound understanding of the power of the law, its impact on the life of the people whose path it crosses and the important role that our of the profession has on the life of those it serves. I now know how I fit in life's puzzle. I know my chosen career path and this is without a doubt the greatest lesson learned.

EXTERNSHIP STUDENTS

Externship programs draw much of their strength from their students, and in this way externship students offer contributions to the social justice mission of clinical legal education apart from those attributable to externship programs. For example, supervisors with a passion for social justice are interested in engaging externs who can help validate their social justice practice. Taking on unpopular cases can be lonely work. Having law students work with lawyers can provide personal validation as well as legal support. It sends a powerful message: not only does the lawyer think this case or issue is important, but a student values it enough to work with the lawyer—and a law school values it enough to send a student to apprentice. This message can be important not only to the supervising lawyer, but also to other actors in the larger legal community, from judges to opposing counsel.

Students in an externship can also help improve the profession as a whole. Working with students may reenergize and improve the practice of a lawyer whose passion for social justice work has gradually burned out over a career of taking on emotionally demanding and financially draining work. When a fresh and energetic student comes to work with a lawyer, she will find herself looking at her work through the eyes of the newcomer. Students may question established practices, from filing systems to client management to billing, which may stimulate new thinking about how the office is run. When facing an ethical dilemma, which the supervisor must also explain to a student, the lawyer may be motivated to take the "better" path even if it is not the most expedient. Externs can thus serve as an external conscience for the lawyers with whom they practice. As supervising lawyers see themselves in the mirror of the student's eyes, their posture—in this case their professional posture—improves.

A third value to involving externship students in practice is that they can make explicit the value of supervision in legal work. When a student is paying for an experience (through tuition), and an institution is providing external support, students and faculty supervisors expect that the on-site supervisor will provide a level of supervision not usually demanded in routine law practice. Externship supervisors are required to give clear directions, involve students in planning, give students timely and descriptive feedback on their legal work, and give students an opportunity to apply the lessons learned (within the limits of their skill and experience).

Finally, externship students can become activists in their own right. Once they return to campus, students bring back lessons from the externship and may be able to put them into practice immediately. Consider this example:

> A student, having completed a public interest externship with a state's Division of Children and Families (DCF), enrolled in an advanced externship course supervised by a lawyer with the Child Protection Unit at the Office of the Attorney General for the state. The unit's attorneys represent the DCF in child-abuse and child-neglect proceedings in juvenile courts. In both externships she was exposed to the Court Appointed Special Advocates (CASA) program, through which trained volunteers are appointed to gather and transmit to the court information about the needs and interests of children involved in child protection proceedings—information critical to the safety and well-being of those children. In part because of difficulties in volunteer recruitment and retention, very few children actually had access to the benefits of the CASA program. As a result, courts far too often were required to make decisions about children based on inaccurate and incomplete information. The student became convinced that she and her classmates could help address this problem by expanding the state's pool of CASA volunteers, but she also knew that law students would have a hard time attending the mandatory CASA training. Working with the CASA program and with help from a member of the faculty, she managed to restructure the volunteer training so that law students could complete the training program and enroll as CASA volunteers.

EXTERNS GLOBALLY AND LOCALLY

What sorts of things do externs do? Sometimes the extern's work is dramatic and visible. Students who provide criminal defense, and especially those who work with postconviction and innocence projects, do work that is recognized and valued by lawyers and by the public. Externs also perform a great deal more pedestrian legal work, which advances the cause of social justice just as significantly as does more visible practice. Students who provide day-to-day civil legal services, either working with legal services organizations or with volunteer lawyers, provide access to justice for those who could not otherwise afford it. Students who work with legislators and legislative counsel help draft and pass legislation that protects the environment or provides funds to help with education and health care. Students who work with prosecutors have the chance to help make the criminal justice system work fairly. Students in externships with judges and with ethics counsel and boards bring a perspective and energy that enhances the ability of decision-makers to reach complete and reflective judgments.

Most of the time students work in settings within their own countries. Students in the United States work with thousands of nongovernmental organizations (NGOs), such as the Natural Resources Defense Council, the Alliance for Justice, the National Partnership for Woman and Families, and the Center on Race, Poverty, and the Environment. Externships also are an important part of the social justice mission of the global clinical movement. Externship students can leave their home school and apprentice wherever lawyers practice. Externs work with international tribunals including the International Criminal Tribunal for the former Yugoslavia (ICTY), the International Criminal Tribunal for Rwanda (ICTR), and the International Criminal Court (ICC), and with prosecutors and defense counsel appearing in these same courts. They work with the United Nations and with the Global Environment Facility Secretariat of the World Bank. They help human refugees and immigrants by externing with Amnesty International, and they protect highly migratory fish as externs with the Food and Agriculture Organization of the United Nations. They fight slavery in Mauritania and work for environmental justice in Madagascar, Japan, and Costa Rica. They advocate for Palestinians with agencies of the European Union. They contribute to the work of human rights organizations and Truth and Reconciliation Commissions in many countries throughout the world. Currently most international externships mean students from higher income country go to lower and middle-income countries but that is something that can change. Moreover, students are likely to move across many more cultural, social, and financial borders as international LLM programs develop courses of study that include an apprenticeship component.

LOOKING TO THE FUTURE

Thirty years ago, just a handful of schools awarded credit for externship-based learning. Today almost every law school in the United States offers opportunities to earn academic credit in an external setting. Externships are common in clinical programs in other countries as well. For example, a number of law schools in Argentina are modeling clinical programs after an externship agreement between an NGO, the Centre for Social and Legal Studies, and Buenos Aires National University.[1] It is not as clear, however, whether these off-campus field-based opportunities will become an integral part of legal education, or whether

---

1. This externship is described in Chapter 5, which covers clinical programs in Latin America.

they will become instead an adjunct to the job-focused work of career services offices. Law schools, students, and lawyers can all make contributions to helping make externships tools for teaching and for furthering the cause of social justice.

What can law schools do? They can screen and train externship supervisors, prepare students for the work at the externship site, and support students during the period of the externship. While a student may know that there are legal issues that must be addressed in a far away region of the country, without the structure and support provided by an externship program the student may not know how to find the capable and experienced lawyers doing the sort of work that makes a difference; and if the student does find the right lawyer, he may not have the confidence that the lawyer will offer a sufficiently worthwhile externship experience. Law schools can integrate the value of practicing social justice by establishing service as a goal for all law students and allowing externships to be one way to meet that goal.

What are some of the things students can do to help make externships most effective? First and foremost, they can encourage their schools to offer them. They can ask about externships in the admissions process and insist that their school makes externships available to all. Second, they can share their experience on their return to campus. Sharing interests other students in enrolling, and brings some of the insight and learning individual students have gained back to their classmates and teachers. Finally, they can be informed consumers and refuse to pay for "externships" in which they obtain neither academic credit nor meaningful experience and reflection overseen by skilled teachers.

What are some of the things practicing lawyers can do to make externships most effective? First, they can make a commitment to take the time to give timely and descriptive feedback. Most experienced supervisors understand that their own practice improves when they are able to integrate capable and well-trained law students into their practices. The quid pro quo, in an externship context, is quality teaching and supervision on the part of the supervising attorney. Second, they can take on a small number of cases which advance the cause of social justice, and which they could not otherwise take on without apprentices. This will provide even richer learning for students and will advance the cause of social justice through direct legal service to the needy. Finally, lawyers can consider teaching externs as part of their obligation to improve the profession. Taking that approach to their supervising role will not only reinforce professional pride in what they do, but could also lead them to model that professional contribution for the other lawyers in the community.

If the legal academy—both teachers and students—and the profession can accomplish these tasks, then externships will become an even more significant part of the global clinical movement and its mission to educate lawyers for social justice.

LIST OF REFERENCES

Richard L. Abel, *Choosing, Nurturing, Training and Placing Public Interest Law Students*, 70 FORDHAM L. REV. 1563 (2002).

James H. Backman, *Where Do Externships Fit? A New Paradigm Is Needed: Marshaling Law School Resources to Provide an Externship for Every Student*, 56 J. LEGAL EDUC. 615 (2006).

Liz Ryan Cole, *Lessons from a Semester in Practice*, 1 CLINICAL L. REV. 173 (1994).

Bernadette T. Feeley, *Training Field Supervisors to Be Efficient and Effective Critics of Student Writing*, 15 CLINICAL L. REV. 211 (2009).

Peter A. Joy, *Evolution of ABA Standards Relating to Externships: Steps in the Right Direction?*, 10 CLINICAL L. REV. 681 (2004).

Harriet N. Katz, *Counseling Externship Students*, 15 CLINICAL L. REV. 239 (2009).

PAUL MAHARG, TRANSFORMING LEGAL EDUCATION: LEARNING AND TEACHING THE LAW IN THE EARLY TWENTY-FIRST CENTURY (Ashgate Publishing Ltd., 2007).

Susan K. McClellan, *Externships for Millennial Generation Law Students: Bridging the Generation Gap*, 15 CLINICAL L. REV. 255 (2009).

Tan N. Nguyen, *An Affair to Forget: Law School's Deleterious Effect on Student's Public Interest Aspirations*, 7 CONN. PUB. INT. L.J. 95 (2008).

J. P. OGILVY, LEAH WORTHAM, & LISA G. LERMAN, LEARNING FROM PRACTICE: A PROFESSIONAL DEVELOPMENT TEXT FOR LEGAL EXTERNS (West 2007).

Donald A. Schön, *Educating the Reflective Legal Practitioner*, 2 CLINICAL L. REV. 231 (1995).

ROBERT STOVER, MAKING IT AND BREAKING IT: THE FATE OF PUBLIC INTEREST COMMITMENT DURING LAW SCHOOL (Howard S. Erlanger ed., University of Illinois Press 1989).

23. SETTING AN AGENDA FOR THE GLOBAL CLINICAL MOVEMENT

MARGARET (PEGGY) MAISEL

INTRODUCTION

A global clinical movement crystallized in 1999 at the first meeting of the Global Alliance for Justice Education (GAJE) in Trivandrum India. That conference built on a growing number of international exchanges and collaborations during the 1990s in which experienced clinical law teachers traveled to countries with law faculties concerned with social justice issues and interested in reforming their curriculum to include clinical programs. Clinicians representing more than twenty countries met at the GAJE conference to exchange information and ideas on justice education, particularly clinical legal education. Linked to the conference was a training workshop that focused on how to develop and teach law school clinical and Street Law courses, and to use clinical teaching methods in some doctrinal courses.[1]

Since that first meeting, the global clinical movement has begun to develop a shared mission and an organizational structure, as demonstrated at subsequent GAJE conferences held biannually around the world. On the plus side, it continues to grow, and its accomplishments include a whole host of activities documented elsewhere in this book. On the other hand, funding and other internal issues have resulted in the movement having a fluid membership, and it still seems to lack a clear vision of how it wants to influence legal education over the next decades and an agenda for how to continue to grow and increase its influence. The goal of this chapter is therefore to help fill that gap by first articulating a unifying vision for the movement and then suggesting what an agenda needed to reach that vision could look like. Included in the latter discussion will be examples of strategies and models of how to succeed.

In articulating a vision for what the global clinical movement should strive to accomplish, I am guided by three goals which are widely shared by clinicians around the world: increased access to justice for previously unrepresented groups; a system of legal education that ensures future lawyers have the knowledge, skills, and values needed to help solve the world's complex problems; and a legal profession that is more diverse, skilled, and committed to

---

1. The history of GAJE, including its various worldwide meetings, is discussed in Chapter 25.

serving social needs.[2] This chapter is organized around the three parts of this vision and how they form a global agenda, including the structures and resources that will be needed for the global clinical movement to implement its strategies and sustain its work. The final section discusses how the movement needs to develop organizationally in order to accomplish this ambitious agenda.

Any effort to propose a global clinical agenda must begin with the key principle that the work needs to encompass the full variety of approaches to clinical education that exist currently both between and within different countries. Up to this point, clinical law teachers around the world have, for the most part, been careful not to impose one model of clinical education as best or even suitable in all countries and law schools. Instead, law school clinical programs have tried to respond to the system of legal education in each country and to address local legal needs. It is imperative to continue and even strengthen this approach, especially for clinicians from the United States where clinical education has existed longest and is best resourced, so that the movement avoids the pitfalls of legal imperialism that undercut the effectiveness of the US-led Law and Development Movement in the 1960s.[3] (Maisel, 2008) In addition, international organizations such as GAJE must continue to promote leadership that is not dominated by Western voices but instead is shared by representatives from all regions of the world, so that they can then bring together the worldwide clinical movement needed to implement a truly global agenda.

PROMOTE ACCESS TO JUSTICE

Access to justice is a core component of the agenda for the clinical movement in developing countries. This is no longer the case to the same extent in the United States and other developed countries, although it was a major motivating factor in the development of law clinics in their early history prior to the expansion of government and philanthropically supported legal aid organizations.[4] Recently, clinical legal education in the developed world has focused more on its educational value rather than on its mission of representing low-income communities. This change has been reinforced by the recognition that similar to clinical rotations in medical schools, live-client legal clinics, with their low student-faculty ratio and intensive supervision, are the best place in legal education to combine theory and practice. As a result, the legal practice in these clinics has expanded from traditional legal aid to other areas of practice, such as intellectual

---

2. The goals and values of a global clinical movement are discussed in more detail in Chapter 18.

3. The law and development movement and its relationship to the global clinical movement are discussed in Chapter 9.

4. See Chapter 10 for a discussion of the legal aid origins of clinical legal education.

property or business deals, although the focus of these clinics is usually on representing minority businesses or low-income groups. In contrast, the newer university-based law school clinics, mostly in developing countries with limited or no legal aid structure, are still asked to fill the legal services needs of disadvantaged clients while they also educate students and others in the community on the continuing need for greater access to justice for the poor. (Wilson, 2009; Bloch, 2008; Burman, 2002; Wilson, 2004)

The reality in most developing countries is that if university-based law clinics are to be instituted and sustained, they must receive government funds as part of a national scheme for providing legal aid. This is true both because universities cannot afford the additional faculty needed to supervise student casework and the percentage of low income people in these countries is much greater than in developed nations.

Three suggestions are made here for how the global clinical movement can increase its chances of success in improving access to justice worldwide. First, the clinical movement in each country should work in partnership with local government legal aid schemes and nonprofit organizations to design the most effective legal delivery system while avoiding duplication of services. Second, the global movement needs to help increase the number of legal representatives for the poor by advocating for changes in practice rules to allow law students to provide direct representation to clients under the supervision of attorneys. And third, to further maximize available resources, the global clinical movement should encompass legal literacy and Street Law programs so that law students learn about the importance of integrating community education and client representation while clients are empowered to either advocate for themselves when a legal representative is not available or take preventative measures to avoid legal problems in the future. Strategies for each of these are described below.

Partnerships between Law Schools, Government Legal Aid, and Legal NGOs

With scarce resources to provide access to justice, it is vital that the global clinical movement provide leadership in establishing collaboration between government legal aid schemes, law schools, and legal NGOs by helping to organize national and regional meetings of key members of these groups to determine the most effective national legal delivery scheme. A key topic would be the best way to distribute limited resources, a discussion that could lead to opening up of clinical courses to more, or possibly every, law student at relatively little additional cost. This would increase resources available for representation while also graduating law students better prepared to enter the profession, more knowledgeable about the legal needs of the poor, and, hopefully, committed to providing greater access to justice.

This approach was adopted by some law schools in the early days of clinical education in the United States. For example, Antioch Law School collaborated in the early 1970s with the then new national Legal Services Corporation (LSC) to establish a clinical program with its core funding each year coming from the LSC. The law students, beginning in their first year, enrolled in a clinic every semester and provided free legal services in all types of matters. (Kay, 2002; Barry et. al, 2000). Another example, in the 1980s, was the Legal Services Institute founded by Gary Bellow at Harvard Law School, which received federal funding for legal services lawyers to supervise Harvard and Northeastern law students on cases in Boston, as well as to learn about and contribute to research on best practices. (Charn, 2003) In South Africa, representatives from every law school participated in a series of national forums in the late 1990s and early twenty-first century to discuss how best to establish a more effective legal services delivery system. In addition, the coordinating body for university-based law clinics, the Association of University Legal Aid Institutions (AULAI), has two representatives on the national legal aid board. South Africa has also led the way in university-based clinics providing backup legal services to community-based paralegals. (Maisel, 2007)

Such coordination could also take a different path of placing law students in off-campus locations to be supervised by lawyers who work there.[5] This would also increase the number of law students who can have a clinical experience at relatively low cost, thereby again improving the chances of low-income people obtaining legal representation.

One barrier to collaboration between national legal aid schemes and law school clinical programs may be a perceived competition for funds. Antioch Law School and the Legal Services Institute were often criticized by LSC-funded project directors for costing more than a staff attorney model of legal services delivery. Some collaboration between law schools and legal services offices continues in the United States, but most often in the more limited form described above of sending law students to legal services offices for externship credit.

The issue of resource allocation is even more complex at the global level because the scheme to distribute funds differs in each country, so that different groups of people are involved in decision-making about legal services delivery and funding. In most countries, the majority of university law faculties are publicly funded by the national or regional governments. But even in public universities, law clinics often have to be established and sustained by donor funding because of limited government funds. At privately funded law schools, law school clinics receive funding from different sources. All of this makes collaboration more difficult. Nonetheless, promoting law school clinics as a means to increase access to justice will help maximize the limited resources available to provide the highest quality legal representation for the poor—and, while doing so, provide more professionally and socially responsible education of future lawyers.

---

5. See Chapter 22 for a discussion of externships.

Promote Law Student Practice Rules

Where student practice rules exist, law students work in the role of lawyers and can handle their own case load under faculty supervision, either directly or with the cooperation of a supervising attorney. Allowing law students to represent clients not only increases legal resources available to indigent clients, but also enhances the clinical learning experience. For these reasons, a concrete agenda item for the global clinical law movement is to work for the institutionalization of law student practice rules in every country.

Although certification requirements may differ from country to country, depending on the type of work most students would do and the forums where they would most likely appear, the global effort should be to maximize the operation of student practice rules. When certification is limited, the number of law students who enroll in clinical courses and are available to represent indigent people decreases substantially. For example, in 2007 the certification process was changed in Florida (in the United States, lawyers are licensed by the states), making it much harder and more expensive to be certified as a law student. The result was an abrupt drop in the number of law students working through law school clinics and at agencies such as the public defender's office. As South African clinician David McQuoid-Mason has noted, if every law student spent vacation time representing indigent clients, then most criminally accused might have the opportunity for some legal help. (Maisel, 2004)

Lobbying government or the courts to adopt student practice rules requires leadership from the global clinical movement to educate rule-makers on the importance and benefit of law student practice. These rule-makers must be sure that law students will have the necessary supervision to provide high-quality legal representation so that clients will not be hurt, and law students will learn to set high professional standards. They also need to be shown that law students representing low-income clients will not take business away from practicing lawyers but instead will provide representation for clients who otherwise have no access to lawyers.

Legal Literacy and Street Law Programs

One of the most effective ways of promoting access to justice has been through law school legal literacy and Street Law programs.[6] In these programs, law students provide community legal education about legal rights and responsibilities in all types of settings, such as secondary schools, prisons, and community groups. These programs often operate separate from, but alongside, law school clinics that provide direct client representation. In countries such as Cambodia, where there are only a few lawyers, legal literacy programs may be the only way of providing legal knowledge to the public to help them access the legal system without a lawyer.

---

6. Street Law and legal literacy clinics are discussed in chapters 15 and 16.

The agenda for the global clinical movement should, therefore, include teaching law students about both legal literacy and direct client representation and offering both through law school clinics. In some instances, these two functions may be combined, such as in South Africa, where law students provide support and consultation at community-based clinics staffed by paralegals, or by establishing pro se clinics to support individuals or groups in representing themselves with law students acting as consultants. The Bridges Across Borders Southeast Asia Community Legal Education Initiative (BABSEA CLE) International Law Student Internship Program is a model of how law students from around the world can work with local attorneys to develop and deliver community legal education.[7] By implementing such strategies, the global clinical movement will again greatly increase access to justice for disadvantaged groups while teaching law students about community outreach, community education, and legal representation.

REFORMING LEGAL EDUCATION: INSTITUTIONALIZING CLINICAL LEGAL EDUCATION AROUND THE GLOBE

Until relatively recently, law school clinics and clinical legal education existed in only a few countries, most notably in the United States, Australia, and England.[8] The Ford Foundation and other funders have supported the expansion and growth of clinical legal education, beginning primarily in Eastern and Central Europe when the Cold War ended, and then in other parts of the globe. Today clinical legal education and university-based legal aid clinics exist in law schools in countries in every region of the world.

While this growth is encouraging, it by no means ensures the continued vitality of clinical legal education. Indeed, the brief history of the clinical movement in developing countries in Central and Eastern Europe, Africa, and Asia indicates that these programs all experience problems with sustainability once donor funding runs out. For this reason, probably the key goal for the global clinical movement is to find a way to institutionalize clinical legal education into the curriculum of all law schools. A three-part strategy is suggested here: changing nationally mandated law school curricula to include clinical courses, whether it be by the government for public law schools or other law school accrediting bodies; developing best practices for clinical legal education in each country; and hiring and training permanent members of law school faculties capable of teaching clinical courses.

---

7. BABSEA CLE programs are discussed in Chapter 3, which covers clinics in South and Southeast Asia.

8. The first wave of clinical legal education is described in Chapter 1.

Mandatory Clinical Education

An important part of the agenda for the global movement is to expand opportunities for clinical education so that every law student has a clinical experience before graduation. This is needed as a simple curricular matter: only through clinical education can students learn how to integrate legal knowledge, skills, and values; prepare for actual legal practice; and understand the legal needs of the poor and the social impact of a lack of access to justice. If clinical courses are voluntary, some law students will graduate with major gaps in their legal education.

In many countries, instituting such a requirement will mean eliminating other currently required courses and instituting new teaching methodologies. This in turn will require a change in the standards set by national accrediting bodies. Fortunately, there already are precedents for such action. In the past five years, several African countries—Kenya, Lesotho, and Nigeria, for example—have held national conferences involving judges, bar association leaders, government ministers, and law school administrators and faculty to decide on the national legal curriculum. In each instance, a consensus was reached to introduce a clinical experience at both the undergraduate and graduate levels. Members of the global clinical movement in other countries need to learn from the actions taken in these three nations in order to influence local decision-makers to reach a similar result—and to ensure that law schools get the assistance they need to implement the new curriculum mandates.

Best Practices for Legal Education

A major challenge facing legal education around the world is how to prepare law students with the knowledge, skills, and values to fill different roles (transactional attorney, litigator, negotiator, legal adviser) in a wide variety of substantive legal areas. Clinical programs can play a key role in meeting this challenge because they focus directly on preparing future lawyers for the legal practice needed in a particular country. The form of practice taught clinically can vary widely and may include litigation, alternative dispute resolution, policy or legislative advocacy, community education, or transactional practice.[9] The same is true for the location of a clinical practice, since clinically trained law students can work comfortably in many settings: from the local community to a national or international practice; in a law firm, a government office, or nonprofit legal organization; or even outside what is thought of traditionally as law practice, with a lobbyist or public official.

---

9. A number of these areas of clinical practice are covered in other chapters of this book: Chapter 17 (alternative dispute resolution), Chapters 13 and 14 (policy and legislative advocacy), Chapters 15 and 16 (community education), and Chapter 11 (transactional practice).

Given these advantages, the global clinical movement is well positioned to lead a reform of legal education that identifies and teaches best practices. An example of this took place in the United States, where the Clinical Legal Education Association (CLEA) undertook a reform project, called the Best Practices Project, to influence change in legal education. This project, which was initiated in 2001, culminated with the publication of the book, *Best Practices for Legal Education* in 2007. *Best Practices* provides a general framework for best practices for legal education, including, for example, setting goals for a program of instruction, delivering instruction, assessing student learning, and assessing institutional effectiveness—all of which are important in educating future lawyers. (Stuckey and Others, 2007) The part of the project directly related to clinical education is its identification of best practices for three types of experiential courses using clinical methodology: simulation-based courses, in-house clinics, and externships. The book provides standards for each type of clinical setting, including a framework for assessing the merit of the course and the students' learning.

There have been similar, if less comprehensive, projects elsewhere. These include one in Australia that dealt with the issue of assessment and another in the United Kingdom that focused on teaching legal skills such as interviewing. In South Africa, the national clinical organization AULAI held a workshop in 2009 to discuss, develop, and publish best practices for South African law clinics.

Best practices for experiential legal education and university-based law clinics will differ around the world, depending on the goals of clinical legal education in each country, the nature and quality of existing clinical courses, and the resources available. For example, the *Best Practices* book does not include best practices for—or even discuss—legal literacy or Street Law courses that are outside the mainstream of the clinical curriculum in the United States but are among the most widely used forms of experiential education at law schools in developing countries around the world. The Best Practices Project and book can serve, however, as useful resources in developing different standards for clinical legal education throughout the world and, more importantly, they demonstrate the influence the clinical movement can have on best practices in any given country.

Given other priorities, the question remains as to whether developing best practices belongs high on the agenda of a global clinical movement. In my opinion, the answer is "yes" for several reasons. First, the Best Practices Project involved—and continues to involve—a cross section of clinical law teachers and experts from other disciplines from across the United States and other parts of the world. It therefore increased collaboration and cooperation among a wide variety of academics that has helped broaden and strengthen the clinical movement. Second, the project has had a positive influence on the future of legal education in the United States, which could stimulate similar efforts in other countries and lead to a broader dialogue about best practices for both clinical and nonclinical legal education. Finally, best practices are needed also for law students studying and working abroad, including international clinical legal work and clinics collaborating across country borders on, for example, international human rights issues. Given this need, the global clinical movement is in the best position to undertake such a task.

Train Legal Educators in Clinical Pedagogy and How to Teach Legal Skills

A third strategy—educating and training the law teachers and lawyers required to staff clinics—needs to be implemented to ensure the sustainability of the global clinical movement. As discussed below, clinical teaching is quite different from traditional legal pedagogy; therefore, teaching the knowledge and skills needed to become effective clinical educators requires a separate effort from the training of traditional law faculty. This is a major task that will expand as the clinical education movement extends its reach into new law schools, sometimes in countries where clinical or even formal legal education previously did not exist. To reach the desired goal, the movement needs to create mechanisms and forums for an exchange of materials and information about effective training projects—and also to train trainers who can design and deliver training programs for new and experienced clinicians around the world (through so-called "Train-the-Trainer" workshops). This can be done through international conferences and meetings and by developing and distributing materials, but it also should include clinical faculty mentoring and exchanges between law schools in different countries. The latter may not only prove to be more cost effective in the long run, but it also increases networking and an exchange of ideas that will increase the overall strength and effectiveness of the global clinical movement.

Effective clinical teaching involves skills and knowledge not taught in law schools or in other disciplines, except possibly education. An effective clinician must, for example, understand adult learning theory, be skilled in using experiential teaching techniques, have excellent supervision skills, including being able to give effective feedback, and be able to incorporate social justice principles and legal ethics into the clinical curriculum. Formal extended training programs to educate clinicians exist already and can serve as models if the global movement recognizes, publicizes, critiques, and disseminates information about them. For example, a training center for clinical law teachers from twelve sub-Saharan African countries is now in its third year. The Human Rights Development Institute in Pretoria has trained new African clinicians from eight sub-Saharan countries who are now back at their law schools developing and teaching in law clinics. The institute brings the new clinicians to Pretoria for five months, where they learn clinical methodology and teaching skills and plan how to implement clinical programs with a particular focus on providing legal services regarding HIV/AIDS when they return to their home law schools. A second example is a week-long institute held at Georgetown University Law School in the United States, which exposes newer clinicians to creative teaching methodologies and theory that can improve their teaching and supervision skills. A third example is a two-and-a-half day workshop developed by the Legal Services Corporation in 1981 that has been adapted to train US clinical law faculty and externship mentors in supervision skills. Shorter versions of this workshop have been offered successfully in South Africa and at the 2008 GAJE conference in the Philippines.

Beyond these extended programs, national and regional clinical law organizations have taken a leading role in setting up or supporting shorter term training conferences for new and experienced clinicians. Indeed, many hold annual conferences where clinicians meet and teach each other.[10] On the worldwide level, GAJE has been a leader at its biannual international conferences in providing training for justice educators and by fostering regional conferences between worldwide conferences.

Finally, clinicians in different countries have hosted each other for exchange visits and there are an increasing number of LLM programs and clinical teaching fellowships that allow new clinicians to learn how to teach while working in a clinical program. The Ford Foundation and others have supported international exchanges and training programs for clinicians in many parts of the world. The global clinical movement should study all of these existing programs and then find ways to replicate them for clinicians in parts of the world where such training is not currently available. This may require providing financial support and finding ways to overcome language barriers and operational differences between legal systems, particularly between civil and common law countries. Despite the difficulties that will be encountered, this particular goal is essential to the success of the global clinical movement, lest there be insufficient staff for the law clinics emerging worldwide.

THE LEGAL PROFESSION

The third part of the vision for the global clinical movement proposed here is to promote a legal profession that is more diverse, skilled, and committed to serving social justice. People and nations today have become much more interconnected through technology, travel, and trade. Likewise, lawyers and legal systems are increasingly interdependent and there is more emphasis in law schools on teaching international law. As a result, it is not enough to work to improve the quality of the legal profession in any one country or group of countries. Legal educators everywhere have an interest in supporting the development of a more diverse, skilled, and socially committed profession around the world.

---

10. The work of these organizations is discussed in Chapter 19, which covers national and regional clinical organizations.

The first step in achieving this aspect of the global clinical agenda must be to strengthen the legal profession's commitment to educating law students who will have the skills, knowledge, and commitment to serve social needs and to develop ways for law schools and professional bodies to work more closely together to promote these goals. The movement thus must help ensure that a fully diverse student body—race, gender, income, cultural background—is recruited into law schools and helped to qualify for the bar.

It will not be enough just to educate a diverse group of students; the work must continue after graduation from law school. Thus, the global clinical movement needs to develop and implement strategies that assist law school graduates to continue to serve social needs and to promote access to justice in their legal practice. It is most critical in this regard that ongoing training and support be available to graduates who go into solo practice or to small firms, since they will likely be the practitioners who provide representation to low- and middle-income communities. Paralleling this effort is the need to teach law students to confront corruption in the legal system after they graduate, especially those in government service, and to work with the professional bodies regulating lawyers to provide continuing education about ethical issues and problems of corruption.

Support Law Graduates in Solo Practice, Small Firms, and Public Interest Work

In order to further its agenda of supporting those law school graduates who want to practice law in the service of the underrepresented, the global clinical movement will have to focus support on small firms and solo practitioners. Even with their clinical experience in law school, newly graduated attorneys will need further help on such matters as how to set up and run a solo legal practice, how to bill and collect fees and keep proper accounts, and how to solve legal problems they have never before encountered. One way to do this is to work with bar associations to provide them with materials and training that they can pass on to attorneys in solo practice or in small firms. Similarly, law schools must understand that their obligation to their students does not end at graduation; that they too need to help create programs in collaboration with the bar, government, and others to support law school graduates who are willing to go into underserved urban communities and rural areas to serve a vast majority of people who have no access to justice. Fortunately, a few models for doing this type of work exist already on a small scale. Perhaps more importantly, proposals have been discussed in various countries that would take a much broader approach to ensuring representation for the underserved. The global clinical movement can study and critique all of these efforts and proposals so that they can be implemented and possibly expanded or modified for use in different countries and contexts.

One model implemented at a particular institution is the Community Legal Resource Network (CLRN) started at the City University of New York in 1998. This program networks law graduates in solo or small practices committed to providing affordable legal services to those who would not otherwise have access. (Glen, 2006) CLRN provides free training, client referrals, and various means by which new lawyers practicing alone or starting small firms can share information and assist each other in their practices. Symbiosis Law School in Pune, India, recently followed the CLRN model and started a similar program for its graduates.

A much broader proposal to promote a legal profession serving social needs that has been advanced in several contexts is to create programs for law graduates to work in communities serving clients who would not otherwise have access to justice—or even require a mandatory year of service at these types of programs. For example, a mandatory year of community service for all law graduates was proposed for South Africa by the Chief Judge of the Constitutional Court, Arthur Chaskalson. It was not adopted, although a similar program was instituted for all medical school graduates. Additional examples include voluntary programs in the United States, such as Americorps, through which attorneys work with nonprofit organizations on a subsistence stipend.

A third model is to provide alternative methods for law graduates to qualify to practice. In many countries, law graduates serve a year or more of apprenticeship to qualify to practice. In Haiti, law graduates must write a dissertation after finishing their law school course work in order to be admitted to the bar. In the United States, law graduates must pass a state bar examination before being admitted to practice law. Such requirements often do not test for the skills and values that are important components of law practice and often disproportionately disqualify law graduates from less privileged educational backgrounds for various reasons, resulting in a less diverse legal profession. Therefore, the global clinical movement's agenda should include working with licensing authorities around the world to develop alternatives to bar examinations or better apprenticeship programs that will help law graduates continue to develop the skills and values necessary for the effective practice of law. For example, law graduates could qualify for the bar by demonstrating their skills to mentors or examiners while working on legal aid or other cases providing access to justice for underrepresented communities.

Ending Corruption in the Profession, Legal System, and Judiciary

One of the key challenges to socially responsible law practice identified by clinical educators around the world is corruption in legal systems by prosecutors, judges, magistrates—and even within law schools when professors receive bribes for grades or other benefits. The global clinical movement agenda needs to focus attention on ending all such corruption in order to create a just and impartial legal system worldwide. One key strategy for achieving this goal is to ensure that legal education includes significant course work that teaches ethical behavior, allows for discussions of values, and actually confronts and resolves ethical issues in clinical practice on real cases. In effect, law schools must create the foundation for the ethical practice of law so that their graduates personally adhere to the highest standards of professionalism and also work to combat corruption elsewhere in the legal system. And as with ongoing educational support discussed earlier, the schools' obligation on this issue cannot end at graduation; rather law schools must continue to offer or support programs in ethics for lawyers while they are in practice, perhaps in conjunction with bar associations.

THE ORGANIZATIONAL AGENDA

As stated at the beginning of this chapter, a global agenda requires the participation of clinicians throughout the world. Fostering such participation has always been one of the most important goals of GAJE and is one of the reasons it moves its biannual conferences around the world, thereby allowing for easier and less costly access to both established and emerging clinical programs in the local region. Many in the organization have therefore resisted creating too elaborate and formal a structure, fearing such a move would stifle the entry of new participants. The type of ambitious agenda proposed here cannot be accomplished, however, without the establishment of a broader and more formal organizational structure, promoting greater communication among members, and establishing mechanisms for the assessment of progress. Ideas for how to move forward in each of these areas are presented below.

Global Structures

GAJE has developed over the past decade into a major international organization that brings together lawyers and law faculty members from around the world who want to learn about and support the development of clinical legal education and university-based law clinics, as well as other nontraditional forms of justice education. GAJE is therefore ideally suited to be the organization that undertakes and leads a discussion of a future agenda for global clinical legal education. Any such effort must have the broadest level of participation, which can be achieved most likely through one or more major global gatherings preceded by a series of regional and countrywide conferences or meetings to debate the key issues facing the global clinical movement. The initial goal of these meetings would be to reach consensus on what each country or region believes is important to include in the global agenda and then to have representatives bring those ideas to the international conference. In addition, such meetings could form the basis for the creation of less formal but nevertheless ongoing organizations able to respond to particular issues of local concern.

Understandably, there may be logistical and cost considerations that make it difficult to hold in-person conferences in some countries or regions, but hopefully the types of organizations that have financed previous efforts to develop and expand clinical legal education will support projects to come together to build and implement a global agenda for change. To the extent that such support is not available, technology offers less expensive methods for ongoing dialogue on these issues by a wide range of clinical teachers through conference calls, e-mail, and other online forms of communication.

Organizing regional groupings may involve considerable effort, but they can be held in collaboration with existing national and regional organizations that have been so important to the development of clinical legal education around the world.[11] For example, the Committee of Chinese Clinical Legal Educators (CCCLE) holds frequent conferences for those clinical law teachers and others trying to implement clinical legal education at their universities. In Africa, continent-wide and country-specific conferences and organizations have brought clinical educators together, including two all-Africa colloquia on clinical legal education. In Nigeria and South Africa, two of the largest countries in the region, clinical educators meet frequently under the auspices of their respective national clinical organizations to plan workshops and other activities to support clinical legal education.

Once the agenda has begun to take shape, additional input can be sought from other organizations concerned with legal education more generally. One possibility is the relatively new International Association of Law Schools (IALS), which has started to bring together law school deans and faculty from around the world. Another possibility is the International Bar Association (IBA).

The final structural issue concerns leadership, since the success of any movement depends on the education, support, and development of leaders to implement its agenda. There have been a number of key individuals both nationally and internationally who have committed significant time and energy to the development of clinical legal education. These pioneers should be acknowledged and honored. Nevertheless, it is always important to develop new leaders, and therefore leadership development, including identification, training, and support of lawyers and legal educators with the skills and interest to help design and implement a global clinical agenda, must be part of that agenda. Given the diversity within the global clinical movement, it is crucial that its leaders reflect that diversity in terms of gender and economic, cultural, religious, and racial background. Only in that way will these leaders be able to reach out effectively to different groups of stakeholders from around the world, including law teachers, lawyers and judges, and various client communities.

Communication and Materials Development

Beyond simply creating more formal structures, implementation of the type of global clinical agenda proposed here will require improvements in the methods

---

11. National and regional clinical organizations are discussed in Chapter 19, including their role in the global clinical movement.

through which interested parties communicate, mentor, and train each other, including the development and sharing of materials. Fortunately, some of this activity is already underway through the ongoing exchanges between law schools in different countries that have exposed legal educators around the world to new ideas and models for clinical education. The relationships built on these exchanges also provide for ongoing support when the participants return to their own country and try to implement new ideas. One way to further enhance such exchanges and formally improve the education of future clinicians would be to establish LLM or PhD programs in global clinical legal education, which would also help generate research and develop new ideas for implementing a global agenda.

Technology, primarily in the form of computers with internet access, is a key to increasing the exchange of ideas and support for a global clinical legal education agenda. Internet access allows clinical educators to join the existing national and international electronic mailing lists that provide a means to share ideas and resources, including ways to solve problems faced by individuals or law schools and to view Web sites that have been developed by the various national and international organizations involved in clinical legal education, including GAJE. In addition, a growing number of newsletters that discuss national and international clinical developments are posted electronically. And finally, with Internet access, clinicians can communicate directly with each other to exchange information and ideas through video conferencing using such programs as Skype.

Parallel to the need to exchange information and ideas is the need to share various types of teaching materials and resources. An important source in this regard is the growing literature of clinical scholarship.[12] In addition, resource manuals and textbooks have been written in several countries that provide useful information on how to develop a law school clinic, some of which provide resource materials for use in a seminar or classroom component of a clinic. There is also a rich literature of skills training materials and simulations—both formal and informal—that can be used by clinicians to teach all types of legal skills.

The obvious problem is how to acquire the resources needed to provide computers with Internet access and these written materials to clinics in developing countries where Internet access is limited and library assets are meager. This is a problem in virtually all areas of legal education, but it must be part of the agenda for the global clinical movement if all law schools and clinics are to be able to participate effectively in this movement. Clinical legal educators must, therefore, join with others to develop strategies to address the resource issue.

---

12. The role that clinical scholarship can play in the global clinical movement is the subject of Chapter 21.

Assessment

Those of us who work in the area of clinical legal education have a sense of how well clinical courses, programs, and methodologies prepare law students for the legal profession. But without being able to demonstrate their impact and effectiveness to others, it is difficult to justify adding new—or shifting—resources to this area of legal education. Also, clinical legal educators need information that will help them revise and improve their methodologies to make them even more effective. Therefore, no agenda for the clinical legal education movement would be complete unless it includes a form of rigorous, ongoing assessment of the impact of this work.

Clinicians have already begun to look seriously at how to define and then assess legal education outcomes.[13] Clinical legal educators will need to learn these assessment techniques and then incorporate them into their work. Information from other disciplines will be useful in this effort, but in order to implement a global clinical agenda it will be necessary to figure out how best to measure the impact that these courses, programs, and methodologies have on carrying out that agenda: providing greater access to justice, improving legal education, and creating a more diverse and skilled legal profession.

CONCLUSION

The premise of this chapter is that a clear agenda is needed to guide the development of clinical education globally if it is to expand both in size and influence. To help instigate the development of such an agenda, I have suggested a vision for the global clinical movement, what will be needed to be done to implement that vision, and possible strategies to help in its implementation. Hopefully, enough has been presented to spark ongoing discussion aimed at developing such an agenda. Clearly there is much work left to be done. Clinicians around the world, including many of the authors of the chapters of this book, have started the process; now is the time for a concerted effort to consolidate what has been achieved and to set an ambitious yet realistic agenda for the future.

LIST OF REFERENCES

Anthony G. Amsterdam, *Clinical Legal Education—A 21st-Century Perspective*, 34 J. Legal Educ. 612 (1984).

Margaret Martin Barry, Jon C. Dubin, and Peter A. Joy, *Clinical Education for This Millennium: The Third Wave*, 7 Clinical L. Rev. 1 (2000).

---

13. One such effort is described in Chapter 24.

Frank S. Bloch, *New Directions in Clinical Legal Education: Access to Justice and the Global Clinical Movement*, 28 WASH. U. J.L. & POL'Y 111 (2008).

John M. Burman, *The Role of Clinical Legal Education in Developing the Rule of Law in Russia*, 2 WYO. L. REV. 89 (2002).

Jeanne Charn, *Service and Learning: Reflections on Three Decades of the Lawyering Process at Harvard Law School*, 10 CLINICAL L. REV. 75 (2003).

Jay M. Feinman, *The Future History of Legal Education*, 29 RUTGERS L. J. 475 (1998).

Jeff Giddings, *A Vision of Clinical Education in Australia*, 1 ALTERNAT. LAW J. 86 (2007).

Kristin Booth Glen, *Haywood Burns: A Commemoration: To Carry It On: A Decade of Deaning After Haywood Burns*, 10 N.Y. CITY L. REV. 7 (2006).

Herma Hill Kay, *Women Law School Deans: A Different Breed, or Just One of the Boys?*, 14 YALE J.L. & FEMINISM 219, 223 (2002).

Peggy Maisel, *An Alternative Model to United States Bar Examinations: The South African Community Service Experience in Licensing Attorneys*, 20 GA. ST. U.L. REV. 977 (2004).

Peggy Maisel, *Expanding and Sustaining Clinical Legal Education in Developing Countries: What We Can Learn from South Africa*, 30 FORDHAM INT'L L.J. 374 (2007).

Peggy Maisel, *The Role of U.S. Law Faculty in Developing Countries: Striving For Effective Cross-Cultural Collaboration*, 14 CLINICAL L. REV. 465 (2008).

Roy T. Stuckey, *Preparing Students to Practice Law: A Global Problem in Need of Global Solutions*, 43 S. TEX. L. REV. 649 (2002).

ROY STUCKEY AND OTHERS, BEST PRACTICES FOR LEGAL EDUCATION (Clinical Legal Education Association 2007).

Richard J. Wilson, *Training for Justice: The Global Reach of Clinical Legal Education*, 22 PENN St. INT'L L. REV. 421 (2004).

Richard J. Wilson, *Western Europe: Last Holdout in the Worldwide Acceptance of Clinical Legal Education*, 10 GERMAN L.J. 823 (2009).

24. NORMATIVE ATTRACTIONS TO LAW AND THEIR RECIPE FOR ACCOUNTABILITY AND SELF-ASSESSMENT IN JUSTICE EDUCATION

ADRIAN EVANS

INTRODUCTION

Not many legal education institutions (LEIs), including law schools and other providers of practical legal training, see themselves as having a responsibility to deliver justice education—that is, education in the social responsibility of the law and the legal profession. Were LEIs to consider if their mission ought to expand to include education in the justice paradigm of law, or, if they already aspire to it, to reassess whether that paradigm is in fact being achieved, the question arises: according to what criteria might such a self-assessment proceed? For the first time, this chapter provides a set of suggested criteria (or recipes) to allow that process of introspection to occur.

There are numerous contexts in which to address education in social responsibility. Lawyers and nongovernmental organizations (NGOs) working for justice and justice education, or even thinking about the possibility, are confronted with a bewildering variety of interrelated complexities. These include, for example, the links between poverty and preventing terrorism, human rights and access to resources, taxation and wealth distribution, even legal ethics and the difficulties in withstanding global warming. And yet so little seems, at times, to be achieved by those of us who try to use the law as an instrument to achieve sustainable improvement in many of these fields. Thus, Canadian Harry Arthurs observes that "[a]ll too often, constitutions are adopted, judicial institutions are established, rights are declared, remedies are created, litigation is commenced, landmark judgments are pronounced . . . [and] not much changes" because all these positive outcomes (favoring the rule of law) occur inside the larger and more pervasive trends to neoliberalism and globalization. (Arthurs, 2001 at 14) These larger movements may be checked from time to time by threatened financial meltdown and recession, but the actual core value of our species might increasingly be considered "growth" rather than equality before the law. Consequently, Arthurs thinks that hardly anyone believes nowadays in the progressive potential of law—and if this is true, we have to ask why anyone would think there is much to be gained from attempts to encourage and occasionally self-assess our own efforts at justice education?

The answer, if there is one, must lie in a sense of optimism that there is purpose to a struggle to improve access to justice regardless of past setbacks, because such setbacks are never complete, and gradually advances are achieved. One such advance could be to encourage those LEIs that might like to self-assess their own attitudes to justice education. This chapter seeks to do just that by proposing a "recipe book" approach to self-assessment in justice education and providing at least some of the potential recipes.

THE CONTEXT OF SELF-ACCOUNTABILITY

Within the field of legal ethics, which is an indirect contributor to social justice education and a particular responsibility of LEIs and law-resourced NGOs, the mood for moral accountability has slowly returned because of major ethical scandals. Recent stories from the world of corporate regulation provide a context for revisiting the problem Arthurs refers to, and a possible remedy.

The end of giant corporations like Enron and the collapse of Arthur Andersen, one of the world's largest accounting firms, led to proscriptive regulation which initially bit hard in the United States. However, the "black-letter law" regulatory reaction was limited to matters of internal corporate probity and had no real impact on integrity in borrowing and ethical vigilance over the broad spectrum. The risks of debt-based trading were not truly accepted in the Enron collapse and general financial deregulation expanded. Greed remained the unofficial driver of the global enterprise in this "preclimate change" period. The progressive collapse of the subprime mortgage market in the United States in 2008 caused the insolvency of mortgage financiers and Wall Street investment "banks" and resulted in a tightening of liquidity that rippled across the world economy. Cumulatively, these events demonstrated again—to a new generation—that fiduciary obligation and access to housing and employment will lose out to a profit lust if the stakes are high enough and, perhaps, if professionals' own sense of moral accountability is allowed to dissipate.

Contrast these events in the United States with what occurred in Australia following the 2000 decline and collapse of HIH, one of its largest insurers, shortly before the US implosions of Enron and Arthur Andersen. Banking regulation *and* governance education were seen as equally important, and a series of corporate governance guidelines for stock exchange listing showed an educative, moral development approach to the failures of both business and the professions. As a result, the later Wall Street turmoil of 2008 did not produce a runaway confidence nosedive.

Simon Longstaff, director of the St. James Ethics Centre in Sydney, recognized this connectivity between regulation and moral accountability when he spoke of the implicit contract between a professional and society: a contract that requires the professional to hold the line against self-interest in return for certain privileges. Noting that society cannot be protected from circumstances that put it most at risk by "a formal system of regulation and surveillance,"

Longstaff looks instead to "groups of people who at a more informal level act as gatekeepers and not just guns for hire."[1]

"GATEKEEPER" FORMATION: LEGAL ETHICS AS LAWYERS' NECESSARY ASPIRATION

Longstaff would argue that the assessment of the gatekeeper (in the context of legal education, whether understood as the individual lawyer or LEI, or both) is crucial in fostering moral accountability. Law students at least are aware that all is not well. They "pick up" on the social and political cynicism and are increasingly doing their time in tertiary and preadmission education with a mixture of weary determination and a "what choice is there?" attitude. (Asimow, 2005) Other disciplines are likewise affected, though not all are resigned to coping a day at a time or content just with hand-wringing. If that were the case, there would be no Médecins Sans Frontières, no International Commission of Jurists, no Global Alliance for Justice Education, and no Engineers Without Borders; Lawyers Without Borders are now, belatedly, on the Internet also.

Nevertheless, the repetitive and sometimes biased reporting of less than ideal professional behavior among lawyers is a constant reminder that the "problem" is receiving more attention than possible approaches to it. Evan Whitton's caustic description of much of the legal mystique as a profound role denial is a measure of social suspicion, perhaps even contempt:

> David Luban . . . says: ". . . the standard conception (of legal ethics) simply amounts to an institutionalised immunity from the requirements of conscience." Law professor Murray L Schwartz, of the University of California, Los Angeles, says: "When acting as an advocate for a client, a lawyer . . . is neither legally, professionally, nor morally accountable for the means used or the ends achieved." Dr. Elizabeth O'Brien, a Sydney psychiatrist, says: "That sounds like psychopathy." Psychopaths have no conscience. (Whitton, 2002 at 7)

Clients and consumers have always been cautious of lawyers, and allegations about lawyers' bad or inadequate behavior are not a recent phenomenon. And not without reason; notorious and well-publicized cases of aberrant behavior and the circumstances surrounding their investigation are all too common. Increasing client dissatisfaction with their lawyers, rather than just lawyers in general, is profoundly destabilizing not just for the profession, but also, potentially, for society as a whole. (Evans, 1995) Law societies have shown concern, commissioning their own studies and those of consultants as to how lawyers are perceived by the

---

1. Quoted in Fiona Buffini, *The Decline of Ethical Behaviour*, AUSTL. FIN. REV., Apr. 19, 2002, at 57.

community,[2] while commentators and bar associations have repeatedly called for an invigoration of professional commitment, most recently through the development of greater *pro bono publico* efforts by lawyers.[3] Some of these matters have had very disturbing properties which ought to add urgency to efforts by LEIs to limit their repetition. Lawyers' sense of morality is on the critical list. Academic legal opinion agrees.

LEGAL ETHICS AND JUSTICE EDUCATION

Anthony Kronman, former Dean of Yale Law School, asserted in 1999 that "[A] new and aggressive culture of commercial values, which claims for itself a moral as well as a material superiority, is spreading through the profession as a whole." (Kronman, 1999 at 90; *see also* Rhode, 2000 at 31–38) But there are also real signs that the earlier, almost slavish focus on "zealous advocacy" and "neutral partisanship" as the basis of professional legal ethics in the United States ought now to be moderated by the view that "ethical lawyering involves not the suspension of moral judgment but rather the exercise of it." (Dolovich, 2002 at 1629–30)

Some law firms would have us believe that *all* ethical strategies are win-win in nature: that the present dominant culture of legal practice fully supports ethical behavior and that any ethical challenge can be met without hurting short-term profits. Ethical behavior, according to this view, is just pragmatic (that is, good business)—it has nothing to do with altruism. But if ethical behavior is only pragmatic (sensible) behavior, why are *ethical standards* failing to inspire, let alone cajole, the best behavior? Why are financiers, some with law degrees, among those implicated in the collapse of global corporations, contributing to poverty and injustice? Could part of the answer be that morality, altruism, and even justice are in reality ignored in lawyers' ethical education and that this is occurring because ethical principles are never sufficiently examined and promoted by LEIs themselves?

While much of the global problem with professionalism and access to justice seems to be laid at the door of Western—and particularly US—legal culture, it is not fair to so label that country or its legal educators. Academic response to the perceived decline in ethical standards has in fact been strongest in the United States. Deborah Rhode has complained of a lack of evaluation of professionalism

---

2. *See, for example,* Roy Morgan Research Centre Pty Ltd., *The General Public's Perception of the Standing of Solicitors in New South Wales,* December 1989; E. Skondaki and C.F. Willis, Law Society of England and Wales/Research and Policy Planning Unit, *Public Use and Perception of Solicitors' Services,* 1989.

3. *See, for example,* Linda Cauchi, *An Obligation to Serve? Ethical Responsibilities and the Legal Profession,* 27 ALT. L. J. 3, 133–135 (2002).

initiatives, suggesting that US bar leaders should just forget "incivility" as of any real importance and use the disciplinary process routinely. Reflecting frustration with the lack of change, Rhode is almost at the point of discarding professionalism as a goal for what she sees as the major public concern: access to justice, particularly indigent defense. (Rhode, 2003) Christine Parker affirms Rhode's view, noting that "the most serious potential pathology of the legal profession is its failure to comprehend its role in a broader access to justice agenda." (Parker, 1999 at 85)

And Robert Gordon is one of those who, at least in the US context, make no bones about the real priorities of role morality:

> [L]awyers at the apex of their profession have hardly renounced their claims to elite incomes, elite status, or elite influence in legal policy making. Lawyers remain perfectly happy to deploy that influence to advance their own interests, and their clients' and to maneuver around the controls of democratically elected law if it gets in the way. All they have renounced are the social responsibilities traditionally attached to the power and opportunity conferred by elite status. The sense of paralyzed helplessness descends upon them only when they are asked to consider other interests besides their clients' and their own. (Gordon, 2002 at 1445; *see also* Gordon, 2005)

Sharon Dolovich goes a bit further and calls not just for passive resistance to inequality but also for active subversion of injustice, referring to David Luban's endorsement of the "betrayal by the lawyer of a client's projects, if the lawyer persists in the conviction that they are immoral or unjust." (Dolovich, 2002 at 1648, quoting Luban, 1988 at 174) Dolovich also calls for "institutional support" in the cultivation of integrity, which in turn requires "a broad-based collective commitment to meaningful institutional change." (Dolovich, 2002 at 1687) Might this institutional support include concrete methods of encouraging better behavior in sectors of the global profession? In fact, could we not aspire to a system of self-assessment of legal ethics education as a method of institutional strengthening among LEIs? We could, and we could extend that methodology further to all legal education, assisting its justice imperative.

SELF-ASSESSMENT OF JUSTICE EDUCATION

Self-assessment of legal ethics education is a part of the wider issue of encouraging and supporting justice education. While much of the discussion that follows treats LEIs (and a host of international placement programs involving law students) as the institutions in which legal ethics and social responsibility are taught, there are also many NGOs doing similar things either unilaterally or in conjunction with LEI outreach programs. The principles discussed here apply, with necessary modification, to those NGOs.

The link between legal ethics and justice education is now recognized, in large part because of the efforts of clinicians and clinical legal education. In the United States, Roy Stuckey and others have developed a list of best practices in legal education which prominently links legal ethics and clinical legal education as key tools of justice education (Stuckey and others, 2007) while the 2007 Carnegie Foundation report on legal education attempts to deal with the US reality that "[i]n their all-consuming first year, students are told to set aside their desire for justice." (Sullivan, 2007 at 4) David Chavkin and many others cogently advocate clinical method as the best ethical preparation for legal practice (Chavkin, 2007), while Clark Cunningham and Paul Maharg are leading an international team working on empirical methods to measure a critical accountability dimension: client communication standards. (Barton et al., 2006) In Australia, the Committee of Australian Law Deans (CALD) is beginning to consider standards for Australian law schools which will strengthen clinical legal education and the internalization of better values and legal ethics in future lawyers. In 2001, a Global Alliance for Justice Education (GAJE) preconference workshop explored the idea that LEIs might be monitored for their contribution to social justice, but it did not result in any positive recommendations or major discussion perhaps because the possible monitoring mechanisms were seen as too vague. (Global Alliance for Justice Education, 2001)

All this work was important, but it does not go far enough: it provides no vehicle for lawyers' and LEIs' own reflection on these issues and offers no international recipes which could allow for comparison. The possibility that a common approach to justice education efforts is possible, and perhaps desirable, is not that surprising; but the corollary is more challenging: it is less understood that justice education (however defined) in LEIs ought to be an *internationally required* part of their curricula. (Cunningham, 2008) It is also time to develop and empirically test criteria to help LEIs assess their own educative performance in the interests of justice and social responsibility. Before criteria can be proposed, however, LEIs must address a major jurisprudential debate if they are to adapt to some international comparability in their programs.

POSITIVIST AND NORMATIVE TRADITIONS

There is a long debate in jurisprudence and legal education between those who regard the law as *written* to be the (entire) law, sufficient unto itself and requiring neither contextual addition in its implementation nor outside overriding objectives for its validity—loosely described as the *positivist tradition*—and those who understand the written word of the law as always just a part of the story of justice and injustice, to which it is accountable—the *normative tradition*. (*e.g.*, Dworkin, 1977; Ziv, 2004; Evans, 2008) This debate also characterizes the continuing struggle for liberal legal education in Western law schools.

The debate is not really about disagreements among those on the left and right in terms of political persuasion. A normative position can occasionally be very conservative; for example, the neoconservative perspective, which for a time dominated the post-9/11 US political environment. Nevertheless, normative and positivist perspectives on the teaching and practice of law take different perspectives: normative analyses tend to promote social connectivity and a sense of responsibility for the cultural consequences of law; positivist approaches prefer internal, law-as-text reference points to explain what law is and what its objectives are. Although a positivist approach is in some circumstances less uncertain and perhaps more stable than is the case when law is, by definition, *always* relative to its context, the normative perspective is inherently attractive to those who teach in clinics and practice law for clients whose rights are nearly always marginalized—and not without reason. If law is seen as "just the rules," socially active lawyers can find it much harder to locate within those rules the discretion that is needed to achieve justice for impoverished clients. The corruption of law into an oppressive system is perhaps easier to accomplish in a positivist analytical framework.

This wider jurisprudential debate between certainty and flexibility seems unlikely to be resolved, but its implications are real and significant for those seeking to teach social responsibility through clinical experience and similar techniques of engagement. Clinical teachers must inevitably deal with law by reference to the justice it produces in any one case, rather than as an exercise which sees most of its value in the provision of some additional certainty about what law is or might be. Defining law as rules alone unfairly simplifies the positivist perspective, but the preference for *regulating* solutions to social problems (as opposed to educating about options) does capture a punitive tendency in positivism and can leave social justice collaboration out in the cold. In the end, social improvement is a more explicit objective of the normative perspective of law.

So the question becomes: how can the law and, by extension, LEIs take seriously any claims to be interested in affirming and teaching justice and producing graduates who value, when necessary, justice *before* rules, if neither seeks to be accountable for those priorities? And if an LEI does accept such accountability and seeks to align its courses—or itself—to various social justice priorities, would it not need a structure which allows it to self-assess the likelihood of achieving those priorities? An affirmative response seems logical, despite the irony that such a structure will be regulatory and positivist in nature.

Regardless of any preferred analytical framework for law and its purposes, there is a clear case for LEIs to influence students directly in their understanding and acceptance of ethical and social justice priorities. But this objective, without some monitoring process, is increasingly insufficient. The justice community can benefit from reforming the structures of legal education by progressively self-assessing the courses and the personnel that teach ethics, supervise in clinics (especially those who might tend toward positivist skills instruction rather than normative education in social responsibility), and deliver courses with critical content involving social responsibility.

FOUR INSTRUMENTS TO MEASURE JUSTICE EDUCATION

It is one thing to discuss the theoretical purposes and difficulties in assessing justice education and another to consider how LEIs that are attracted to these ideals might achieve self-assessment in practice. The four tables that follow in the appendices propose instruments for assessable components of legal ethics and social responsibility education, clinical and pro bono programs, staff selection, and LEIs as institutions. These four areas in particular are likely to be important to self-monitoring because each combines an overall indicator of justice education and a number of tangible submeasures or components that are relatively accessible to observation and recording. The various instruments can then be used to determine whether an institution "passes" the self-assessment process.

The presence or absence of legal ethics and social responsibility courses in a law school are tangible indicators of the commitment of the LEI to normative legal education in its students. Clinical education is a key component of justice education, as testified to throughout this book; assessing the quality of a clinic must be a part of any LEI efforts to judge for itself the quality and sufficiency of its own efforts at justice education. These obvious areas for self-assessment are followed by two which testify to the underlying social justice infrastructure of an LEI. Staff selection issues are critical because they can support or undermine all other strategies to achieve justice education. And the characteristics of an LEI as an institution in itself will strongly influence the extent to which it plays a supportive or spoiling role in justice education.

The approach for each criterion, which is explained in more detail in the sections below, is to provide an instrumental mechanism for "scoring" several subcriteria according to a numerical value in the "Totals" column of the relevant table. While it would be possible to prescribe a minimum score in order to help an institution decide if it is sufficiently adequate as a justice educator, initially it is probably better to undertake the self-assessments without regard to suggested minimums. If participating LEIs could be persuaded to publish the results, so much for the better. In due course, a threshold score might be thought feasible, but the suggestions in this chapter are untried and are altogether too tentative in nature to allow a credible attempt at setting a minimum score for an LEI.

Self-assessment of justice education will not be easy, not just because of the positivist-normative debate outlined above but also because the actual mechanisms will remain contentious. Some proposals involve judgments about individual law teachers that could be misused and may be criticized for their utopian quality. But if the objective is considered, these instruments or protocols may nevertheless be found helpful in a utilitarian context.

Assessment of Legal Ethics and Social Responsibility Education

Self-assessment in legal ethics and social responsibility education involves some determination of whether an LEI's efforts to teach legal ethics and social responsibility are adequate. (Duncan & Chandler, 2006) Deciding adequacy requires in itself several preliminary definitions in order to set the scene. The *academic phase* of legal education is either undergraduate or postgraduate and provides law students with a prescribed and culturally specific set of substantive (doctrinal) courses and, increasingly, values and skills, in respect of which their proficiency is individually examined, leading to a basic academic qualification in law. A *substantive law course* is a "black-letter law" or doctrinal course. These courses may be compulsory or elective in nature. In many jurisdictions, there is a "core" of compulsory substantive law courses that each student must take to be eligible to graduate. A *Social Responsibility (SR) module* is a course which makes explicit the principle that law is a normative concept which can assist or inhibit just relationships, and illustrates this reality with appropriate case studies.

A number of key criteria are proposed in order for LEIs to self-assess the adequacy of their teaching of legal ethics and social responsibility. These particular criteria have been chosen because their presence in an LEI are most likely to lead to reflective graduates, capable of the complex ethical judgments that dominate professional practice.

There is general agreement within legal education that best practice in legal ethics education involves the insertion (integration) of legal ethics content and concepts into other courses within the overall law school curricula. This approach is also often referred to as *pervasive*, or *incremental*, legal ethics education. (Rhode, 1992; Noone & Dickson, 2002; Shestack, 1998) Further, an ethics module is a course which defines "ethical behavior" as *considered* behavior, that which takes account of competing ethical principles and intentionally chooses a position and a course of action that is held bona fide by its author. Critically, such a module would not define ethical behavior primarily in terms of behavior that falls on one side of a line rather than the other, e.g., compliance with professional conduct rules. Two consequences follow from this understanding of ethical behavior: first, that students in an ethics course are encouraged in some way to explore and, if possible, understand their own values' structures; and second, that the ethics course will provide a lawyers' typology of some description (e.g., lawyers are either zealous advocates or responsible to the courts) to help them understand their likely behaviors. (Parker & Evans, 2007; Kohlberg, 1984; Cunningham, 2008)

Developing students' self-understanding of values and ethical typologies is therefore included because of their importance to lawyers' ethical resilience in subsequent practice environments. Appendix 1 contains suggested criteria to allow LEIs to self-assess the presence or absence of these "markers" (and other self-explanatory measures of the relative importance of legal ethics curricula) in their institution. The right-hand column and concluding row for "totals" allows LEIs to construct an overall numerical measure of their own institution's performance in this set of criteria, to allow them to build up a chronological picture of their performance over several self-assessment periods.

Self-Assessment of Clinical Programs

There is a significant debate internationally about whether LEI clinics should primarily address law student education or seek to serve clients, or whether these objectives are, in fact, fully compatible. (Bloch & Prasad, 2006) Although there is no consensus, it might be thought reasonable to suggest that clinical programs which orient themselves toward delivering justice ahead of purely educational objectives may be making a stronger contribution to justice education. There is also the issue whether those clinical programs which adopt a normative stance and consciously develop critical, compassionate thinking (or teach by omission a conservative silence by focusing on skills development as a morally neutral technical attribute) are also making a more definite contribution to justice education. (Aiken, 1997) Although periodic reviews of clinical programs can be seen two ways—as an indication of self-aware justice education or as a sign of LEI attempts at cost-cutting (Evans & Hyams, 2008)—they are included for their potential indication of a commitment to justice education.

With respect to the criteria suggested in Appendix 2, some definitions are again necessary. A *clinical program* is a single course or series of courses which expose(s) students to real or simulated clients with real or simulated legal issues, and requires them to be responsible for those clients. A *pro bono placement program* is organized by an LEI in an NGO or other community setting for the purpose of assisting the community via direct service, policy development, or advocacy.

An important method of self-assessing the presence of social responsibility education is the existence of credible pro bono programs for law students within LEI curricula. Whether these programs are mandatory or merely an option is important because it is likely that optional programs will fail to attract the mass of law students to engage in professional service. It is also probable that an LEI which consciously attempts to select and appoint academic staff that is aware of these criteria and their significance actually prioritizes these issues, as opposed to merely producing written policies to this effect.

Attributes of Law Teachers

Since the attitudes and attributes of academic staff are critical to the effectiveness of normative teaching and scholarship, it is reasonable to suggest self-rating these qualities as contributing factors to the overall self-assessment of an LEI's justice education. Appendix 3 proposes the issues that a prospective LEI staff member might be asked about when being considered for a new position, on a probationary basis. These issues are partially derivative of the criteria proposed in the previous appendices and are concerned with awareness of pro bono as a community responsibility of the profession, the importance of lawyers' ethical type to attitudes to practice, consciousness of normative versus positivist jurisprudential debates, and finally, an understanding of the importance of emotional intelligence (EQ) as a law graduate attribute. (Committee of Australian Law Deans, 2008; Shaffer & Cochran, 1994; Luban, 1988; Parker & Evans, 2007; Brayne, 2002; James, 2005)

Certification of LEIs as Justice Educators

When the process of self-assessing courses and teachers is completed, the question arises as to whether the whole self-assessment exercise necessarily also involves LEIs asking themselves whether, as institutions, they measure up to their own goals as justice educators. If the quality of LEI infrastructure is relevant to the issue of the adequacy of justice education, then LEIs should self-certify according to the suggested criteria in Appendix 4. These criteria include the issues of diversity of governance structures, publication of equal opportunity policies, Web site statements about commitment to justice education, a low-income student scholarship program, and a self-assessment "score" which allows the LEI to rate itself according to how it has performed in the self-assessment exercise as a whole.

CONCLUSION

This book seeks to explore the ins and outs of clinical approaches and purposes not in isolation from any paradigm, but in the context of the provision of justice education. Many other chapters speak explicitly or implicitly of the potential for clinics to achieve social justice through justice education. Yet not many law schools and perhaps very few providers of practical legal training see themselves as having a responsibility to deliver justice education.

This chapter seeks to promote such an effort by offering a set of recipes for self-assessment of an LEI's commitment to and delivery of justice education. The truly global LEI is one that will elevate justice education to a front rank objective, not as something merely alongside other objectives, such as final student grade averages, graduate destinations, and alumni endowments—but over and above them all.

The best case that can be made for implementing these instruments is their tangible contribution to a moral rearmament of law graduates and future lawyers, recognizing that there is no longer a lot of patience in the wider community—locally and internationally—for lawyers and lawyer-dominated businesses which persist with positivist denial of justice objectives and an individual preoccupation with last-century monetary gain.

Whether the instruments proposed here are seen as opportunities to deepen and strengthen (as all quality assurance processes are intended), or as radical devices designed to transform legal education, depends on individual LEIs. A commitment to a normative and not a positivist orientation may turn out to be a distinguishing characteristic. But if future lawyers are to be "justice artificers," as opposed to technicians, if they are to be better known for their integrity rather than their income level, and if the global realities of overpopulation, environmental stress, and the politics of terror are all to be tackled by law rather than military budgets—then legal educators, and especially deans, will need to increase the moral awareness and resilience of their graduates. The tools they choose to self-improve their educational mission cannot fail to play a vital role in that task.

LIST OF REFERENCES

Jane H. Aiken, *Striving to Teach "Justice Fairness and Morality,"* 4 CLINICAL L. REV. 1 (1997).

Harry Arthurs, *The World Turned Upside Down: Are Changes in Political Economy and Legal Practice Transforming Legal Education and Scholarship, or Vice Versa?*, 8 INT'L J. LEGAL PROF. 11 (2001).

Michael Asimow et al., *Perceptions of Lawyers—A Transnational Study of Student Views of Law and Lawyers,* 12(3) INT'L J.LEGAL PROF. 407 (2005).

Karen Barton et al., *Valuing What Clients Think: Standardized Clients and the Assessment of Communicative Competence,* 13 CLINICAL L. REV. 1 (2006).

Frank S. Bloch & M. R. K. Prasad, *Institutionalizing a Social Justice Mission for Clinical Legal Education: Cross-National Currents from India and the United States,* 13 CLINICAL L. REV. 165 (2006).

Hugh Brayne *Learning to Think Like a Lawyer: One Law Teacher's Exploration of the Relevance of Evolutionary Biology,* 9 INT'L J.LEGAL PROF. 283 (2002).

David F. Chavkin, Experience Is the Only Teacher: Meeting the Challenge of the Carnegie Foundation Report (2007), NYLS Clinical Research Institute, Paper No. 07/08-3, *available at* http://papers.ssrn.com/sol3/papers. cfm?abstract_id=1008960.

COMMITTEE OF AUSTRALIAN LAW DEANS, DRAFT STANDARDS FOR AUSTRALIAN LAW SCHOOLS (2008).

Clark D. Cunningham, *How Can We Give Up Our Child: A Practice-Based Approach to Teaching Legal Ethics,* 42 LAW TEACHER 312 (2008).

Sharon Dolovich, *Ethical Lawyering and the Possibility of Integrity,* 70 FORDHAM L. REV. 1629 (2002).

Nigel Duncan et al., *Learning Professional Ethics: An International Perspective,* 9 LEGAL ETHICS 160 (2006).

RONALD DWORKIN, TAKING RIGHTS SERIOUSLY (Harvard University Press 1977).

Adrian Evans, *Acceptable, But Not Entirely Satisfied: Client Perceptions of Victorian Lawyers*, 20 ALT L.J. 2 (1995).

Adrian Evans, *Justice Before Rules*, 82 (4) L. INST. J. 76 (2008).

Adrian Evans & Ross Hyams, *Independent Evaluations of Clinical Legal Education Programs: Appropriate Objectives and Processes in an Australian Setting*, 17 GRIFFITH L. REV. 52 (2008).

Global Alliance for Justice Education, Report on the Second World Conference of the Global Alliance for Justice Education: Reconciliation, Transformation, and Justice (2001), http://www.gaje.org/Durban%20Conference%20report.htm.

Robert W. Gordon, *Portrait of a Profession in Paralysis*, 54 STAN. L. REV. 1427 (2002).

Robert W. Gordon, *A New Role for Lawyers? The Corporate Counsellor After Enron*, in LAWYERS' ETHICS AND THE PURSUIT OF SOCIAL JUSTICE: A CRITICAL READER (Susan D. Carle ed., New York University Press 2005).

Colin James, *Seeing Things As We Are: Emotional Intelligence and Clinical Legal Education*, 6 INT'L J. LEGAL PROF EDU. 123 (2005).

LAWRENCE KOHLBERG, THE PSYCHOLOGY OF MORAL DEVELOPMENT, (Harper and Row 1984).

Anthony T. Kronman, *Professionalism*, 2 J. INST. STUDY LEGAL ETHICS 89 (1999).

DAVID LUBAN, LAWYERS AND JUSTICE: AN ETHICAL STUDY (Princeton University Press 1988).

Mary Anne Noone & Judith Dickson, *Teaching Towards a New Professionalism: Challenging Law Students to Become Ethical Lawyers* 4 LEGAL ETHICS 127 (2001).

CHRISTINE PARKER, JUST LAWYERS, (Oxford University Press 1999).

CHRISTINE PARKER & ADRIAN EVANS, INSIDE LAWYERS' ETHICS, (Cambridge University Press 2007).

Deborah L. Rhode, *Ethics by the Pervasive Method*, 42 J. LEGAL EDUC. 31 (1992).

DEBORAH L. RHODE, IN THE INTERESTS OF JUSTICE: REFORMING THE LEGAL PROFESSION (Oxford University Press 2000).

Deborah L. Rhode, *Defining the Challenges of Professionalism: Access to Law and Accountability of Lawyers*, 54 S.C. L. REV. 889 (2003).

THOMAS L. SHAFFER & ROBERT F COCHRAN, JR., LAWYERS, CLIENTS AND MORAL RESPONSIBILITY (West 1994).

Jerome J. Shestack, *Taking Professionalism Seriously*, 84 A.B.A. J. 70 (1998).

ROY STUCKEY AND OTHERS, BEST PRACTICES FOR LEGAL EDUCATION (Clinical Legal Education Association 2007).

WILLIAM M. SULLIVAN ET AL., EDUCATING LAWYERS: PREPARATION FOR THE PROFESSION OF LAW (Jossey Bass 2007).

Evan Whitton, *Client Versus Ethics: No Legal Contest*, THE AGE, June 22, 2002.

Neta Ziv, *Lawyers Talking Rights and Clients Breaking Rules: Between Legal Positivism and Distributive Justice in Israeli Poverty Lawyering*, 11 CLINICAL L. REV. 209 (2004).

APPENDIX 1. PROPOSED SELF-ASSESSMENT CRITERIA REGARDING THE ADEQUACY OF TEACHING OF LEGAL ETHICS AND SOCIAL RESPONSIBILITY (SR)

Suggested Criteria	Proposed Numerical Measures of Ethics and SR Courses		Totals
All students will encounter legal ethics education in some sense within the academic phase of legal education.	No = 0	Yes = 1	
There are stand-alone courses on legal ethics topics.	0	1	
Relative importance of professional conduct rules in relation to the underlying principles of moral responsibility in the stand-alone ethics curriculum.	Conduct rules dominate the course = 0	Theories of moral responsibility and/or ethical type dominate = 1	Balance between the two = 2
Stand-alone ethics courses are taught by a full member of academic staff.	0	1	
Stand-alone legal ethics courses propose at least one method of classifying "lawyer types" as an aid to student understanding of legal ethics pedagogy.	0	1	
Stand-alone legal ethics courses encourage law students to understand their own values as relevant to the type of lawyer they aspire to.	0	1	
Legal ethics courses are assessable.	0	1	
Social Responsibility units are compulsory.	0	1	
SR units are assessable.	0	1	
Clinical-ethics interface: students explore ethics and social responsibility debates in clinical live-client placements under the auspices of law school staff.	No = 0	Some but not all elements are present = 1	Yes = 2

APPENDIX 1. (cont.)

Suggested Criteria	Proposed Numerical Measures of Ethics and SR Courses	Totals
Ratio of number of ethics/SR courses to the number of compulsory substantive courses in the academic phase (e.g., if there are 3 ethics courses & 11 compulsory courses, ratio is 3:11 or .27).		Insert ratio [.27]
Relative presence of integrated legal ethics education: the ratio of the number of substantive law courses which include ethics modules to the total number of compulsory substantive law courses.		Insert ratio
Relative importance of ethics/ SR courses in the academic phase: the ratio of teaching staff to students in ethics/SR units is no less than in substantive law units.		Insert the ratio of one to the other

Total for legal ethics and social responsibility education

LEI comments on exceptions and clarifications:

APPENDIX 2. SELF-ASSESSMENT CRITERIA FOR CLINICAL AND PRO BONO PROGRAMS

Suggested Criteria	Proposed Numerical Measures of Credible Clinical and Pro Bono Programs			Totals
	No	Yes		
A clinical program is in existence.	0	1		
The clinical program is periodically reviewed by an external team.	0	1		
Is the clinical program law student–education centered, client-service centered, or a balance of the two?	Law student–education centered = 1	Client-service centered = 2	Some active balance of the two = 3	
Does the clinical program focus on skills development or promote a normative/critical emphasis?	Unclear = 0	Skills development = 1	Normative emphasis = 2	
There is a for-credit, pro bono placement program for students.	0	1		
Is there an optional or compulsory (but not for-credit) pro bono program for students?		Optional = 1	Compulsory = 2	
New academic staff is oriented for their awareness of the significance of the above criteria.	0	1		
Total for clinical and pro bono programs				

LEI comments on exceptions and clarifications:

APPENDIX 3. SELF-ASSESSMENT CRITERIA FOR STAFF SELECTION

Suggested Criteria	Suggested Numerical Measures of Staff-Selection Processes			Totals
Potential academic staff member has a positive attitude to the idea of pro bono work for law students and lawyers.	No clear opinion= 0	Mildly in favor = 1	Strongly in favor = 2	
Existence of a track record of personal pro bono activity?	None = 0	< 2 hrs pw =1	> 2 hrs pw = 2	
Potential academic has normative views about the purpose of law and legal practice (accepting that a normative view is also at one level a positivist perspective).	Positivist view = 0	Normative view = 1		
Potential academic has an awareness of the pedagogical debates concerning competing legal ethical perspectives.	Not aware = 0	Aware = 1		
Potential academic possesses qualifications to practice law (and therefore supervise in clinical legal practice).	Not qualified = 0	Qualified = 1	Qualified and currently licensed = 2	
Potential academic is aware of the importance of emotional intelligence.	Not aware, or aware & dismissive = 0	Aware & supportive = 1	Undertaken EQ assessment = 2	
Total for staff selection				

LEI comments on exceptions and clarifications:

APPENDIX 4. POSSIBLE SELF-ASSESSMENT CRITERIA FOR LEIs AS INSTITUTIONS

Suggested Criteria	No	Yes		Totals
The LEI expressly advocates, preferably on its Web site, a responsibility to promote justice awareness in its students.	0	1		
The LEI has a published equal opportunity staff employment policy.	0	1		
Self-assessments of no more than [X] of the criteria specified in appendices 1–3 above are considered inadequate in the self-assessment exercise.	> 3 criteria are considered inade-quate = 0	2–3 criteria are consid-ered inade-quate= 1	< 2 criteria are considered inade-quate= 3	
The LEI has a student scholarship program which supports low-income student enrollments amounting to X% of its overall enrollments.	No such program= 0	< 5% of students= 1	> 5% of students= 2	
The LEI has a [XX:X] ratio of academic staff to support staff.	> 10:1 = 0	Ratio between 10:1 and 5:1 = 1	< 5:1 = 2	
The LEI has an advisory board or governance structure that includes representatives of consumer groups, political parties, major religious traditions, and an NGO which is primarily concerned with issues of social responsibility.	< 2 of these stake-holders= 0	2–3 of these stake-holders= 1	All these stake-holders= 2	
Total for LEI as an institution				

LEI comments on exceptions and clarifications:

25. THE GLOBAL ALLIANCE FOR
JUSTICE EDUCATION

EDWARD SANTOW AND GEORGE MUKUNDI WACHIRA

INTRODUCTION

The Global Alliance for Justice Education (GAJE) is an informal international organization that has served, since the late 1990s, as a key player in the emerging global clinical movement. The essence of GAJE is captured in its original mission statement, which describes the organization as "a global alliance of persons committed to achieving justice through education."[1] The main focus of the organization is on "justice education"—a term that is intended to encompass clinical legal education without limiting its scope of influence to law school–based clinical programs. Thus, GAJE seeks to advance justice education by supporting other forms of "socially relevant legal education," such as projects and programs aimed at educating practicing lawyers, judges, nongovernmental organizations (NGOs), and the lay public.

The purpose of this chapter is to place GAJE and its brief history in the broader context of the global clinical movement. It begins with a description of how and why GAJE came into being. It then charts the development of GAJE's organizational structure and how that structure supports GAJE's social justice agenda. The chapter next examines some of GAJE's key projects and how those projects have helped advance justice education around the world. Finally, the chapter seeks to situate GAJE in the global clinical legal education movement.

HISTORICAL DEVELOPMENT OF GAJE

Consistent with its informal status, it is difficult to say exactly at what point GAJE came into existence. One could say that GAJE was formed in 1997, following a series of meetings and discussions by legal academics and members of the legal fraternity aimed at establishing an international organization to advance socially relevant legal education. (Cunningham, 2005; McCrimmon, 2000) Another key year was 1999, when a group of the participants at those meetings

---

1. Many of the details in this chapter about GAJE's institutional history and structure are drawn from material available on GAJE's Web site at http://www.gaje.org. The authors acknowledge in particular the contribution of Clark Cunningham's excellent paper, "Clinical Education Changing the World and the World Changing Clinical Education: The Global Alliance for Justice Education," also posted on the GAJE Web site.

organized and staged GAJE's first international conference in India. A third possibility is 2001, when GAJE's constitution was formally adopted. Each of these periods was significant in the formation of GAJE as it exists today; together they describe the key moments in the organization's history.

Setting the Stage: Three Meetings in India, the United States, and Australia

A series of events and interactions among clinical law teachers, as well as practicing and academic lawyers, were integral to GAJE's establishment. The first of these was a clinical legal education teaching course at the National Law School of India University in 1995, which was attended by law teachers and legal practitioners from South Asia. The three-week course was facilitated and taught by experienced clinical legal educators from—in addition to India—the United Kingdom, the United States, Bangladesh, and Australia. The content, teaching methodology, and diversity of participants in the course provided impetus for reflection on gaps in the existing models, and opportunities for the establishment of an international clinical legal education organization.

An opportunity arose to follow up some of the ideas that emerged from that informal reflection at the Association of American Law Schools (AALS) Annual Conference on Clinical Education in 1996. The theme of that conference was "Expanding the Frame: Crossing the Border to Other Countries and Disciplines," and it drew a number of delegates from outside the United States. The conference opened with a keynote address entitled "In Defense of Socially Relevant Legal Education" by Dr. N. R. Madhava Menon, the founding director of the National Law School of India University and the organizer of the clinical teaching course in 1995. A group of individual delegates, including Dr. Menon and some of the instructors at the clinical legal education course in India, held a series of informal meetings to consider how to harness their expertise and diversity, with a view to promoting collaboration and the sharing of information on issues relating to clinical legal education. The participants agreed to establish a working party to explore the feasibility of establishing a global organization to further that ideal.

The practical turning point in GAJE's formation is accordingly traced to the first working party meeting held at the Centre for Legal Education in Sydney, Australia on September 4, 1996, during an international legal education conference sponsored by the Australasian Professional Legal Education Council. That meeting, attended by twenty-one individuals from eleven countries, proposed the formation of an organization tentatively titled the International Council for the Advancement of Socially Relevant Legal Education.

The preparatory meetings, correspondence, and discussions about the formation of GAJE clearly spelled out that the organization would be global and would avoid domination by any single nationality or region. There was emphasis on international cooperation in seeking to achieve social justice through the reform of legal education. Participants also felt it was imperative to broaden the scope of activities to promote socially relevant legal education beyond the traditional models of clinical legal education. That would ensure that the organization did not champion a particular format or model of legal education, but would instead permit the accommodation of specific national and regional requirements. It would also ensure that, in addition to law teachers, other groups and individuals involved in justice education—especially members of nongovernmental organizations, activists, practicing lawyers, judges, and the general public—would have an active role to play in GAJE's activities.

By mid-1997, the first signs of an organizational structure began to appear with the creation of an e-mail list to facilitate discussion among the participants at the various preparatory meetings. The list members then selected the name "Global Alliance for Justice Education" for the organization, together with the following mission statement:

> GAJE is GLOBAL, seeking to involve persons from as many countries in the world as possible, avoiding domination by any single country, and especially committed to meaningful participation from less affluent countries, institutions, and organizations. GAJE is an ALLIANCE of persons committed to achieving JUSTICE through legal education. Clinical education of law students is a key component of justice education, but this organization also works to advance other forms of socially relevant legal education, which includes education of practicing lawyers, judges, non-governmental organizations and the lay public.

The list members articulated three preliminary goals for the organization, drawing on the earlier discussions in Miami and Sydney. The first was to convene by the end of 1999 a global conference at a low-cost location, with a view to facilitating the participation of persons from developing countries. The other two goals were to receive and administer funds to support the development of innovative justice education, especially in less affluent countries, and to serve as a clearinghouse of teaching methods and materials. A temporary steering committee was established to further these goals, with members representing Argentina, Australia, Canada, Fiji, India, South Africa, the United Kingdom, and the United States.

The Inaugural Conference in Thiruvananthapuram

GAJE was launched informally during its inaugural conference held in Thiruvananthapuram, Kerala, India, on December 8–17, 1999. The conference was attended by 125 persons from 20 countries, a majority of whom were from developing countries. The conference was structured in three parts. First was a one-day preconference workshop designed to "set the stage for the main conference by encouraging cross-cultural interaction between the participants" and also to "address the practical as well as theoretical issues of how a justice dimension to legal education can be practically achieved." The second part was the main conference, which focused on legal education in a number of social justice contexts, such as women's rights and working with NGOs. A deliberate decision was made to limit plenary sessions to brief presentations on chosen themes, so as to devote the maximum amount of time to smaller breakout groups where the themes could be discussed in a less formal and more interactive setting. A business meeting was also held during the main conference, which addressed a number of issues relating to GAJE's future governance. Critical among those was how GAJE should be structured and run. Delegates opted to constitute a steering committee with a geographically diverse membership of men and women, and this group took primary responsibility for organizing a second international conference in two years' time. In the interim, various subcommittees were established to consider issues such as a constitution for GAJE, as well as communication and outreach to new members. After the conclusion of the main conference, the third part was a week-long postconference workshop consisting of Train-the-Trainer sessions aimed at delegates interested in acquiring practical clinical teaching skills. The principal focus of these interactive sessions was on using clinical methodologies in a social justice context.

The GAJE Constitution

Until 2001, GAJE continued to operate as an informal organization with interim structures, but without a constitution. GAJE's constitution was drafted by a committee set up at the business meeting during the 1999 conference and chaired by Professor Clark Cunningham. The committee prepared a report that was circulated to all members of the GAJE e-mail list; it was debated and ratified on December 9, 2001, at GAJE's second international conference in Durban, South Africa.

The GAJE constitution is a simple, eight-clause document with provisions on the organization's name, purpose and goals, membership, general meetings, and steering committee, and on some key administrative matters including amending the constitution, incorporation and regional chapters, and dissolution. The constitution enshrines, in terms of governance through the steering committee, the principles discussed in India of broad geographical and gender representation. It also lists GAJE's main goals:

(1) To facilitate international information sharing and collaboration on justice education.
(2) To support, develop, and implement advocacy projects on a regional and global basis.
(3) To convene global conferences, workshops, and training sessions on justice education at locations accessible and affordable for persons from developing countries.
(4) To receive and administer funds to support the development of innovative justice education, especially in developing countries.
(5) To serve as a clearinghouse of teaching methods and materials.

The 2001 constitution establishes GAJE's two main governance structures. The highest decision-making organ is the general meeting, which meets approximately every two years at GAJE's international conferences. The organization's steering committee is elected at these general meetings, where all GAJE members have equal voting rights. The steering committee consists of two members (a man and a woman) from each of the following eight regions: North America; South and Central America; Africa; South and Central Asia (including the Middle East); East Asia; Western Europe; Eastern Europe, including Russia; and Australasia, including the Pacific Islands.

The steering committee manages the affairs of the organization and "may take any action on behalf of GAJE which, in its opinion, will further the objects of GAJE." Steering committee members work on a voluntary basis and serve for four-year terms but are eligible for reelection. The steering committee elects a convenor, who chairs meetings and manages the administration of the committee and other functions of the organization. Decisions of the steering committee are arrived at by discussion (usually via e-mail) and consensus. The steering committee can create standing and ad hoc working committees on specific issues such as fund-raising, membership and recruitment, conference organizing, communication, and nomination of new members.

Appointing an Executive Committee and General Secretary

To expedite decision-making on urgent matters, the steering committee decided in 2004 to delegate some of its powers to an executive committee. According to the constitution, the only powers the executive committee cannot exercise are those relating to appointment and removal of members of the steering committee and officers as well as amendment of bylaws or the constitution. Ordinarily, the decisions of the executive committee must be sanctioned by the steering committee.

In the period since 2007, GAJE has explored various ways to reduce some of the administrative burden from the steering committee generally and the convenor in particular. For a period, the steering committee appointed a general secretary. The role, which carried a modest honorarium, involved providing administrative support to the steering committee, general membership correspondence, and overseeing the organization's fund-raising efforts. The office of the general secretary is presently under review, with the steering committee seeking to determine the most effective means of performing a broader secretariat function, and communicating with the members and others interested in justice education, including via the GAJE Web site. At the same time, the steering committee and other GAJE members began discussing the option of formalizing the organization's status as a legal entity separate from its membership. This discussion was motivated in part by the desire to facilitate GAJE raising funds in its own name for carrying out its various activities. The organization had thus far relied mainly on funds generated at its biannual worldwide conferences, including some fees paid by organizations such as the Ford Foundation and the Open Society Institute for delegates from developing countries. Although GAJE has received some modest grants to support its worldwide conferences, it will certainly need additional funds in the future to realize its institutional goals.

GAJE ACTIVITIES AND THEIR CONTRIBUTION TO JUSTICE EDUCATION

In a sense, GAJE's most notable achievement is the simple fact of its existence. GAJE membership has become, in effect, the single most important signature of participation in the global clinical movement. GAJE members consistently make up a significant number—if not the majority—of speakers and delegates at most international conferences and workshops on clinical legal education. GAJE is also cited increasingly in journal articles on global aspects of clinical legal education. Most often, GAJE members' contributions at these international clinical gatherings relate directly to the organization's social justice agenda, as do many journal references to the organization and its activities. The number of activities sponsored directly by GAJE remains small for two reasons. On one level, it simply reflects that GAJE has a very limited operating budget. But it is also because GAJE was always intended to be a catalyst for new social justice projects, simply by bringing together diverse professionals from around the world with a common justice education goal. The result is that many activities associated with GAJE have helped advance justice education around the world and further demonstrate GAJE's influence in the global clinical movement.

Biannual Global Conferences

Since its inception, GAJE has held five biannual worldwide conferences: in India (1999), South Africa (2001), Poland (2004), Argentina (2006), and the Philippines (2008). The locations of the global conferences have been selected to move from one region to another in order to ensure that participants from as many different countries as possible attend and become involved in the organization. As noted earlier, cost and accessibility are also important in determining the location of the GAJE worldwide conferences. Consistent with this aim, at each of its conferences, GAJE has subsidized the cost of participation of persons from developing countries through fee waivers and reductions. Together with outside funding sources, this allows GAJE to provide a substantial number of travel and accommodation grants.

Each conference has been divided into a series of concurrent streams, with each stream representing a particular social justice or clinical legal education theme. Dividing the delegates into smaller groups on this basis not only enables them to attend sessions that best speak to their requirements and interests, but it also allows for greater interactivity among the delegates and increases the opportunity for them to share their expertise and skills. In keeping with this objective, and consistent with the structure of the first international conference in India, there are relatively few plenary sessions and a large number of thematic workshops.

The format of GAJE's international conferences has developed over time. While the first three international conferences were structured, as mentioned earlier, in three distinct parts (a preconference workshop, a main conference, followed by Train-the-Trainer workshops), this format has subsequently been condensed with the aim of capturing the essence of those conferences—especially a focus on information sharing and practical problem-solving in a social justice context—but without demanding such a long period of attendance. As a result, the more recent GAJE conferences were designed to accommodate the divergent needs of sponsors and delegates. For example, some delegates prefer the format of a conventional conference in which issues are addressed through the presentation of conference papers, while other delegates prefer more interaction between a session facilitator and the attendees. Still others attend GAJE conferences with the specific aim of gaining certain legal or teaching skills.

An important feature of all GAJE conferences has been to address social justice problems that are pressing in the region in which the conference is held, focusing especially on the contribution that clinical legal education can make in resolving those problems. For example, delegates at the 2008 international conference in Manila were invited to visit a number of social justice projects, run by local law clinic programs and designed to address issues such as urban poverty, employment rights, women's rights, and environmental rights. One such visit began at the office of the Homeless People's Federation of the Philippines and then continued on to one of the biggest open dumpsites in metropolitan Manila, with a population of over 200,000. The federation brings together diverse Filipino community organizations that work in a wide range of problems affecting the homeless population, including—in addition to housing—income, infrastructure, health, welfare, and access to affordable credit. After the visit, the delegates analyzed the methods used by the clinical program, and how such methods might be applicable in clinical programs in other countries and contexts.

Along the same lines, conference sessions have been enhanced by linking current social justice issues in the host countries through site visits. For example, in South Africa, where one of the conference subthemes was "Access to Justice for People Living with HIV/AIDS," delegates interacted with organizations dealing with the HIV/AIDS pandemic in that country. In Poland, the theme of the main conference—"Using the Experience of Lawlessness to Teach Justice"—was built around a visit to the former concentration camps at Auschwitz-Birkenau. Through related conference sessions before and after the visits, GAJE members were able to explore the role of the law in remedying injustice, as much as how the abuse of the law can lead to atrocities and human rights violations. As stated in the conference report, "the idea behind the visit to the former concentration camps was to let the participants of the conference experience and find out what may happen if the legal system starts serving injustice, to let them comprehend to what extent rights and dignity of people may be violated by other people, and finally to let them try to define the concept of justice by building the definition of justice in opposition to what is symbolized by Auschwitz and Auschwitz-Birkenau."

The most recent GAJE global conference was held in December 2008 in the Philippines, where delegates were encouraged to share resources and strategies on justice education. That conference also incorporated site visits. For example, one group of conference delegates followed the Humanitarian Legal Assistance Foundation to visit two remand centers in Manila. The foundation operates a clinical-style program in which inmates can undertake a course in which they are trained as paralegals. When trained, they assist other inmates, especially those who do not have the literacy or other skills necessary to represent their own interests in pursuing their own cases. The visit showed vividly the need for legal assistance and for legal educators reaching out beyond law students and law schools. It sparked robust debate about how to develop such programs in other places in which resources are very limited.

In addition to disseminating knowledge and skills, GAJE's global conferences have sparked lasting professional relationships and networks. These contacts have helped to establish and expand exchange programs, guest lectures, and invitations to other relevant activities aimed at improving legal education. Over the years, GAJE members have involved each other in consultancies on justice education, notably in Africa, China, Latin America, Eastern Europe, and India.

REGIONAL INITIATIVES

There have been two regional GAJE conferences: the first covering the Australasian region of the South Pacific in 2002, and the second covering North America in 2006.

The Australasian Regional Conference

Clinical legal education in Australia has always been predicated on a desire to promote social justice. (Rice & Coss, 1996) Using clinical legal education to promote other goals—such as the development of practical legal skills—has at times been important, but those other goals have usually been secondary to the focus on social justice. (Noone, 1997) Given the strong alignment between the social justice orientation of Australian clinical legal education and the founding principles of GAJE, it is not surprising that the first regional GAJE conference was hosted in Australia. The conference harnessed the energy generated from the first two worldwide GAJE conferences in 1999 and 2001. This is reflected by the organizing committee, which was led by Professor Les McCrimmon and a group of Australian law students who had accompanied him to the 2001 GAJE international conference.

The Australasian conference—entitled "Social Justice in the Asia-Pacific: Refugees, HIV/AIDS, and Indigenous Peoples" and hosted in Sydney, Australia— attracted legal academics, students, legal practitioners, community groups, advocates, and judges from the Australasian, and broader Asia-Pacific, regions to share their ideas, policies, and expertise, with a view to fostering future collaboration. While Australasia is economically, socially, and ethno-culturally diverse, it is dominated, at least geo-politically and geo-economically, by Australia and New Zealand. Crucially, however, the conference attracted a significant number of delegates from the developing countries in the region, such as Papua New Guinea (PNG) and Fiji.

This regional conference sought to adopt the principal features of GAJE's global conferences, especially in terms of ethos and format, while focusing more specifically on the role of justice education in addressing the social justice issues peculiar to the Australasian region. First, the cost of attendance was minimized, through sponsorship, and a number of means-based scholarships were made available. This encouraged participation from developing countries in the region, as well as students and others with limited financial means. Rather than a narrow focus on legal theories or pedagogical methods, the delegates considered how clinical legal education could play a part in addressing three of the most pressing social justice concerns of the Australasian region at the time: access to justice for asylum seekers; HIV/AIDS and access to justice in developing countries; and justice for indigenous people.

The conference also drew on the features of GAJE conferences by embracing the diversity in the backgrounds and experience of the delegates. It is important to note that the teaching of law in Australasia varies considerably with reference to the relative wealth and the prevailing culture of the different parts of the region. As a result, most of the law schools in Australia and New Zealand resemble, in their fundamental characteristics, those of the United States, the United Kingdom, and other developed countries. In contrast, the vast majority of law schools in the developing nations of Australasia have far fewer resources and operate in states whose legal foundations may be less secure. Nevertheless, many of the problems that the conference addressed transcend national borders, and all of the participants were able to contribute meaningfully to discussion— something that helped in the development of more comprehensive responses to these problems. For instance, the movement of asylum seekers and refugees in Australasia presents differing but interconnected legal problems for all the states in the region. The conference provided a platform for a number of collaborative projects—including a constitutional challenge in PNG, involving local and overseas lawyers, to a joint Australian-PNG agreement to detain on PNG land asylum seekers attempting to travel to Australia.

Finally, the conference was practical and multidisciplinary, attracting delegates from across the legal academy, law students, the practicing profession, policy–makers, and NGOs. The conference sought to achieve practical outcomes, in particular by developing cooperative regional strategies to deal with the issues addressed. For example, the Indigenous Justice stream began with strategies for responding to historical injustice, then moved to a workshop addressing "post-colonial" issues, followed by sessions on key concepts in indigenous justice such as land rights, justice for women and children, and ways for communities to take control of justice systems in their geographical areas. The Asylum Seekers stream included workshops on media training, lobbying, and refugee advocacy skills. Each stream concluded with a report of "three top plans of action" reported back to the closing plenary.

A number of clinical-style projects arose from GAJE's Australasian regional conference, including one led by law students of the University of Sydney that helped to provide legal representation for indigent asylum seekers. That project, which ran for two years before being taken over by an NGO, was unusual in that it was designed and run by law students with no formal assistance from faculty staff. Legal supervision was provided by lawyers working pro bono.

North American Conference

As with the Australasian conference, the North American regional conference was intended to adopt the general structure and ethos of the previous international GAJE conferences. Entitled "International Collaboration in Teaching, Learning, Lawyering, and Scholarship," the conference attracted a geographically broad range of delegates from countries including China, El Salvador, Great Britain, Greece, Israel, Morocco, Pakistan, Poland, Russia, Sweden, and the United States. This conference also facilitated the first publication of a collection of conference papers arising directly from a GAJE event. (Symposium, 2007)

GLOBAL COMMUNICATION NETWORK

GAJE is above all a *network* of people—diverse in origin, in expertise, and in profession—who share the common goal of achieving social justice through education. As such, one of GAJE's early and ongoing priorities has been to facilitate communication among its members and with others interested in learning about and promoting justice education. This has been achieved by, for example, the establishment of a members-only moderated electronic mailing list, a Web site, and a newsletter (in English and Spanish) that is distributed via the electronic mailing list and posted on the Web site. GAJE members use the e-mail list to keep each other abreast of developments in legal education and to post announcements and requests from membership on common issues of interest. GAJE's newsletter reports on members' activities, initiatives, events, and resources of interest.

Research, Conference Presentations, and Publications

GAJE members' international collaboration has resulted in joint projects, publications, invitations to conferences, and guest lectures. A notable publication is a book on creative child advocacy edited by GAJE members Professors Ved Kumari from India and Susan Brooks from the United States, comprising contributions from a number of GAJE members working in the area of child advocacy. The book proposes innovative initiatives to address problems facing children, such as child labor, abuse, neglect, juvenile delinquency, violence, and custody. These strategies include establishing pro bono advocacy centers within commercial law firms, litigation alternatives, and developing a handbook explaining court processes to children. (Kumari and Brooks, 2004) This type of research output by GAJE members helps to expand the list of possible solutions to social justice problems, contributes to teaching resources by law teachers running child advocacy clinics, and suggests new ways for students and practitioners in seeking to achieve social justice outcomes. It was launched during the third GAJE International Conference in Poland.

In February 2008 about twenty GAJE members from around the world participated in an international conference on the future of legal education hosted by Georgia State University in Atlanta. The conference, which was cosponsored by GAJE, brought together prominent legal educators and leaders from the legal profession in the United States and other countries. Presentations and discussions centered on and responded to a critical report by the Carnegie Foundation for the Advancement of Teaching on the state of legal education in the United States. (Sullivan et al., 2007) Participants at that conference identified with the findings of the report in their own jurisdictions and sought ways of addressing challenges they faced in adopting legal curricula that are responsive to social justice problems.

CONCLUSION

The contribution of GAJE to the clinical legal education movement is both immense and subtle. GAJE plays an important role in justifying the existence of clinical legal education. For instance, by providing an international showcase for successful clinical projects that operate within a relatively small local area, it helps to show why such projects perform an important social good.

Most importantly, GAJE brings together a broad range of people who are united primarily by their belief in an abstract concept: justice education. As such, GAJE is not represented by a global empire of offices in law schools and NGOs across the regions in which it is most active. One cannot even point to a large number of publications with "GAJE" in the title. Instead, GAJE acts very much as a network. Using only the Internet and regular international conferences, it unites (and reunites) people from around the world who are seeking to combat social justice problems, using the tools of law and education. Without question those problems differ depending on geography, culture, and economic development. However, time and again, GAJE's international conferences have found those differences to be superficial. As a result, in the field of clinical legal education, GAJE has been a crucial catalyst for meaningful collaboration across borders, and the sharing of ideas about how to achieve social justice.

LIST OF REFERENCES

Clark D. Cunningham, Clinical Education Changing the World and the World Changing Clinical Education: The Global Alliance for Justice Education, Presentation at Flowers in the Desert: Clinical Legal Education, Ethical Awareness and Community Service, Before the Australian Clinical Education Association (July 14, 2005), *available at* http://www.gaje.org.

Global Alliance for Justice Education, Report on the Inaugural Conference and Workshops of the Global Alliance for Justice Education (1999), *available at* http://www.gaje.org.

＿＿＿＿＿＿, Report of the Third International Conference, Structuring a Justice Curriculum for the Future (2004), *available at* http://www.gaje.org.

＿＿＿＿＿＿, Report of the Fifth GAJE International Conference, Manila, Philippines (2008), *available at* http://www.gaje.org.

＿＿＿＿＿＿, Constitution of the Global Alliance for Justice Education, *available at* http://www.gaje.org.

CREATIVE CHILD ADVOCACY: GLOBAL PERSPECTIVES (Ved Kumari & Susan L. Brooks eds., Sage Publications India 2004).

Les McCrimmon, *Transforming Legal Education into Justice Education: GAJE*, 76 REFORM 48 (1992).

Mary Anne Noone, *Australian Community Legal Centres—The University Connection, in* EDUCATING FOR JUSTICE: SOCIAL VALUES AND LEGAL EDUCATION (Jeremy Cooper & Louise G. Trubek eds., Ashgate / Dartmouth 1997).

SIMON RICE & GRAEME COSS, A GUIDE TO IMPLEMENTING CLINICAL TEACHING METHOD IN THE LAW SCHOOL CURRICULUM (Centre for Legal Education 1996).

W. M. SULLIVAN, A. COLBY, J. W. WEGNER, L. BOND, & L. S. SHULMAN, EDUCATING LAWYERS: PREPARATION FOR THE PROFESSION OF LAW (Jossey Bass 2007).

Symposium: Global Alliance for Justice Education ("GAJE") North American Regional Conference, FORDHAM INT'L L. J. 346–454 (2007).

INDEX